the PERENNIAL MATCHMAKER

the PERENNIAL MATCHMAKER

Create Amazing Combinations with Your Favorite Perennials

NANCY J. ONDRA

RODALE

RODALE
wellness

Live happy. Be healthy. Get inspired.

Sign up today to get exclusive access to our authors, exclusive bonuses,
and the most authoritative, useful, and cutting edge information on health,
wellness, fitness, and living your life to the fullest.

Visit us online at RodaleWellness.com
Join us at RodaleWellness.com/Join

Rodale books may be purchased for business or promotional use or for special sales.
For information, please write to:
Special Markets Department, Rodale Inc., 733 Third Avenue, New York, NY 10017.

Printed in China
Rodale Inc. makes every effort to use acid-free ∞, recycled paper ♻.

Book design by Joanna Williams

See photo credits on page 320.

Bloom Buddies illustration © Michael Gellatly

Library of Congress Cataloging-in-Publication Data is on file with the publisher.

ISBN-13: 978–1–62336–538–7

Distributed to the trade by Macmillan

2 4 6 8 10 9 7 5 3 1 hardcover

 RODALE.

Follow us @RodaleBooks on

We inspire and enable people to improve their lives and the world around them.
rodalebooks.com

Euphorbia polychroma with *Heuchera* 'Christa' and *Euphorbia* × *martinii* 'Ascot Rainbow'

CONTENTS

PART 1
MAKING THE PERFECT MATCH:
A PLANT-BY-PLANT GUIDE

Iris ensata 'Variegata' and *Ajuga reptans* 'Catlin's Giant'

Amsonia hubrichtii and *Allium siculum*

Helenium 'Helbro' (Mardi Gras) and *Hemerocallis* 'Nona's Garnet Spider'

Calamagrostis × acutiflora 'Karl Foerster' and *Physocarpus opulifolius* 'Center Glow'

Phlox paniculata 'Eva Cullum' and *Eupatorium maculatum*

Nepeta 'Walker's Low' and *Sedum rupestre* 'Angelina'

PART 2
PERENNIAL MATCHMAKING: EXPLORING MORE OPTIONS

Rudbeckia hirta 'Prairie Sun' and 'Chim Chiminee' with *Euphorbia stricta* 'Golden Foam' and *Kniphofia uvaria* 'Flamenco'

Physostegia virginiana and *Aster novae-angliae*

WELCOME TO *THE PERENNIAL MATCHMAKER!*

Isn't it fascinating how two people can start with the same things and end up with very different results? One person can turn basic ingredients into an unforgettable meal or turn thrift-shop finds into an eye-catching outfit, while another ends up with something barely edible or barely wearable. It's the same with perennials: Two gardeners can shop at the same garden center, but one turns those plants into a gorgeous perennial border and the other simply has a random collection of flowers. Sure, some people can transform the ordinary into the extraordinary just on instinct, but the rest of us need to hone our garden design skills—by learning the basics, taking inspiration from others, and bringing it all together to make our own gardens look amazing. And that's where *The Perennial Matchmaker* comes in.

Whether you're just starting with perennials or are a longtime gardener who wants to fine-tune your plantings for a more cohesive look, *The Perennial Matchmaker* will be your go-to guide for creating stunning plant medleys. And this matchmaker angle is easy to understand—it's a favorite perennial looking for friends!

Are you ready to choose co-stars for perennials that are already in your yard or that you've been longing to plant? Finding the perfect partner starts with identifying one key feature you want to play up on your focus plant, then sorting through possibilities for contrast until you come up with complementary partners. Look up your favorite plants in Part 1, Making the Perfect Match: A Plant-by-Plant Guide, starting on page 1. This encyclopedia of more than 80 popular perennials features photos of simple yet striking perennial partnerships that you can use right away, as well as lots of ideas for crafting other eye-catching color combinations, dramatic

Allium moly with *Dianthus* 'Firewitch' and *Salvia × sylvestris* 'May Night'

textural displays, and stunning seasonal effects with compatible perennial companions. Each entry also includes a quick-reference list of "Bloom Buddies," so you can see at a glance which other perennials are likely to flower at the same time: a huge help if you're trying to plan a spectacular flower garden.

Would you prefer to create your own combinations from scratch? Part 2, Perennial Matchmaking: Exploring More Options, starting on page 261, delves into the thought process behind those breathtaking perennial pairings. You'll learn how to really *look* at a perennial—not just the color of its flowers, but also the shape and size of its blooms and leaves, its special features in each season, and so on— and how to figure out where it wants to grow. Once you can do that, you'll narrow the pool of countless potential partners down to a manageable handful, making it easy to find perfect matches for any perennial, whether you have room for just two or three plants or want to build a whole border.

This how-to guide also includes the scoop on finding design inspiration, working with color, adding seasonal interest, and expanding your plant palette way beyond perennials. You'll learn how to take care of your combinations, too, so your garden will always look its very best.

I've been working with plants since I was a teenager, and over the last several decades I've immersed myself in all things green and colorful and beautiful. In my own gardens and those of others, I've planted and maintained beds and borders in a variety of sites and settings, and I've seen countless amazing plant combinations: Some I made on purpose or by luck, and many other surprising and delightful pairings the plants made on their own. Inspired by this firsthand experience, as well as actual and virtual visits to perennial gardens all over the world, I'm thrilled to have this opportunity to share with you what I've learned about creating breathtaking perennial partnerships. It's my hope that *The Perennial Matchmaker* will become your go-to guide when you're ready to turn your perennial dream garden into a glorious reality. Happy matching!

Nancy J. Ondra

Nan's Top 10 Favorite Perennial Pairings

When I first started making plant combinations, I focused on color, and I still enjoy making high-contrast pairings: particularly bright flowers with dark foliage. Over the years, though, I've come to appreciate more subtle matches, too: similar colors with different flower forms, for instance, or foliage-with-foliage combos. Below are some of my most favorite matches to date. I can't wait to see what new combinations I can come up with this year!

'Kobold' spike blazing star (*Liatris spicata*) with drumstick allium (*Allium sphaerocephalon*). These two flowers are similar color-wise, but their flower forms are distinctly different, providing much-needed visual variety. To be honest, I didn't plant these two together on purpose, but I love the results. This combo peaks in midsummer but looks good well into fall, thanks to the interesting seed heads.

'Karl Foerster' feather reed grass (*Calamagrostis × acutiflora*) with pink muhly grass (*Muhlenbergia capillaris*). One of the first bits of advice I ever got from a gardening expert was to avoid planting grasses with grasses. Since then, I've taken it as a personal challenge to come up with interesting combinations and even whole borders based mostly or completely on ornamental grasses. This simple pairing along my driveway has been one of my favorites for several years. The pink muhly grass blends into the base of the feather reed grass for most of the growing season, but in fall, it explodes into a froth of misty pink flowers.

Variegated sweet iris (*Iris pallida* 'Variegata') with 'Axminster Gold' Russian comfrey (*Symphytum × uplandicum*) and lady's mantle (*Alchemilla mollis*). This trio breaks another "rule": Don't plant two variegated plants next to each other. Yes, the effect *can* look too busy, but I think this one works because the color range is rather limited. It also helps that there are different leaf and plant forms. 'Axminster Gold' Russian comfrey can be hard to find, but it's worth tracking down. Or consider a medium-size, yellow-variegated hosta instead, such as 'Earth Angel' or 'Great Expectations'.

'Sun Power' hosta with Japanese blood grass (*Imperata cylindrica* 'Rubra'). I normally wouldn't combine bright yellow with bright red without including something dark as well, but I really enjoy this strong contrast of color and form, and it looks great from early summer to frost. Because of the concerns about this grass becoming invasive, though, I'm thinking of replacing it with 'Beni-kaze' Hakone grass (*Hakonechloa macra*). That grass is arching instead of upright and mostly green in summer, but it turns red in fall, so the effect will be a bit different but equally interesting.

'Henry Eilers' sweet coneflower (*Rudbeckia subtomentosa*) with great burnet (*Sanguisorba officinalis*). Coneflowers usually have large, bold blooms, but the quilled petals of 'Henry Eilers' sweet coneflower give it a much more delicate appearance. I thought the flowers were beautiful on their own, but once the plant settled in and reached its full size in bloom (about 5 feet), they were just the right height to mingle with the dainty, egg-shaped bloom clusters of great burnet, and they made a charming combination. The coneflower also helps to provide some support for the thin-stemmed burnet blooms, so there's no need for staking—hooray!

Tumbleweed onion (*Allium schubertii*) with golden oregano (*Origanum vulgare* 'Aureum') and giant coneflower (*Rudbeckia maxima*). I never get tired of making matches with ornamental onions. It's so easy to plant these (and many other) bulbs into or close to plants that will carpet the ground around them when they're in bloom and then stick around once the bulbs go dormant. I've tried a number of pairings, and this was one of my best results for both color and form. The tumbleweed onion flowered in early summer and then dried in place, and the oregano provided great support for the seed heads through the rest of the growing season. The broad blue leaves of giant coneflower are a wonderful complement to the pink and yellow of the other plants.

'Pewter Lace' Japanese painted fern (*Athyrium niponicum* var. *pictum*) with dwarf Chinese astilbe (*Astilbe chinensis* var. *pumila*). To be fair, I don't think I've ever seen a combination with Japanese painted fern that I *didn't* like. Texture-wise, its lacy foliage makes a great contrast to the many broad-leaved shade plants; color-wise, it works well with deep greens, cool blues, bright silvers, clear yellows, and deep purples—and even with pink, as in this combo. I'm not a huge fan of astilbes, and they don't care much for me, either, but once this dwarf Chinese astilbe agreed to stick around, I knew right away that I needed to move a nearby 'Pewter Lace' right next to it, and I wasn't disappointed.

'White Nancy' spotted deadnettle (*Lamium maculatum*) with Chinese wild ginger (*Asarum splendens*). This pairing started out as a container combination, and I loved it so much that I transplanted the whole thing to the garden at the end of that growing season. The leaf shapes and colors are very similar but the different leaf sizes supply the element of contrast. It helps that the ginger is mostly green with touches of silver while the deadnettle is mostly silver with just a thin green edge.

'Isla Gold' tansy (*Tanacetum vulgare*) with 'Desert Coral' coreopsis (*Coreopsis*). It took me a while to find a source for 'Isla Gold' tansy, but it was worth the effort. The foliage color is fantastic from spring through fall, and the lacy leaf texture complements many other foliage and flower forms. It does bloom, with clusters of golden yellow buttons, but I sometimes cut them off. Who needs them anyway, with leaves like these? It was just by chance that I put this 'Desert Coral' coreopsis next to it one year, and I thought the effect was stunning.

'Milk Chocolate' and 'Nona's Garnet Spider' daylilies (*Hemerocallis*) with Mellow Yellow spirea (*Spiraea thunbergii* 'Ogon) and 'Royal Purple' smokebush (*Cotinus coggygria*). Purple-leaved smokebushes and yellow-leaved spireas are two of my favorite color companions for perennials. The dark leaves of the smokebush make a great background for bright blooms, and the cheery color and feathery texture of Mellow Yellow spirea pair perfectly with a wide variety of flowering and foliage companions all through the growing season. The yellow foliage also makes a great echo for partners that have some yellow in their flowers.

Iris 'Immortality' and *Scabiosa* 'Butterfly Blue'

PART 1

MAKING THE PERFECT MATCH

A Plant-by-Plant Guide

It's easy to find pictures of breathtaking perennial combinations, but it's often *not* so easy to re-create those images in your own garden: Either you can't find the same plants for sale where you live, or they simply won't grow well in your yard. So while it's fine to use pictures for inspiration, it's much smarter to start with perennials that you're already growing, or that you can easily find at your local garden center. Then you can use those time-tested favorites as building blocks to create your own designer-quality combinations.

In this plant-by-plant guide, you'll discover the best features of more than 80 popular perennials and find advice for choosing many compatible companions. The perennials are presented alphabetically by botanical name, so you can flip directly to a particular plant if you know the genus name; if not, browse the list on the Contents page to find your plant's common name (and, of course, all of the plants appear in the index).

For each of the featured perennials, you'll find general and specific suggestions for other perennials you can use to create soothing harmonies or dramatic contrasts of color or form. You'll learn *when* a particular perennial is in prime form (and when it isn't!), so you can choose co-stars that will make it shine at its peak or carry the show when it's not at its best. Each entry additionally includes a "Bloom Buddies" box: a quick-reference list of other perennials that thrive in the same growing conditions and flower at or around the same time. That sort of information is invaluable for choosing individual companions, of course, but also for expanding simple pairings into a stunning bloom display in an entire bed or border.

Achillea

classic summer perennials

Achillea 'Strawberry Seduction' and *Sedum alboroseum* 'Mediovariegatum'

Achillea 'Coronation Gold' and *Stipa tenuissima*

A Perfect Match

I love making combinations with peachy and salmon colors, and 'Peachy Seduction' and 'Terracotta' yarrows are two of my go-to bloomers in this color range. They're beautiful with 'Black Adder' anise hyssop (*Agastache*), 'Walker's Low' catmint (*Nepeta*), and other purple-blues.

Yarrows (*Achillea*) produce an abundance of tiny blooms clustered into flat-topped flower heads. Among the well-known yarrows with yellow flowers and silvery to gray-green foliage are 3- to 4-foot-tall 'Coronation Gold' and 'Gold Plate' fernleaf yarrow (*A. filipendulina*) and 18- to 24-inch-tall hybrids 'Moonshine' and Anthea ('Anblo'), all of which are hardy in Zones 3 to 9. Common yarrow (*A. millefolium*) and its hybrids, which usually flower at about 2 feet in height, expand the color range to include white, pinks, reds, and oranges, as well as yellows. They typically have very lacy bright green or graygreen leaves and are hardy in Zones 3 to 9.

Color Considerations

Yellow-flowered yarrows make striking partners for blue- to purple-flowering perennials, such as 'Brookside' and Rozanne

('Gerwat') hardy geraniums (*Geranium*), mountain bluet (*Centaurea montana*), and perennial salvias (*Salvia*). The bright yellows, including 'Coronation Gold' and 'Moonshine', also make eye-catching co-stars for equally intense reds and oranges, like those of Arkwright's campion (*Lychnis × arkwrightii*), butterfly weed (*Asclepias tuberosa*), 'Lucifer' crocosmia (*Crocosmia*), and Maltese cross (*Lychnis chalcedonica*), as well as other strong yellows, such as Jerusalem sage (*Phlomis russeliana*) and sundrops (*Oenothera fruticosa*), and crisp whites, like 'Becky' Shasta daisy (*Leucanthemum × superbum*). The bright yellows are excellent for echoing companions that have yellow-centered or -throated blooms, like those of Frikart's aster (*Aster × frikartii*) and many irises and daylilies (*Hemerocallis*).

When you're choosing companions for hybrids of common yarrow, be aware that it's common for their colors to fade as the flowers age. 'Cerise Queen' starts out bright pink and turns light pink, for instance, while 'Apricot Delight' goes from orangey pink to creamy pink, and 'Fireland' (also sold as 'Feuerland') turns from bright red to peachy yellow. Cut off the older blooms if you don't like their softer colors or leave them and select partners with the multicolor effect in mind.

Yarrows in the pink and softer yellow ranges, such as 'Saucy Seduction' and Anthea, look good with blues, purples, creams, and whites, as well as with silver, gray, and blue foliage. 'Inca Gold', 'Terracotta', 'Fanal' (also sold as 'The Beacon'), 'Paprika', and others in the oranges and reds are also interesting with blue leaves, as well as with yellow-variegated foliage and the buff-colored flower and seed heads of summer-blooming ornamental grasses, such

Bloom Buddies
Marvelous Matches for Flowering Combos

Yarrows (*Achillea*) tend to grow best in soil that's on the dry and not-especially-fertile side. They can adapt to more regular watering and richer soil, though they tend to be sprawling there. Below are some other sun lovers that overlap with the peak early- to midsummer bloom period and make great companions for yarrows.

African lilies (*Agapanthus*)

Anise hyssops (*Agastache*)

Bee balms (*Monarda*)

Blackberry lily (*Belamcanda chinensis*)

Blazing stars (*Liatris*)

Blue flax (*Linum perenne*)

Butterfly weed (*Asclepias tuberosa*)

Catmints (*Nepeta*)

Coreopsis (*Coreopsis*)

Echinaceas (*Echinacea*)

Gaura (*Gaura lindheimeri*)

Globe thistles (*Echinops*)

Lavenders (*Lavandula*)

Marguerites (*Anthemis*)

Mountain bluet (*Centaurea montana*)

Mulleins (*Verbascum*)

Penstemons (*Penstemon*)

Perennial salvias (*Salvia*)

Red valerian (*Centranthus ruber*)

Rudbeckias (*Rudbeckia*)

Russian sages (*Perovskia*)

Speedwells (*Veronica*)

Summer phlox (*Phlox paniculata*)

Sundrops (*Oenothera fruticosa*)

Torch lilies (*Kniphofia*)

as blue fescues (*Festuca*), blue oat grass (*Helictotrichon sempervirens*), and tufted hair grass (*Deschampsia cespitosa*).

Shapes and Textures

The yarrows with yellow flowers and silvery leaves are usually clump formers, while common yarrow and its hybrids tend to spread out into broad patches. Most aren't particularly

Achillea 'Pink Grapefruit' with *Callirhoe involucrata* and *Veronica grandis*

distinctive, shape-wise, except for individual clumps of fernleaf yarrow and its taller cultivars, such as 'Gold Plate', which are very upright and contrast well with mounded forms.

The deeply cut foliage gives yarrow plants a fine texture, but that's only obvious in spring and fall. Their primary shape-related feature is their umbel-form blooms (with many small flowers clustered into flat-topped heads). Repeat their strong presence with other perennials that have a similar shape, such as showy stonecrop (*Sedum spectabile*) and wild quinine (*Parthenium integrifolium*); with broad daisy-form flowers, like those of echinaceas (*Echinacea*) and rudbeckias (*Rudbeckia*); or with other large blooms, like those of daylilies and true lilies (*Lilium*).

For contrast, pair yarrows with small, simple flowers, like those of coreopsis (*Coreopsis*) or gaura (*Gaura lindheimeri*); with rounded clusters, like those of drumstick allium (*Allium sphaerocephalon*) and globe thistles (*Echinops*); with airy clusters, like those of catmints (*Nepeta*) and coral bells (*Heuchera sanguinea*); or with spiky blooms, like those of dense blazing star (*Liatris spicata*), penstemons (*Penstemon*), or perennial salvias (*Salvia*). Yarrow flowers look wonderful with the fine foliage textures of Mexican feather grass (*Stipa tenuissima*), New Zealand hair sedge (*Carex comans*), and other ornamental grasses.

Seasonal Features

Yarrows generally begin flowering in late spring in the South and early summer in northern gardens. Fernleaf yarrow and its selections are at their best through midsummer; then you

Achillea 'Apricot Delight' with *Hypericum calycinum* 'Brigadoon' and *Stipa tenuissima*

winter. Other yarrows usually continue to produce new blooms through summer and even into early fall, especially if you regularly remove the finished flower stems. (This will also help to prevent an abundance of unwanted seedlings.)

Special Effects

If you're planning combinations for butterfly gardens, be sure to include pairings of yarrows with other butterfly favorites, such as butterfly weed (*Asclepias tuberosa*), pincushion flowers (*Scabiosa*), phlox (*Phlox*), and red valerian (*Centranthus ruber*).

Common yarrow and its hybrids, with their relatively loose growing habit, also look right at home in meadow gardens, interplanted with relatively low grasses, such as little bluestem (*Schizachyrium scoparium*) and prairie dropseed (*Sporobolus heterolepis*), and other meadowy perennials, such as butterfly weed and rudbeckias.

Yarrows are great in bouquets, too, so they're excellent companions for other long-lasting blooms, like those of coral bells (*Heuchera sanguinea*), lavenders (*Lavandula*), and purple coneflower (*Echinacea purpurea*).

can remove the dead flowering stems (cut them off close to the base of the plant, so the leaves will hide the stubs) or leave them in place to add structural interest in fall and

Managing Your Yarrows

Yarrows (*Achillea*) may be short lived, especially in good soil, and usually benefit from being divided every other year. If you prefer to stick with lower-maintenance plants in your main perennial borders, consider keeping your yarrows—as well as other short-lived perennials, such as black-eyed Susan (*Rudbeckia hirta*), blanket flowers (*Gaillardia*), gaura (*Gaura lindheimeri*), and rose campion (*Lychnis coronaria*)—in a separate area. Interplant them with annuals and tender perennials that need to be replanted each spring anyway, and it won't be a big deal to divide or replace the yarrows at the same time.

Agastache
strikingly spiky

Agastache 'Raspberry Summer' and 'Summer Love' with *Lavandula angustifolia* 'Violet Intrigue' and *Kniphofia* 'Alcazar'

A Perfect Match

When I need a partner for an anise hyssop, I usually look to daisy-form options, such as Shasta daisy (*Leucanthemum × superbum*). But I've been seeing some amazing photos of anise hyssop spikes mingling with the rounded blooms of globe thistles (*Echinops*), and I can't wait to give that idea a try in my own garden. I find it difficult to get globe thistles established, though, so I'll have to go with rattlesnake master (*Eryngium yuccifolium*), instead, for the rounded flowers.

The variety of colors you can find among the agastaches (*Agastache*) offers exciting possibilities for both bold and subtle combinations. As a group, agastaches share several characteristics, including spiky bloom clusters and a months-long flowering period.

The agastaches with purple-blue (or sometimes white) flowers are commonly referred to as anise hyssops. *A. foeniculum* is native to much of northern North America; *A. rugosa*, sometimes called Korean mint, is native to Asia. There are also hybrids, such as 'Black Adder' and 'Blue Fortune'. Anise hyssops are typically hardy in Zones 4 to 9, though some newer selections are less cold-tolerant. Their heights can vary dramatically depending on the growing conditions and the ages of the plants: Though usually in the range of 3 to 4 feet tall, any of these may be as short as 2 feet or reach 5 feet or more (possibly even taller in rich soil).

Bloom Buddies
Marvelous Matches for Flowering Combos

Below are some compatible flowering perennials that overlap or coincide with the main mid- to late-summer bloom period for agastaches (*Agastache*).

Partners for anise hyssops (*A. foeniculum*, *A. rugosum*, and their hybrids) in average to moist but well-drained soil:

Bee balms (*Monarda*)

Crimson scabious (*Knautia macedonica*)

Daylilies (*Hemerocallis*)

Dense blazing star (*Liatris spicata*)

Echinaceas (*Echinacea*)

Fleeceflowers (*Persicaria*)

Heleniums (*Helenium*)

Joe-Pye weeds (*Eupatorium*)

Perennial lobelias (*Lobelia*)

Rattlesnake master (*Eryngium yuccifolium*)

Rudbeckias (*Rudbeckia*)

Shasta daisy (*Leucanthemum × superbum*)

Summer phlox (*Phlox paniculata*)

Threadleaf coreopsis (*Coreopsis verticillata*)

Tuberous-rooted Jerusalem sage (*Phlomis tuberosa*)

Partners for hummingbird mints (such as *A. aurantiaca*, *A. cana*, and *A. rupestris*) in average to dry soil:

Blanket flowers (*Gaillardia*)

Butterfly weed (*Asclepias tuberosa*)

Globe thistles (*Echinops*)

Jerusalem sage (*Phlomis russeliana*)

Lavenders (*Lavandula*)

Ornamental oreganos (*Origanum*)

Penstemons (*Penstemon*)

Perennial salvias (*Salvia*)

Russian sages (*Perovskia*)

Sea hollies (*Eryngium*)

Sedums (*Sedum*)

Torch lilies (*Kniphofia*)

Yarrows (*Achillea*)

Yuccas (*Yucca*)

Agastaches that are native to Mexico and the southwestern United States are generally referred to as hummingbird mints. Orange hummingbird mint (*A. aurantiaca*), reddish pink Texas hummingbird mint (*A. cana*), and salmon orange sunset hyssop (*A. rupestris*), as well as hybrids of these and other species, expand the color range with many rich shades and delicate tints of pink, orange, and yellow. They are generally 2 to 3 feet tall, with some variation either way depending on the species or selection and the growing conditions. Most of these agastaches are rated as hardy in Zones 5 or 6 to 9.

Color Considerations

There are two aspects to the color of agastache flowers: the main one from the flower and sometimes a secondary one from the calyx (the cuplike structure at the base of each bloom).

The flowers of anise hyssops tend to be on the light lavender blue side, though some newer selections, such as 'Black Adder' and 'Blue Boa', are a somewhat richer purple, with touches of violet in their calyces. Repeat their hues with other flowering perennials in the

Agastache 'Black Adder' and *Artemisia* 'Powis Castle' *(above); Agastache rupestris* with *Carex buchananii* and *Stachys byzantina* 'Big Ears' *(right)*

violet-purple-blue range, such as catmints (*Nepeta*), perennial salvias (*Salvia*), and Russian sages (*Perovskia*), and with powder blue foliage, like that of blue fescues (*Festuca*) or 'Dallas Blues' switch grass (*Panicum virgatum*). The purple-blue agastaches also look wonderful with yellow, cream, or white flowers and with artemisias (*Artemisia*), lamb's ears (*Stachys byzantina*), 'Nora Leigh' summer phlox (*Phlox paniculata*), and other plants with silver, gray, or variegated leaves. They're very pretty with pinks and peaches, too, like those you can find in many daylily (*Hemerocallis*) flowers and in some foliage heucheras (*Heuchera*), such as 'Berry Smoothie', 'Caramel', and 'Southern Comfort'.

Colors among the hummingbird mints range from delicate pastels, such as cream-and-pink 'Champagne' and pale pink 'Cotton Candy', to buttery 'Sunset Yellow', rich raspberry pink 'Heat Wave', and vivid orange 'Firebird'. It's not unusual for there to be two or three colors on one plant, because the flowers may fade or change hues as they age; the calyces are often dusky purple to pinkish, too. The pastels are particularly lovely in combinations you'll see up close, where you can appreciate their subtle coloration. Try pairing them with flowering companions in other soft colors, including the purple-blue agastaches, and with silver, gray, blue, or peachy leaves. Purple sage (*Salvia officinalis* 'Purpurascens') and purple-leaved sedums (*Sedum*), such as 'Purple Emperor', as well as silvery purple heucheras, like 'Blackberry Ice', look wonderful in these sorts of combinations, especially when they echo the color of agastaches with dark calyces, such as sunset hyssop and 'Summer Glow'.

Pastel-flowered hummingbird mints pair well with more saturated shades of the same hue, such as 'Acapulco Salmon and Pink' with richly colored 'PowWow Wild Berry' purple coneflower (*Echinacea purpurea*). Or use the reverse approach and combine a bright-flowered selection with a lighter version of the same hue: 'Orange Nectar' hummingbird mint with softer 'Terracotta' yarrow (*Achillea*), for instance. Vibrantly colored hummingbird mints are wonderful with tints and shades of yellow, coral, purple, and blue; with bright silver and deep purple foliage partners; and with the buff to tan seed heads of summer and fall grasses, such as feather reed grass (*Calamagrostis* × *acutiflora*) and fountain grasses (*Pennisetum*).

Shapes and Textures

Agastaches are clump formers that mostly have a mounded form when established. First-year plants tend to be narrower, creating a distinctly vertical effect, especially when in flower. The foliage of the anise hyssops mostly has a medium texture, while the leaves of hummingbird mints tend to be smaller and are often quite narrow, giving them a finer appearance that contrasts well with larger, broader or strappy leaves, like those of irises and yuccas (*Yucca*).

The spikelike flower clusters are the most distinctive textural feature of agastaches. They're normally dense but slender on the anise hyssops; on the hummingbird mints, they're more open and wider, with larger individual blossoms. Both can work well for repeating the form of other spiky flowers, such as Culver's roots (*Veronicastrum*) and penstemons (*Penstemon*). For contrast, use daisy-form flowers, like those of rudbeckias (*Rudbeckia*); large, rounded flowers, like those of daylilies (*Hemerocallis*); umbels, like those of yarrows (*Achillea*); and airy plumes, like those of giant fleeceflower (*Persicaria polymorpha*) and Russian sages. Agastaches also make fantastic co-stars for perennials with globe-like blooms, such as globe thistles (*Echinops*) and rattlesnake master (*Eryngium yuccifolium*).

Seasonal Features

Most agastaches aren't very showy in spring, but 'Golden Jubilee', a selection of anise hyssop

Succeeding with Agastaches

Along with their many wonderful qualities, agastaches (*Agastache*) offer some challenges in perennial combinations. It's quite common for them to live only one or two seasons and then disappear, even in areas where they should be fully cold-hardy. Sometimes this is due to the soil staying a little too moist during the winter months, which may explain why a given species or hybrid can overwinter in Zone 4 or 5 in one area and not below Zone 7 in more humid regions. In other cases, losses are seemingly by chance: Of three clumps growing in the same border, you might lose one or two or none or all. Fortunately, they're quick growing enough that it's worth treating them like annuals. But if you prefer to use longer-lived perennials for lower maintenance, then consider using other spiky plants instead, such as perennial salvias (*Salvia*).

Agastache foeniculum 'Golden Jubilee' with *Geranium* and *Viola tricolor*

with bright yellow foliage, provides brilliant splashes of color that look beautiful with forget-me-nots (*Myosotis*), tulips, and other early bloomers.

The timing of the flowering season can vary quite a bit, depending on the species or hybrid, the age of the plant, and the climate. In warm regions, a late-spring to early-summer start is common; in cooler areas, blooms may not begin to open until midsummer. As you gain experience with how agastaches perform in your garden, you can fine-tune your choice of companions, but in any situation, partners that flower in mid- to late summer are a good bet, and those with colorful foliage are always dependable.

You're likely to find that many agastaches continue flowering into fall, especially if you frequently pinch or clip off the finished spikes through summer. (That will also help to minimize the number of self-sown seedlings, which can be abundant unless you're growing a sterile hybrid, such as 'Black Adder' or 'Blue Fortune'.) Leave them on the plant after that, though, if you'd like to see the dried seed heads in winter.

Special Effects

If you enjoy making combinations that do more than look pretty, agastaches belong in your plant palette.

Want to attract wildlife? There's a good reason that the southwestern species, in particular, are known as hummingbird mints: Their tubular blooms are very appealing to these intriguing creatures. Bees and butterflies also adore agastaches, especially the anise hyssops.

Enjoy having an abundance of fresh bouquets for your home? The spiky blooms of agastaches are wonderful for cutting, so consider adding them to an area where you grow other excellent cutting perennials, such as echinaceas (*Echinacea*), rudbeckias, and yarrows. These mint-family members have edible flowers, too, and the fragrant foliage is flavorful in tea, making them excellent additions to beds based on perennials that are both edible and ornamental.

Agastache 'Blue Fortune' with *Geranium wlassovianum* and *Molinia caerulea* subsp. *arundinacea* 'Skyracer'

Ajuga
ground-covering color

Ajuga reptans 'Atropurpurea' and *Lysimachia nummularia* 'Aurea'

Ajuga reptans 'Burgundy Glow' and *Galium odoratum*

A Perfect Match

After struggling with out-of-control ajugas in other gardens, I was determined that I would never plant any here—until I saw how cute Chocolate Chip was in its little nursery pots and I couldn't resist. Instead of fighting with it, though, I've been pairing it with lamb's ears (*Stachys byzantina*), obedient plant (*Physostegia virginiana*), and other rampant spreaders in a spot out back where I can't get more delicate perennials to grow.

A patch of ajugas (*Ajuga*) in full bloom is a beautiful sight in the spring garden, but it's the ground-hugging rosettes of colorful leaves that carry the show for most of the growing season. Also known as bugleweeds, these plants are typically 3 to 6 inches tall in leaf; in bloom, the spikes usually reach 6 to 8 inches tall. Common ajuga (*A. reptans*), the most well-known species, may have blue, pink, or white flowers, and the foliage may be green, purple, or variegated, as on 'Burgundy Glow' or 'Toffee Chip'. All are hardy in Zones 3 to 9.

Color Considerations

Blue-, pink-, and white-flowered ajugas all look lovely with other spring perennials in those hues and with light to bright yellows. The blues, especially, are wonderful with peachy orange flowers and with peachy to coppery foliage, like that of 'Caramel' heuchera (*Heuchera*) and 'Toffee Twist' weeping brown sedge (*Carex flagellifera*).

It's important to look to the leaf colors when choosing ajuga companions for both spring and beyond. In cool weather, for instance, the leaves of 'Burgundy Glow' are blushed with pink, creating a pleasing harmony with pink-flowering partners, such as bleeding hearts (*Dicentra*). Dark-leaved selections of common ajuga, such as 'Black Scallop' and Chocolate Chip, are also most intensely colored in cool weather but keep at least some of their purple color through the growing season. Use them to echo taller companions that have dark stems, dark markings in their blooms, or dark seed heads. Or create striking contrasts by pairing them with bright yellow or variegated foliage partners.

Shapes and Textures

Ajugas form low, spreading carpets that add variety among mounded and upright companions. The relatively small, tightly packed leaves and short flower spikes give the plants a fine texture: a dramatic contrast to hostas, Siberian bugloss (*Brunnera macrophylla*), and other companions with broad leaves. They also look great weaving around partners with strappy or spiky leaves, such as broadleaf sedge (*C. siderosticha*), irises, and spiderworts (*Tradescantia*).

Seasonal Features

In mild areas, ajugas may jump into bloom as winter ends and finish in late spring; elsewhere, they peak in mid- to late spring or early summer. Either way, they coincide with many popular spring-blooming perennials. Ajugas make great

Bloom Buddies
Marvelous Matches for Flowering Combos

Ajugas (*Ajuga*) can adapt to a range of growing conditions: from full sun in northern gardens (especially if the soil is on the moist side) to dry shade. Below are some suggestions for compatible partners that flower around the same time and are usually sturdy enough to hold their own in a combination with them.

Bearded irises (*Iris* Bearded Hybrids)

Bigroot geranium (*Geranium macrorrhizum*)

Comfreys (*Symphytum*)

Common bleeding heart (*Dicentra spectabilis*)

Golden ragwort (*Senecio aureus*)

Hellebores (*Helleborus*)

'Herman's Pride' yellow archangel (*Lamium galeobdolon*)

Lady's mantle (*Alchemilla mollis*)

Pulmonarias (*Pulmonaria*)

Siberian bugloss (*Brunnera macrophylla*)

Siberian iris (*Iris sibirica*)

Solomon's plume (*Smilacina racemosa*)

Solomon's seal (*Polygonatum odoratum*)

Willowleaf bluestar (*Amsonia tabernaemontana*)

companions for a wide variety of bulbs, providing a "living mulch" that keeps soil from splashing up onto close-to-the-ground blooms, like those of colchicums (*Colchicum*) and crocuses. Ajugas also contribute foliage interest to perennial combinations through summer and fall, and even through much or all of winter in mild climates.

Alchemilla
flowers early on, foliage for later

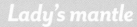
Lady's mantle
Full sun to partial shade; average,
well-drained soil

Alchemilla mollis '**Auslese**'
and *Lavandula angustifolia* '**Hidcote**'

Alchemilla mollis with *Geranium sanguineum*
and *Veronica prostrata* '**Trehane**'

A Perfect Match

A garden edging of chartreuse-y lady's mantle with purple-blue catmint (*Nepeta*) was one of the first plant combinations that ever caught my eye, and I've enjoyed this classic combination ever since. It's living proof that you don't need rare and unusual plants to make amazing perennial partnerships!

The frothy, chartreuse flower clusters of lady's mantle (*Alchemilla mollis*) look delicate, but this pretty perennial is surprisingly tough, adapting well to a wide range of growing conditions. Its clumps of scalloped, furry leaves reach about 1 foot tall; in bloom, the height can reach about 18 inches. Lady's mantle is usually recommended for Zones 3 to 7 or 8.

Color Considerations

Both in and out of bloom, lady's mantle combines beautifully with yellow flowers, like those of yellow foxglove (*Digitalis grandiflora*), as well as with solid yellow or yellow-variegated leaves, like those of 'June' hosta. The gray-green leaves are lovely with silvery, gray-, or blue-leaved companions, such as Japanese painted fern; with white-variegated partners, such as Everest Japanese sedge (*Carex oshimensis* 'CarFit01'); and with deep green leaves, like those of helle-bores (*Helleborus*).

Want a bit more zip? In leaf and in flower, lady's mantle makes a striking partner for reds and oranges, like those of 'Fanal' astilbe (*Astilbe*) and Oriental poppy (*Papaver orientale*); rich pinks and corals, like those of red valerian (*Centranthus ruber*) and 'Coral Charm' peony; and bright white flowers, such as 'White Swirl' Siberian iris (*Iris sibirica*). The greenish yellow blooms also look fantastic with blue-, purple-, or violet-flowered companions, such as cat-mints (*Nepeta*) and Rozanne hardy geranium (*Geranium* 'Gerwat').

Shapes and Textures

Lady's mantle grows in a low, domed mound, repeating the form of many other perennials and contrasting nicely with very upright com-panions. Repeat the rounded outline of its foliage with broad or rounded leaves, like those of heu-cheras (*Heuchera*), Siberian bugloss (*Brunnera mac-rophylla*), and wild gingers (*Asarum*); for variety, pair it with ferny- or narrow-leaved partners, such as Christmas fern (*Polystichum acrostichoides*) or golden Hakone grass (*Hakonechloa macra* 'Aureola'). The frothy flower clusters of lady's mantle look terrific mingling with larger or spiky blooms, like those of 'Sarastro' bellflower (*Campanula*) or perennial salvias (*Salvia*).

Seasonal Features

The blooms of lady's mantles persist for 4 to 6 weeks: late spring to early summer in the warmer parts of its range and early to midsum-mer in the cooler parts. They're terrific with

Bloom Buddies
Marvelous Matches for Flowering Combos

In cooler areas, lady's mantle (*Alchemilla*) can thrive in full sun if the soil is on the moist side. It likes some moisture in partial shade, too (either morning sun and afternoon shade or light all-day shade), but it can tolerate slightly drier condi-tions there, as well. Below is a sampling of com-patible perennials that flower around the same time and complement this lovely perennial.

Astilbes (*Astilbe*)

Baptisias (*Baptisia*)

Bearded irises (*Iris* Bearded Hybrids)

Bellflowers (*Campanula*)

Bleeding hearts (*Dicentra*)

Bluestars (*Amsonia*)

Catmints (*Nepeta*)

Columbines (*Aquilegia*)

Coral bells (*Heuchera*)

Delphiniums (*Delphinium*)

Foxgloves (*Digitalis*)

Greater masterwort (*Astrantia major*)

Hardy geraniums (*Geranium*)

Lupines (*Lupinus*)

Perennial salvias (*Salvia*)

Pincushion flowers (*Scabiosa*)

Red valerian (*Centranthus ruber*)

Siberian iris (*Iris sibirica*)

Speedwells (*Veronica*)

Sweet iris (*Iris pallida*)

Tuberous-rooted Jerusalem sage (*Phlomis tuberosa*)

the many other perennials that flower around this time—including foxgloves (*Digitalis*), irises, and peonies, to name just a few—as well as with the pink, purple, or white globe-shaped blooms of alliums (*Allium*).

Allium
fascinating flower forms

Allium 'Globemaster' with *Geranium macrorrhizum* 'Ingwersen's Variety' and *Viburnum opulus* 'Aureum'

Allium 'Mount Everest' with *Baptisia sphaerocarpa* 'Screamin' Yellow' and *Amsonia*

A Perfect Match

For years, I envied cooler-climate gardeners who could grow gorgeous lupines (*Lupinus*), because those plump spikes look fantastic among the "floating" globes of the big, ball-shaped alliums. Finally, I figured out that I could create a similar effect by combining the alliums with baptisias (*Baptisia*). Sometimes the baptisias don't fully color up until the alliums are almost over—but they're usually close enough to overlap for at least a week.

Alliums (*Allium*), also known as ornamental onions, are invaluable for adding color and fascinating flower forms to perennial combinations. Though individually rather small, the starry or bell-shaped blossoms of alliums are grouped into eye-catching clusters. Some of the most dramatic alliums produce large, ball-shaped blooms atop a stout, straight, leafless stem. *A. hollandicum* 'Purple Sensation' (also sold under *A. aflatunense*), for instance, grows 2 to 3 feet tall, with violet-purple, 3- to 4-inch-wide globes, while giant onion (*A. giganteum*) is taller—usually 3 to 4 feet—with pinkish purple, 4- to 8-inch globes. There are some stunning hybrids with even larger flower clusters, such as 'Ambassador', 'Gladiator', and Globemaster'. Star-of-Persia (*A. cristophii*, also sold as *A. christophii*) is 12 to 18 inches tall, with dense, pinkish lavender globes to about 10 inches across. Tumbleweed onion (*A. schubertii*) is similar in height and color, but its individual flowers are held at varying lengths, giving

Bloom Buddies
Marvelous Matches for Flowering Combos

Alliums (*Allium*) perform best when they get lots of sun while they are actively growing, though the late-spring to early-summer bloomers mostly don't mind if their site is in some shade by midsummer, once their leaves have died down. Average, well-drained soil is generally fine for these terrific partners.

Companions for most alliums in late spring to early summer:

Baptisias (*Baptisia*)

Bearded irises (*Iris* Bearded Hybrids)

Bellflowers (*Campanula*)

Bluestars (*Amsonia*)

Catmints (*Nepeta*)

Columbines (*Aquilegia*)

Euphorbias (*Euphorbia*)

Foxglove penstemon (*Penstemon digitalis*)

Hardy geraniums (*Geranium*)

Jerusalem sages (*Phlomis*)

Lady's mantle (*Alchemilla mollis*)

Lupines (*Lupinus*)

Peonies (*Paeonia*)

Perennial salvias (*Salvia*)

Purple mullein (*Verbascum phoeniceum*)

Siberian iris (*Iris sibirica*)

Sweet iris (*Iris pallida*)

Yarrows (*Achillea*)

Companions for drumstick allium (*A. sphaerocephalon*) in midsummer:

Agastaches (*Agastache*)

Bee balms (*Monarda*)

Blazing stars (*Liatris*)

Echinaceas (*Echinacea*)

Heleniums (*Helenium*)

Mountain fleeceflower (*Persicaria amplexicaulis*)

Nettleleaf mullein (*Verbascum chaixii*)

Ornamental oreganos (*Origanum*)

Rudbeckias (*Rudbeckia*)

Russian sages (*Perovskia*)

Sea hollies (*Eryngium*)

Shasta daisy (*Leucanthemum* × *superbum*)

Summer phlox (*Phlox paniculata*)

Torch lilies (*Kniphofia*)

the flower heads a distinctive starburst appearance.

There are many other amazing allium species, expanding the range of heights, colors, bloom times, and flower sizes. Drumstick allium (*A. sphaerocephalon*), for instance, is a charmer with dense, rosy purple ovals to about 1 inch across atop very slender, 18- to 24-inch-tall stems. Sicilian honey garlic (*A. siculum*, often sold as *Nectaroscordon siculum*) is another eye-catching option, with 3- to 4-foot-tall stems topped with nodding bells that are a combination of cream, green, and pink. It is hardy in Zones 5 to 9, while most other alliums are suited for Zones 4 to 8.

Color Considerations

Pinkish purple to violet-purple is the most common color range among the alliums, especially those with the large, ball-shaped blooms. They're terrific with blue to purple partners in a combination or an entire border based on those colors: Think of anise hyssops (*Agastache*), catmints (*Nepeta*), lavenders (*Lavandula*), perennial salvias (*Salvia*), and Siberian iris (*Iris sibirica*), for instance.

If you'd like to expand the color range of your blue to purple allium combinations, add some touches of magenta, such as rose campion (*Lychnis coronaria*) or winecups (*Callirhoe involucrata*), and deep red to burgundy, as in the flowers of burgundy loosestrife (*Lysimachia atropurpurea*) or crimson scabious (*Knautia macedonica*) or the foliage of Blackbird euphorbia (*Euphorbia* 'Nothowlee'). Or go lighter instead, with pink partners, such as dianthus (*Dianthus*); white flowers, like those of foxglove penstemon (*Penstemon digitalis*); silver-leaved perennials, such as artemisias (*Artemisia*) and lamb's ears (*Stachys byzantina*); or vivid yellow foliage, like that of golden feverfew (*Tanacetum*

parthenium 'Aureum') or golden oregano (*Origanum vulgare* 'Aureum').

Alliums with more intense colors, such as 'Purple Sensation' and drumstick allium, work surprisingly well with orange flowers, like those of butterfly weed (*Asclepias tuberosa*) or 'Fireglow' Griffith's spurge (*E. griffithii*), as well as silver or bright yellow foliage.

White-flowered selections of tall, large-clustered alliums, such as 'Mont Blanc' and 'Mount Everest', are wonderful with other whites in a moon garden or white border, along with silver, gray, and blue foliage. They're also terrific paired with the more common pinkish purple alliums and with the blue- and pink-flowered partners. The creamy bells of Sicilian honey garlic are charming with soft blues in flowers or leaves—like those of bluestars (*Amsonia*) or 'Fragrant Blue' hosta—and with pink flowers and plum-colored foliage to pick up their darker markings.

Shapes and Textures

It's easy to find room for alliums because they take up very little ground space, and their straight, unbranched stems look fantastic popping up through lower-growing, mounded perennials, such as hardy geraniums (*Geranium*) and perennial salvias, or the foliage of daylilies (*Hemerocallis*) or hostas. There are also practical benefits from this sort of pairing: For instance, the lower companions help to provide some support, keeping the allium stems upright. And, since allium foliage often turns yellow around or soon after flowering, the bushier plants around their bases cover up the declining leaves and bare stem bases.

Allium sphaerocephalon and *Agastache* 'Cotton Candy'

In bud, in bloom, and even in seed, the ball-shaped heads of the larger alliums tend to steal the show in any combination. Let them be the stars of a small bed or border by pairing them with small flowers or simple shapes, such as catmints and lesser calamint (*Calamintha nepetoides*). Or use them to add drama to a mass planting of a low- to medium-height ornamental grass, such as Mexican feather grass (*Stipa tenuissima*) or prairie dropseed (*Sporobolus heterolepis*). This sort of combination can also work well in some shade if you pair the alliums with bushy, upright ferns instead, such as common lady fern (*Athyrium filix-femina*) or male fern (*Dryopteris filix-mas*), or with shade-loving golden Hakone grass (*Hakonechloa macra* 'Aureola').

Of course, with such fun flower shapes, it's hard to resist pairing alliums with other striking partners, particularly spikes, like those of agastaches (*Agastache*), Jerusalem sages (*Phlomis*), lupines (*Lupinus*), mulleins (*Verbascum*), and perennial salvias. Alliums can also hold their own with other bold blooms, like those of bearded irises and Oriental poppies (*Papaver orientale*).

Seasonal Features

Alliums send up their leaves relatively early, in early to mid-spring. 'Purple Sensation' and Sicilian honey garlic are usually among the first of the taller alliums to flower in late spring, followed a week or two later by giant onion and similar species and hybrids, and then star-of-Persia and tumbleweed onion by early summer. The bloom periods of these alliums overlap or coincide with many border

Allium schoenoprasum and *Iris pallida* 'Argentea Variegata'

classics, including bellflowers (*Campanula*), delphiniums (*Delphinium*), peonies, and Siberian iris (*Iris sibirica*), as well as roses. Drumstick allium peaks several weeks later, around midsummer, and combines delightfully with daylilies, purple coneflower (*Echinacea purpurea*), yarrows (*Achillea*), and other summer favorites.

Most alliums hold their color for about 3 weeks, then develop into interesting seed heads, extending their season of interest through much of summer, at least. All but the latest-flowering alliums (such as 8- to 10-inch-tall *A. thunbergii* 'Ozawa', which produces its purplish pink blooms in October) are dormant by early fall. This is usually when you'll see them for sale with daffodils, tulips, and other dormant, hardy bulbs, so it's a good time to add them to your garden.

Amsonia
multiseason features

Amsonia 'Blue Ice'
and *Carex oshimensis* 'Evergold'

Amsonia hubrichtii
and *Baptisia* 'Purple Smoke'

A Perfect Match

Arkansas bluestar is one of my must-have perennials: not for its flowers, but for its fine-textured foliage and fantastic fall color. I've made some memorable seasonal pairings by planting it around shrubs with showy fall foliage—particularly viburnums (*Viburnum*). When cool autumn weather arrives, the reds of the viburnums and the gold of the bluestar make a hot combination.

Tough and practically trouble-free, bluestars (*Amsonia*) bring multiseason features to your combinations: first flowers, then foliage texture, and finally fall color. Willowleaf bluestar (*A. tabernaemontana*), with slender, tapered foliage, and Arkansas or threadleaf bluestar (*A. hubrichtii*), with nearly needlelike leaves, take a few years to fill out but eventually reach 3 to 4 feet tall and wide. They both bear clusters of starry, spring or early-summer flowers that may range in color from pale blue to nearly white. You can also find crosses, such as 'Seaford Skies', that share the traits of both parent species. The foliage of hybrid 'Blue Ice' looks rather like that of willowleaf bluestar, but it's shorter (to about 18 inches tall and 24 inches wide), with deep blue buds and medium blue to lavender blue flowers. Willowleaf bluestar is generally recommended for Zones 3 to 9, the others for Zones 4 to 9.

Color Considerations

The soft blues of bluestars are perfectly suited to pairings with a wide range of pinks, like those of common chives (*Allium schoenoprasum*), 'Coral Charm' peony, and red campion (*Silene dioica*). Flowers and foliage in pale, clear, or greenish yellows are also lovely: Think of buttery Anthea yarrow (*Achillea* 'Anblo') or yellow foxglove (*Digitalis grandiflora*) with Arkansas or willowleaf bluestars, for instance, or vibrant yellow 'Screamin' Yellow' yellow false indigo (*Baptisia sphaerocarpa*) or 'Citronelle' heuchera (*Heuchera*) with the slightly darker 'Blue Ice'.

Bluestars are exquisite paired with white-flowered partners for a cool, fresh effect, and there's an abundance of options to choose from: Consider foxglove penstemon (*Penstemon digitalis*), giant fleeceflower (*Persicaria polymorpha*), 'Snow Hill' perennial salvia (*Salvia*), 'White Star' columbine (*Aquilegia*), or white irises, such as 'Immortality' bearded iris or 'White Swirl' Siberian iris (*Iris sibirica*), to name just a few.

If you enjoy creating sophisticated combinations within one color range, try pairing bluestars with other tints, tones, and shades of blue and purple-blue that appear around the same time, like those of catmints (*Nepeta*), perennial salvias (*Salvia*), Siberian irises, and speedwells (*Veronica*) for flowers and blue hostas and blue fescues (*Festuca*) for foliage. Silver and gray leaves and white flowers also look terrific as accents in blue-based bluestar combos.

Shapes and Textures

Bluestars have a broad, mounded form that repeats the form of many other perennials,

Bloom Buddies
Marvelous Matches for Flowering Combos

Bluestars (*Amsonia*) are sturdy, dependable perennials that can adapt to a range of conditions, as long as the site isn't constantly soggy or in heavy shade. That makes it easy to find lots of compatible flowering companions, including the perennials listed below.

Ajugas (*Ajuga*)

Baptisias (*Baptisia*)

Bearded irises (*Iris* Bearded Hybrids)

Bleeding hearts (*Dicentra*)

Blue flax (*Linum perenne*)

Catmints (*Nepeta*)

Chives (*Allium schoenoprasum*)

Columbines (*Aquilegia*)

Delphiniums (*Delphinium*)

Dianthus (*Dianthus*)

Foxglove penstemon (*Penstemon digitalis*)

Green-and-gold (*Chrysogonum virginianum*)

Hardy geraniums (*Geranium*)

Jacob's ladders (*Polemonium*)

Lady's mantle (*Alchemilla mollis*)

Lupines (*Lupinus*)

Meadow rues (*Thalictrum*)

Mountain bluet (*Centaurea montana*)

Peonies (*Paeonia*)

Perennial salvias (*Salvia*)

Pincushion flowers (*Scabiosa*)

Siberian iris (*Iris sibirica*)

Woodland phlox (*Phlox divaricata*)

such as baptisias (*Baptisia*) and hardy geraniums (*Geranium*), and makes an interesting contrast for strongly upright companions, such as foxgloves (*Digitalis*), 'Karl Foerster' feather reed grass (*Calamagrostis* × *acutiflora*), and summer phlox (*Phlox paniculata*). Bluestars are particularly useful for covering the "bare ankles" of plants that tend to have few leaves at the bases of their tall stems at bloom time, such as Brazilian vervain (*Verbena bonariensis*), golden lace (*Patrinia scabiosifolia*), Joe-Pye weeds (*Eupatorium*), and New England asters (*Aster novae-angliae*).

Foliage-wise, willowleaf bluestar and 'Blue Ice' have a medium-fine texture, while Arkansas bluestar is definitely on the fine side. They all look sharp contrasted with perennials that have broad or rounded leaves, such as 'Big Ears' lamb's ears (*Stachys byzantina*), hostas, and lady's mantle (*Alchemilla mollis*), and with broad,

strappy or spiky leaves, like those of bearded irises, daylilies (*Hemerocallis*), and yuccas (*Yucca*).

Seasonal Features

In southern gardens, bluestars start flowering around the end of April; in cooler regions, they usually peak in May or June. Arkansas bluestar and willowleaf bluestar generally bloom for 3 to 4 weeks; 'Blue Ice' tends to last 4 to 6 weeks. Their bloom period overlaps or coincides with many other border classics, including dianthus (*Dianthus*), hardy geraniums, irises, and peonies.

After flowering, the foliage provides an interesting textural accent, and its rich green color is useful for separating potentially uncomfortable color pairings, such as orangey pinks with bluish pinks or pale purples with orangey yellows. It's also a neutral but beautiful backdrop for flowers that offer intricate shadings and color combinations, such as those of many hybrid daylilies and true

Amsonia 'Blue Ice' and *Forsythia* 'Fiesta'

Amsonia tabernaemontana and *Iris sibirica* 'Butter and Sugar'

lilies (*Lilium*), and for partners with variegated, yellow, or silvery leaves.

Fall color isn't a feature that most people associate with perennials, but the autumn display of bluestars can rival that of many deciduous shrubs and trees. Arkansas bluestar is most spectacular, ranging from brilliant yellow to orangey yellow to reddish orange, but the yellows of willowleaf bluestar and 'Blue Ice' are also very attractive. Make the most of their late-season show by pairing bluestars with other perennials that show a striking seasonal color change, such as hardy geraniums, Japanese blood grass (*Imperata cylindrica* 'Rubra'), leadwort (*Ceratostigma plumbaginoides*), prairie dropseed (*Sporobolus heterolepis*), and switch grasses (*Panicum*).

To bring even more color into your autumn garden, combine bluestars with bright fall blooms, including asters, azure monkshood (*Aconitum carmichaelii*), chrysanthemums, goldenrods (*Solidago*), and pink muhly grass (*Muhlenbergia capillaris*). And don't forget seed heads! Fall-colored bluestars make a great contrast to

Amsonia hubrichtii with *Muhlenbergia capillaris*, *Miscanthus sinensis*, and *Panicum virgatum* 'Northwind'

the brown-black seed heads of echinaceas (*Echinacea*) or rudbeckias (*Rudbeckia*) and the flattened, reddish heads of upright sedums (*Sedum*), such as 'Autumn Fire'.

Exploring More Options: Partners beyond Perennials

Arkansas bluestar (*Amsonia hubrichtii*) and willowleaf bluestar (*A. tabernaemontana*), particularly, combine beautifully with spring bulbs. These bluestars tend to be upright in bloom, so you can easily tuck early bulbs around their bases; then the bluestars' stems spread out to fill the space left when the bulbs die back to the ground in summer. For bulb partners that bloom at the same time as bluestars, consider camassias (*Camassia*), Sicilian honey bells (*Allium siculum*), summer snowflake (*Leucojum aestivum*), and late-flowering tulips. The alliums (*Allium*) with large, globe-shaped blooms, such as 'Gladiator' and 'Globemaster', make excellent co-stars for bluestars.

Bluestars are superb partners for shrubs in mixed borders. These perennials are tough enough to compete with spreading shrub roots for moisture, and they can adapt to a good bit of shade as their woody partners get larger. They're especially handy for filling the space around spiny shrubs, such as hardy orange (*Poncirus trifoliata*), hollies (*Ilex*), and roses, because you don't have to do a lot of fussing close to prickly leaves or stems.

Anemone
it's all about the flowers

Anemone hupehensis and *Verbena bonariensis*

Anemone × *hybrida* 'Honorine Jobert' and *Hakonechloa macra* 'Aureola'

A Perfect Match

There are lots of pinks, purples, and yellows to choose from for fall combinations, but not many bright whites, so I treasure 'Honorine Jobert' Japanese anemone. It's exquisite in front of 'Morning Light' miscanthus (*Miscanthus sinensis*), which has a fine white leaf edge that's a subtle but elegant echo of the anemone's crisp white petals. I've also seen it look stunning set against a cobalt blue wall. It may be time to give my garden shed a new coat of paint so I can try that for myself.

Delicate in appearance but sturdy by nature, anemones (*Anemone*) offer beautiful blooms to bridge the seasons. Snowdrop anemone (*A. sylvestris*), with bright white flowers on individual, 12- to 18-inch-tall stems, shines in late spring to early summer. It's generally hardy in Zones 3 to 8. There are a number of later-blooming species, hybrids, and selections that typically flower from late summer into fall. Their names are a bit jumbled: The entire group is often referred to as Japanese anemones, but you may see cultivars listed under *A.* × *hybrida*, *A. japonica*, or *A. tomentosa*, or under Chinese anemone (*A. hupehensis*) or grapeleaf anemone (*A. vitifolia*). By any name, they're beautiful perennials, reaching 1 to 2 feet in leaf and 3 to 5 feet in flower, with single, semidouble, or double pink or white flowers atop branching stems. Most are recommended for Zones 5 to 7 or 8, but 'Robustissima' may overwinter as far north as Zone 3.

Bloom Buddies
Marvelous Matches for Flowering Combos

Anemones (*Anemone*) generally grow best with morning sun and afternoon shade. The more sun they get, the more moisture they need (particularly in warmer areas), but they don't like soggy soil, especially in winter. Here's a sampling of perennials that can thrive in similar conditions and complement their elegant blooms.

Partners for snowdrop anemone (*A. sylvestris*):

Ajugas (*Ajuga*)

Bergenias (*Bergenia*)

Columbines (*Aquilegia*)

Common bleeding heart (*Dicentra spectabilis*)

'Georgia Blue' speedwell (*Veronica umbrosa*)

Lady's mantle (*Alchemilla mollis*)

Leopard's banes (*Doronicum*)

Mourning widow geranium (*Geranium phaeum*)

Robb's spurge (*Euphorbia amygdaloides* var. *robbiae*)

Siberian bugloss (*Brunnera macrophylla*)

Solomon's seals (*Polygonatum*)

Wild geranium (*Geranium maculatum*)

Willowleaf bluestar (*Amsonia tabernaemontana*)

Wood poppy (*Stylophorum diphyllum*)

Partners for later-flowering anemones (such as *A. × hybrida*, *A. japonica*, and *A. vitifolia*):

Asters (*Aster*)

August lily (*Hosta plantaginea*)

'Autumn Bride' heuchera (*Heuchera villosa*)

Bugbanes (*Cimicifuga*)

Culver's roots (*Veronicastrum*)

False aster (*Boltonia asteroides*)

Hardy begonia (*Begonia grandis*)

Joe-Pye weeds (*Eupatorium*)

Monkshoods (*Aconitum*)

Mountain fleeceflower (*Persicaria amplexicaulis*)

'Superba' Chinese astilbe (*Astilbe chinensis* var. *taquetii*)

White Japanese burnet (*Sanguisorba tenuifolia* 'Alba')

White mugwort (*Artemisia lactiflora*)

Woodland sage (*Salvia koyamae*)

Color Considerations

The blooms of snowdrop anemone and Japanese anemones look lovely with blue, gray, or silver leaves, especially as part of a "white garden" with other white blooms and white-variegated foliage. Or pair pink Japanese anemones with flowering partners in other tints and shades of pink, such as pale 'Max Vogel' Japanese anemone with hot pink 'Alma Potschke' New England aster (*Aster novae-angliae*) or bright pink 'Pamina' Chinese anemone with lighter pink hardy begonia (*Begonia grandis*).

To introduce more variety, try pink or white anemones with blue flowers: snowdrop anemone with forget-me-nots (*Myosotis*) or 'Origami Blue' columbine (*Aquilegia*), for example, or Japanese anemones with Frikart's aster (*A. × frikartii*) or monkshoods (*Aconitum*). Pale-flowered anemones also show off beautifully against a backdrop of

Anemone sylvestris and *Matteuccia struthiopteris*

Shapes and Textures

Individual anemone plants have an upright habit, but they all tend to spread to form broad patches. The leaves of snowdrop anemone are deeply cut, those of 'Robustissima' Chinese anemone are broad but lobed, and those of other Japanese anemones are usually separated into three parts; overall, they have a medium to fine texture in both leaf and bloom. They're not particularly distinctive in either form or texture, so consider giving them companions that *are* distinctive, such as strongly upright Culver's root (*Veronicastrum virginicum*) or 'Karl Foerster' feather reed grass (*Calamagrostis × acutiflora*); strappy-leaved daylilies (*Hemerocallis*) or irises; bold-leaved hostas; or cloud-like tufted hair grass (*Deschampsia cespitosa*).

Seasonal Features

Snowdrop anemone begins blooming in April in the warmest parts of its range and May in other areas, often continuing into early summer, at least. In some areas, it may continue to produce scattered new flowers through the rest of the growing season or have a short rebloom period in late summer or fall. The flowers are followed by clusters of fluffy white seed heads; they add interest in summer, but removing them may encourage rebloom. Make the most of the late-spring show by pairing them with other perennials and bulbs that flower around their peak period, such as willowleaf bluestar (*Amsonia hubrichtii*) and wood poppy (*Stylophorum diphyllum*), then use companions with colorful foliage to carry the show through the rest of the season.

dark foliage, like that of deep purple 'Hillside Black Beauty' bugbane (*Cimicifuga simplex*).

Anemone blossoms have bright yellow centers that you can echo with yellow-flowered partners, such as lady's mantle (*Alchemilla mollis*) with snowdrop anemones or goldenrods (*Solidago*) or woodland sage (*Salvia koyamae*) with Japanese anemones. Perennials with solid yellow or yellow-variegated leaves, such as golden meadowsweet (*Filipendula ulmaria* 'Aurea'), golden Hakone grass (*Hakonechloa macra* 'Aureola'), or variegated blue lilyturf (*Liriope muscari* 'Variegata'), work well with anemones whatever the season.

Anemone × hybrida 'Honorine Jobert' with *Ilex verticillata*

as late July, while most selections listed under *A. × hybrida* begin in early to mid-fall. Despite the variation, it's easy to find plenty of complementary companions: late bloomers like asters, Joe-Pye weeds (*Eupatorium*), 'Superba' Chinese astilbe (*Astilbe chinensis* var. *taquetii*), and turtleheads (*Chelone*); interesting berries and seed heads, like those of doll's eyes (*Actaea pachypoda*) and purple coneflower (*Echinacea purpurea*); and fall-colored foliage, like that of foamy bells (× *Heucherella*) and hardy geraniums (*Geranium*). Japanese anemones also produce fluffy white seed heads as their flowers finish in fall; then they disappear for winter.

Special Effects

Both snowdrop and Japanese anemones can be vigorous creepers, especially in loose, rich soil, so instead of combining them with delicate perennials in your borders, consider pairing them with other sturdy perennials that seed or spread freely to fill space around shrubs. Some candidates to consider include ajugas (*Ajuga*), blue mistflower (*Eupatorium coelestinum*), comfreys (*Symphytum*), golden ragwort (*Senecio aureus*), lamb's ears (*Stachys byzantina*), lily-of-the-valley (*Convallaria majalis*), and obedient plant (*Physostegia virginiana*).

Japanese anemones tend to sprout late in spring, so they make good partners for bulbs and perennials that are showy early in the season, such as bleeding hearts (*Dicentra*) and tulips. As the early bloomers die back, the anemone leaves fill in.

Most Japanese anemones flower for 6 to 8 weeks in late summer to early fall, though the start and length of their bloom period varies depending on the weather and cultivar. 'Robustissima', for instance, may begin as early

Exploring More Options: Partners beyond Perennials

Japanese anemones look terrific with deciduous shrubs that have late-season flowers, such as 'Tardiva' and 'Unique' panicle hydrangea (*Hydrangea paniculata*); bright fall berries, like those of purple beautyberries (*Callicarpa*) and viburnums (*Viburnum*); or showy autumn colors, like those of fothergillas (*Fothergilla*) or summersweets (*Clethra*).

Aquilegia
old-fashioned favorites

Aquilegia flabellata 'Nana' and Sedum ternatum

Aquilegia canadensis with Matteuccia struthiopteris and Hyacinthoides hispanica

A Perfect Match

I've never seen a columbine I didn't like, but I'm particularly fond of the superdark ones, such as 'Black Barlow'. They can easily get lost among leafy green companions, though, so I like to set them in front of a lighter background. One of my favorite flowering partners for them is the appropriately named fragrant abelia (*Abelia mosanensis*), which has pink buds and powerfully perfumed white blooms that contrast prettily with the dark columbine blossoms.

The demurely nodding blooms of these old-fashioned favorites are charming for spring-into-summer combinations. Held atop slender, 1- to 3-foot-tall stems, the flowers of many columbine (*Aquilegia*) species and hybrids are distinctive for their short or long, straight or curved "spurs," which are filled with nectar and very attractive to bees, hawk moths, and hummingbirds.

Wild or eastern columbine (*A. canadensis*), native to the eastern half of North America, and crimson or western columbine (*A. formosa*), native to the western half, both bear scarlet-and-yellow blooms. Common or European columbine (*A. vulgaris*) and hybrid columbine (*A. × hybrida*) offer a wide range of flower forms—from single to double and spurred to spurless—and a rainbow of colors. Fan columbine (*A. flabellata*) tends to be shorter than the others (to about 1 foot), with blue-green leaves and short-spurred flowers that are usually solid blue, solid white, blue and white, or pink and white. All of these columbines are generally hardy in Zones 3 to 8 or 9.

Color Considerations

There's a columbine color to suit almost any combination. The whites and pastels of common columbine, hybrid columbines, and fan columbines harmonize beautifully with similarly colored flowering partners, as well as with silver, gray, blue, or peach-colored foliage. Or pair a pastel columbine with a more saturated version of the same color: pale purple-blue 'Tower Light Blue' with darker blue false indigo (*Baptisia australis*), for instance. Columbines that come in bright or deep colors, such as sunny yellow 'Denver Gold', ruby red 'Ruby Port', and superdark 'Black Barlow', add a welcome touch of intensity among softer spring colors.

It's quite common to find bicolor columbines—usually white or yellow with some other color in the same flower—and you can use those colors to inspire your choice of companions. 'William Guiness', for instance, has deep purple-and-white blooms that would look great paired with the dark leaves of 'Purple Petticoats' heuchera (*Heuchera*) and white blossoms of snowdrop anemone (*Anemone sylvestris*). Or you could use a partner with yellow foliage, such as 'All Gold' Hakone grass (*Hakonechloa macra*), golden meadowsweet (*Filipendula ulmaria* 'Aurea'), or 'Little Aurora' hosta, to pick up the yellow in the blooms of scarlet-and-yellow wild columbine.

One of the most important color-related issues for columbines is their tendency to cross

Bloom Buddies
Marvelous Matches for Flowering Combos

In most areas, columbines (*Aquilegia*) look best in a site with morning sun and afternoon shade or light all-day shade, but they can do well in full sun, especially if the soil is on the moist side (though not waterlogged). Here's a sampling of compatible companions that bloom around the same time as peak columbine season.

Ajugas (*Ajuga*)

Baptisias (*Baptisia*)

Bearded irises (*Iris* Bearded Hybrids)

Bleeding hearts (*Dicentra*)

Bluestars (*Amsonia*)

Catmints (*Nepeta*)

Creeping phlox (*Phlox stolonifera*)

Crested iris (*Iris cristata*)

Geums (*Geum*)

Hardy geraniums (*Geranium*)

Jacob's ladders (*Polemonium*)

Lady's mantle (*Alchemilla mollis*)

Lupines (*Lupinus*)

Masterworts (*Astrantia*)

Peonies (*Paeonia*)

Perennial salvias (*Salvia*)

Siberian bugloss (*Brunnera macrophylla*)

Siberian iris (*Iris sibirica*)

Snowdrop anemone (*Anemone sylvestris*)

Sweet iris (*Iris pallida*)

Woodland phlox (*Phlox divaricata*)

if you grow more than one kind, resulting in seedlings in a range of colors. That's not necessarily a bad thing—the variety can be a delightful surprise—but it can be disappointing

Aquilegia × hybrida 'Biedermeier Mix' and *Dicentra spectabilis (left); Aquilegia vulgaris* 'Clementine Rose' and *Corydalis lutea (above)*

if you are counting on combinations based on specific colors. In that case, try to stick with one species or cultivar, or buy named plants or seed strains as needed to replace old clumps instead of letting them self-sow.

Shapes and Textures

In leaf, columbines are distinctly mounded; in bloom, the shorter cultivars are still mounded while the taller ones are more upright. For a contrasting habit, consider pairing them with carpeting or broadly mounded perennials, such as European wild ginger (*Asarum europaeum*) or bloody cranesbill (*Geranium sanguineum*), or those with a distinctly upright form, like that of foxgloves (*Digitalis*).

Multipart leaves and dainty blossoms give columbines a fine texture. They look striking paired with broad or spiky leaves, like those of heucheras (*Heuchera*), hostas, and sweet iris (*Iris pallida*), and with big, bold blooms, like those of large-flowered alliums (*Allium*), bearded irises, and peonies.

Seasonal Features

Wild columbine and crimson columbine tend to be the earliest to open—usually in early to mid-spring—while other species and hybrids start in late spring; then they continue to bloom for 6 to 8 weeks. That means they're around to co-star with lots of other spring to early-summer perennials and bulbs, such as bluestars (*Amsonia*), cushion spurge (*Euphorbia polychroma*), epimediums (*Epimedium*), and hybrid tulips—to name just a few—as well as cool-season annuals and biennials, such as forget-me-nots (*Myosotis*) and honesty (*Lunaria annua*).

Once the flowers finish, leave some or all of the flowering stems in place to form seeds, if you want to get self-sown seedlings to expand your planting or to have a steady supply of new plants. (Columbines tend to be short lived, so expect to replace the clumps every 2 to 3 years.) Or cut off the flowering stems—or the whole plant, if the leaves look tired or damaged—a few inches above the ground to get a flush of new growth by the end of summer.

Artemisia
some for foliage, one for flowers

Artemisia 'Powis Castle' and *Geranium* 'Gerwat' (Rozanne)

Artemisia lactiflora 'Guizhou' and *Echinacea purpurea*

A Perfect Match

It's so easy to make high-contrast pairings with silvery artemisias and bright flowers or dark foliage that I sometimes have to challenge myself to try something more subtle. One of my successes was combining feathery 'Powis Castle' with the broad, fuzzy foliage of 'Big Ears' lamb's ears (*Stachys byzantina*). Their colors were similar, but the difference in height, habit, and texture offered just the right amount of variety.

Artemisias (*Artemisia*), also known as wormwoods, are invaluable for adding interesting foliage to perennial pairings. There are several species and selections with bright silver to silver-gray leaves, varying in height and habit. Two well-known low growers—to about 6 inches tall, but at least twice as wide—are silvermound artemisia (*A. schmidtiana* 'Silver Mound' or 'Nana') and beach wormwood (*A. stelleriana*). Both are hardy in Zones 3 to 9 but usually perform best in 3 to 7 or 8.

Hybrid 'Powis Castle' forms a larger, shrubby mound that's usually 2 to 3 feet tall, branching out to twice as wide or even wider in ideal conditions. It's possibly hardy in Zones 5 to 9 but may not overwinter dependably north of Zone 7 without excellent drainage. Western mugwort (*A. ludoviciana*) is similar in size: around 3 feet tall for 'Silver King' and 'Silver Queen' and 2 feet for 'Valerie Finnis'. Best suited for Zones 3 to 9, the plants spread freely by rhizomes to form broad patches, to the

Bloom Buddies
Marvelous Matches for Flowering Combos

Silvery artemisias (*Artemisia*) typically prefer full sun and average to dry soil, while white mugwort (*A. lactiflora*) can adapt to sun or partial shade and average to moist soil. Below are some compatible flowering companions that will complement the silvery foliage or white flowers.

Pairings for silver-leaved artemisias:

Bearded irises (*Iris* Bearded Hybrids)

Butterfly weed (*Asclepias tuberosa*)

Daylilies (*Hemerocallis*)

Dianthus (*Dianthus*)

Echinaceas (*Echinacea*)

Knautias (*Knautia*)

Ornamental oreganos (*Origanum*)

Penstemons (*Penstemon*)

Perennial salvias (*Salvia*)

Sedums (*Sedum*)

Sweet iris (*Iris pallida*)

Torch lilies (*Kniphofia*)

Verbenas (*Verbena*)

Yarrows (*Achillea*)

Pairings for white mugwort (*A. lactiflora*):

Giant coneflower (*Rudbeckia maxima*)

Japanese anemones (*Anemone*)

Japanese burnet (*Sanguisorba tenuifolia*)

Monkshoods (*Aconitum*)

New England aster (*Aster novae-angliae*)

Perennial lobelias (*Lobelia*)

Perennial sunflowers (*Helianthus*)

Turtleheads (*Chelone*)

point that they can crowd out less vigorous companions.

White mugwort (*A. lactiflora*), also known as ghost plant, is very different from more common artemisias. Its leaves are green rather than silver, and it produces showy plumes of creamy white flowers atop 3- to 6-foot-tall stems from mid- or late summer into fall. Plants sold as 'Guizhou' or Guizhou Group have purple-flushed green leaves and purple stems. White mugwort is hardy in Zones 3 to 9.

Color Considerations

Silvery artemisias have small greenish yellow blooms that are not particularly interesting;

with them, you focus on the foliage. They harmonize beautifully with white flowers (more on that under "Special Effects" on page 34); with blue and blue-purple blooms, like those of balloon flower (*Platycodon grandiflorus*), catmints (*Nepeta*), and pincushion flowers (*Scabiosa*); and with gray and blue leaves, like those of dianthus (*Dianthus*), donkey-tail spurge (*Euphorbia myrsinites*), and many sedums (*Sedum*).

Silvery artemisias mix comfortably with pastel-flowering partners, such as peachy 'Ruffled Apricot' daylily (*Hemerocallis*) or soft pink 'Bright Eyes' summer phlox (*Phlox paniculata*) or Lancaster geranium (*Geranium sanguineum* var. *striatum*). They look wonderful with soft to bright yellows: Consider lady's mantle (*Alchemilla mollis*), 'Moonshine' yarrow (*Achillea*), or 'Prairie Sun' black-eyed Susan (*Rudbeckia hirta*) for blooms, for example, or golden oregano (*Origanum vulgare* 'Aureum') or Sunshine Blue blue mist shrub (*Caryopteris incana* 'Jason') as leafy companions.

For a bit more intensity, pair silvery artemisias with perennials that have bright or deep green leaves, or go for an even stronger contrast with maroons or dark purples, like the flowers of 'Black Ambrosia' daylily or 'Hello Darkness' bearded iris or the leaves of 'Chocolate' white snakeroot (*Eupatorium rugosum*) or 'Obsidian' heuchera (*Heuchera*). Add some purple coneflower (*Echinacea purpurea*), 'Purple Emperor' sedum (*Sedum*), red valerian (*Centranthus ruber*), or another rosy pink perennial to a silver-and-"black" pairing for a combo that's sure to catch the eye. Silvery artemisias are also stunning as a setting for brilliantly colored blooms, such as magenta rose campion (*Lychnis coronaria*), glowing red 'Firebird' penstemon (*Penstemon*), scarlet-orange 'Allegro' Oriental poppy (*Papaver orientale*), or vibrant 'Homestead Purple' verbena (*Verbena*).

With white mugwort, the flowers are the main color feature. Use them to repeat other later-season whites, such as false aster (*Boltonia asteroides*); choose pastel companions, such as 'Harrington's Pink' New England aster (*Aster novae-angliae*); or go for more intense partners, such as rich blue azure monkshood (*Aconitum carmichaelii*), vivid purple New York ironweed (*Vernonia noveboracensis*), or sunny yellow 'Lemon Queen' perennial sunflower (*Helianthus*). Echo the purple stems of 'Guizhou' with a dark-leaved co-star, such as 'Chocolate' white snakeroot (*Eupatorium rugosum*) or Black Beauty elderberry (*Sambucus nigra* 'Gerda').

Shapes and Textures

The low, spreading forms of silvermound artemisia and beach wormwood work well around the bases of larger mounds and upright growers. The broad mounds of 'Powis Castle' and expanding patches of western mugworts contrast with low, spreading or trailing companions, such as hardy geraniums (*Geranium*), and strongly vertical stems or spiky blooms, like those of dense blazing star (*Liatris spicata*), summer phlox (*Phlox paniculata*), and torch lilies (*Kniphofia*). It's not unusual for 'Powis Castle' and western mugworts to lose their lower leaves by late summer, especially in humid areas, so consider placing them behind partners that will cover their bare lower stems.

Texture-wise, slender or deeply cut leaves give the silvery artemisias a fine texture. Use them to echo partners with ferny or lacy leaves, or contrast them with companions that have broad, rounded, or strappy foliage, such as

Artemisia schmidtiana 'Silver Mound' and *Stachys byzantina* 'Big Ears'

agaves (*Agave*), bearded irises, 'Big Ears' lamb's ears (*Stachys byzantina*), heucheras (*Heuchera*), and yuccas (*Yucca*).

Upright in form and lacy in leaf, white mugwort contrasts handsomely with mounded companions and broad or grassy foliage, like that of ligularias (*Ligularia*) and 'Dallas Blues' switch grass (*Panicum virgatum*). Its plumy blooms add welcome variety among the many daisy-form perennials that are in flower around the same time, including echinaceas (*Echinacea*) and rudbeckias (*Rudbeckia*). You can also contrast them with slender spikes, like those of Culver's roots (*Veronicastrum*), and broad, branching bloom clusters, like those of Joe-Pye weeds (*Eupatorium*).

Seasonal Features

Silvery artemisias are showy from the time they sprout in spring. If hot, humid, or rainy weather in midsummer causes the leaves to look tired or drop off, trim the plants back by about half; they'll resprout in a few weeks and look good for the rest of the growing season, even into winter in mild areas.

White mugwort usually starts flowering in late summer and continues into early or even mid-fall, overlapping or coinciding with the bloom period of many other later-blooming perennials, including asters, obedient plant (*Physostegia virginiana*), perennial sunflowers (*Helianthus*), and turtleheads (*Chelone*), as well as warm-season ornamental grasses, such as miscanthus (*Miscanthus*) and switch grasses (*Panicum*).

Special Effects

The silvery artemisias and white mugwort are all excellent choices for evening gardens. The pale leaves and flowers reflect any available light—from moonlight, streetlights, or solar garden lights, for instance—so you can appreciate the plants even if you don't get outside until dinner is done and the evening is coming to a close. Combine them with white-flowering partners, such as 'David' summer phlox (*P. paniculata*), gaura (*Gaura lindheimeri*), Shasta daisy (*Leucanthemum × superbum*), and Iceberg rose (*Rosa* 'Korbin'), and with white-striped foliage, like that of variegated sweet iris (*Iris pallida* 'Variegata').

Western mugwort and its cultivars can spread too quickly to make good companions in typical beds and borders, so consider setting aside a separate "wild garden" area for them and for other perennials that can be aggressive spreaders, such as ajugas (*Ajuga*), bee balms (*Monarda*), loosestrifes (*Lysimachia*), and obedient plant (*Physostegia virginiana*).

Artemisia stelleriana 'Silver Brocade' with *Salvia officinalis* 'Berggarten' and *Thymus vulgaris*

Asarum
an element of elegance

Asarum europaeum and *Hakonechloa macra* 'Aureola'

Asarum canadense and *Polygonatum × hybridum* 'Striatum'

A Perfect Match

When I need a perennial to fill in around either hostas or ferns, wild gingers are among the first companions I consider. Canada wild ginger is particularly handy for covering the ground around larger partners, such as 'Krossa Regal' hosta, and I've even seen it hold its own with ostrich fern (*Matteuccia struthiopteris*), which can easily crowd out less vigorous partners.

With their simple leaf shapes and soothing range of greens, wild gingers (*Asarum*) are great go-to perennials for adding a finishing touch to shady combinations. Wild gingers do bloom, but their small, brownish flowers are mostly hidden by their heart-shaped to nearly rounded leaves.

Canada wild ginger (*A. canadense*) is medium to deep green, with a covering of short, soft hairs that give its foliage a velvety appearance. It's rated for Zones 2 or 3 to 8. There are also several evergreen species with smooth, glossy, deep green leaves, including solid green European wild ginger (*A. europaeum*), best suited to Zones 4 to 7, and Chinese wild ginger (*A. splendens*), with larger, silver-splotched foliage, for Zones 5 to 9.

Color Considerations

The gorgeous greens of wild gingers combine easily with any other color but are especially eye-catching with white-flowered

Bloom Buddies
Marvelous Matches for Flowering Combos

The lovely leaves of wild gingers (*Asarum*) complement the beautiful blooms of many other shade-loving perennials that also appreciate average to moist (but not soggy) soil. Below is just a sampling of companions to consider.

Astilbes (*Astilbe*)

Bleeding hearts (*Dicentra*)

Columbines (*Aquilegia*)

Corydalis (*Corydalis*)

Creeping phlox (*Phlox stolonifera*)

Dwarf goatsbeard (*Aruncus aethusifolius*)

Epimediums (*Epimedium*)

Foamflowers (*Tiarella*)

Foamy bells (× *Heucherella*)

Hardy begonia (*Begonia grandis*)

Heucheras (*Heuchera*)

Pulmonarias (*Pulmonaria*)

Solomon's seals (*Polygonatum*)

Wild geranium (*Geranium maculatum*)

Woodland phlox (*Phlox divaricata*)

Some other striking co-stars for foliage color include powder blues, like those of 'Halcyon' hosta or blue wood sedge (*Carex flaccosperma*), and bright yellows: 'Gold Heart' common bleeding heart (*Dicentra spectabilis*), for instance.

Shapes and Textures

Wild gingers grow in low, spreading patches that are usually 6 to 8 inches tall: They're ideal for filling in around mounding and upright-growing partners, such as hostas and toad lilies (*Tricyrtis*). Or create a tapestry effect by planting wild gingers in drifts with other low-growing shade perennials, such as crested iris (*Iris cristata*) and epimediums (*Epimedium*), for a gorgeous groundcover under trees and shrubs.

The rounded or heart-shaped leaves of wild gingers provide welcome visual variety among feathery foliage, like that of many ferns. Their shape contrasts pleasingly with spiky or strappy foliage, too, like that of 'Banana Boat' broadleaf sedge (*Carex siderosticha*).

Seasonal Features

Canada wild ginger works in combinations all through the growing season because it sprouts in early spring, and its leaves remain interesting well into fall before dying back to the ground for winter. European and Chinese wild gingers also send up fresh new foliage in spring, but they look attractive through winter, as well. The two are particularly useful in groupings with other four-season perennials, such as Allegheny pachysandra (*Pachysandra procumbens*), dwarf mondo grass (*Ophiopogon japonicus* 'Nana'), and 'Evergold' Japanese sedge (*C. oshimensis*).

partners, such as dwarf white fan columbine (*Aquilegia flabellata* 'Nana Alba'), and with white-variegated foliage, like that of 'Stairway to Heaven' creeping Jacob's ladder (*Polemonium reptans*).

Silver and gray foliage, like that of Japanese painted fern (*Athyrium niponicum* var. *pictum*) or 'Samurai' pulmonaria (*Pulmonaria*), looks great with wild gingers, contrasting with the solid green kinds and echoing the markings of silver-and-green species and selections.

Asclepias
intriguingly intricate flowers

Asclepias tuberosa **and** Sedum 'Xenox'

Asclepias incarnata **and**
Calamagrostis × acutiflora
'Karl Foerster'

A Perfect Match

Swamp milkweed grows wild in my meadow, where it often chooses bright purple New York ironweed (*Vernonia noveboracensis*) as a partner. In the garden, I enjoy pairing its rosy pink blooms with cool blue grasses, such as 'Dewey Blue' bitter panic grass (*Panicum amarum*) or 'Dallas Blues' switch grass (*P. virgatum*).

The intriguingly intricate flowers of milkweeds (*Asclepias*) are grouped into showy clusters that always attract attention. There are many species to choose from, in varying heights and colors. Some are vigorous spreaders that are too aggressive for traditional borders, but there are some beauties that grow in distinct clumps. Two of the most popular—and well-behaved— species for perennial beds and borders are butterfly weed (*A. tuberosa*), commonly with orange flowers on 1- to 3-foot-tall stems, and swamp milkweed (*A. incarnata*), with pink or sometimes white blooms atop 3- to 5-foot-tall stems. Both are generally hardy in Zones 3 to 9.

Color Considerations

Though the blooms of butterfly weed can range from red to yellow, most appear in shades of bright orange with a touch of

Bloom Buddies
Marvelous Matches for Flowering Combos

While milkweeds (*Asclepias*) can adapt to a range of soil conditions, butterfly weed (*A. tuberosa*) is best suited for average to dry soil, while swamp milkweed (*A. incarnata*) prefers average to moist conditions, so keep that in mind when choosing companions. Below is a sampling of perennials that are adapted to similar site conditions and complement their beautiful blooms.

Companions for butterfly weed (*A. tuberosa*):

Blanket flowers (*Gaillardia*)

Blazing stars (*Liatris*)

Catmints (*Nepeta*)

Coreopsis (*Coreopsis*)

Echinaceas (*Echinacea*)

Globe thistles (*Echinops*)

Goldenrods (*Solidago*)

Lavenders (*Lavandula*)

Orange hummingbird mint (*Agastache aurantiaca*)

Perennial salvias (*Salvia*)

Purple prairie clover (*Dalea purpurea*)

Rudbeckias (*Rudbeckia*)

Russian sages (*Perovskia*)

Sea hollies (*Eryngium*)

Sedums (*Sedum*)

Sundrops (*Oenothera fruticosa*)

Sunset hyssop (*Agastache rupestris*)

Torch lilies (*Kniphofia*)

Verbenas (*Verbena*)

Yarrows (*Achillea*)

Companions for swamp milkweed (*A. incarnata*):

Anise hyssop (*Agastache foeniculum*)

Bee balms (*Monarda*)

Culver's roots (*Veronicastrum*)

Daylilies (*Hemerocallis*)

Dense blazing star (*Liatris spicata*)

Echinaceas (*Echinacea*)

Ironweeds (*Vernonia*)

Joe-Pye weeds (*Eupatorium*)

'Karley Rose' Oriental fountain grass (*Pennisetum orientale*)

Obedient plant (*Physostegia virginiana*)

Rattlesnake master (*Eryngium yuccifolium*)

Rose mallow (*Hibiscus moscheutos*)

Rudbeckias (*Rudbeckia*)

Summer phlox (*Phlox paniculata*)

White mugwort (*Artemisia lactiflora*)

---

yellow. They're bold enough to hold their own with other vibrant colors, including rich reds, like those of 'Paprika' yarrow (*Achillea*); vivid purples, like those of 'Homestead Purple' verbena (*Verbena*); and intense magentas, like those of winecups (*Callirhoe involucrata*).

Butterfly weeds are beautifully harmonious with other orange partners, like 'Oranges and Lemons' blanket flower (*Gaillardia × grandiflora*) and 'Southern Comfort' heuchera (*Heuchera*), and

with bright yellow flowers and leaves, too: Consider 'Prairie Sun' black-eyed Susan (*Rudbeckia hirta*), 'Zagreb' threadleaf coreopsis (*Coreopsis verticillata*), and yellow-striped 'Color Guard' or 'Golden Sword' Adam's needle (*Yucca filamentosa*). Their bright orange flowers are also striking with blue- or silver-leaved partners, such as 'Siskiyou Blue' fescue (*Festuca*) or 'Powis Castle' artemisia (*Artemisia*), and with purple foliage, like that of 'Purple Emperor' sedum (*Sedum*).

Swamp milkweed flowers are primarily pink with a touch of white, which you could complement with white-flowered partners, such as 'Becky' Shasta daisy (*Leucanthemum* × *superbum*) or white mugwort (*A. lactiflora*). For zippy combinations, try swamp milkweed with bright yellow companions, such as 'Chicago Gold Strike' daylily (*Hemerocallis*), or blues and purple-blues, like those of balloon flower (*Platycodon grandiflorus*). Or go for a profusion of pinks by combining swamp milkweed with Joe-Pye weeds (*Eupatorium*), purple coneflower (*Echinacea purpurea*), 'Robert Poore' summer phlox (*Phlox paniculata*), and other mid- or late-summer perennials that have rosy pink to purplish pink flowers.

Shapes and Textures

Butterfly weed usually has an upright, mounded form that contrasts nicely with lower, spreading companions, such as creeping verbenas (*Verbena*). Its small leaves have a fine texture, as do its tiny individual blossoms, but those blossoms are clustered into larger heads that, combined with their bright color, give them a somewhat bold effect. Emphasize this boldness with other large blooms and bloom clusters, like those of echinaceas (*Echinacea*), rudbeckias (*Rudbeckia*), and yarrows (*Achillea*). Or provide some contrast with spiky flowers or foliage, like that of dwarf blazing star (*Liatris microcephala*) or yuccas (*Yucca*). Butterfly weed is lovely with graceful grasses, such as Mexican feather grass (*Stipa tenuissima*) or prairie dropseed (*Sporobolus heterolepis*).

Swamp milkweed has more of a vertical habit, especially when young, though it eventually forms broad mounds. For contrast, use lower mounded plants, such as compact daylilies (*Hemerocallis*), or taller, upright or fountain-shaped partners, such as Culver's roots (*Veronicastrum*) or 'Morning Light' miscanthus (*Miscanthus sinensis*).

Seasonal Features

Milkweeds are slow to sprout in spring, often not even peeking above the ground until late spring. They make up for that quickly, though: They usually begin blooming sometime in midsummer and continue into late summer. Regularly clipping off the finished clusters can help to extend the flowering period. The plants also typically develop bright yellow fall color, complementing perennial partners that feature late-season flowers, interesting seed heads, or fall foliage color, such as asters, hardy geraniums (*Geranium*), and many ornamental grasses.

Asclepias tuberosa 'Hello Yellow' and *Heuchera villosa* 'Palace Purple'

Aster
stars of the later-season garden

Aster × frikartii and *Echinacea purpurea* 'Fatal Attraction'

Aster 'Wood's Purple' and *Heuchera* 'Peach Melba'

A Perfect Match

When I hear gardeners complain about the typical fall asters looking too "wild and weedy," I like to recommend 'October Skies' aromatic aster as an alternative. It forms dense, neatly rounded mounds that look like tightly clipped shrubs, but with no pruning necessary. It's terrific in front of loose, somewhat sprawly companions, such as 'Brookside' hardy geranium (*Geranium*) or 'Full Moon' coreopsis (*Coreopsis*), providing support without getting smothered itself.

You'll hardly notice asters (*Aster*) for the first few months of the growing season, but once their flowers start opening, you'll know why they're considered the stars of the late-summer and fall garden. Most classic garden asters are still sold under the genus name *Aster*, but you may also see the North American species listed under their newer names, including *Symphyotrichum* and *Eurybia*. There are so many species, selections, and hybrids of asters to choose from, you can find at least one for just about any site.

Many excellent asters thrive in full sun and average to somewhat dry soil. Frikart's aster (*A. × frikartii*) has bluish lavender flowers atop loose, 2- to 3-foot-tall clumps from midsummer into fall, for Zones 5 to 9. Bushy aster (*A. dumosus* [*Symphyotrichum dumosum*]) features purple-blue, pink, or white flowers on 1- to 2-foot-tall mounds from late summer to mid-fall, for Zones 4 to 8. Smooth aster (*A. laevis* [*S. laeve*]) sports light purple to blue flowers atop upright, 2- to 4-foot-tall stems in early to mid- or late fall, for Zones 3 to 8. And aromatic aster (*A. oblongifolius* [*S. oblongifolium*]) has purple to purple-blue flowers on dense, 2- to 3-foot-tall mounds in early to mid-fall, for Zones 4 to 9.

For average to moist sites in full sun, consider some of the many selections of New England aster (*A. novae-angliae* [*S. novae-angliae*]). Hardy in Zones 3 to 8, most grow somewhere between 3 and 6 feet tall and flower in early to mid-fall, primarily in shades of purple and pink.

For average, well-drained sites that get some shade, consider white wood aster (*A. divaricatus* [*Eurybia divaricata*]), with tiny white flowers on near-black, 1- to 2-foot-tall stems, or blue wood aster (*A. cordifolius* [*S. cordifolium*]), with tiny, light blue flowers on 2- to 3-foot-tall stems. Both form upright, loosely branched clumps that flower from late summer or early fall to mid-fall and can grow in Zones 3 to 8.

Color Considerations

As a group, asters offer many tints and shades of purple, purple-blues, and pinks, as well as white. Their flowers have yellow to orange-yellow centers, which you can complement with yellow-flowered companions, such as perennial sunflowers (*Helianthus*), as well as leaves that turn yellow, like those of bluestars (*Amsonia*), purple moor grass (*Molinia caerulea*), and Siberian iris (*Iris sibirica*).

New England asters offer some particularly strong pinks, including 'September Ruby' and the even more intense 'Alma Potschke', and rich purples, as on 'Purple Dome'. They can pair well with other bright pinks and purples, as

Bloom Buddies
Marvelous Matches for Flowering Combos

There's no shortage of fantastic flowering companions for asters (*Aster*) in late summer to mid-fall. Here are some perennial partners to consider.

Combinations in full sun to light shade:

Catmints (*Nepeta*)

Chrysanthemums (*Chrysanthemum*)

Daylilies (*Hemerocallis*, reblooming types)

Echinaceas (*Echinacea*)

False aster (*Boltonia asteroides*)

Golden lace (*Patrinia scabiosifolia*)

Goldenrods (*Solidago*)

Heleniums (*Helenium*)

Japanese burnet (*Sanguisorba tenuifolia*)

Joe-Pye weeds (*Eupatorium*)

Lesser calamint (*Calamintha nepetoides*)

Monkshoods (*Aconitum*)

Montauk daisy (*Nipponanthemum nipponicum*)

Mountain fleeceflower (*Persicaria amplexicaulis*)

Obedient plant (*Physostegia virginiana*)

Perennial sunflowers (*Helianthus*)

Rudbeckias (*Rudbeckia*)

Sedums (*Sedum*, upright types)

Combinations in partial shade:

Blue lilyturf (*Liriope muscari*)

Bugbanes (*Cimicifuga*)

Hardy begonia (*Begonia grandis*)

Japanese anemones (*Anemone*)

Obedient plant (*Physostegia virginiana*)

Toad lilies (*Tricyrtis*)

Yellow waxbells (*Kirengeshoma palmata*)

Aster oblongifolius 'October Skies' and *Muhlenbergia capillaris*

well as oranges and yellows: Think of bold late-season bloomers, such as goldenrods (*Solidago*) and rudbeckias (*Rudbeckia*), for instance. If you aren't comfortable putting bright colors right next to each other, separate them with the foliage of a warm-season ornamental grass, such as prairie dropseed (*Sporobolus heterolepis*) or switch grass (*Panicum virgatum*).

The various other pinks, purples, and purple-blues in the asters offer many more opportunities for late-season combos. They, too, work well with rudbeckias and other yellows, as well as with pinks, purples, blues, and peach-colored flowers and green, blue, gray, silver, and yellow- to cream-variegated foliage. White asters look great with all of those colors and with white-variegated leaves, like those of 'Francee' hosta and variegated obedient plant (*Physostegia virginiana* 'Variegata').

Shapes and Textures

Most asters have a mounded habit, with tightly or loosely branched clumps, but some—including most New England asters—are rather upright, with branching mostly along the upper half of the stems. Their leaves tend to be on the small and narrow side, giving the plants a fine texture. Overall, they aren't particularly interesting for either shape or texture, except for aromatic aster, which naturally forms quite dense domes, 18 to 24 inches wide. To give your aster combinations some zip, include companions with contrasting features, such as a low, spreading habit or broad or spiky leaves, like those of bearded irises or yuccas (*Yucca*). Upright asters, in particular, benefit from having lower, mounded partners, such as hardy geraniums (*Geranium*), to cover their often-bare lower stems.

Flower-wise, asters are all fairly similar, with relatively small to tiny, daisy-form blooms that have very narrow petals. If you'd like some repetition, echo their shape with larger daisy-type flowers, like those of orange coneflower (*R. fulgida*), perennial sunflowers, or purple coneflower (*Echinacea purpurea*). Make sure you add some contrast, though, with companions that are spiky, such as fountain grasses (*Pennisetum*) and obedient plant (*Physostegia virginiana*); with plumed blooms, like those of flame grass (*Miscanthus* 'Purpurascens') and goldenrods (*Solidago*); or with broad, clustered flower heads, like those of Joe-Pye weeds (*Eupatorium*) and upright sedums (*Sedum*).

Seasonal Features

Frikart's aster tends to be the earliest bloomer in this genus, possibly starting in early summer in southern gardens but in midsummer in most areas: just in time to fill the gap between the early and late show with other summer favorites, such as daylilies (*Hemerocallis*), Russian sage (*Perovskia*), showy stonecrop (*S. spectabile*), and summer phlox (*Phlox paniculata*).

Frikart's aster continues into late summer, eventually joined by other asters for the late-season spectacle. Bushy aster is usually first, at the end of summer, with the others joining in at some point in early fall. Their bloom period overlaps with quite a few other perennials: earlier bloomers that are flowering again after a break, such as catmints (*Nepeta*) and coreopsis (*Coreopsis*); summer bloomers that are still producing new flowers, such as purple coneflower; and late-summer and fall bloomers, such as chrysanthemums, goldenrods, heleniums (*Helenium*), and Japanese anemones (*Anemone*). In shade, white wood and blue wood asters make charming co-stars for other late-flowering shade perennials, such as bugbanes (*Cimicifuga*) and toad lilies (*Tricyrtis*).

For additional companions, look beyond flowers to perennials and grasses with colorful leaves, as well as those whose foliage turns from green to other hues in fall. Try yellow to orange bluestars (*Amsonia*), deep red Bowman's roots (*Gillenia*), golden to purple balloon flower (*Platycodon grandiflorus*), coppery little bluestem (*Schizachyrium scoparium*), and orangey prairie dropseed (*Sporobolus heterolepis*). And don't forget

Delay the Display

A little pruning can work wonders on asters, delaying the flowers of Frikart's aster (*Aster × frikartii*) to late summer and holding the others off for an additional few weeks so they can make a real end-of-the-season spectacle. (This is especially useful in warmer zones, where unpruned asters may be just about finished by the time fall actually arrives.) Pruning is also invaluable on the upright types, such as smooth aster (*A. laevis*) and the taller New England asters (*A. novae-angliae*), keeping them lower and bushier to minimize the chances of their sprawling. Trim lightly, removing just 1 to 2 inches from the tips, every few weeks from mid-spring to early July, or do one hard pruning sometime in early summer, cutting back the stems by about half their height at the time.

the many dark seed heads of the fall season, such as the ball-shaped clusters of echinaceas (*Echinacea*) and rudbeckias and the spikes of Culver's roots (*Veronicastrum*). Those seed heads, along with the dried stems and seed heads of ornamental grasses, join the lingering structure of woody-stemmed aromatic aster and New England aster to make a wonderful show well into winter.

Special Effects

With their abundance of small, daisy-form flowers, asters of all kinds are favorites with butterflies as well as bees and other beneficial insects. If you'd like to attract more of these creatures to your yard, pair your asters with other pollinator-friendly perennials, such as blazing stars (*Liatris*), goldenrods, oxeye (*Heliopsis helianthoides*), perennial sunflowers, and summer phlox.

Asters are native to many parts of the United States, so there's little wonder that they look right at home in naturalistic gardens. (These natives also tend to self-sow freely, which is less of a problem in these casual settings.) Enjoy the sun lovers in meadow-style plantings with other native perennials and grasses, such as echinaceas, heleniums, ironweeds (*Vernonia*), Joe-Pye weeds, rudbeckias, and little bluestem.

The shade-tolerant white wood and blue wood asters are, not surprisingly, wonderful for woodland gardens, as a late-season follow-up to early-blooming native and nonnative companions, such as epimediums (*Epimedium*), foamflowers (*Tiarella*), hostas, and Solomon's seals (*Polygonatum*)—all of which happen to have showy fall foliage color, too.

Aster dumosus 'Sapphire' and *Rudbeckia fulgida (left)*; *Aster ericoides* 'Snow Flurry' and *Thymus pseudolanuginosus (above)*

Though they generally don't like constantly soggy soil, New England asters are well adapted to sites that are on the moist side, and they can tolerate short periods of flooding, so they're well suited to sunny rain gardens (see page 158). Pair them with other perennials that can thrive in those conditions, such as Culver's root (*Veronicastrum virginicum*), rose mallow (*Hibiscus moscheutos*), switch grass, three-lobed coneflower (*R. triloba*), and turtleheads (*Chelone*).

Most asters are bushy or upright, but 'Snow Flurry' heath aster (*A. ericoides*) is distinctly different, with a low, spreading habit just 4 to 6 inches tall. It makes an out-of-the-ordinary, fall-flowering groundcover for sunny, average to dry sites in Zones 5 to 8. Let it mingle with other low-growers, such as creeping thymes (*Thymus*) and two-row sedum (*Sedum spurium*), on a slope or atop a retaining wall.

Aster novae-angliae 'Harrington's Pink' with *Helianthus* 'Lemon Queen' and *Solidago rugosa* 'Fireworks'

Exploring More Options: Partners beyond Perennials

Asters are ideal companions for border-size, summer-flowering shrubs that also offer great fall color, such as 'Hummingbird' summersweet (*Clethra alnifolia*), which turns bright yellow; smokebushes (*Cotinus*), with their brilliant reds and oranges; and southern bush honeysuckle (*Diervilla sessilifolia*), with deep reds and muted tones of orange and yellow. Try 'Tor' birchleaf spirea (*Spiraea betulifolia*) to end the season with fiery reds accented with touches of orange and gold.

Add a touch of the unexpected to your autumn aster combinations with late-flowering bulbs, such as light purple fall crocus (*Crocus speciosus*) or pink or white colchicums (*Colchicum*) in sun and pink hardy cyclamen (such as *Cyclamen hederifolium* and *C. purpurascens*) in some shade. These little gems reach only 4 to 6 inches tall, so keep them close to the front of the border, paired with lower asters, such as aromatic aster (*Aster oblongifolius*), blue wood aster (*A. cordifolius*), bushy aster (*A. dumosus*), and 'Purple Dome' New England aster (*A. novae-angliae*).

Need some height to complement taller asters in your fall combinations? Many tall-growing tender perennials are at their peak from late summer to frost. Salvias (*Salvia*) are especially good for autumn color: Consider anise-scented sage (*S. guaranitica*), hybrid 'Indigo Spires', and rosebud sage (*S. involucrata*), to name just a few. Cannas, with their bold foliage and rich colors, are also excellent aster companions. And don't forget dahlias, which produce an abundance of bloom as temperatures begin to cool in early fall.

Astilbe
showy blooms for summer color

Astilbe chinensis 'Visions' and *Hosta* 'American Halo'

Astilbe 'Deutschland' and
Physocarpus opulifolius 'Monlo'
(Diabolo)

A Perfect Match

Astilbes come in wonderful red, pink, purplish, and peachy hues for colorful shade combinations. But one of the most memorable partnerships I've ever seen was one of the simplest: brilliant white 'Deutschland' astilbe with white-variegated 'Francee' hosta. This simple combo would work with any white astilbe or with another hosta that has a bright white edge, such as 'Antioch'.

The showy plumes of astilbes (*Astilbe*) in bloom are sure to be the star of any combination. Most of the commonly available astilbes are hybrids sold under the name *A. × arendsii* or Arendsii Group, but there are also some excellent selections of several species, including star astilbe (*A. simplicifolia*) and Chinese astilbe (*A. chinensis*). They come in a variety of colors and a range of heights, from just 8 inches or so to 5 feet or more. Astilbes generally perform best in Zones 3 to 8.

Color Considerations

Astilbe leaves are interesting enough—mostly shades of green, though sometimes bronzy or reddish—but their flowers are really the focus when you're choosing them for color. Pastels are most abundant, from light pink 'Erica' to purplish pink 'Visions in Pink', salmon pink 'Peach Blossom' and 'Sister

Theresa', and rosy purple 'Purple Candles' (also sold as 'Purpurkerze'), to name just a few. Besides combining comfortably with each other, these pastels are pretty paired with white-, pink-, or lavender-flowered partners, such as hostas or purple coneflower (*Echinacea purpurea*).

Pastels are also lovely with blue leaves, like those of 'Blue Angel' and 'Fragrant Blue' hostas; silvers and grays, like those of 'Looking Glass' Siberian bugloss (*Brunnera macrophylla*) and 'Pewter Lace' Japanese painted fern (*Athyrium niponicum* var. *pictum*); and white or yellow variegates, such as variegated blue lilyturf (*Liriope muscari* 'Variegata') and variegated Solomon's seal (*Polygonatum odoratum* 'Variegatum').

There are some exceptional red-flowered cultivars among the astilbes, such as deep red 'Glow' and vibrant 'Red Sentinel'. They are invaluable when you're trying to bring some of the bright colors of sunny summer borders into your shady areas. Match their intensity with vivid red cardinal flower (*Lobelia cardinalis*) and red-leaved 'Fire Alarm' heuchera (*Heuchera*); bright yellow foliage, like that of Bowles' golden sedge (*Carex elata* 'Aurea') and 'Sun Power' hosta; and orangey leaves, like those of 'Buttered Rum' foamy bells (× *Heucherella*) and 'Southern Comfort' heuchera. Red astilbes look very rich paired with deep purple-leaved partners, such as 'Britt-Marie Crawford' ligularia (*Ligularia dentata*) and 'Hillside Black Beauty' bugbane (*Cimicifuga simplex*).

There's no lack of white flowers for shade, but those of 'Bridal Veil', 'Deutschland', and other white astilbes are so brilliant that they practically glow. Complement them with silvery or blue foliage and with white-variegated leaves, like those of variegated sweet flag (*Acorus*

Bloom Buddies
Marvelous Matches for Flowering Combos

In the cooler parts of their growing range, astilbes (*Astilbe*) can tolerate full sun as long as their soil doesn't dry out; in warmer zones, partial shade with dependable moisture is vital for success. Keep these needs in mind, as well as the specific flowering periods of the astilbes you're considering, so you can make sure that you choose compatible companions that will be in bloom around the same time. Below are some perennials that typically make charming summer co-stars for astilbes.

Daylilies (*Hemerocallis*)

Globeflowers (*Trollius*)

Hostas (*Hosta*)

Japanese iris (*Iris ensata*)

Joe-Pye weeds (*Eupatorium*)

Lady's mantle (*Alchemilla mollis*)

Louisiana irises (*Iris* Louisiana Hybrids)

Masterworts (*Astrantia*)

Northern blue flag iris (*Iris versicolor*)

Perennial lobelias (*Lobelia*)

Rabbit-ear iris (*Iris laevigata*)

Siberian iris (*Iris sibirica*)

Southern blue flag iris (*Iris virginica*)

Spiderworts (*Tradescantia*)

Turtleheads (*Chelone*)

calamus 'Variegatus'). They're wonderful with other white flowers, of course, as well as with pink- or blue-flowered companions, such as 'Pink Chablis', 'Therese' spiderworts (*Tradescantia*), or 'Butterflies in Flight' Japanese iris (*Iris ensata*).

Shapes and Textures

Most astilbes grow in dense clumps that are mounded in leaf but distinctly upright in bloom: terrific for adding vertical accents among hostas and other mounded perennials. A grouping of very short astilbe selections, such as 6- to 8-inch-tall 'Perkeo', or a planting of the 1-foot-tall, vigorously creeping dwarf Chinese astilbe (*A. chinensis* var. *pumila*), is much more horizontal, creating a low carpet around taller mounding or upright partners.

The deeply lobed or divided leaves of astilbes have a jagged to lacy look. They repeat the foliage shape of companions like bleeding hearts (*Dicentra*) and ferns and make a striking contrast next to broader-leaved bedmates, such as bergenias (*Bergenia*), heucheras, and pulmonarias (*Pulmonaria*).

With tiny individual blossoms that are grouped into branching clusters, astilbe blooms typically have a feathery, pyramidal form, though you can also find some that are more open and arching, like 'Ostrich Plume' (also sold as 'Straussenfeder'), or that have dense, narrower, tapered clusters, like 'Superba' Chinese astilbe (*A. chinensis* var. *taquetii*). Use any of these to repeat the shapes of other plumy perennials, such as filipendulas (*Filipendula*) and goatsbeards (*Aruncus*), or to echo partners with more slender, spiky bloom clusters, such as bugbanes (*Cimicifuga*) and Culver's roots (*Veronicastrum*). For contrasting flower shapes, consider daisy-form or "dot-like" blooms, like those of masterworts (*Astrantia*); airy, cloud-like bloom clusters, like those of lady's mantle (*Alchemilla mollis*) or tufted hair grass (*Deschampsia cespitosa*); or large, bold blooms, like those of daylilies (*Hemerocallis*) or irises.

Seasonal Features

The leaves of astilbes are attractive from the time they emerge in spring (especially those with bronzy to bright red shoots, such as 'Fanal' and 'Montgomery') through the rest of the growing season, as long as the soil doesn't get too dry. The flowering period typically lasts 3 to 5 weeks, with peak bloom in June and July, but "early" types, such as 'Deutschland' and 'Rheinland', may start in late spring in the warmer parts of their range, and "late" types—particularly the Chinese astilbes—usually begin in late summer and may continue into early fall. If you leave the flower clusters in place as they finish, they'll dry a golden brown to deep brown color and linger for months, providing welcome interest in fall and winter and contrasting nicely with evergreen perennials, such as bergenias and hellebores (*Helleborus*).

Astilbe × *arendsii* 'Fanal' with *Polygonatum* × *hybridum* 'Striatum' and *Carex oshimensis* 'Evergold'

Athyrium
feathery fronds for terrific texture

Athyrium niponicum var. pictum and *Primula sieboldii*

Athyrium niponicum var. pictum and Hosta 'Blue Cadet'

A Perfect Match

Of the many marvelous foliage partners for Japanese painted ferns, my favorites are those with dark leaves. Heucheras (*Heuchera*) offer lots of options, but where the soil stays moist enough, my pick is 'Britt-Marie Crawford' bigleaf ligularia (*Ligularia dentata*). It's a terrific textural contrast as well as an excellent echo for the dark stems and shadings of the fern fronds.

Athyriums (*Athyrium*) are among the most popular ferns for perennial gardens, contributing a variety of habits, textures, and colors to shady combinations.

Common lady fern (*A. filix-femina*), for Zones 3 to 9, produces feathery, light green fronds that typically reach 2 to 3 feet tall. There are a number of named selections, including tatting fern ('Frizelliae'), with very narrow fronds holding tightly crinkled leaflets, and 'Lady in Red', with green fronds on red to maroon stems, to name just two.

Japanese painted fern (*A. niponicum* var. *pictum*) is distinctive for its colorful fronds, with dark stems and varying amounts of silver-gray, gray-green, and burgundy in the leaflets. It, too, has a number of named cultivars, some with more emphasis on the silver (such as 'Silver Falls') and some with more burgundy (such as 'Regal Red'). Japanese painted ferns typically reach 1 to 2 feet tall and are best suited to Zones 4 to 9.

Bloom Buddies
Marvelous Matches for flowering Combos

Common lady fern (*Athyrium filix-femina*), Japanese painted fern (*A. nipponicum* var. *pictum*), and their hybrids can tolerate dryish soil if they get full shade. In partial shade, they thrive in evenly moist but well-drained soil: the same conditions that favor many beautiful bloomers, including those mentioned below.

Astilbes (*Astilbe*)

Bleeding hearts (*Dicentra*)

Columbines (*Aquilegia*)

Creeping phlox (*Phlox stolonifera*)

Foamflowers (*Tiarella*)

Foamy bells (× *Heucherella*)

Foxgloves (*Digitalis*)

Goatsbeards (*Aruncus*)

Hardy begonia (*Begonia grandis*)

Hostas (*Hosta*)

Jacob's ladders (*Polemonium*)

Siberian bugloss (*Brunnera macrophylla*)

Woodland phlox (*Phlox divaricata*)

There are hybrids between common lady fern and Japanese painted fern, with the height and mostly upright habit of the former and the silvery gray to gray-green fronds of the latter, such as 'Branford Beauty' and 'Ghost'. They're generally hardy in Zones 3 to 9.

Color Considerations

The light green fronds of common lady fern work well in any flower or foliage color combination.

They're particularly useful when you're trying to combine two or more variegated plants and need something solid green to separate them a bit, so the grouping isn't too chaotic. If you'd like to emphasize the dark stems of 'Lady in Red', consider a companion that has deep red or bronzy foliage, such as 'Burnished Bronze' foamy bells (× *Heucherella*) or 'Cajun Fire' heuchera (*Heuchera*).

Japanese painted ferns and the silver-gray hybrid athyriums are excellent for echoing other shade perennials with solid silver or silver-marked foliage, such as Chinese wild ginger (*Asarum splendens*), 'Jack Frost' Siberian bugloss (*Brunnera macrophylla*), or 'Samurai' pulmonaria (*Pulmonaria*), as well as gray-blue leaves, like those of 'Burning Hearts' bleeding heart (*Dicentra*) or 'Halcyon' hosta. Their pale gray color is also similar to that of weathered wood or cement, which can help to connect a planting visually with nearby paths, edgings, benches, and garden ornaments.

Japanese painted ferns show off beautifully among glossy or deep greens, like those of bergenias (*Bergenia*) and European wild ginger (*A. europaeum*). Or emphasize the purple color in the fronds and stems with partners that have solid purple or purple-and-green leaves. Imagine them underplanted with the glossy black leaves of black mondo grass (*Ophiopogon planiscapus* 'Nigrescens') or 'Black Scallop' common ajuga (*Ajuga reptans*). Or go for a high-contrast combo by pairing the particularly silvery or gray ones with bright yellow leaves, like those of 'Piedmont' hosta, or a reddish or orangey heuchera, such as 'Berry Smoothie', 'Georgia Peach', or 'Southern Comfort'.

All lady ferns are lovely with white-flowering partners, and the silver-gray selections are particularly pretty with pinks, like those of wild geranium (*Geranium maculatum*), and blues, such as 'Clouds of Perfume' woodland phlox (*Phlox divaricata*) and forget-me-nots (*Myosotis*).

Shapes and Textures

Common lady fern and its hybrids tend to have upright fronds, so they're distinctly vertical at first but more broadly mounded as they mature and spread out a bit. Japanese painted ferns, on the other hand, have more arching fronds, creating broad mounds right from the start. Both look terrific rising out of lower, carpeting companions: short ones, such as Chocolate Chip common ajuga (*A. reptans* 'Valfredda') or woodland sedum (*Sedum ternatum*), for painted ferns and somewhat taller ones, like Canada wild ginger (*A. canadense*), for the lady ferns and hybrids.

For textural interest, repeat the lacy leaflets of these ferns with companions that also have deeply cut or jagged foliage, such as bugbanes (*Cimicifuga*) or goatsbeards (*Aruncus*). Partners with slender or strappy leaves, such as blue lilyturf (*Liriope muscari*) or silver sedge (*Carex platyphylla*), add a bit more variety. For even more contrast, pair these ferns with bold-textured leaves: Think of heucheras, hostas, Jack-in-the-pulpits (*Arisaema*), and lady's mantle (*Alchemilla mollis*), to name a few.

Seasonal Features

Common lady fern usually unfurls its fronds starting in early spring, while Japanese painted ferns may not appear until mid- or late spring. Either way, there's room around them for small, early-blooming bulbs, such as snowdrops (*Galanthus*). The silvery and purple colors of Japanese painted ferns are most intense in spring and the early part of summer, becoming more muted but still usually noticeable later on. Unless browned by dry soil or too much sun, the fronds of these ferns remain attractive until frost, then die back to the ground for winter.

Athyrium niponicum var. *pictum* 'Pewter Lace' with *Rodgersia pinnata* and *Astilbe chinensis* var. *pumila*

Baptisia
beautiful and dependable

Baptisia sphaerocarpa 'Screamin' Yellow' and *Anthemis* 'Susanna Mitchell'

Baptisia australis and *Persicaria polymorpha*

A Perfect Match

Bearded irises make spectacular partners for baptisias in bloom, and there are thousands to choose from to create whatever sort of contrast or harmony you'd like. 'Edith Wolford' is my own favorite, because its blue-and-yellow flowers work equally well with solid blue or all-yellow baptisias.

Baptisias (*Baptisia*), also known as false indigos or wild indigos, are a blessing for gardeners who appreciate easy-care plants. But these adaptable perennials are more than just sturdy and long lived: Their spiky bloom clusters are very striking in late-spring or early-summer combinations.

Blue false indigo (*B. australis*), with blue to purple-blue flowers and bluish green leaves, is one of the most widely grown species. It typically grows 3 to 5 feet tall and wide and is hardy in Zones 3 to 9. White false indigo (usually sold as *B. alba*), suited to Zones 4 to 9, is similar in size but more open in habit, with dusky gray stems and white flowers.

Yellow false indigo (*B. sphaerocarpa*), with bright yellow flowers and light green leaves, tends to be more compact at 2 to 3 feet tall and wide, though it may reach a foot or so taller. It's hardy in Zones 4 or 5 to 9.

There are many stunning hybrids of these and other

species, such as light yellow 'Carolina Moonlight', soft purple 'Purple Smoke', and Twilite Prairieblues ('Twilite'), with violet, purple-blue, and yellow in each bloom. Most reach 3 to 4 feet tall in bloom and are adapted to Zones 4 to 9.

Color Considerations

Baptisias that bloom in the blue to purple range complement a number of similarly colored perennials that typically flower around the same time, including bellflowers (*Campanula*), catmints (*Nepeta*), and Siberian irises (*Iris sibirica*), to name a few. They (and the white and yellow baptisias, too) are outstanding with white-flowered partners, such as "Festiva Maxima" peopny (*Paeonia lactiflora*); bright to soft yellow flowers, like those of 'Moonshine' yarrow (*Achillea*) and yellow meadow rue (*Thalictrum flavum* subsp. *glaucum*); and delicate to warm pink blooms, like those of Lancaster geranium (*Geranium sanguineum* var. *striatum*) and red valerian (*Centranthus ruber*).

The blue and purple baptisias—particularly the darker ones, such as 'Dutch Chocolate'—may blend into a dark background, so consider siting them against a lighter backdrop, such as a pale fence or wall or a yellow-leaved shrub, such as golden elderberry (*Sambucus nigra* 'Aurea').

Many of the hybrid baptisias include two or more colors in their flowers or change color as the blooms age. Pictures can give you some idea of what to expect, but if you want to take best advantage of them, you may wish to watch them through at least one bloom period to see how they look in your garden before choosing permanent companions. Consider using bearded or Dutch irises to pick up some

Bloom Buddies
Marvelous Matches for flowering Combos

Baptisias (*Baptisia*) thrive in full sun but can take light shade, and they'll grow in either dry or moist soil (even in clayey soil, as long as the site isn't constantly wet). That gives you lots of potential flowering companions to choose from, including those listed below.

Bearded irises (*Iris* Bearded Hybrids)

Bellflowers (*Campanula*)

Carolina phlox (*Phlox carolina*)

Columbines (*Aquilegia*)

Coral bells (*Heuchera sanguinea*)

Coreopsis (*Coreopsis*)

Dianthus (*Dianthus*)

Echinaceas (*Echinacea*)

Gas plant (*Dictamnus albus*)

Meadow phlox (*Phlox maculata*)

Oriental poppy (*Papaver orientale*)

Penstemons (*Penstemon*)

Peonies (*Paeonia*)

Pincushion flowers (*Scabiosa*)

Red valerian (*Centranthus ruber*)

Siberian iris (*Iris sibirica*)

Sweet iris (*Iris pallida*)

Yarrows (*Achillea*)

of the more unusual colors and shading, such as purple-and-bronze 'Lion King' Dutch iris to echo the orangey touches in 'Solar Flare'.

Once the flowering period is over, the foliage is the main color feature. Repeat the blue-green leaf color present on many baptisias with perennials that have a similar foliage color, such as 'Dallas Blues' switch grass (*Panicum virgatum*),

Baptisia 'Carolina Moonlight' with *Allium* 'Gladiator' and *A. hollandicum* 'Purple Sensation'

dianthus (*Dianthus*), and yuccas (*Yucca*). Expand the palette a bit with gray to silver leaves, like those of artemisias (*Artemisia*), lamb's ears (*Stachys byzantina*), and rattlesnake master (*Eryngium yuccifolium*), or go for more zip with solid yellow or brightly variegated foliage, like that of 'Isla Gold' tansy (*Tanacetum vulgare*) or 'Nora Leigh' summer phlox (*Phlox paniculata*).

Shapes and Textures

Baptisia plants eventually form broad, domed mounds in leaf. It takes them several years to reach their full spread, though, so consider using annuals around them until they're established; then you can place perennial partners where they won't get smothered by the baptisias. The bottom third of the stems can be somewhat bare, so use lower, bushy companions, such as hardy geraniums (*Geranium*) or mountain bluet (*Centaurea montana*), in front of your baptisia clumps. For a contrast in form, use tall, vertical perennials, such as Culver's root (*Veronicastrum virginicum*) or 'Northwind' switch grass (*P. virgatum*), behind them.

Plants with columnar flower clusters, such as delphiniums (*Delphinium*) and lupines (*Lupinus*), repeat the shape of the baptisias in bloom, while slender spikes, like those of perennial salvias (*Salvia*) and spike speedwell (*Veronica spicata*), echo the vertical look in a more refined form. For variety, pair the chunky spikes of in-bloom baptisias with equally bold globe- or bowl-shaped blooms, like those of 'Mount Everest' or 'Purple Sensation' alliums (*Allium*), Oriental poppy (*Papaver orientale*), or peonies. Baptisia blooms also contrast well with daisy-form or flat-clustered flowers, such as purple coneflower (*Echinacea purpurea*) or yarrows, and with airy or plumy flower heads, like those of columbine meadow rue (*Thalictrum aquilegifolium*) or giant fleeceflower (*Persicaria polymorpha*).

Seasonal Features

In the southern parts of their range, baptisias usually sprout in early spring and begin to bloom in mid-spring; in northern gardens, they emerge in mid- or late spring and flower in late spring to early summer. The gray to grayish purple stems of white false indigo and its hybrids are most noticeable early in the growing season. You might choose to echo them with similarly colored flowers or leaves, like those of 'Blackberry Ice' heuchera (*Heuchera*) or 'Queen of Night' tulip.

Once their flowers begin to open, baptisias are usually in bloom for 3 to 4 weeks. Cut them back by about half after flowering to keep the plants denser and bushier, or leave them alone to get the inflated or rounded seedpods for later interest. From early or midsummer to frost, the key features of baptisias are their handsome form and foliage.

Brunnera

for flowers, form, and foliage

Brunnera macrophylla 'Looking Glass'
and 'Jack Frost' with *Osmunda claytoniana*

Brunnera macrophylla 'Jack Frost'
and *Muscari*

A Perfect Match

With so many eye-catching silvery cultivars of Siberian bugloss to choose from, it's easy to overlook the beauty of the ordinary green-leaved species. Instead of discarding the solid green seedlings I find from the fancier hybrids, I like to move them into gaps between equally sturdy but showier shade lovers, such as 'Painter's Palette' jumpseed (*Persicaria virginiana* var. *filiformis*) and variegated Solomon's seal (*Polygonatum odoratum*).

Siberian bugloss (*Brunnera macrophylla*) is a beauty in bloom, but it's even more valuable for its form and foliage, which extend its season of interest through the whole growing season. In spring, it sends up loose clusters of small but abundant flowers—usually sky blue, but sometimes blue-and-white or pure white—that reach a height of 12 to 18 inches. Then the 1-foot-tall mounds of heart-shaped leaves take over. They are commonly deep green, but there are a number of selections with silver markings or frosting, as well as some with variegated foliage. Siberian bugloss is best suited for Zones 3 to 7 or 8.

Color Considerations

In bloom, the sky blue flowers of Siberian bugloss are a perfect echo for blue forget-me-nots (*Myosotis*), and they're exquisite mingling with other shades of blue to purple-blue, such as those

Bloom Buddies
Marvelous Matches for Flowering Combos

Siberian bugloss (*Brunnera macrophylla*) flowers most freely and looks most lush in partial shade with fertile, evenly moist soil: the same conditions that favor many other spring-flowering shade-garden favorites, including the sampling listed below.

Ajugas (*Ajuga*)

Bleeding hearts (*Dicentra*)

Columbines (*Aquilegia*)

Cowslip (*Primula veris*)

Creeping phlox (*Phlox stolonifera*)

Foamflowers (*Tiarella*)

Foamy bells (× *Heucherella*)

Jacob's ladders (*Polemonium*)

Lady's mantle (*Alchemilla mollis*)

Leopard's banes (*Doronicum*)

Solomon's plume (*Smilacina racemosa*)

Solomon's seals (*Polygonatum*)

Spotted deadnettle (*Lamium maculatum*)

Wild geranium (*Geranium maculatum*)

Woodland phlox (*Phlox divaricata*)

astilbes (*Astilbe*) and columbines (*Aquilegia*). It's also a top-notch co-star for vividly colored leaves, like those of bright yellow 'Gold Heart' bleeding heart (*Dicentra spectabilis*) and golden meadowsweet (*Filipendula ulmaria* 'Aurea'); showy variegated foliage, like that of 'Snow Cap' broadleaf sedge (*Carex siderosticha*) and many hostas; and gray, blue, or silver leaves, like those of Japanese painted fern (*Athyrium niponicum* var. *pictum*) and pulmonarias.

Siberian bugloss cultivars with silver-and-green leaves, such as 'Emerald Mist' and 'Langtrees', look great in pairings with silvery, blue, or gray foliage. Selections that are mostly silver with just a touch of green, such as 'Jack Frost', pair perfectly with rich green companions to pick up their green veining or edging: Think of hellebores (*Helleborus*), for instance, or Robb's spurge (*Euphorbia amygdaloides* var. *robbiae*) or wild gingers (*Asarum*). You could also use them to repeat other silvery perennials throughout a border. Or create eye-catching combinations with deep purple- to black-leaved partners: 'Black Scallop' common ajuga (*Ajuga reptans*), 'Chocoholic' bugbane (*Cimicifuga*), and black mondo grass (*Ophiopogon planiscapus* 'Nigrescens'), for instance. For a really striking grouping, try a silvery Siberian bugloss with a red- or pink-leaved heuchera, such as 'Berry Smoothie' or 'Fire Alarm', and a red-flowered bleeding heart, such as 'Bacchanal'.

Shapes and Textures

Siberian bugloss plants form dense mounds of large, broad leaves that are ideal for repeating the bold forms of hostas, heucheras (*Heuchera*),

in the blooms of Jacob's ladders (*Polemonium*) or pulmonarias (*Pulmonaria*). Whites, pinks, and yellows are also charming with the blue flowers.

In leaf, solid green Siberian bugloss makes a great companion for any flowering or foliage partners, but it's particularly handsome with white and pale blooms, like those of many

Brunnera macrophylla 'Looking Glass' with *Polygonatum odoratum* 'Variegatum', *Lamium maculatum* 'White Nancy', and *Arrhenatherum elatius* var. *bulbosum* 'Variegatum' *(left)*; *Brunnera macrophylla* and *Dicentra spectabilis (above)*

and ligularias (*Ligularia*). For variety, pair them with upright companions, such as variegated Solomon's seal (*Polygonatum odoratum* 'Variegatum') or toad lilies (*Tricyrtis*), and fill in around them with lower, carpeting partners, such as epimediums (*Epimedium*) or spotted deadnettle (*Lamium maculatum*). You can make dramatic contrasts by using them with other shade lovers that have jagged leaves, such as Allegheny pachysandra (*Pachysandra procumbens*) and goatsbeards (*Aruncus*); strappy to spiky leaves, like those of golden Hakone grass (*Hakonechloa macra* 'Aureola') or spiderworts (*Tradescantia*); or finely cut foliage, like that of ferns and bleeding hearts (*Dicentra*).

Seasonal Features

In the warmer parts of its range, Siberian bugloss begins blooming in early spring; farther north, it starts in mid-spring. The 3- to 4-week flowering period coincides with that of many other early-flowering perennials and with lots of spring bulbs, too, including daffodils and tulips. When the flowers finish, it's a good idea to cut off the bloom stalks close to the base of the plant: Otherwise, the plants are likely to produce lots of seedlings, which won't have the same markings as the parent. The foliage usually looks good through the rest of summer and fall, and it can linger well into winter in mild areas.

Calamagrostis
fluffy flower plumes

Calamagrostis × acutiflora 'Karl Foerster' with *Sambucus racemosa* 'Sutherland Gold', *Amsonia hubrichtii*, and *Geranium wlassovianum*

Calamagrostis brachytricha with *Aster novae-angliae* 'Harrington's Pink' and *Cornus sericea* 'Sunshine'

A Perfect Match

'Karl Foerster' feather reed grass is so distinctly upright that it makes a great divider or screen in a narrow bed or border: between a walkway and a wall, for instance, or around a deck or patio. I often pair it with tall-stemmed pink flowers, such as 'Black Beauty' Orienpet lily (*Lilium*) or sweet Joe-Pye weed (*Eupatorium dubium*), but I've also admired it planted with purple-blues, like those of lavenders (*Lavandula*) or Russian sages (*Perovskia*).

Feather reed grasses (*Calamagrostis*) are a great choice when you need a tall grass for a summer combination. 'Karl Foerster' feather reed grass (*C. × acutiflora*) typically tops out at 4 to 6 feet tall when its plumy flowers reach their full height in early to midsummer. It's suited for Zones 3 to 9. Korean feather reed grass (*C. brachytricha*) is a bit shorter—usually 3 to 4 feet in leaf and 4 to 5 feet when it flowers in late summer to early fall—and a bit less hardy: usually Zones 4 to 9.

Both of these feather reed grasses are clump formers, so while the individual plants will expand a bit each year, you don't have to worry about them taking over a border with creeping roots. 'Karl Foerster' is also seed sterile, so it won't produce seedlings, either (something Korean feather reed grass can do, though usually not to the point of being a serious problem).

Bloom Buddies
Marvelous Matches for Flowering Combos

While full sun and average to moist but well-drained soil suit both types of feather reed grasses (*Calamagrostis*), these beauties can also grow in partial shade—particularly Korean feather reed grass—and somewhat dry soil. Below are some of the compatible companions that bloom around their peak flowering periods.

Combine with feather reed grass (*C. × acutiflora*):

- Anise hyssops (*Agastache*)
- Bee balms (*Monarda*)
- Blazing stars (*Liatris*)
- Carolina phlox (*Phlox carolina*)
- Echinaceas (*Echinacea*)
- Fleeceflowers (*Persicaria*)
- Globe thistles (*Echinops*)
- Knautias (*Knautia*)
- Meadow phlox (*Phlox maculata*)
- Perennial salvias (*Salvia*)
- Pincushion flowers (*Scabiosa*)
- Queen-of-the-prairie (*Filipendula rubra*)
- Rattlesnake master (*Eryngium yuccifolium*)
- Rudbeckias (*Rudbeckia*)
- Shasta daisy (*Leucanthemum × superbum*)
- Summer phlox (*Phlox paniculata*)
- Tuberous-rooted Jerusalem sage (*Phlomis tuberosa*)
- Yarrows (*Achillea*)

Combine with Korean feather reed grass (*C. brachytricha*):

- Asters (*Aster*)
- Caryopteris (*Caryopteris*)
- False aster (*Boltonia asteroides*)
- Goldenrods (*Solidago*)
- Ironweeds (*Vernonia*)
- Japanese anemones (*Anemone*)
- Japanese burnet (*Sanguisorba tenuifolia*)
- Joe-Pye weeds (*Eupatorium*)
- Monkshoods (*Aconitum*)
- Montauk daisy (*Nipponanthemum nipponicum*)
- Mountain fleeceflower (*Persicaria amplexicaulis*)
- Perennial sunflowers (*Helianthus*)
- Russian sages (*Perovskia*)
- Turtleheads (*Chelone*)

Color Considerations

In leaf, feather reed grasses are mostly a rich, glossy green that works well with a wide range of flower and foliage colors. There are a few variegated cultivars of *C. × acutiflora*, including white-striped 'Avalanche' and 'Overdam' and yellow-striped 'Eldorado', all of which are usually a foot or so shorter than 'Karl Foerster'. Emphasize their markings with white- or yellow-flowering partners, such as daffodils or tulips in spring or Shasta daisy (*Leucanthemum × superbum*) or coreopsis (*Coreopsis*) in summer.

The flower plumes of feather reed grasses tend to have a light purplish pink blush, which you could emphasize with pink-flowering partners appropriate to their bloom time. Match 'Karl Foerster' with purple coneflower (*Echinacea* purpurea) or red valerian (*Centranthus ruber*) in early to midsummer, for instance, or pair Korean feather reed grass with obedient plant (*Physostegia virginiana*) in late summer. The plumes of feather reed grasses are also pale enough to hold up well with white-flowered partners, such as giant fleeceflower (*Persicaria polymorpha*) for 'Karl Foerster' and false aster (*Boltonia asteroides*) for the Korean species, or with white-variegated leafy companions for either.

As the aging plumes turn tan, echo their color with peachy to tan heucheras (*Heuchera*), such as 'Caramel'; bronzy New Zealand sedges (*Carex*), such as 'Toffee Twist' weeping brown sedge (*C. flagellifera*); or the seed heads of other grasses, like those of fountain grasses (*Pennisetum*) or tufted hair grass (*Deschampsia cespitosa*).

Shapes and Textures

Feather reed grasses have a distinctly upright form. Use single clumps as accents among lower perennials: They make a particularly striking contrast to mounded bedmates, such as aromatic aster (*Aster oblongifoliums*), blue mist shrub (*Caryopteris* × *clandonensis*), and bluestars (*Amsonia*). Or match them with other tall growers, such as ironweeds (*Vernonia*) or 'Lemon Queen' perennial sunflower (*Helianthus*).

With their long, narrow leaves, slender stems, and fluffy flower plumes, these fine-textured grasses add variety when paired with strong bloom shapes: Combine them with large, daisy-form flowers, like those of echinaceas (*Echinacea*) or rudbeckias (*Rudbeckia*), for instance, or with the bold blooms of daylilies (*Hemerocallis*) or hardy hibiscus (*Hibiscus*). Or emphasize their vertical inflorescences with other plumy perennials, such as Russian sages (*Perovskia*), or with partners that have slender, spiky bloom clusters, such as mountain fleeceflower (*P. amplexicaulis*).

Seasonal Features

Feather reed grasses are quick to send up their foliage as soon as the soil starts to warm up in spring. The flower plumes of 'Karl Foerster' and other selections of *C.* × *acutiflora* usually open in June, while August or early September is more typical for Korean feather reed grass. The aging plumes turn tan, dry in place, and linger into winter, along with the skeletons and seed heads of asters, purple coneflower (*Echinacea purpurea*), upright sedums (*Sedum*), and other winter-persistent perennials.

Calamagrostis × *acutiflora* 'Karl Foerster' with *Pennisetum orientale* 'Karley Rose' and *Rudbeckia fulgida*

Campanula
classics for purples and blues

Campanula '**Birch Hybrid**' with *Spiraea japonica* '**Walbuma**' (Magic Carpet), *Alchemilla mollis*, and *Geranium sanguineum*

Campanula 'Sarastro' and *Stachys byzantina*

A Perfect Match

I've always admired bellflowers in other gardens, but so far the only one that's been dependable for me is 'Sarastro'. I don't feel deprived, though: Its abundant, blue-purple bells are gorgeous. My first choice for its partner was 'All Gold' lemon balm (*Melissa officinalis*), with brilliant yellow foliage, and that was a winner. More recently, I've been enjoying it with white-variegated leaves: 'Snow Fairy' bluebeard (*Caryopteris divaricata*) makes a great background for its showy flowers.

Blooming primarily in tints and shades of purple-blue, bellflowers (*Campanula*) are a classic choice for beds and borders, particularly where summertime temperatures don't get too hot. Most perform best in Zones 4 to 7, but they may also grow a zone cooler or warmer.

There are many species and selections of bellflowers, in a range of heights and habits. When it comes to considering them for combinations, it's easiest to divide them into two groups: the low growers and the upright kinds.

Among the low growers—which typically reach 6 to 8 inches tall and about twice as wide—are Carpathian bellflower (*C. carpatica*), with cupped, upward-facing flowers; Dalmatian bellflower (*C. portenschlagiana*), with funnel-shaped, upward-facing blooms; and Serbian bellflower (*C. poscharskyana*), with starry, upward-facing blooms.

Among the most popular upright species are peachleaf

Bloom Buddies
Marvelous Matches for Flowering Combos

Bellflowers (*Campanula*) bloom most freely in full sun but can also grow in some shade, especially in the warmer parts of their growing range. The exact flowering period varies by location and species, but peak bloom time for most is early to midsummer. Below are some potential co-stars that flower around the same time and thrive in similar light conditions and average, well-drained soil.

Alliums (*Allium*)

Anise hyssops (*Agastache*)

Astilbes (*Astilbe*)

Baby's breaths (*Gypsophila*)

Bearded irises (*Iris* Bearded Hybrids)

Bistort (*Persicaria bistorta*)

Bluestars (*Amsonia*)

Carolina phlox (*Phlox carolina*)

Catmints (*Nepeta*)

Columbines (*Aquilegia*)

Coreopsis (*Coreopsis*)

Delphiniums (*Delphinium*)

Dianthus (*Dianthus*)

Feverfew (*Tanacetum parthenium*)

Foxgloves (*Digitalis*)

Italian alkanet (*Anchusa azurea*)

Jacob's ladders (*Polemonium*)

Masterworts (*Astrantia*)

Meadow phlox (*Phlox maculata*)

Meadow rues (*Thalictrum*)

Perennial salvias (*Salvia*)

Shasta daisy (*Leucanthemum × superbum*)

Siberian iris (*Iris sibirica*)

Spiderworts (*Tradescantia*)

Summer phlox (*Phlox paniculata*)

Yarrows (*Achillea*)

bellflower (*C. persicifolia*), with upward- or outward-facing bells on 2- to 3-foot-tall stems; milky bellflower (*C. lactiflora*), with funnel-shaped, upward-facing blooms on 3- to 5-foot-tall stems; and giant bellflower (*C. latifolia*), with outward-facing bells on 4- to 5-foot-tall stems. 'Sarastro' is a dependable 18- to 24-inch-tall hybrid with large, nodding, bell-shaped blooms.

Color Considerations

The various species and selections bloom in a wide range of purple-blues, as well as some pinks and whites. All blend beautifully with other pastel-flowered perennials: soft pink Lancaster geranium (*Geranium sanguineum* var. *striatum*) to rosy pink red valerian (*Centranthus ruber*), for example. Or try combining them with peachy irises or roses, soft yellow foxgloves (*Digitalis grandiflora* and *D. lutea*), or 'Moonbeam' threadleaf coreopsis (*Coreopsis verticillata*).

The purple-blues are excellent additions to all-blue or primarily blue borders, too, with 'Black Adder' or 'Blue Fortune' anise hyssop (*Agastache*), catmints (*Nepeta*), perennial salvias (*Salvia*), and other perennials in the same color range. They're outstanding with white blooms, like those of baby's breaths (*Gypsophila*) or 'Miss Lingard' Carolina phlox (*Phlox carolina*), and with white-variegated leaves, like those of 'Loraine Sunshine' oxeye (*Heliopsis helianthoides*). Silver, gray, or blue foliage partners work well: Think of lacy silver 'Powis Castle' artemisia (*Artemisia*), for instance, or fuzzy lamb's ears (*Stachys byzantina*), or the powder blue tufts of 'Elijah Blue' blue fescue (*Festuca glauca*).

Blue-purple bellflowers—especially those on the darker side, such as 'Sarastro'—also look

Choose Bellflowers Carefully

Many bellflowers (*Campanula*) are perfectly well behaved in borders, or at least are easy to control. But some spread aggressively by creeping roots, to the point that they can take over significant areas and crowd out less vigorous companions, and it can be a nightmare to deal with getting rid of them. Creeping bellflower (*C. rapunculoides*) is one of the most notoriously thuggish species; Korean bellflower (*C. takesimana*) and spotted bellflower (*C. punctata*), too, may be very aggressive. Clustered bellflower (*C. glomerata*) also has the potential to become problematic.

The easiest option is to choose a clump-forming bellflower instead, but if you really want to try one of the creepers, give them a bed of their own—as a groundcover under a tree or shrub, perhaps. Or combine them with other strong spreaders, such as ajugas (*Ajuga*), bee balms (*Monarda*), lily-of-the-valley (*Convallaria*), and obedient plant (*Physostegia virginiana*), in a spot surrounded by an edging strip so they can't escape into adjacent lawn areas.

great with flowering and foliage companions in vibrant, clear, greenish, or golden yellows, such as lady's mantles (*Alchemilla*), 'Moonshine' yarrow (*Achillea*), and golden feverfew (*Tanacetum parthenium* 'Aureum').

Shapes and Textures

Low-growing bellflowers form spreading carpets that combine comfortably with other ground-hugging perennials, such as creeping sedums (*Sedum*), dianthus (*Dianthus*), and thymes (*Thymus*), along paths and steps, atop retaining walls, or on slopes. Or use them to fill in around mounded or spiky companions, such as coreopsis and dwarf daylilies (*Hemerocallis*), at the front edge of a border. The upright bellflowers are useful for adding height among bluestars (*Amsonia*), hardy geraniums, and other mounded perennials, or for repeating the forms of other upright plants, such as columbines (*Aquilegia*) and lupines (*Lupinus*).

Bellflowers mostly have medium-size leaves and blooms, so they work well with both fine textures, like that of airy Bowman's roots (*Gillenia*), and bold flower forms, like those of alliums (*Allium*), irises, and lilies (*Lilium*).

Seasonal Features

One of the tricky parts of using bellflowers in combinations is figuring out when, and for how long, they will bloom in your particular conditions. In the warmer parts of their range, most are in bloom by late spring; in cooler areas, they may not begin until early summer. Once their peak period is done (4 to 6 weeks for most), cutting back the low growers by about half and removing the spent flowers of the upright types may encourage more flowers to appear later in summer or in fall.

Bellflowers that are most dependable for a long season of bloom (through much of summer, at least) include Carpathian, Dalmatian, and Serbian bellflowers, as well as 'Birch Hybrid' and 'Sarastro'.

Carex
outstanding for foliage

Carex elata 'Aurea' and *Ajuga reptans*

Carex flagellifera 'Toffee Twist' and *Stachys byzantina* 'Big Ears'

A Perfect Match

Granted, the brown-leaved sedges are a bit of an acquired taste, but I've had a lot of fun making combinations with them. One year, I paired upright leatherleaf sedge (*C. buchananii*) with trailing 'Sweet Caroline Bronze' sweet potato vine (*Ipomoea batatas*) and bushy 'Wellington Bronze' toatoa (*Haloragis erecta*) in a container, and the brown-on-brown effect was surprisingly striking.

Sedges (*Carex*) are excellent plants to consider when you'd like the look of an ornamental grass in a site that's too shady for most true grasses to thrive. They're useful in many other situations, too: Quite a few can grow in sun, and some are ideal for wet sites. Sedges also offer some outstanding foliage effects that you can't get from most other perennials.

There are well over 1,000 species of sedges, though only a small fraction of them are readily available to gardeners. That still leaves plenty of options, however. One feature to keep in mind when choosing among them for combinations is whether they are primarily clump forming or creeping.

Clump-forming sedges work well singly as accent plants in combinations, or in groups to fill in larger areas. Some of the most widely available clump formers are 6- to 12-inch-tall plantainleaf sedge (*C. plantaginea*), for Zones 3 to 8; 6- to 12-inch-tall blue wood sedge (*C. flaccosperma*), for Zones 5 to 8; and

Bloom Buddies
Marvelous Matches for Flowering Combos

Sedges (*Carex*) have a reputation for liking shade and moisture, but that doesn't apply to all species, so it's important to check their preferences before choosing companions. Below is just a sampling of the many terrific flowering partners that can pair well with these top-notch foliage perennials.

Companions for full sun to light shade and average to moist but well-drained soil (with New Zealand sedges, such as *C. buchananii*, *C. comans*, and *C. flagellifera*):

Agastaches (*Agastache*)

Asters (*Aster*)

Carolina phlox (*Phlox carolina*)

Coreopsis (*Coreopsis*)

Heleniums (*Helenium*)

Heucheras (*Heuchera*)

Irises (*Iris*)

Meadow phlox (*Phlox maculata*)

Purple coneflower (*Echinacea purpurea*)

Sedums (*Sedum*)

Summer phlox (*Phlox paniculata*)

Yarrows (*Achillea*)

Companions for full sun and moist soil or partial shade and average, well-drained soil (with blue sedge [*C. flacca*], Bowles' golden sedge [*C. elata* 'Aurea'], Gold Fountains sedge [*C. dolichostachya* 'Kaga-Nishiki'], and palm sedge [*C. muskingumensis*]):

Astilbes (*Astilbe*)

Candelabra primrose (*Primula bulleyana*)

Hostas (*Hosta*)

Japanese iris (*Iris ensata*)

Japanese primrose (*Primula japonica*)

Ligularias (*Ligularia*)

Meadowsweet (*Filipendula ulmaria*)

Perennial lobelias (*Lobelia*)

Rodgersias (*Rodgersia*)

Siberian iris (*Iris sibirica*)

Turtleheads (*Chelone*)

Companions for partial to full shade with average to moist but well-drained soil (with blue wood sedge [*C. flaccosperma*], broadleaf sedge [*C. siderosticha*], Bunny Blue sedge [*C. laxiculmis* 'Hobb'], 'Ice Dance' and 'Ice Ballet' sedge, Japanese sedge [*C. oshimensis*], plantainleaf sedge [*C. plantaginea*], and sparkler sedge [*C. phyllocephala* 'Sparkler']):

Bleeding hearts (*Dicentra*)

Columbines (*Aquilegia*)

Epimediums (*Epimedium*)

Foamflowers (*Tiarella*)

Foamy bells (× *Heucherella*)

Pulmonarias (*Pulmonaria*)

Spotted deadnettle (*Lamium maculatum*)

1-foot-tall Bunny Blue sedge (*C. laxiculmis* 'Hobb'), Gold Fountains sedge (*C. dolichostachya* 'Kaga-nishiki'), and Japanese sedge (*C. oshimensis*; also sold as *C. hachijoensis* or *C. morrowii*), for Zones 5 to 9. The 1- to 2-foot-tall Bowles' golden sedge (*C. elata* 'Aurea') grows in Zones 5 to 9, while the 2- to 3-foot-tall palm sedge (*C. muskingumensis*) is for Zones 3 to 9. New Zealand sedge species—such as 1-foot-tall New Zealand hair sedge (*C. comans*), 12- to

18-inch-tall weeping brown sedge (*C. flagel-lifera*), and 1- to 2-foot-tall leatherleaf sedge (*C. buchananii*)—are all for Zones 6 or 7 to 9. They tend to stay in distinct clumps, as does 1- to 2-foot-tall sparkler sedge (*C. phyllocephala* 'Sparkler'), for Zones 7 to 9.

Creeping sedges may be a bit too vigorous to pair well with delicate companions but are great co-stars for sturdy perennials, such as medium-size and large hostas, in larger borders. Some sedges that are more likely to spread than to stay in tidy clumps are 6- to 12-inch-tall broadleaf sedge (*C. siderosticha*) and 'Ice Ballet' and 'Ice Dance' sedge (often listed under *C. morrowii*), as well as 10- to 16-inch-tall blue sedge (*C. flacca* or *C. glauca*), all for Zones 4 to 9.

Color Considerations

The flowers of most sedges are small and not especially interesting, so foliage is the key feature to consider for combinations. Some sedges with solid green leaves include 'Everdi' Japanese sedge, palm sedge, and plantainleaf sedge. These and other all-green sedges are easy to combine with any flower color and are excellent as "neutral" additions to combinations that already include bright yellow or showily variegated foliage.

There are many variegated sedges, too. Some are on the subtle side: 'Ice Dance', for instance, has thin white leaf edges, and 'Island Brocade' sedge is narrowly edged with yellow. They're elegant up close, but you may not notice their understated markings from a distance. The pin-striping on the superslender leaves of Japanese sedge selections, such as Everest ('Carfit01'), with bright white edges, and 'Evergold', with creamy yellow centers, and on Gold Fountains sedge, with yellow edging, also shows up best in combinations that you see at close range. For more dramatic markings, consider sparkler sedge, 'Spark Plug' (its more-compact version), or 'Snow Cap' broadleaf sedge, all with white edging, or bright-yellow-and-green 'Banana Boat' broadleaf sedge. All of these are ideal for repeating the variegated foliage of hostas and other larger-leaved or taller partners, for echoing the blooms of white- or yellow-flowered companions, and for adding a bit of zip among ferns and other green-leaved bedmates.

Carex **'Island Brocade'** and *Polygonatum humile*

Sedges with bright yellow leaves are especially striking color accents in combinations. Bowles' golden sedge is actually variegated, because its foliage has a thin green edge, but it looks solid yellow even at fairly close range. Some other particularly good choices here are solid yellow 'Everillo' Japanese sedge and 'Lemon Zest' broadleaf sedge. All of these are terrific with flowering partners in shades of blue and purple, such as 'Big Blue' and 'Caesar's Brother' Siberian irises (*Iris sibirica*). The yellow sedges pair well with pinks, such as 'Ostrich Plume' astilbe (*Astilbe*); reds, such as 'Ruby Wedding' masterwort (*Astrantia major*); and oranges, such as candelabra primrose (*Primula bulleyana*).

For foliage companions to yellow sedges, consider dark green partners, such as Lenten roses (*Helleborus × hybridus*); deep purples to blacks, like those of black mondo grass (*Ophiopogon planiscapus* 'Nigrescens') and 'Ravenswing' cow parsley (*Anthriscus sylvestris*); yellow variegates, such as variegated meadowsweet (*Filipendula ulmaria* 'Variegata'); and blues, such as 'Blue Mouse Ears' or 'Love Pat' hostas.

Speaking of blues: There are some splendid blue-leaved sedges, including blue wood sedge, 'Blue Zinger' blue sedge, and Bunny Blue sedge. Pair them with white or pastel blooms, like those of columbines (*Aquilegia*), or with other blue, gray, or silver leaves, like those of 'Halcyon' hosta or 'Majeste' pulmonaria (*Pulmonaria*). They also partner with rich green foliage, like that of bergenias (*Bergenia*) or European wild ginger (*Asarum europaeum*), or with bright yellows, such as 'Sun King' Japanese spikenard (*Aralia racemosa*).

The leaves of New Zealand sedges offer some particularly distinctive color options: shades of copper and bronze, often with some touches of pink, if you look closely. They make a great front-of-the-border echo for the seed heads (and winter color, too) of many ornamental grasses, including feather reed grasses (*Calamagrostis*). Use them to pick up the colors in orangey-leaved heucheras, such as 'Caramel', or peachy to bronzy blooms, like those of 'Copper Classic' bearded iris, Lady of Shalott rose (*Rosa* 'Ausnyson'), 'Milk Chocolate' daylily (*Hemerocallis*), or sunset hyssop (*Agastache rupestris*). Or make intriguing combinations by pairing them with purples, like the leaves of 'Purple Emperor' sedum (*Sedum*) or the blooms of

Carex muskingumensis 'Oehme' with *Allium sphaerocephalon* buds, *Geranium sanguineum*, and *Spiraea japonica* 'Walbuma' (Magic Carpet)

'Wood's Purple' aster, or with partners that have bright yellow foliage, such as 'Angelina' sedum (*Sedum rupestre*) or 'Aztec Gold' prostrate speedwell (*Veronica prostrata*).

Shapes and Textures

Most common sedges have a mounded or tufted form. For contrast, set them among even shorter, carpet- or mat-forming companions, such as spotted deadnettle (*Lamium maculatum*) or woodland sedum (*S. ternatum*), or in front of taller, upright perennials, such as 'Ghost' lady fern (*Athyrium*).

Sedge leaves are typically long and narrow, giving the plants a fine, grassy texture that's excellent for adding visual variety to combinations with larger leaves, like those of hostas and ligularias (*Ligularia*). Sedges with arching leaves, such as Japanese sedge, New Zealand hair sedge, and plantainleaf sedge, contrast with irises and other spiky partners. Those that are spiky themselves, such as broadleaf sedge, palm sedge, and sparkler sedge, contrast with companions that have broad or rounded foliage, such as heucheras (*Heuchera*) and Siberian bugloss (*Brunnera macrophylla*).

Seasonal Features

Sedges are valuable for foliage texture and color all through the growing season, or even longer. For early color around deciduous species—those that die back to the ground over winter, such as Bowles' golden sedge, broadleaf sedge, and palm sedge—use early-blooming bulbs, such as snowdrops (*Galanthus*) and winter aconite (*Eranthis hyemalis*).

Carex elata 'Aurea' with *Myosotis sylvatica* 'Ultramarine', *Heuchera* 'Caramel', and *Geum*

Many other sedges can be ideal for four-season interest, depending on where you live. The New Zealand sedges tend to keep their color all year long, for instance, as do 'Ice Ballet' and 'Ice Dance', Japanese sedge, Gold Fountains sedge, and the blue-leaved species and selections, so they can be superb with other perennials that have persistent foliage, such as Allegheny pachysandra (*Pachysandra procumbens*), bergenias, and hellebores (*Helleborus*). These "evergreen" sedges may get winter damaged in the cooler parts of their growing ranges, though, especially when snow cover is lacking, so you may end up needing to trim off the browned tips or shear them an inch or two above the ground in early spring to make room for fresh new leaves.

Caryopteris
intriguing leaves, then fall flowers

Caryopteris × clandonensis 'Longwood Blue' with *Calamagrostis × acutiflora* 'Karl Foerster' and *Sedum* 'Matrona'

Caryopteris divaricata 'Snow Fairy' and *Anemone × hybrida* 'Honorine Jobert'

A Perfect Match

One of my favorite caryopteris combinations to date is 'Longwood Blue' blue mist shrub in front of *Leucanthemella serotina*, an out-of-the-ordinary perennial that looks like a Shasta daisy (*Leucanthemum × superbum*) but doesn't begin blooming until September. If you can't find *Leucanthemum*, consider Montauk daisy (*Nipponanthemum nipponicum*), perhaps, or 'Honorine Jobert' Japanese anemone (*Anemone × hybrida*).

Blue mist shrubs (*Caryopteris × clandonensis, C. incana,* and their hybrids) technically are deciduous shrubs, but you'll usually find them sold with perennials. Prized for their clusters of blue flowers in late summer and fall, they may also offer showy foliage. Hardy in Zones 5 to 9, blue mist shrubs typically grow 2 to 4 feet tall and wide.

Bluebeard (*C. divaricata*) shares the late-blooming trait of its woody-stemmed cousins, but it's purely perennial, with airy, branching heads of dainty blue blooms. It's most commonly available as the 3- to 4-foot-tall, variegated cultivar 'Snow Fairy'. It, too, is hardy in Zones 5 to 9.

Color Considerations

The leaves of most caryopteris add at least some color interest from the time they appear in spring. The usual gray-green of

flowers, such as daylilies (*Hemerocallis*), true lilies (*Lilium*), and roses.

The yellow-leaved blue mist shrubs are dramatic border accents in their own right. Use them to repeat the colors of other bright yellow foliage perennials, such as golden oregano (*Origanum vulgare* 'Aureum'); of yellow variegates, such as variegated lemon thyme (*Thymus citriodorus* 'Variegatus'); and of greenish yellow blooms, like those of many euphorbias (*Euphorbia*). They're gorgeous with flowering companions in shades of blue to purple, such as balloon flower (*Platycodon grandiflorus*) and bellflowers (*Campanula*), and stunning with oranges and reds, like those of butterfly weed (*Asclepias tuberosa*) and 'Pardon Me' daylily. For dramatic contrast, pair the yellow-leaved blue mist shrubs with dark leaves, like those of 'Black Jack' sedum (*Sedum*) or 'Mocha' heuchera (*Heuchera*).

The blue flowers of in-bloom caryopteris make elegant partners for late-season whites, such as false aster (*Boltonia asteroides*) and kalimeris (*Kalimeris*). They're also charming with yellow flowers, like those of goldenrods (*Solidago*) and rudbeckias (*Rudbeckia*); with pink blooms, like those of colchicums (*Colchicum*) and 'Vera Jameson' sedum (*Sedum*); and with peachy colors, like those of 'Sheffield Pink' chrysanthemum.

Shapes and Textures

The shrubby mounds of caryopteris repeat the shape of many other border perennials. For contrast, pair them with lower, spreading plants, such as dianthus (*Dianthus*) and ornamental oreganos (*Origanum*), or with distinctly upright partners, such as summer phlox (*Phlox paniculata*) and switch grass (*Panicum virgatum*).

blue mist shrubs is a particularly pleasing complement to white and pastel flowers, and it looks equally good paired with deep green, white-variegated, or silver foliage.

Variegated versions of caryopteris, such as white-and-green 'Snow Fairy' bluebeard and yellow-and-green 'Summer Sorbet' blue mist shrub, are so showy that they make eye-catching border accents set among partners with solid green or blue leaves. Small blooms may get lost against the vivid leaf markings, so consider companions that have large, vibrant

The small leaves of most caryopteris give the plants a relatively fine texture. For variety, use them with broader leaves, like those of 'Big Ears' lamb's ears (*Stachys byzantina*), or strappy foliage, like that of agaves (*Agave*), bearded irises, or yuccas (*Yucca*).

Seasonal Features

In the cooler parts of their growing range, caryopteris are often slow to start growing in spring. (If the shrubby types are damaged by winter cold, they may have to resprout from ground level.) Take advantage of the open space around them with spring bulbs, such as reticulated iris (*Iris reticulata*). In summer combinations, enjoy them for their foliage. Flowering usually begins sometime in late summer and continues until frost: just in time for a splendid autumn show with asters, chrysanthemums, and other late-blooming perennials, as well as showy fall foliage colors.

Caryopteris incana 'Jason' (Sunshine Blue) with *Heuchera* 'Plum Pudding' and *Sedum rupestre* 'Angelina' (*above*); *Caryopteris* × *clandonensis* 'Summer Sorbet' with *Zinnia* 'Profusion Orange' and *Melissa officinalis* 'All Gold' (*below*)

Centranthus
striking with spiky partners

Centranthus ruber and Nepeta 'Walker's Low'

Centranthus ruber and Artemisia 'Powis Castle'

A Perfect Match

One of the most memorable companions I've seen for red valerian is Mexican fleabane (*Erigeron karvinskianus*), a low-growing, long-blooming beauty with dainty white daisies that blush to pink as they age. I've not had luck reproducing this pairing because neither plant cares for the winter-wet soil of my Pennsylvania garden. But if I lived in a warmer zone (Mexican fleabane is usually recommended for Zones 7 or 8 to 10), I'd definitely give it a try.

Red valerian (*Centranthus ruber*) is a long-blooming beauty where it is happy: mostly in areas of Zones 3 to 8 that aren't subject to high summer heat and humidity. The bushy plants typically reach 2 to 3 feet tall (sometimes 4 feet), with slender, grayish green leaves and tiny but abundant blooms grouped into showy clusters.

Color Considerations

Red valerian's key color feature is its flowers, which can range from light pink to a rich reddish pink. If you have a particular shade of pink in mind for a combination, it's best to buy plants in bloom. All but the reddest shades of red valerian flowers tend to work well with other pink-flowered perennials, such as dianthus (*Dianthus*), 'Pink Grapefruit' yarrow (*Achillea*), and purple coneflower (*Echinacea purpurea*).

Red valerian looks lovely with blues and purples, too—think of bellflowers (*Campanula*), catmints (*Nepeta*), and lavenders (*Lavandula*), for instance—as well as a range of yellows, from greenish yellow euphorbias (*Euphorbia*) and lady's mantles (*Alchemilla*) to brighter yellow coreopsis (*Coreopsis*), and 'Moonshine' yarrow (*Achillea*). Or try pairing red valerian with white flowers. It's particularly pretty with those that have a bit of pink or red in them, such as 'Arctic Fire' dianthus or 'Whirling Butterflies' gaura (*Gaura lindheimeri*).

Shapes and Textures

Red valerian plants form bushy, upright mounds. Fill in around them with lower mounded or carpeting companions, such as mountain bluet (*Centaurea montana*) or snow-in-summer (*Cerastium tomentosum*), or use them to contrast with a more vertical co-star, such as a delphinium (*Delphinium*) or annual larkspur (*Consolida ajacis*).

Overall, red valerian mostly has a medium texture, so it benefits from having a partner with a more distinct flower or foliage form. Strongly spiky blooms, like those of perennial salvias (*Salvia*), work well, as do bold blooms, like those of bearded irises, and daisy-form flowers, like those of pyrethrum daisy (*Tanacetum coccineum*). Red valerian also makes an interesting partner for fine-textured ornamental grasses, such as Mexican feather grass (*Stipa tenuissima*) or prairie dropseed (*Sporobolus heterolepis*).

Seasonal Features

In the warmest parts of its growing range, red valerian is in full bloom by late spring; in cooler

Bloom Buddies
Marvelous Matches for flowering Combos

Sites with lots of sun and average to dry (and ideally neutral to alkaline) soil are ideal for red valerian (*Centranthus ruber*), and those conditions also suit the suggested perennial companions below.

Baby's breaths (*Gypsophila*)

Bellflowers (*Campanula*)

Carolina phlox (*Phlox carolina*)

Catmints (*Nepeta*)

Coreopsis (*Coreopsis*)

Dianthus (*Dianthus*)

Gaura (*Gaura lindheimeri*)

Hardy geraniums (*Geranium*)

Jerusalem sage (*Phlomis russeliana*)

Meadow phlox (*Phlox maculata*)

Mexican fleabane (*Erigeron karvinskianus*)

Mountain bluet (*Centaurea montana*)

Mulleins (*Verbascum*)

Penstemons (*Penstemon*)

Perennial salvias (*Salvia*)

Pincushion flowers (*Scabiosa*)

Pyrethrum daisy (*Tanacetum coccineum*)

Summer phlox (*Phlox paniculata*)

Verbenas (*Verbena*)

Wood betony (*Stachys officinalis*)

Yarrows (*Achillea*)

areas, it usually begins in June. It's typically filled with flowers for a month or so; after that, it may continue to bloom through the rest of summer—especially if you keep the finished flower clusters trimmed off—or it may produce few or no new blooms after the early-summer show.

Chelone
an out-of-the-ordinary option

Chelone lyonii 'Hot Lips' and *Lamium maculatum*

Chelone lyonii 'Hot Lips'
and *Astilbe chinensis* var. *pumila*

A Perfect Match

It took me a while to appreciate the appeal of turtleheads, probably because I'd only seen them in wet meadows, where they looked somewhat scrawny growing among wild grasses. But when I saw what they could do in the good soil of a friend's big garden border—a broad clump of 'Hot Lips' pink turtlehead balanced with a shrub-size mound of 'Gibraltar' bush clover (*Lespedeza thunbergii*)—I immediately bought some for my own garden.

Turtleheads (*Chelone*) are ideal for later-season combinations in shady or wet-soil sites. Typically growing 2 to 3 feet tall, though sometimes taller, the plants have glossy green leaves on upright stems. Pink turtlehead (*C. lyonii*) has pink flowers; rose turtlehead (*C. obliqua*) has rosy pink to purplish pink flowers; and white turtlehead (*C. glabra*) has pinkish white to greenish white flowers. The blooms appear in spikelike clusters at the tops of the stems, opening over a period of 4 to 8 weeks. Turtleheads are hardy in Zones 3 to 8.

Color Considerations

Shades of pink are common in turtleheads, making them great choices for pairing with Chinese astilbe (*Astilbe chinensis*), summer phlox (*Phlox paniculata*), and other late-summer pinks. Similarly, white turtleheads are elegant with other white-flowered or white-variegated perennials, such as 'Miss Manners' obedient plant (*Physostegia virginiana*) or variegated Japanese iris (*Iris ensata* 'Variegata').

If you're looking for more intense color combinations, consider pairing rich pink 'Hot Lips' or compact Tiny Tortuga ('Armtipp02')—both selections of pink turtlehead—with bright yellows, such as goldenrods (*Solidago*) for flowers or Bowles' golden sedge (*Carex elata* 'Aurea') for foliage. Blue- to purple-flowered companions also work well. White turtlehead can look wonderful with brilliant red cardinal flower (*Lobelia cardinalis*), too.

Shapes and Textures

Best suited to medium-size or large borders, turtleheads tend to spread by creeping roots to form broad, dense patches of upright stems. For contrast in plant shape, pair them with lower mounded or carpeting companions, such as hostas or dwarf Chinese astilbe (*A. chinensis* var. *pumila*), or taller, more open background perennials, such as bugbanes (*Cimicifuga*).

Turtlehead blooms are held in spikelike heads, but not all of the flowers are open at the same time, so the blooms tend to appear more as clusters. You could use them to complement the form of other strongly spiky perennials, such as perennial lobelias (*Lobelia*), or of fluffy, vertical plumes, like those of white mugwort (*Artemisia lactiflora*). Turtleheads contrast pleasingly with the graceful, slender leaves of ornamental grasses, such as golden Hakone grass (*Hakonechloa macra* 'Aureola'); strappy foliage, like that of Japanese iris; and bold, broad leaves, like those of ligularias (*Ligularia*), rodgersias (*Rodgersia*), and umbrella plant (*Darmera peltata*).

Bloom Buddies
Marvelous Matches for Flowering Combos

Turtleheads (*Chelone*) can grow in full sun if the soil doesn't dry out; in a site with half-day sun or light all-day shade, average to moist soil is fine. Below are some other later-flowering perennials that can adapt to similar conditions.

Bugbanes (*Cimicifuga*)

Cardinal flower (*Lobelia cardinalis*)

Chinese astilbe (*Astilbe chinensis*)

Culver's roots (*Veronicastrum*)

Great blue lobelia (*Lobelia siphilitica*)

Japanese anemone (*Anemone × hybrida*)

Joe-Pye weeds (*Eupatorium*)

Purple coneflower (*Echinacea purpurea*)

Rose mallow (*Hibiscus moscheutos*)

Swamp milkweed (*Asclepias incarnata*)

White mugwort (*Artemisia lactiflora*)

Seasonal Features

White turtlehead is usually the first of the three common species to flower, starting in mid- to late July and continuing until early fall. Pink and rose turtlehead typically begin a few weeks later, in early to mid-August, and continue through September, or even into October. Their bloom periods overlap with those of many other later-season perennials, so there's no lack of flowering partners to choose from. For interest earlier in the growing season, pair them with colorful foliage, like that of bright yellow, powder blue, or vibrantly variegated hostas.

Chrysanthemum
eye-catching colors

Chrysanthemums

Full sun to light shade; average to moist but well-drained soil

Chrysanthemum 'Sheffield Pink' and *Aster oblongifolius*

A Perfect Match

'Sheffield Pink' mum is one of the last perennials to bloom in my garden, but I don't mind the wait. The plants form tidy mounds even without summer pruning, and the large, peachy pink daisies are a delight in late-season bouquets. In the garden, I like to pair them with ornamental grasses for some contrast in form and texture. Grasses that develop yellow fall color, such as 'Heavy Metal' switch grass (*Panicum virgatum*), are particularly pretty partners.

Few flowers are more traditional for sunny fall gardens than chrysanthemums (*Chrysanthemum*)—often simply referred to as mums. Their single, semidouble, or double flowers come in a wide range of colors, so there are lots of options for creating interesting pairings, and when you buy them already in bloom, it's easy to create instant combinations. The wide variety of species and hybrids available makes it possible to enjoy their beauty over a long period.

The typical garden mums (*C. × morifolium*, also known as *Dendranthema × grandiflorum*) are commonly sold in bud or bloom in late summer to early fall. That's very convenient if you want to use them in combinations, because you can see exactly what color and flower form you're getting. On the downside, planting them when they're in bloom gives them little time to settle their roots before winter, so they may not return in spring. You can also buy hybrid garden mums through mail-order suppliers for spring planting, which greatly increases their chances of living through the first winter, though you'll have to depend on catalog descriptions and pictures.

Rubellum chrysanthemums (variously sold as *C. zawadskii* var. *latilobum*, *C. × rubellum*, or *Dendranthema zawadskii*) are normally available in spring or summer, like other perennials. The two most common cultivars are 'Clara Curtis', with pink flowers, and 'Mary Stoker', with yellow flowers that develop a pink or peachy blush as they age, particularly in cool weather. The rubellum chrysanthemums tend to spread at a good clip after a year or two, but it's not hard to pull out unwanted shoots in spring if they get too enthusiastic.

Among the latest-flowering chrysanthemums are the Korean hybrids, such as the peachy pink selection sold variously as 'Sheffield Pink', 'Hillside Pink Sheffield', and 'Single Apricot', and the even-later 'Mei-Kyo', with small, fully double, lavender pink flowers that usually lighten to pale pink as they age.

All of these chrysanthemums can reach 2 to 3 feet tall and are generally hardy in Zones 4 to 9 if you plant them in spring to early or midsummer.

Color Considerations

Chrysanthemums come in many colors, so it's easy to work them into a variety of combinations. If you prefer a pastel palette, pair pink, peachy, or soft yellow selections—such as 'Clara Curtis', 'Mary Stoker', and 'Sheffield Pink'—with partners in lighter tints or slightly deeper shades of the same colors, such as 'Apricot Sunrise' orange hummingbird mint

---

Bloom Buddies
Marvelous Matches for Flowering Combos

Chrysanthemums (*Chrysanthemum*) can grow in light shade but are bushier and bloom better in full sun, and they thrive in average to moist (but not soggy), compost-enriched soil. Below are some suggestions of perennial partners that can complement them in bloom.

Partners for the main chrysanthemum season (late summer to early fall):

Agastaches (*Agastache*)

Asters (*Aster*)

Blue lilyturf (*Liriope muscari*)

Blue mistflower (*Eupatorium coelestinum*)

Caryopteris (*Caryopteris*)

Goldenrods (*Solidago*)

Japanese anemones (*Anemone*)

Joe-Pye weeds (*Eupatorium*)

Kalimeris (*Kalimeris*)

Mountain fleeceflower (*Persicaria amplexicaulis*)

Perennial sunflowers (*Helianthus*)

Rudbeckias (*Rudbeckia*)

Sedums (*Sedum*, upright types)

Verbenas (*Verbena*)

Partners for late-flowering chrysanthemums, such as 'Mei-Kyo' and 'Sheffield Pink' (mid- to late fall):

Aromatic aster (*Aster oblongifolius*)

Montauk daisy (*Nipponanthemum nipponicum*)

October daphne (*Sedum sieboldii*)

Pink muhly grass (*Muhlenbergia capillaris*)

Tatarian aster (*Aster tataricus*)

Chrysanthemum 'Harmony' with *Amsonia hubrichtii* and *Gillenia stipulata*

(*Agastache aurantiaca*), Autumn Charm sedum (*Sedum* 'Lajos'), or purple coneflower (*Echinacea purpurea*). They also pair beautifully with soft purples and blues, like those of aromatic aster (*Aster oblongifolius*) or blue mist shrub (*Caryopteris* × *clandonensis*).

Silver, gray, blue, or peachy foliage partners, such as artemisia (*Artemisia*), blue fescues (*Festuca*), or 'Caramel' heuchera (*Heuchera*), work well with pastel chrysanthemums, too. White-flowered chrysanthemums are charming with all of these pastels, as well as with other white blooms, like those of 'Whirlwind' Japanese anemone (*Anemone* × *hybrida*), and white-variegated leaves, like those of variegated obedient plant (*Physostegia virginiana* 'Variegata').

If you enjoy warmer colors in your late-season gardens, rich red, orange, and yellow garden mums are right at home with other autumnal reds, rusts, bronzes, golds, and purples in flowering or foliage partners, such as Japanese blood grass (*Imperata cylindrica* 'Rubra'), 'Toffee Twist' weeping brown sedge (*Carex flagellifera*), 'Golden Fleece' dwarf goldenrod (*Solidago sphacelata*), 'Obsidian' heuchera, and 'Wood's Purple' aster.

Shapes and Textures

The form of chrysanthemum plants depends a good deal on how you handle them. Potted, already-in-bloom mums are fine for creating instant combinations in fall, and their tightly mounded forms make an interesting contrast to the looser look of fall borders. But if you like your perennials to have a more natural form—and to increase their odds of overwintering, too—spring planting is usually the better way to go with chrysanthemums. With a bit of light pruning, as explained in "Seasonal Features" (see opposite page), hybrid mums will form broad to rounded mounds, and that's the usual form of the rubellum and Korean types, too. For some contrast in form, combine them with carpeting or low-mounded companions, such as bloody cranesbill (*Geranium sanguineum*) or dwarf fleeceflower (*Persicaria affinis*). These lower companions will also help to cover the "bare ankles" of the chrysanthemum stems.

Their relatively small and deeply lobed leaves give chrysanthemum plants a fine texture in spring and summer. In bloom, the texture usually ranges from medium to fine, depending on the size and form of the flowers. For variety, pair them with different flower and foliage shapes, such as fuzzy, broad-leaved 'Big Ears' lamb's ears (*Stachys byzantina*), spiky-leaved bearded irises or yuccas (*Yucca*), or gracefully arching grasses, such as fountain grasses (*Pennisetum*) or Mexican feather grass (*Stipa tenuissima*). Repeat the daisy-form flowers with perennials that bloom in similar shapes, such as asters or kalimeris (*Kalimeris*), or contrast them with spiky companions, such as mountain fleeceflower (*Persicaria amplexicaulis*) or the fall rebloom of perennial salvias (*Salvia*).

Seasonal Features

Spring-planted and established chrysanthemums benefit from a light pinch or snip (about 1 inch off each shoot tip) in late spring to early summer and again every 2 to 3 weeks until early or mid-July, or else a single shearing by half of their height in early summer. This sort of pruning will encourage the stems to branch, producing lower, bushier clumps and delaying bloom until late summer. Without pruning, 'Clara Curtis' is likely to begin blooming in July and may be finished flowering before fall. Most other chrysanthemums begin blooming sometime in late summer and continue into early fall, while late bloomers, such as 'Sheffield Pink' and 'Mei-Kyo', generally wait until October and may still be going in November. Their bloom periods overlap with those of many repeat-flowering, long-flowering, and late-flowering perennials, as well as with fall bulbs, such as autumn crocus (*Colchicum autumnale*).

Think of other seasonal features, too, when you're planning chrysanthemum combinations, such as interesting seed heads—like those of echinaceas (*Echinacea*), rudbeckias (*Rudbeckia*), ornamental grasses, and upright sedums (*Sedum*). Also consider perennial partners with fall-colored foliage, such as balloon flower (*Platycodon grandiflorus*), bluestars (*Amsonia*), Bowman's roots (*Gillenia*), flame grass (*Miscanthus* 'Purpurascens'), hardy geraniums (*Geranium*), and prairie dropseed (*Sporobolus heterolepis*).

Chrysanthemums make wonderful partners for cool-season annuals, such as ornamental cabbages and kales (*Brassica oleracea*), pot marigold (*Calendula officinalis*), sweet alyssum (*Lobularia maritima*), and violas (*Viola*). Don't forget tender perennials, too: Think of cannas, dahlias, and Mexican bush sage (*Salvia leucantha*), to name just a few.

Chrysanthemum 'Rhumba' and *Cornus kousa*

Cimicifuga
made for shade

Cimicifuga simplex **Atropurpurea Group,** *Athyrium niponicum* **var.** *pictum* **'Burgundy Lace', and** *Aquilegia*

Cimicifuga simplex 'Brunette' and *Anemone × hybrida* **'Whirlwind'**

A Perfect Match

When I want a companion for a dark-leaved bugbane, I usually choose a paler partner, such as a bright yellow hosta or silvery Siberian bugloss (*Brunnera macrophylla*). Ever since I saw a photo of a purple-leaved bugbane with a rich red masterwort (*Astrantia*), though, I've been looking forward to trying that combination in my own garden.

These big beauties are a stunning sight in shady gardens, providing welcome height, vertical interest, and lush, lacy leaves. It's easy to enjoy using them in combinations; the hard part is getting their names straight. Generally referred to as bugbanes—or fairy candles or snakeroots, among other common names—they are widely sold under the genus name *Cimicifuga*, but they're also listed under *Actaea*. The species names are quite jumbled, too, so it's often more useful to look at the cultivar names and tag or catalog descriptions to make sure you're getting the traits you're searching for. As a group, bugbanes are suited for Zones 3 to 9.

Black cohosh (*C. racemosa* or *A. racemosa*), also known as black snakeroot, is native to parts of eastern North America. It is quite variable: The height in bloom can be anywhere from 3 to 8 feet, and the flowering time can range from May and June in the mildest parts of its range to July and August in cooler areas. It holds its white blooms in branching heads of slender, tapering spikes.

The next species to bloom—in late summer to early fall—is an Asian native listed as *C. simplex, C. ramosa, A. simplex,* or *A. ramosa.* The exact name doesn't matter so much: From the perspective of making combinations, it's important to know that these are the bugbanes that often have deliciously dark foliage and pinkish flower buds that open to white or very pale pink. The leaves of those sold as part of the Atropurpurea Group range from purple-tinged green to purplish brown (as on 'Brunette') to practically black (as on 'Hillside Black Beauty'). Those two selections typically reach 4 to 6 feet in bloom. There are a number of more compact cultivars, such as 'Chocoholic', which generally reaches 2 to 3 feet tall in flower.

The latest blooming of the bunch is another Asian native commonly known as autumn bugbane or Kamchatka bugbane (*C. simplex* var. *matsumurae* or *A. matsumurae*). You'll most often find it sold as the cultivar 'White Pearl', with 3- to 5-foot-tall, pure white blooms that open in fall.

Color Considerations

Bugbanes in bloom are a beautiful source of white for the summer or fall garden. They work well with any other color, from vivid reds, oranges, and yellows to more delicate hues of peach, pink, or blue. (See "Bloom Buddies," right, for specific suggestions depending on the season.) They're outstanding with cream- or white-variegated companions, such as 'Patriot' hosta or 'River Mist' sea oats (*Chasmanthium latifolium*).

The bugbanes with dark foliage offer exciting opportunities for creating memorable color

Bloom Buddies
Marvelous Matches for Flowering Combos

Bugbanes (*Cimicifuga*) generally do best with morning sun and afternoon shade or light all-day shade and compost-enriched soil that's on the moist side. Below is a sampling of beautiful flowering companions that can thrive in similar conditions.

Companions for black cohosh (*C. racemosa*) in early to midsummer:

Astilbes (*Astilbe*)

Bleeding hearts (*Dicentra*)

Hostas (*Hosta*)

Lady's mantles (*Alchemilla*)

Masterworts (*Astrantia*)

Meadow rues (*Thalictrum*)

Spiderworts (*Tradescantia*)

Companions for dark-leaved bugbanes (*C. simplex*) in late summer to early fall:

Cardinal flower (*Lobelia cardinalis*)

Chinese astilbe (*Astilbe chinensis*)

Japanese anemones (*Anemone*)

Joe-Pye weeds (*Eupatorium*)

New England aster (*Aster novae-angliae*)

Turtleheads (*Chelone*)

White mugwort (*Artemisia lactiflora*)

Companions for 'White Pearl' autumn bugbane (*C. simplex* var. *matsumurae*) in early to mid-fall:

Blue wood aster (*Aster cordifolius*)

Hardy begonia (*Begonia grandis*)

Japanese anemones (*Anemone*)

Smooth aster (*Aster laevis*)

Toad lilies (*Tricyrtis*)

White wood aster (*Aster divaricatus*)

Yellow waxbells (*Kirengeshoma palmata*)

Cimicifuga racemosa with *Acer palmatum* 'Red Emperor' and *Polygonatum odoratum* 'Variegatum'

robbiae), or 'White Nancy' spotted deadnettle (*Lamium maculatum*). In bloom, bugbanes have a distinctly vertical stance, contrasting well with hostas and other mounded companions.

Bugbane leaves have a lacy form that repeats the look of many other shade lovers, such as astilbes (*Astilbe*), goatsbeards (*Aruncus*), and ferns. For visual variety, pair them with broad leaves, like those of ligularias (*Ligularia*) and Siberian bugloss (*Brunnera macrophylla*), or with grassy or strappy leaves, like those of Bowles' golden sedge (*Carex elata* 'Aurea') or 'Sweet Kate' spiderwort (*Tradescantia*). The upright to arching, fuzzy bloom spikes of bugbanes are lovely paired with plumy blooms—think of astilbes, Korean feather reed grass (*Calamagrostis brachytricha*), or white mugwort (*Artemisia lactiflora*), for instance—or contrasted with large, bold blooms, like those of daylilies (*Hemerocallis*), hydrangeas (*Hydrangea*), or true lilies (*Lilium*).

effects. They're especially striking paired with bright yellow or yellow-variegated leaves, like those of 'Banana Boat' broadleaf sedge (*Carex siderosticha*), and with white-variegated partners, such as variegated Solomon's seal (*Polygonatum odoratum* 'Variegatum').

Shapes and Textures

Bugbanes take a few years to settle in and fill out, eventually forming bushy mounds of divided foliage. Fill in around tall species and selections with lower, mounded plants, such as Lenten rose (*Helleborus* × *hybridus*) and wild geranium (*Geranium maculatum*), and around compact cultivars with carpeting companions, such as Allegheny pachysandra (*Pachysandra procumbens*), Robb's spurge (*Euphorbia amygdaloides* var.

Seasonal Features

Well-established bugbanes can fill a space several feet across in summer and fall, but in spring, their ferny shoots are narrowly upright. Take advantage of that space by filling in around them with early-blooming bulbs and wildflowers, such as snowdrops (*Galanthus*) and Virginia bluebells (*Mertensia virginica*), which will go dormant as the bugbanes expand in early summer. For the earliest bloom season, consider black cohosh; it's followed later in summer by the dark-leaved bugbanes. 'White Pearl' opens in time to mingle with perennial and shrubby companions that have equally late blooms, interesting seed heads, beautiful berries, or showy fall foliage color.

Coreopsis
cheery colors for summer combos

Coreopsis

Full sun to light shade; average, well-drained soil

Coreopsis verticillata 'Zagreb' and *Hyssopus officinalis*

Coreopsis 'Jethro Tull' with *Baptisia sphaerocarpa* 'Screamin' Yellow' and *Spiraea betulifolia* 'Tor'

A Perfect Match

For a long time, our color options for perennial coreopsis were limited to light yellow, bright yellow, and golden yellow. Those yellows are still excellent for combinations, but I can't help falling for the rich hues and intricate shading on many of the newer hybrids, even if they tend to fizzle out after 1 year in my garden. I've made some great matches with rich reddish pink 'Limerock Ruby' and dark-leaved partners, such as 'Obsidian' heuchera (*Heuchera*) and 'Merlot' lettuce.

Coreopsis (*Coreopsis*) belong in every color-loving gardener's plant paint box. Though the plants tend to be short lived, often lasting just a season or two, they bloom so readily and for so long that they earn their keep even if you have to replace them every year or two. They're ideal for filling space around perennials that take several years to reach their full width, such as baptisias (*Baptisia*) and bluestars (*Amsonia*).

Among the well-known yellow-flowered species are lanceleaf coreopsis (*C. lanceolata*) and the very similar large-flowered coreopsis (*C. grandiflora*), with single, semidouble, or double golden yellow blooms. Threadleaf coreopsis (*C. verticillata*) has single flowers in a range of yellows (golden yellow on 'Golden Showers' and 'Zagreb', for example, to soft yellow on 'Moonbeam'). It's also distinctive for its very slender foliage. These three coreopsis can grow 1 to 3 feet tall, depending on the cultivar, and are hardy in Zones 3 to 9.

Bloom Buddies
Marvelous Matches for Flowering Combos

Full sun brings out the best bloom and sturdiest stems on coreopsis (*Coreopsis*). The yellow-flowered types can often adapt well to dry sites, but in general, coreopsis perform beautifully in the same border conditions that suit many complementary partners, such as those listed below.

Agastaches (*Agastache*)

Bee balms (*Monarda*)

Bellflowers (*Campanula*)

Blanket flowers (*Gaillardia*)

Blazing stars (*Liatris*)

Catmints (*Nepeta*)

Daylilies (*Hemerocallis*)

Dianthus (*Dianthus*)

Echinaceas (*Echinacea*)

Feverfew (*Tanacetum parthenium*)

Globe thistles (*Echinops*)

Hardy geraniums (*Geranium*)

Lavenders (*Lavandula*)

Penstemons (*Penstemon*)

Perennial salvias (*Salvia*)

Pincushion flowers (*Scabiosa*)

Red valerian (*Centranthus ruber*)

Rudbeckias (*Rudbeckia*)

Sea hollies (*Eryngium*)

Shasta daisy (*Leucanthemum × superbum*)

Speedwells (*Veronica*)

Torch lilies (*Kniphofia*)

Verbenas (*Verbena*)

Yarrows (*Achillea*)

Pink coreopsis (*C. rosea*) has, as you may guess, pink flowers. It generally reaches 12 to 18 inches tall but much wider, because it is a vigorous spreader. Its leaves are very slender, like those of threadleaf coreopsis, and it too is hardy in Zones 3 to 9, but it tends to like more moisture than the yellow species.

There are many coreopsis hybrids, expanding the range from yellows and pinks to ruby reds, such as 'Mercury Rising' and 'Red Satin', and peachy oranges, such as Crème Caramel ('Novcorcar') and 'Sienna Sunset'. Quite a few have intricate shadings, as on coral-and-peach 'Desert Coral' and peach, pink, and yellow 'Tahitian Sunset', or contrasting markings, as on 'Cosmic Eye' (with bright yellow flowers that have a deep red eye) and 'Star Cluster' (with white flowers that can have deep purple markings). Most of these hybrids grow 1 to 2 feet tall. Hardiness zones can range from 4 or 7 to 9, so be sure to check catalog descriptions or plant tags before selecting specific hybrids for your combinations.

Color Considerations

While the yellow-flowered coreopsis are fairly consistent, color-wise, it's common for the hybrids to vary in color through the growing season. Their hues (particularly the pinks and reds) tend to be more intense early and late in the growing season, when temperatures are on the cooler side and the sun is not too strong. The flowers may be significantly paler during the hottest part of summer, losing much or all of their reddish coloring (as on 'Autumn Blush' and 'Starlight') or even developing touches of white (as on 'Mercury Rising'). You may need to experiment with several different flowering companions before finding perfect color matches, or else grow new hybrids in a holding bed for a full season and observe how they perform in your specific conditions before choosing ideal color companions. Or pair them with heucheras (*Heuchera*), sedums (*Sedum*), or other foliage partners that will provide consistent, complementary color for your chosen coreopsis through the growing season.

Vivid yellow coreopsis species and hybrids are terrific for high-impact combinations in bright-and-bold borders. Use them to repeat other strong yellows, like those of 'Coronation Gold' fernleaf yarrow (*Achillea filipendulina*), mulleins (*Verbascum*), and rudbeckias (*Rudbeckia*), or contrast them with rich blues and purples, like those of 'Caradonna' perennial salvia (*Salvia nemorosa*), mountain bluet (*Centaurea montana*), 'Nicky' summer phlox (*Phlox paniculata*), or 'Sarastro' bellflower (*Campanula*). 'Early Sunrise', 'Zagreb', and other bright yellow coreopsis also look terrific with orange or red flowers or leaves, like those of blanket flowers (*Gaillardia*), butterfly weed (*Asclepias tuberosa*), 'Cheyenne Sky' switch grass (*Panicum virgatum*), or Japanese blood grass (*Imperata cylindrica* 'Rubra').

If you prefer a pastel palette, there are plenty of coreopsis cultivars to choose from, such as buttery yellow 'Moonbeam', peachy 'Sienna Sunset', and pink 'Heaven's Gate', among many others. Try them with cool blues and purples, like those of 'Boulder Blue' blue fescue (*Festuca glauca*) or lavenders (*Lavandula*). Or pair them with pink-flowered partners, such as 'Bath's Pink' dianthus (*Dianthus*), purple coneflower (*Echinacea purpurea*), or red valerian

Coreopsis 'Full Moon' with *Allium hollandicum* 'Purple Sensation', *Veronica grandis*, and *Sanguisorba obtusa*

(*Centranthus ruber*). Try combining with creamy yellow flowers or leaf markings, like those of 'Pineapple Popsicle' torch lily (*Kniphofia*) or variegated sweet iris (*Iris pallida* 'Variegata'). Or try them with peachy partners, such as 'Just Peachy' orange hummingbird mint (*Agastache aurantiaca*) or 'Ruffled Apricot' daylily (*Hemerocallis*).

Coreopsis hybrids offer some wonderful options for "sunset" borders based on warm pinks, oranges, corals, and dusky purples. 'Limerock Dream' and 'Tahitian Sunset', for instance, include shades of gold, pink, and peach in each bloom, while 'Desert Coral' flowers combine orange and coral. Complement them with bearded irises that include similar colors or with bronzy or purple foliage, like that of 'Bronze Beauty' heuchera (*Heuchera villosa*) or 'Purple Emperor' sedum (*Sedum*).

Coreopsis cultivars with bicolor blooms offer intriguing opportunities for creating color echoes in combinations. The raspberry red petals of 'Ruby Frost', for instance, have a white frosting on the edge, which you could pick up with a white-variegated companion, such as 'Avalanche' feather reed grass (*Calamagrostis × acutiflora*) or 'Snow Fairy' bluebeard (*Caryopteris divaricata*). Partners with yellow flowers or foliage are ideal for echoing the yellow color in the center of many coreopsis blooms.

Coreopsis 'Limerock Dream' and *Weigela florida* 'Bramwell' (Fine Wine)

Shapes and Textures

Coreopsis plants mostly have a mounded form and fine-textured foliage. For contrast, use lower, trailing or carpeting partners, such as creeping sedums (*Sedum*) or ornamental oreganos (*Origanum*), or vertical companions, such as dense blazing star (*Liatris spicata*) or summer phlox (*Phlox paniculata*). They also work well with strappy foliage, like that of bearded irises and yuccas (*Yucca*), or grassy partners, such as leatherleaf sedge (*Carex buchananii*) or Mexican feather grass (*Stipa tenuissima*).

It's easy to find co-stars that repeat the daisy form of most coreopsis flowers: Think of asters, heleniums (*Helenium*), and rudbeckias (*Rudbeckia*), to name a few. For variety, choose companions with other flower forms, such as airy catmints (*Nepeta*), plumy Russian sages (*Perovskia*), flat-topped upright sedums, spiky speedwells (*Veronica*), or funnel-shaped penstemons (*Penstemon*).

Seasonal Features

Most coreopsis are in bloom by early summer. The threadleaf types, however, can be slow to come up in spring, especially in the cooler parts of their range, where they may not begin until almost midsummer. Shearing your coreopsis plants lightly after the first wave of flowers is done (or snipping off individual spent flowers, if you have the patience) can encourage the plants to flower again, and they may continue to produce new blooms well into fall. Left to dry in place, the seed heads add winter interest and supply winter food for backyard birds.

Delphinium
the stars of any combination

Delphinium **New Zealand Hybrids** with *Persicaria polymorpha*, *Hemerocallis*, and *Silene* **'Rollie's Favorite'**

Delphinium grandiflorum **'Diamonds Blue'** with *Lilium* **'Monte Negro'** and *Filipendula ulmaria* **'Aurea'**

A Perfect Match

I've been hearing great things about the New Zealand Hybrids: They sound like an excellent choice for those of us who struggle with growing the classic hybrid delphiniums. Until I can try them for myself, I'll stick with annual larkspur (*Consolida ajacis*) when I want delphinium-like blue, pink, or white spires in an early-summer combination. Like their perennial relatives, they're particularly pretty rising out of a cloud of tiny blooms, like those of baby's breath (*Gypsophila paniculata*).

Delphiniums (*Delphinium*) aren't particularly distinctive in leaf, but in bloom, they tend to be the stars of any combination. Classic favorites include Elatum Group delphiniums, such as the 4- to 7-foot-tall Pacific Hybrids, with dense, columnar or tapering bloom spikes, and the 3- to 4-foot-tall Belladonna Group hybrids, with looser, branching bloom spikes and lacier leaves. They're generally best in Zones 3 or 4 to 7 but can go as far sound as Zone 10 where summers don't get too hot. The New Zealand Hybrids, such as the New Millennium strains, offer the dramatic spires of those older favorites but on sturdier-stemmed plants that are more tolerant of heat and humidity.

Selections of Chinese delphinium (*D. grandiflorum*, also sold as *D. chinensis*), such as 'Blue Butterfly' and 'Blue Mirror', are also a bit more heat tolerant (Zones 3 to 8), but they tend to be short lived, often blooming for just a year or two. They're also quite compact—in the range of 12 to 30 inches.

Bloom Buddies
Marvelous Matches for flowering Combos

Delphiniums (*Delphinium*) love sun in the cooler parts of their growing range but often appreciate afternoon shade or light all-day shade south of Zone 5. They thrive in compost-enriched soil—ideally on the neutral to slightly alkaline side—that stays somewhat moist. Below are just a few compatible companions whose bloom times overlap with delphiniums.

Bellflowers
(*Campanula*)

Carolina phlox
(*Phlox carolina*)

Catmints (*Nepeta*)

Coreopsis (*Coreopsis*)

Daylilies (*Hemerocallis*)

Foxgloves (*Digitalis*)

Irises (*Iris*)

Lady's mantle
(*Alchemilla mollis*)

Meadow rues
(*Thalictrum*)

Peonies (*Paeonia*)

Perennial salvias
(*Salvia*)

Pincushion flowers
(*Scabiosa*)

Rose campion
(*Lychnis coronaria*)

Summer phlox
(*Phlox paniculata*)

(*Leucanthemum* × *superbum*); pink-flowered partners, such as purple coneflower (*Echinacea purpurea*); and a wide range of yellows. For a high-impact combination, try rich purple or blue delphiniums with vivid orange, scarlet, or red flowers, like those of Oriental poppy (*Papaver orientale*) or 'Totally Tangerine' geum (*Geum*).

Shapes and Textures

The very vertical, tall delphiniums pair well with large, bushy partners, such as goatsbeard (*Arunucus dioicus*) or shrub roses, which will remain to fill the space when the delphiniums are done blooming. More-compact hybrids and the Chinese delphiniums work well closer to the front or middle of the border, contrasted with mounded companions, such as coreopsis (*Coreopsis*) and hardy geraniums (*Geranium*).

Both the strongly spiky delphiniums and the more open Belladonna and Chinese delphiniums work well with a range of other bloom shapes, from big-and-bold alliums (*Allium*) and Oriental poppy (*Papaver orientale*) to daisy-form flowers. They also look terrific with spiky plumes, like those of astilbes (*Astilbe*).

Color Considerations

Blue and purple-blue delphiniums are outstanding in "all-blue" or mostly blue borders with other flowering perennials in the same color range. Just keep in mind that pure blue delphiniums may not look good right next to lavender-blue companions, such as Frikart's aster (*Aster* × *frikartii*).

Delphiniums of all sorts are gorgeous with white flowers, like those of Shasta daisy

Seasonal Features

In most areas, delphiniums begin blooming in late spring to early summer, just in time to join many other classic border perennials, including irises, lupines (*Lupinus*), and peonies, as well as roses. They usually continue into midsummer, at least, so you can also match them with summer favorites, such as daylilies (*Hemerocallis*), echinaceas (*Echinacea*), hollyhocks (*Alcea rosea*), and true lilies (*Lilium*).

Dianthus
small in size, big on charm

Dianthus 'Rosish One'
and *Iris pallida* 'Variegata'

Dianthus 'Frosty Fire' and *Amsonia* 'Blue Ice'

A Perfect Match

It was just by chance that I planted 'Bath's Pink' dianthus with 'Immortality' iris, but it turned out to be an excellent partnership. They're both beautiful in bloom—the dainty pink dianthus makes a pretty complement to the bold, bright white iris flowers—and are equally pleasing long after, as well. Though very similar in color, the fine foliage of the dianthus and the bold, spiky leaves of the iris make a terrific textural contrast.

Dianthus (*Dianthus*) are small in size, but they're big on charm. Though some last just 1 or 2 years, there are truly perennial kinds, too: Among them are cheddar pinks (*D. gratianopolitanus*), cottage or grass pinks (*D. plumarius*), maiden pinks (*D. deltoides*), and many hybrids, including the Allwood pinks (*D. × allwoodii* or Allwoodii Alpinus Group). Most reach 3 to 6 inches tall in leaf and 6 to 12 inches tall in bloom. The winter hardiness of the different species and hybrids varies a bit, and many don't tolerate heat and humidity well, but most can grow in Zones 3 or 4 to 7 or 8.

Color Considerations

Dianthus are often referred to as pinks, due to the jagged or "pinked" edges on their petals, but that name could just as easily apply to their most common color range: from pale pink to rich

Bloom Buddies
Marvelous Matches for Flowering Combos

Though they can tolerate light shade, dianthus (*Dianthus*) prefer full sun and average, well-drained to dryish soil that's on the neutral to alkaline side. Below are some compatible perennials that can make beautiful bloom partners during the main dianthus flowering period.

Baby's breaths (*Gypsophila*)

Bearded irises (*Iris* Bearded Hybrids)

Bellflowers (*Campanula*)

Bluestars (*Amsonia*)

Catmints (*Nepeta*)

Coreopsis (*Coreopsis*)

Foxgloves (*Dianthus*)

Hardy geraniums (*Geranium*)

Mountain bluet (*Centaurea montana*)

Perennial salvias (*Salvia*)

Red valerian (*Centranthus ruber*)

Speedwells (*Veronica*)

Sweet iris (*Iris pallida*)

for example, or purple-blue catmints (*Nepeta*) and pincushion flowers (*Scabiosa*). With richer pinks, like those of 'Rosish One' or 'Ruby Sparkles', and reds, like those of 'Desmond' and 'Red Beauty', consider making a dramatic contrast with yellows, like those in the flowers of lady's mantle (*Alchemilla mollis*) or the leaves of 'Aztec Gold' prostrate speedwell (*Veronica prostrata*). Or go for an elegant effect by pairing them with striking silvers or soft grays, like those of 'Silver Brocade' beach wormwood (*Artemisia stelleriana*) or woolly thyme (*Thymus pseudolanuginosus*).

Dianthus offer some of the crispest white blooms you can find, so they are wonderful for a white-themed bed or border. Use cultivars such as 'Aqua' and 'Greystone' to repeat other bright white flowers, like those of 'Miss Lingard' Carolina phlox (*Phlox carolina*), along with leaves that are bright to deep green, silver, or gray. White dianthus are also gorgeous with blue to purple-blue blooms, like those of 'Blue Butterfly' Chinese delphinium (*Delphinium grandiflorum*) or lavenders (*Lavandula*), or with blue to gray-blue leaves, like those of 'Beyond Blue' blue fescue (*Festuca glauca*).

Shapes and Textures

Dianthus plants grow as dense mounds or low carpets that are ideal for planting at the edge of a border or along a path, where you can appreciate the dainty blooms up close. Use them in front of mounded or upright partners, such as perennial salvias (*Salvia*) or showy sedum (*Sedum spectabile*). Or pair them with other low-growing perennials, such as moss

rosy or purplish pink. There are also some stunning reds and brilliant white cultivars. The blooms may be a solid color or have a lighter or darker center or edge. You can emphasize these markings by choosing co-stars that have the same color: A red-leaved heuchera (*Heuchera*), for instance, such as 'Fire Alarm', would do a beautiful job echoing the deep red "eye" on the white blooms of 'Arctic Fire' dianthus.

Light pink dianthus, such as 'Bath's Pink' and Blushing Maiden ('Valda Judith'), are lovely with other soft colors, particularly in the blue to purple range: cool blue bluestars (*Amsonia*),

Dianthus 'Bath's Pink' with *Artemisia* 'Powis Castle', *Amsonia* 'Blue Ice', and *Iris* 'Immortality' *(above)*; *Dianthus deltoides* with *Liriope muscari* 'Variegata', *Callirhoe involucrata*, and *Origanum vulgare* 'Dr. Ietswaart' *(right)*

phlox (*Phlox subulata*), snow-in-summer (*Cerastium tomentosum*), two-row sedum (*S. spurium*), and woolly yarrow (*Achillea tomentosa*), to create a tapestry groundcover to fill a dry, sunny spot or to cover a slope.

Their small, short, slender leaves give dianthus plants a fine texture. Echo their look with short to medium-size grasses, such as blue fescue (*Festuca glauca*) or blue oat grass (*Helictotrichon sempervirens*), or with wider, spiky leaves, like those of bearded irises or yuccas (*Yucca*). Or go for a striking contrast with broader leaves, like those of 'Berggarten' common sage (*Salvia officinalis*) or 'Big Ears' lamb's ears (*Stachys byzantina*).

Dianthus flowers may be single or double and relatively simple or charmingly frilly. They contrast prettily with spiky-flowered partners, such as lavenders and Royal Candles spike speedwell (*Veronica spicata* 'Glory'), or with large blooms, like those of dwarf bearded irises or star-of-Persia (*Allium cristophii*).

Seasonal Features

Peak bloom season for most dianthus is late spring or early summer, but many modern hybrids can produce additional flowers through the rest of summer or even into fall, especially if you remove the blooms as they fade. Even on those with just one main show, shearing off the faded flowers right above the leaves tidies the plants and lets you enjoy the beautiful gray-blue to silvery blue leaves. They remain attractive through winter, too, making them handsome companions for other low, evergreen perennials and shrubs, such as 'Angelina' sedum (*S. rupestre*) and dwarf conifers.

Dicentra
charming hearts for the garden

Dicentra spectabilis and Brunnera macrophylla 'Jack Frost'

Dicentra spectabilis 'Gold Heart' and Omphalodes cappadocica 'Starry Eyes'

A Perfect Match

One of my first gardening mentors hated pink paired with yellow, so for a long time, I automatically avoided that color combination myself. 'Gold Heart' common bleeding heart changed my mind, though. Its rosy pink blooms and bright yellow leaves look brilliant together: a showy combination all on one plant. I like it best with quiet partners, such as the deep green leaves of hybrid hellebores (*Helleborus* × *hybridus*) or blue-leaved hostas.

The distinctive blooms of bleeding hearts (*Dicentra*) are an elegant addition to late-spring and early-summer combinations. Common bleeding heart (*D. spectabilis*, also known as *Lamprocapnos spectabilis*), grows in 2- to 3-foot-tall clumps with gracefully arching stems that are tipped with chains of dangling, heart-shaped flowers. Fringed or wild bleeding heart (*D. eximia*), western or Pacific bleeding heart (*D. formosa*), and related hybrids are much more compact: typically just 10 to 15 inches tall in bloom. Bleeding hearts are generally hardy in Zones 3 to 8.

Color Considerations

Though the color range of their blooms is somewhat limited—primarily pinks, reds, and white—bleeding hearts offer lots of possibilities for creating outstanding combinations. Common bleeding heart has both pink and white in its flowers, so you can easily create harmonies by choosing partners in either of those colors: 'Dayglow Pink' foamy bells (× *Heucherella*) or white 'Mr. Morse' Siberian bugloss (*Brunnera macrophylla*) for flowers, for instance, or 'Midnight Rose' heuchera (*Heuchera*) or 'Snow Cap' broadleaf sedge (*Carex siderosticha*) for foliage. The pink-flowered fringed and western bleeding hearts and hybrids also work well with white flowers and white-variegated leaves.

If pastels are your passion, pair any of the pink bleeding hearts with gray or blue foliage, like that of Japanese painted fern (*Athyrium niponicum* var. *pictum*) or 'Halcyon' hosta, or with soft yellow flowers, like those of bicolor barrenwort (*Epimedium × versicolor* 'Sulphureum') or 'Corbett' wild columbine (*Aquilegia canadensis*). Baby blues also look lovely with pink bleeding hearts: Consider 'Blue Ridge' creeping phlox (*Phlox stolonifera*), forget-me-nots (*Myosotis*), 'Stairway to Heaven' creeping Jacob's ladder (*Polemonium reptans*), or Virginia bluebells (*Mertensia virginica*), to name a few possibilities.

Looking for a bit more intensity? Combine your pink bleeding hearts with companions that have dark flowers or foliage, such as mourning widow geranium (*Geranium phaeum*), 'Queen of Night' tulip, 'Hillside Black Beauty' bugbane (*Cimicifuga simplex*), and 'Obsidian' heuchera. Or start with bleeding heart selections with flowers that are on the red side, such as Valentine ('Hordival') common bleeding heart or hybrid 'Red Fountain'; then, go bold with bright yellow co-stars, such as golden Hakone grass (*Hakonechloa macra* 'Aureola'), 'Sun Power' hosta, 'Stoplight' foamy bells, or wood poppy (*Stylophorum diphyllum*), and orangey partners,

Bloom Buddies
Marvelous Matches for flowering Combos

Bleeding hearts (*Dicentra*) can grow in full sun in the coolest parts of their growing range where the soil stays moist; south of Zone 6, partial shade with average to moist but well-drained soil is best. Below are some compatible perennial companions for their peak late-spring to early-summer bloom period.

Ajugas (*Ajuga*)

Columbines (*Aquilegia*)

Creeping Jacob's ladder (*Polemonium reptans*)

Creeping phlox (*Phlox stolonifera*)

Crested iris (*Iris cristata*)

Epimediums (*Epimedium*)

Foamflowers (*Tiarella*)

Foamy bells (× *Heucherella*)

Foxgloves (*Digitalis*)

Jack-in-the-pulpits (*Arisaema*)

Snowdrop anemone (*Anemone sylvestris*)

Solomon's seals (*Polygonatum*)

Virginia bluebells (*Mertensia virginica*)

Wood poppy (*Stylophorum diphyllum*)

Woodland phlox (*Phlox divaricata*)

Yellow corydalis (*Corydalis lutea*)

such as *Epimedium × warleyense* or 'Sweet Tea' foamy bells. Reds are outstanding in matches with whites in flowering and foliage companions, and with silver-leaved partners, such as 'Looking Glass' Siberian bugloss (*Brunnera macrophylla*).

Dicentra spectabilis 'Alba' and *Galium odoratum (left); Dicentra spectabilis* 'Gold Heart' and *Spiraea japonica* 'Walbuma' (Magic Carpet) *(above)*

Bleeding hearts offer some wonderful whites of their own—'Aurora' western bleeding heart and white ('Alba') common bleeding heart, to name just two—and it's easy to find compatible white companions: 'Bruce's White' creeping phlox (*P. stolonifera*) and 'White Nancy' spotted deadnettle (*Lamium maculatum*) for flowers, for instance, or perhaps variegated Solomon's seal (*Polygonatum odoratum* 'Variegatum') for foliage. Add some blue, gray, or silver foliage here, as well, for an unforgettable show.

Don't forget to take advantage of the beautiful foliage of your bleeding hearts. 'Gold Heart' is a stunning selection of common bleeding heart with brilliant yellow leaves. Use it among greens as an accent; echo it with yellow-variegated leaves, like those of 'Oehme' palm sedge (*Carex muskingumensis*); complement it with bright blue or silver leaves, like those of 'Fragrant Blue' hosta; or contrast it with 'Britt-Marie Crawford' ligularia (*Ligularia dentata*) or

other companions with dark foliage. Bleeding hearts with blue-green to gray-green leaves, such as 'Ivory Hearts' and 'Langtrees', show off beautifully against perennial partners with deep green leaves, such as European wild ginger (*Asarum europaeum*) or Lenten rose (*Helleborus × hybridus*), or with bright yellow foliage, like that of 'Citronelle' heuchera (*Heuchera*) or 'Maui Buttercups' hosta.

Shapes and Textures

Common bleeding heart plants have a broad, bushy form that works well behind lower mounded or carpeting plants, such as pulmonarias (*Pulmonaria*) and woodland phlox (*P. divaricata*). Fringed bleeding heart and similar hybrids have a more compact, mounded shape, while western bleeding heart and its hybrids tend to have a more open, somewhat creeping habit. Both work well around larger, mounded companions and behind low growers, such as common ajuga (*Ajuga reptans*). For contrast, pair any of your bleeding hearts with upright perennials, such as columbines (*Aquilegia*), foxgloves (*Digitalis*), and Solomon's seals (*Polygonatum*).

Bleeding hearts have divided leaves, giving the plants a lacy look, particularly on the low-growing species and hybrids. They repeat the leaf shape of many other shade lovers, including astilbes (*Astilbe*), bugbanes (*Cimicifuga*), goatsbeards (*Aruncus*), and ferns, so separate them with contrasting shapes, such as rounded to oval bergenias (*Bergenia*), hostas, or wild gingers (*Asarum*) and grassy to strappy foliage, like that of crested iris (*Iris cristata*), sedges (*Carex*), and spiderworts (*Tradescantia*).

Seasonal Features

Beautiful in leaf as soon as they sprout, bleeding hearts quickly add their blooms to the show. The flowers of fringed bleeding heart and its hybrids typically begin in mid-spring followed within a few weeks by western bleeding heart and common bleeding heart and continuing into early summer. Their peak period coincides with that of many other shade-loving perennials and wildflowers (see "Bloom Buddies" on page 93 for lots of ideas) as well as late-spring bulbs, such as bluebells (*Hyacinthoides*), late tulips, and summer snowflake (*Leucojum aestivum*).

After flowering, common bleeding heart tends to decline or disappear altogether in mid- to late summer, especially if the soil dries out, potentially leaving a large gap in your border. To prevent that problem, consider combining it with later-rising companions, such as hardy begonia (*Begonia grandis*) or Japanese anemones (*Anemone*), or with large hostas that will expand to fill their space, such as 'Krossa Regal' or 'Sum and Substance'.

Fringed and western bleeding hearts and hybrids may continue producing new blooms through the rest of summer, and even into fall. Match them with pink, red, or white astilbes (*Astilbe*) or Asiatic lilies (*Lilium* Asiatic Hybrids), with hosta flowers and foliage, or with colorful leafy partners to take advantage of their extended bloom period.

Dicentra 'Luxuriant' with *Carex siderosticha* 'Snow Cap' and *Lamium maculatum* 'White Nancy'

Digitalis
dramatically vertical

Digitalis purpurea with *Miscanthus sinensis* 'Variegatus' and *Iris sibirica*

Digitalis × *mertonensis* and *Polemonium boreale* 'Heavenly Habit'

A Perfect Match

The elegant spires of common foxglove are glorious, but I have much better luck growing strawberry foxglove. Its rich raspberry sorbet color and chunky bells are lovely with the dainty, purple-blue blooms of catmints. As a finishing touch, I like to add a bit of yellow: The frothy flower clusters of lady's mantle (*Alchemilla mollis*) are always winners.

Foxgloves (*Digitalis*) all share the same basic form: dense, leafy rosettes that send up strongly vertical stems lined at the top with tubular to bell-like flowers. Common foxglove (*D. purpurea*) blooms in shades of pink, peach, cream, and white on stems that usually reach 3 to 5 feet tall. Strawberry foxglove (*D.* × *mertonensis*) is a bit stockier looking, with rosy pink flowers on 2- to 3-foot-tall stems. Yellow foxglove (*D. grandiflora*, also sold as *D. ambigua*) and straw foxglove (*D. lutea*) are also in that height range. They both have soft yellow flowers, but straw foxglove's blossoms are much daintier. All of these foxgloves are usually hardy in Zones 3 or 4 to 9.

Color Considerations

The pinks, peaches, whites, and yellows of foxgloves pair beautifully with blues and purples, from brilliant blue Italian alkanet (*Anchusa azurea*) and rich purple-blue delphiniums (*Delphinium*) to softer tints and tones in catmints (*Nepeta*) and hardy geraniums (*Geranium*), such as 'Brookside'.

For other peaches and pinks, think of astilbes (*Astilbe*), such as 'Peach Blossom' and 'Rheinland', for similar height. Closer to the front of the border, consider hybrid bleeding hearts (*Dicentra*) or dianthus (*Dianthus*).

To create an elegant, all-white effect, try white foxgloves with white Siberian irises, such as 'Gull Wings' or 'White Swirl'; white astilbes, such as 'Bridal Veil' or 'White Gloria'; and white rose campion (*Lychnis coronaria* 'Alba').

Shapes and Textures

The spiky blooms of foxgloves have a dramatically vertical form. For contrast, pair them with perennials that have mounded shapes, such as peonies and hostas, or large, rounded blooms, like those of 'Gladiator' allium (*Allium*) or pink or white Oriental poppies (*Papaver orientale*). Or repeat their form with other spiky-flowered partners, such as lupines (*Lupinus*) and mulleins (*Verbascum*).

Seasonal Features

Foxgloves put on their best show around early summer, starting a bit earlier in warmer climates and extending into midsummer in cooler areas: just in time to pair perfectly with bellflowers (*Campanula*), irises, peonies, and many other classic border perennials.

Common foxglove tends to die after flowering and setting seed, but it will produce an abundance of seedlings if you leave the spent flower stalks on the plants so the seeds can mature in late summer—a fine solution in informal sites,

Bloom Buddies
Marvelous Matches for flowering Combos

Foxgloves (*Digitalis*) grow well in full sun in cooler areas, particularly if the soil doesn't dry out. They also perform well in partial shade in most areas with average to moist but well-drained soil. Below are some companions that thrive in the same conditions and flower around the same time.

Baptisias (*Baptisia*)

Bearded irises (*Iris* Bearded Hybrids)

Bellflowers (*Campanula*)

Bluestars (*Amsonia*)

Carolina lupine (*Thermopsis villosa*)

Catmints (*Nepeta*)

Columbines (*Aquilegia*)

Delphiniums (*Delphinium*)

Dianthus (*Dianthus*)

Jacob's ladders (*Polemonium*)

Lady's mantle (*Alchemilla mollis*)

Lupines (*Lupinus*)

Meadowsweet (*Filipendula ulmaria*)

Perennial salvias (*Salvia*)

Siberian iris (*Iris sibirica*)

Yellow meadow rue (*Thalictrum flavum* subsp. *glaucum*)

such as woodland gardens. For high-visibility sites, you may prefer to buy or start new plants each summer and transplant them in fall, placing them where you want them to bloom the following year. Then pull them out after they flower and fill in with spiky-flowered summer annuals, such as angelonias (*Angelonia*) or a white or pink Texas sage (*Salvia coccinea*).

Echinacea
colorful and versatile

Echinacea purpurea 'Magnus' with *Calamagrostis × acutiflora* 'Karl Foerster', *Agastache* 'Blue Blazes', and *Sedum* 'Matrona'

Echinacea 'Evan Saul' (Sundown) and *Agastache* 'Salmon and Pink'

A Perfect Match

Ordinary purple coneflowers thrive in my Pennsylvania garden, but I've had a hard time with many of the showier hybrids. One that *has* done well for me is Sundown ('Evan Saul'). The rich orange color of its newly opened blooms is eye-catching, but I like it even better a day or two later, when it softens to peachy pink. At either stage, it shows off beautifully against a taller, dark-leaved companion, such as Summer Wine ninebark (*Physocarpus opulifolius* 'Seward').

Echinaceas (*Echinacea*), often known as purple coneflowers, are equally at home in elegant borders and casual country gardens. They grow in such a wide variety of conditions, in such a range of sizes and colors, and flower for such a long time that they offer endless possibilities for subtle to stunning combinations.

The most common purple coneflower (*E. purpurea*) can range in height from about 18 inches to 4 feet or more, depending on the cultivar, with relatively broad, rough leaves and large, daisy-form flowers that have prominent, conical centers and outward-facing or somewhat drooping ray florets (the technical name for what we gardeners call "petals"). Narrowleaf purple coneflower (*E. angustifolia*) is similar but is usually just around 2 feet tall, while 2- to 4-foot-tall pale purple coneflower (*E. pallida*) has very thin, downward-pointing petals; both species have slender leaves. These purple coneflowers are generally hardy in Zones 3 to 9.

There are also many hybrids of these and other echinacea species, expanding the color range from pinks and whites to include shades of red, orange, and yellow. These hybrid echinaceas are stunning once they get established, but it can be difficult to get the vigor and dependability from them that you can usually expect from the time-tested favorites. The usual advice with these is to keep the flowering stems cut off the first year so the plants put their energy into making roots instead of blooms: a good approach if you can make yourself remove the flowers, but frustrating if you want to make combinations with them right away. If there are unusual colors and/or flower forms that you simply can't resist, consider planting them in a holding bed for their first year, then moving them to your garden the next year for making matches.

Color Considerations

Whatever your color preferences, you can probably find an echinacea in your favorite hues, except for true purples and blues. Keep in mind that photographs of the flowers may not represent their colors accurately—particularly those of the brighter hybrids—and that petal colors often soften as the flowers age, so it's a good idea to see the blooms in person before you finalize your combination if you're trying to make careful color matches.

Think pinks. It's a shame that these plants aren't known as "pink coneflowers," since that's the most common color range: from pale pink selections like 'Hope' to rosy pink ' Prairie Splendor' to vibrant magenta pink 'PowWow Wild Berry'. There are loads of other

Bloom Buddies
Marvelous Matches for flowering Combos

Echinaceas (*Echinacea*) typically thrive in full sun and average to moist but well-drained soil, but they can adapt to partial shade and drier soil. Many terrific perennial partners, such as those mentioned below, overlap or coincide with their long bloom period.

Agastaches
 (*Agastache*)

Bee balms (*Monarda*)

Blazing stars (*Liatris*)

Bowman's roots
 (*Gillenia*)

Culver's roots
 (*Veronicastrum*)

Daylilies
 (*Hemerocallis*)

Filipendulas
 (*Filipendula*)

Fleeceflowers
 (*Persicaria*)

Globe thistles
 (*Echinops*)

Hollyhocks (*Alcea*)

Jerusalem sages
 (*Phlomis*)

Joe-Pye weeds
 (*Eupatorium*)

Knautias (*Knautia*)

Milkweeds (*Asclepias*)

Obedient plant
 (*Physostegia
 virginiana*)

Ornamental oreganos
 (*Origanum*)

Penstemons
 (*Penstemon*)

Perennial salvias
 (*Salvia*)

Pincushion flowers
 (*Scabiosa*)

Purple prairie clover
 (*Dalea purpurea*)

Rudbeckias
 (*Rudbeckia*)

Russian sages
 (*Perovskia*)

Sea hollies (*Eryngium*)

Shasta daisy
 (*Leucanthemum ×
 superbum*)

Stoke's aster
 (*Stokesia laevis*)

Summer phlox
 (*Phlox paniculata*)

Torch lilies
 (*Kniphofia*)

Turtleheads (*Chelone*)

Yarrows (*Achillea*)

Echinacea purpurea 'Virgin' and *Sedum telephium* 'Sunkissed'

summer-flowering perennials in the same color range—Joe-Pye weeds (*Eupatorium*), ornamental oreganos (*Origanum*), pink and rose turtleheads (*Chelone lyonii* and *C. obliqua*), queen-of-the-prairie (*Filipendula rubra*), summer phlox (*Phlox paniculata*), and tuberous-rooted Jerusalem sage (*Phlomis tuberosa*), to name a few—so it would be easy to build a whole border around pink flowers. Magenta to reddish pinks may not look good right next to soft pinks or lavender pinks, though, so consider using some green, gray, or silver foliage between them.

Pink-petaled echinaceas look terrific with white flowers and white-variegated foliage, as well as with yellows, blues, and purples, especially if you match the intensity of the hues. With vivid 'Burgundy Fireworks', for instance, consider a strong yellow, like that of 'Lemon Popsicle' torch lily (*Kniphofia*), or a rich purple-blue, such as 'Caradonna' perennial salvia (*Salvia nemorosa*). Rosy pink–purple coneflowers can also work surprisingly well with oranges that have some pink in them, such as 'Orange Perfection' summer phlox (*P. paniculata*) or sunset hyssop (*Agastache rupestris*).

Wonderful whites. White cultivars of purple coneflower, such as 'Jade', 'Milkshake', 'Pow-Wow White', and 'White Swan', match well with a wide range of other white-flowered perennials: Think of 'David' summer phlox, 'Floristan White' dense blazing star (*Liatris spicata*), and wild quinine (*Parthenium integrifolium*), among others. To complete the theme for a marvelous moon garden or a bridal-white border for a summer wedding, include white-striped foliage, like that of variegated Japanese iris (*Iris ensata* 'Variegata') and variegated obedient plant (*Physostegia virginiana* 'Variegata'), and silver-leaved perennials, such as artemisias (*Artemisia*).

Blue with white is an elegant color theme for a bed or border, and it's easy to accomplish: Simply expand the previous ideas for white echinacea combinations to include blue and purple-blue perennials, such as anise hyssops (*Agastache*), catmints (*Nepeta*), lavenders (*Lavandula*), and Russian sages (*Perovskia*), along with silvery blue to blue-gray foliage, like that of 'Dallas Blues' switch grass (*Panicum virgatum*) or 'Sapphire Skies' beaked yucca (*Yucca rostrata*).

Delicate pastels. Besides the pastel pinks of the purple coneflowers, echinacea hybrids expand the range of soft colors to include peachy orange, as on Summer Sky ('Katie Saul') and 'Supreme Cantaloupe', and buttery yellow, as on 'Sunrise'. Combine any of them with other summer perennials in sorbet colors— Anthea ('Anblo') or 'Apricot Delight' yarrow (*Achillea*), for instance, or 'Apricot Sunrise' or

'Summer Glow' hummingbird mints (*Agastache*)—and with soft blues and lavender purples. They also combine beautifully with foliage that's striped with creamy yellow, like that of 'Color Guard' or 'Golden Sword' Adam's needle (*Yucca filamentosa*) or variegated sweet iris (*Iris pallida* 'Variegata'), and with the tan to golden brown seed heads of feather reed grasses (*Calamagrostis*), Mexican feather grass (*Stipa tenuissima*), and other ornamental grasses.

Echinacea 'Firebird' and *Asclepias tuberosa*

Bright and bold. New echinacea cultivars in particularly bright reds, corals, oranges, and yellows are appearing every year, with breeders attempting to produce selections that hold on to their rich petal colors longer. Many of these colors are already available among the rudbeckias (*Rudbeckia*) on less expensive and more vigorous plants, but the echinacea hybrids do provide some other heights and flower forms. Any of the hybrids can be vibrant additions to summer borders with other bold bloomers, such as Asiatic lilies (*Lilium* Asiatic Hybrids), bee balms (*Monarda*), daylilies (*Hemerocallis*), and heleniums (*Helenium*), perhaps with 'Powis Castle' artemisia (*Artemisia*) and other silver leaves for extra sparkle or 'Black Truffle' cardinal flower (*Lobelia cardinalis*), 'Obsidian' heuchera (*Heuchera*), and other dark foliage for depth.

Consider the Cones

As the tiny, tightly packed "disc florets" in the center of echinacea (*Echinacea*) flowers open, they typically have a reddish orange to golden orange cast against a deep green to dark brown base. Instead of going for the obvious petal color when choosing a companion for echinaceas, consider those secondary colors instead to create more subtle echoes. Form harmonies with flowering and foliage partners in similar colors, such as butterfly weed (*Asclepias tuberosa*) or 'Mango Popsicle' torch lily (*Kniphofia*), for instance. Or create contrast by setting them against a partner with very dark or bright foliage, such as deep purple 'Royal Purple' smokebush (*Cotinus coggygria*) or vivid yellow Mellow Yellow spirea (*Spiraea thunbergii* 'Ogon').

You can match other foliage colors with the bright echinaceas for intriguing combinations: orangey 'Southern Comfort' heuchera with 'Flame Thrower' or 'Marmalade' echinaceas, for instance, or red-tipped Japanese blood grass (*Imperata cylindrica* 'Rubra') or 'Shenandoah' switch grass (*P. virgatum*) with 'Firebird' or Sombrero Salsa Red ('Balsomsed') echinacea.

Shapes and Textures

With echinaceas, it's all about the flowers, even from a form and texture perspective. Because the flowers are large and close together, established clumps tend to have a broad, horizontal appearance in bloom, and that's emphasized on cultivars that have outward-facing petals. They benefit from having mounded companions, such as catmints or hardy geraniums (*Geranium*) in front of them, for lower color, and more narrowly upright companions, such as Culver's root (*Veronicastrum virginicum*) and 'Heavy Metal' switch grass (*Panicum virgatum*), behind them for contrast.

The horizontal bloom form of many echinaceas pairs well with shorter or taller partners that have blooms packed into broad clusters, such as showy sedum (*Sedum spectabile*) or yarrows (*Achillea*). Ball-shaped blooms, like those of drumstick allium (*Allium sphaerocephalon*), rattlesnake master (*Eryngium yuccifolium*), or globe thistles (*Echinops*), do a great job repeating the prominent center cones of echinaceas.

The big, bold blooms of single-flowered echinaceas also lend themselves well to dramatic shape contrasts. Pair them with spiky-flowered companions, such as blazing stars (*Liatris*) and obedient plant (*Physostegia virginiana*), or with plumy blooms, like those of giant fleeceflower (*Persicaria polymorpha*), Korean feather reed grass (*Calamagrostis brachytricha*), Russian sages, or white mugwort (*Artemisia lactiflora*).

Echinacea purpurea 'White Swan' and *Kniphofia (above);*
Echinacea purpurea and *Veronicastrum virginicum (right)*

Some echinaceas have such eye-catching flower forms that they deserve to be the star of a combination. The slender, drooping petals of pale purple coneflower, for instance, have a very dainty, delicate look, while many hybrids and selections are distinctive for their quilled petals, frilly centers, or other unusual features. Instead of drawing attention away from them with a strongly contrasting flower shape, focus mostly on foliage companions, or consider combining them with much smaller daisy-form blossoms, like those of asters, coreopsis (*Coreopsis*), feverfew (*Tanacetum parthenium*), and pincushion flowers (*Scabiosa*). Or let them mingle with tiny blossoms, like those of catmints, Bowman's roots (*Gillenia*), flowering spurge (*Euphorbia corollata*), or lesser calamint (*Calamintha nepetoides*).

Echinacea purpurea with *Molinia caerulea* subsp. *arundinacea* 'Skyracer' and *Solidago rugosa* 'Fireworks'

Seasonal Features

In southern gardens, echinaceas are typically in bloom by mid- to late spring; in cooler areas, early to midsummer is the usual beginning of their flowering season. The plants may take a break during the worst heat of southern summers, but mostly they continue flowering through the summer months, especially if you clip off the old flowers as they finish. Their long bloom period gives you a wide range of flowering partners to choose from: daylilies (*Hemerocallis*), summer phlox, and many more. (See "Bloom Buddies" on page 99 for other suggestions.)

Keeping up with regular deadheading through summer may prolong the flowering season into fall, when your echinaceas can mingle with asters, chrysanthemums, and other late bloomers, as well as with fall-colored foliage. Or stop deadheading after midsummer and leave the finished flowers in place to dry into interesting seed heads for fall and winter. Besides providing welcome food for winter birds, they also look great with the seed heads of blazing stars (*Liatris*), Culver's roots (*Veronicastrum*), and goldenrods (*Solidago*), and with the dried remains of ornamental grasses.

Special Effects

Purple coneflower species, such as *E. angustifolia*, *E. pallida*, and *E. purpurea*—and the older, single-flowered cultivars, too, such as 'Magnus' and 'White Swan'—look perfectly at home in naturalistic plantings with other native perennials and grasses, such as little bluestem (*Schizachyrium scoparium*), milkweeds (*Asclepias*), prairie dropseed (*Sporobolus heterolepis*), wild bergamot (*Monarda fistulosa*), and wild quinine (*Parthenium integrifolium*).

Eryngium
fascinating flower heads

Eryngium × zabelii 'Big Blue' and *Lychnis coronaria*

Eryngium yuccifolium with *Panicum virgatum* 'Dallas Blues' and *Rudbeckia fulgida*

A Perfect Match

A combo I've seen in photos and want to try for myself is a blue sea holly with drumstick allium (*Allium sphaerocephalon*). The shape of the allium is almost a perfect match for the center cone of the sea holly, but with a terrific contrast between the silvery blue of the sea holly and the rich reddish purple of the allium. Kudos to the gardeners who came up with that one!

Eryngiums (*Eryngium*), also known as eryngos, produce fascinating flower heads that can make striking combinations. The flowers themselves are tiny, but they're tightly packed into dense clusters.

On the kinds known as sea hollies, the rounded to conical clusters are surrounded by a ruff of spiky, petal-like bracts. Complementing their interesting form is their unique color: a silvery to intense blue that usually extends down into the upper parts of the stems. The common perennial species, such as amethyst sea holly (*E. amethystinum*) and flat sea holly (*E. planum*), and hybrids, such as *E. × zabelii* 'Big Blue' and 'Sapphire Blue' (also sold as 'Jos Eijking'), are typically in the 2- to 3-foot-tall range and best adapted to Zones 4 to 9.

Rattlesnake master (*E. yuccifolium*), also known as button eryngo, is different in form and color but equally striking, with spiky foliage and greenish white, globe-shaped flower heads in branching clusters atop 3- to 5-foot-tall stems. Unlike its blue cousins, which need excellent drainage to thrive and do best in not-very-fertile soil, rattlesnake master is much more adaptable to typical border conditions ranging from moist to dry. It's hardy in Zones 3 to 9.

Color Considerations

Sea hollies blend beautifully with other silvery blues and purple-blues, like those of globe thistles (*Echinops*), lavenders (*Lavandula*), and Russian sages (*Perovskia*), and with silver, gray, and blue foliage, like that of artemisias (*Artemisia*), 'Berggarten' common sage (*Salvia officinalis*), and blue oat grass (*Helictotrichon sempervirens*). To expand that color range, consider rosy pinks to pinkish purples, like those of drumstick allium (*Allium sphaerocephalon*), ornamental oreganos (*Origanum*), purple coneflower (*Echinacea purpurea*), and red valerian (*Centranthus ruber*), or try buttery yellows and peachy oranges, like those of many daylilies (*Hemerocallis*) and hummingbird mints (*Agastaches*).

Whites also work well with the blues of sea hollies: Consider 'David' summer phlox (*Phlox paniculata*), for instance, or white rose campion (*Lychnis coronaria* 'Alba'). Bright yellow foliage, like that of Sunshine Blue blue mist shrub (*Caryopteris incana* 'Jason'), makes a dramatic backdrop for 'Big Blue' and other intensely blue sea hollies.

With its grayish foliage and greenish white flower heads, rattlesnake master is an excellent choice for moon gardens and white borders with companions such as 'Floristan White' dense blazing star (*Liatris spicata*), 'White Swan' purple coneflower, and wild quinine (*Parthenium integrifolium*). It looks lovely with pastel cultivars

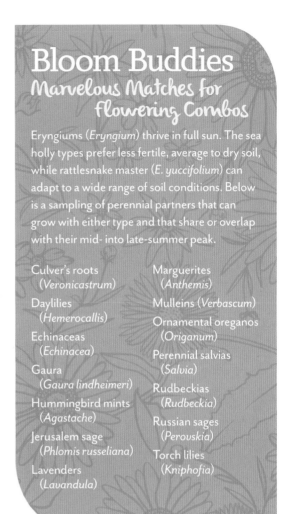

Bloom Buddies
Marvelous Matches for Flowering Combos

Eryngiums (*Eryngium*) thrive in full sun. The sea holly types prefer less fertile, average to dry soil, while rattlesnake master (*E. yuccifolium*) can adapt to a wide range of soil conditions. Below is a sampling of perennial partners that can grow with either type and that share or overlap with their mid- into late-summer peak.

Culver's roots (*Veronicastrum*)

Daylilies (*Hemerocallis*)

Echinaceas (*Echinacea*)

Gaura (*Gaura lindheimeri*)

Hummingbird mints (*Agastache*)

Jerusalem sage (*Phlomis russeliana*)

Lavenders (*Lavandula*)

Marguerites (*Anthemis*)

Mulleins (*Verbascum*)

Ornamental oreganos (*Origanum*)

Perennial salvias (*Salvia*)

Rudbeckias (*Rudbeckia*)

Russian sages (*Perovskia*)

Torch lilies (*Kniphofia*)

of daylilies and summer phlox, and with purple-blues to powder blues in flowers and foliage, like those of balloon flower (*Platycodon grandiflorus*) and 'Dallas Blues' switch grass (*Panicum virgatum*).

Shapes and Textures

Sea hollies start as low mounds of leathery, lobed leaves, then send up branching flowering

Eryngium planum 'Jade Frost' with *Perovskia* 'Longin' and *Leucanthemum* × *superbum* 'Becky'

companions, such as gaura (*Gaura lindheimeri*), and with soft- or wispy-looking partners, such as 'Karley Rose' Oriental fountain grass (*Pennisetum orientale*), Mexican feather grass (*Stipa tenuissima*), or Russian sages.

Rattlesnake master, with its long, spiky leaves, makes an excellent midborder contrast for mounded companions or a superb echo for similar-looking agaves (*Agave*) and yuccas (*Yucca*), as well as upright ornamental grasses, such as 'Heavy Metal' switch grass (*Panicum virgatum*) or 'Prairie Blues' little bluestem (*Schizachyrium scoparium*). Repeat the rounded forms of its blooms with globe thistles or the cone-centered flowers of echinaceas (*Echinacea*) or rudbeckias (*Rudbeckia*), or contrast them with Culver's root (*Veronicastrum virginicum*) or other spikes.

Seasonal Features

The foliage provides some interest in spring, particularly on rattlesnake master. Sea holly flowers typically form in early summer, developing their best color by midsummer and continuing into late summer. Rattlesnake master begins blooming in early summer in southern gardens and midsummer in the northern half of the country, and it, too, continues through summer.

The long-lasting seed heads dry in place and can hold their form for months. That makes them excellent for winter interest, though some, such as flat sea holly, may self-sow freely. If that worries you, cut off the flowering stems once the blooms are finished, or grow a sterile cultivar of sea holly, such as 'Sapphire Blue', instead.

stems. They look great rising behind lower mounded companions; just keep in mind that they don't like to be crowded to the point that their leaves are shaded. If the plants do sprawl—as some of the taller ones are prone to do, especially in good soil—their spiny blooms can be very unpleasant to touch or brush against, so you may not want to use them close to a path unless you plant them behind a sturdy, bushy companion that can prop them up, such as a clump of common sage or a lavender.

In bloom, sea hollies make striking contrasts with spiky-flowered sun lovers, such as dense blazing star (*Liatris spicata*), mulleins (*Verbascum*), and perennial salvias (*Salvia*), and with the flat to slightly domed heads of upright sedums (*Sedum*) and yarrows (*Achillea*). Sea hollies with large flower heads, such as 'Sapphire Blue', pair particularly well with small-flowered

Eupatorium
easy to grow and easy to use

Eupatorium dubium 'Little Joe' with
Pennisetum alopecuroides Cassian and
Miscanthus sinensis 'Morning Light'

Eupatorium coelestinum and *Amsonia
hubrichtii* in fall color

A Perfect Match

Joe-Pye weeds grow wild in my meadow, where they're right at home with native grasses such as Indian grass (*Sorghastrum nutans*) and big bluestem (*Andropogon gerardii*). I like to copy those pairings in my perennial borders but often substitute selections of ornamental grasses, such as 'Morning Light' miscanthus (*Miscanthus sinensis*) or 'Karl Foerster' feather reed grass (*Calamagrostis × acutiflora*). The combinations still have a natural look, but with a touch of refinement, too.

Though they vary in height and color, eupatoriums (*Eupatorium*) share a similar form in bloom, with many tiny blossoms grouped into dense but fluffy-looking flower heads. Their common and botanical names are somewhat difficult to keep straight, but the plants themselves are easy to grow and easy to use in later-season combinations. Many are native to North America; below are just some of the most widely grown kinds.

The common name Joe-Pye weed applies to several eupatorium species—among them, *E. dubium*, *E. fistulosum*, *E. maculatum*, and *E. purpureum*. (You'll also see these plants sold under the genus name *Eutrochium*.) These butterfly magnets produce domed heads of pink or white flowers atop stems that can reach 8 feet tall (even higher in rich, moist soil). That's too large for most borders, but fortunately, there are some more-compact cultivars, such as 'Gateway' (to about 6 feet), 'Little Joe' (4 to 5 feet tall), and

Bloom Buddies
Marvelous Matches for Flowering Combos

Eupatoriums (*Eupatorium*) are diverse in appearance but fairly similar in their growth preferences: full sun to light shade and average to moist but well-drained soil. (White snakeroot [*E. rugosum*] may do better in partial shade if your soil is not consistently moist.) Below are some compatible flowering partners for a great show during their late-summer into fall peak.

Asters (*Aster*)

Caryopteris (*Caryopteris*)

Culver's roots (*Veronicastrum*)

Echinaceas (*Echinacea*)

False aster (*Boltonia asteroides*)

Goldenrods (*Solidago*)

Heleniums (*Helenium*)

Japanese anemones (*Anemone*)

Obedient plant (*Physostegia virginiana*)

Rose mallow (*Hibiscus moscheutos*)

Rudbeckias (*Rudbeckia*)

Sedums (*Sedum*, upright species)

Summer phlox (*Phlox paniculata*)

Swamp milkweed (*Asclepias incarnata*)

Turtleheads (*Chelone*)

White mugwort (*Artemisia lactiflora*)

flowers, can reach 6 feet tall but is usually more like 3 to 4 feet. It's lovely for white flowers in late summer and fall, but be warned: It can spread by creeping roots and may self-sow freely if you don't cut off the blooms before they set seed. You're most likely to find it for sale as 'Chocolate', a form that emerges with dark purple-brown leaves. White snakeroot performs best in Zones 3 to 8.

Blue mistflower or hardy ageratum (*E. coelestinum*, also known as *Conoclinium coelestinum*), with light bluish purple flowers on 2- to 3-foot-tall stems, is another one to enjoy with caution, because of its creeping roots. Instead of letting it loose in a front-yard bed or border, where it may crowd out less vigorous companions, consider enjoying it in a less visible "wild garden" area with other spreaders, such as bee balms (*Monarda*) and obedient plant (*Physostegia virginiana*), to provide welcome food for bees and butterflies and an ample supply of flowers for cutting, too.

Color Considerations

Joe-Pye weeds primarily come in rosy to slightly purplish pinks: the same color range as many other later-summer perennials, including pink and rose turtleheads (*Chelone lyonii* and *C. obliqua*), purple coneflower (*Echinacea purpurea*), summer phlox (*Phlox paniculata*), and showy sedum (*Sedum spectabile*). You can echo their bloom color with grasses that include a bit of pink, as in the flower heads of 'Dallas Blues' switch grass (*Panicum virgatum*) or 'Karley Rose' Oriental fountain grass (*Pennisetum orientale*), or in the stems of 'The Blues' little bluestem (*Schizachyrium scoparium*).

'Baby Joe' (3 to 4 feet tall), which are much easier to fit into a home-garden setting. Joe-Pye weeds are usually suited to Zones 3 or 4 to 9.

White snakeroot (*E. rugosum*, also known as *Ageratina altissima*), with loose heads of white

To pep up the pinks, include some whites, like those of Culver's root (*Veronicastrum virginicum*), 'Ice Ballet' swamp milkweed (*Asclepias incarnata*), and white mugwort (*Artemisia lactiflora*). Or go for a warmer color theme all around: Joe-Pye weeds look wonderful with rich purples and purple-blues, like those of ironweeds (*Vernonia*) and many asters, and with rich yellows, like those of goldenrods (*Solidago*), perennial sunflowers (*Helianthus*), and rudbeckias (*Rudbeckia*).

Like Joe-Pye weeds, white snakeroot and blue mistflower complement many pastel-flowered perennials, including pink or blue asters or pink Japanese anemones (*Anemone*). They're lovely with richer purple-blues, too, like those of balloon flower (*Platycodon grandiflorus*) or 'Blue Paradise' summer phlox, and with white-flowered partners, such as false aster (*Boltonia asteroides*), 'Miss Manners' obedient plant (*Physostegia virginiana*), or white turtlehead (*C. glabra*).

The stems of Joe-Pye weeds often have dark spotting or are a solid deep reddish purple color, as on 'Baby Joe' or 'Gateway'. If you'd like to emphasize these features, try matching them with dark-leaved perennial or shrub partners, such as 'Chocolate' white snakeroot or 'Royal Purple' smokebush (*Cotinus coggygria*).

Eupatorium maculatum 'Gateway' with *Lobelia* 'Ruby Slippers' and *Iris ensata* 'Variegata'

'Chocolate' white snakeroot is also useful for echoing flowering partners with dark centers or markings, such as 'Lionheart' Asiatic lily (*Lilium*) or rudbeckias, or dark flowers, like those of 'Jungle Beauty' or 'Midnight Oil' daylilies (*Hemerocallis*). This sort of echoing works best in early to mid- or late summer, when the leaves of 'Chocolate' have their richest color—by the time 'Chocolate' blooms, its leaves are often more on the purplish green to deep green side.

A Timely Trim

Taller Joe-Pye weeds (*Eupatorium*), such as 'Gateway', and white snakeroot (*E. rugosum*), too, can get a bit too tall or sprawling in rich, moist soil. If you want to keep them shorter, cut the stems back by about half in early summer to get bushier growth. Giving Joe-Pye weeds another trim (by about one-third) a few weeks later can delay the start of their bloom period into late summer: a plus if you'd like to have them around for fall combinations.

Shapes and Textures

Eupatoriums generally grow in broad clumps of upright stems. Joe-Pye weeds, with their height and stout stems, have a particularly vertical effect, pairing well with densely to loosely mounded companions, such as 'Fireworks' rough goldenrod (*Solidago rugosa*) and rudbeckias. They also make great partners for other tall, late-summer into fall bloomers, such as 'Henry Eilers' sweet coneflower (*R. subtomentosa*), 'Lemon Queen' perennial sunflower (*Helianthus*), and New York ironweed (*Vernonia noveboracensis*). White snakeroot and blue mistflower are more mounded and benefit from some contrast with vertical companions, such as 'Karl Foerster' feather reed grass (*Calamagrostis* × *acutiflora*) or white mugwort.

The fluffy-looking flowers of eupatoriums complement other soft-looking flowers, like those of false aster (*Boltonia asteroides*), Korean feather reed grass (*Calamagrostis brachytricha*), or fountain grasses (*Pennisetum*). Too much fluffiness can all blend together, though, so think about including some large, bold blooms, like those of daylilies (*Hemerocallis*), purple coneflower (*Echinacea purpurea*), or hardy hibiscus (*Hibiscus*), for contrast.

Seasonal Features

Other than 'Chocolate' white snakeroot, which offers showy foliage as soon as it sprouts, eupatoriums are best for later-season combinations. Joe-Pye weeds begin flowering in midsummer, while white snakeroot and blue mistflower typically start in late summer. Once they begin blooming, the flowers are colorful for about 6 weeks. As white snakeroot and blue mistflower finish, shear off the flower heads to prevent self-sowing. Joe-Pye weeds can self-sow, too, but usually not to the point of being problematic, so consider leaving their seed heads to dry in place for winter interest.

Eupatorium rugosum 'Chocolate' and *Aster novae-angliae*

Euphorbia
multiseason interest

Euphorbia polychroma and *Ajuga reptans* 'Valfredda' (Chocolate Chip)

Euphorbia griffithii 'Fireglow' and *Cotinus coggygria* 'Royal Purple'

A Perfect Match

When cushion spurge is in flower, you can't miss those brilliant yellow bracts. 'Bonfire' takes it up another notch, with purple-red foliage: a light-and-dark combo that I can't resist. One of my favorite partners for it is a yellow-leaved spirea (*Spiraea × bumalda* 'Monhub'), such as 'Limemound'. The plant forms are very similar, and the spurge bracts and spirea leaves are the same color, but the dark spurge leaves make for an eye-catching contrast well into summer.

Euphorbias (*Euphorbia*), also known as spurges, are an intriguingly diverse group of plants, including annuals, hardy perennials, and tender species with succulent or woody stems. They grow in a range of colors and are adapted to a variety of growing conditions. One thing they do share is a sticky, milky sap; another is their interesting floral structure, with tiny true blooms clustered with showier, petal-like bracts to create what we gardeners refer to as the flowers. What follows is just a handful of the most common euphorbias that make excellent additions to perennial gardens.

Hardy herbaceous euphorbias. Some hardy species grow from the ground each spring and flower on those new stems. Of these herbaceous species, cushion spurge (*E. polychroma*, also known as *E. epithymoides*) is a classic for spring color, with yellow flowers atop 12- to 18-inch-tall, dense mounds of light green leaves, for Zones 3 to 8. Griffith's spurge (*E. griffithii*), best

Bloom Buddies
Marvelous Matches for Flowering Combos

Euphorbias (*Euphorbia*) vary in their growth needs, so keep that in mind when choosing companions. Below is a sampling of flowering partners to consider for beautiful bloom combinations.

Companions for cushion spurge (*E. polychroma*) or Martin's spurge (*E. × martinii*) in full sun to light shade and average, well-drained soil:

Baptisias (*Baptisia*)

Bearded irises (*Iris* Bearded Hybrids)

Columbines (*Aquilegia*)

Dianthus (*Dianthus*)

Forget-me-nots (*Myosotis*)

Moss phlox (*Phlox subulata*)

Peonies (*Paeonia*)

Perennial candytuft (*Iberis sempervirens*)

Purple rock cresses (*Aubrieta*)

Sweet iris (*Iris pallida*)

White rock cresses (*Arabis*)

Companions for Griffith's spurge (*E. griffithii*) in full sun to light shade and average to moist but well-drained soil:

Alliums (*Allium*)

Asiatic lilies (*Lilium* Asiatic Hybrids)

Bellflowers (*Campanula*)

Carolina lupine (*Thermopsis villosa*)

Coreopsis (*Coreopsis*)

Delphiniums (*Delphinium*)

Geums (*Geum*)

Hardy geraniums (*Geranium*)

Lady's mantle (*Alchemilla mollis*)

Perennial salvias (*Salvia*)

Siberian iris (*Iris sibirica*)

Speedwells (*Veronica*)

Spiderworts (*Tradescantia*)

Sundrops (*Oenothera fruticosa*)

Companions for wood spurge (*E. amygdaloides*) and Robb's spurge (*E. amygdaloides* var. *robbiae*) in partial shade and average, well-drained soil:

Ajugas (*Ajuga*)

Bleeding hearts (*Dicentra*)

Creeping phlox (*Phlox stolonifera*)

Epimediums (*Epimedium*)

Foamflowers (*Tiarella*)

Foamy bells (× *Heucherella*)

Mourning widow (*Geranium phaeum*)

Siberian bugloss (*Brunnera macrophylla*)

Snowdrop anemone (*Anemone sylvestris*)

Virginia bluebell (*Mertensia virginica*)

Wild columbine (*Aquilegia canadensis*)

Wild geranium (*Geranium maculatum*)

Woodland phlox (*Phlox divaricata*)

known as the cultivars 'Dixter' and 'Fireglow', spreads by creeping roots to form 2- to 3-foot-tall patches of reddish stems clad in deep green leaves and topped with orange to red flowers. It's usually best in Zones 4 to 8.

Elegant evergreens. Martin's spurge (*E.* × *martinii*) is an evergreen euphorbia that forms shrubby, 2- to 3-foot-tall mounds, for Zones 6 or 7 to 9. Wood spurge (*E. amygdaloides*), too, has upright stems, usually reaching 18 to 24 inches when in flower. Robb's spurge (*E. amygdaloides* var. *robbiae*, also sold as *E. robbiae*) is a creeping variety of wood spurge with particularly dense, deep green leaves. Wood spurges are best suited to Zones 5 or 6 to 8.

Color Considerations

Some euphorbias are most interesting in bloom, while others are fantastic foliage accents.

Colorful flower combos. The spring blooms of cushion spurge, Martin's spurge, wood spurge, and Robb's spurge are greenish yellow to bright yellow: ideal for echoing the bright yellow spring foliage of perennial and shrubby companions, such as 'Golden Jubilee' anise hyssop (*Agastache foeniculum*), 'Gold Heart' bleeding heart (*Dicentra spectabilis*), 'Lime Marmalade' heuchera (*Heuchera*), and Mellow Yellow spirea (*Spiraea thunbergii* 'Ogon'). Or use these euphorbia blooms to echo partners that have yellow centers or markings in their flowers, such as wild columbine (*Aquilegia canadensis*) or 'White Swirl' Siberian iris (*Iris sibirica*).

Yellow-flowered euphorbias work with many other hues, as well. They are exceptionally pretty paired with blues and purples, like those of ajugas (*Ajuga*), Virginia bluebell (*Mertensia virginica*), or woodland phlox (*Phlox divaricata*), and with purplish to rosy pinks, like those of many alliums (*Allium*) and dianthus (*Dianthus*). Yellow euphorbias create elegant combinations with bright white partners, such as perennial candytuft (*Iberis sempervirens*) and snow-in-summer (*Cerastium tomentosum*). Or go bold by partnering them with bright reds and oranges, like those of 'Fire Alarm' heuchera or 'Orange Emperor' tulip.

Griffith's spurge starts blooming slightly later, with orangey red flowers. Like the other euphorbias, they're fantastic with bright yellow foliage partners and with rich purples and blues, like those of 'Caesar's Brother' Siberian iris (*I. sibirica*) or Italian alkanet (*Anchusa azurea*).

Euphorbia amygdaloides var. *robbiae* and *Heuchera* **'Key Lime Pie'**

They also look great with deep red to dark purple foliage companions, such as 'Red Dragon' fleeceflower (*Persicaria microcephala*).

Euphorbias for foliage. Selections with showy leaves greatly extend the season for striking color combinations. Several euphorbia cultivars, such as hybrid Blackbird ('Nothowlee') and Ruby Glow ('Waleuphglo') wood spurge, have deep reddish purple to dark purple leaves. Use them to repeat the color of dark-flowered partners, such as 'Samobor' mourning widow geranium (*Geranium phaeum*) or 'Queen of Night' tulip, or to echo purple markings in the leaves of other perennials, such as Japanese painted fern (*Athyrium niponicum* var. *pictum*) or 'Marvelous Marble' alumroot (*Heuchera americana*). If you prefer some contrast, try them with artemisias (*Artemisia*), lamb's ears (*Stachys byzantina*), or other silvery leaves. All of these partners also work well with Excalibur ('Froeup'), a selection that has gray-green leaves with a silvery midrib.

Robb's spurge has green foliage so dark that it makes a handsome contrast with lighter-colored leaves. Try blue or silver foliage—blue hostas, such as 'Prairie Sky', for instance, or silvery pulmonarias (*Pulmonaria*), such as 'Samurai' or 'Silver Bouquet'—or bright yellow leaves, like those of Bowles' golden grass (*Milium effusum* 'Aureum') or golden Hakone grass (*Hakonechloa macra* 'Aureola'). White-variegated shade lovers, such as 'Snow Cap' broadleaf sedge (*Carex siderosticha*) and variegated Solomon's seal (*Polygonatum odoratum* 'Variegatum'), look crisp and clean against the extra-dark greens of Robb's spurge.

Shapes and Textures

Cushion spurge, Martin's spurge, and some kinds of wood spurge are densely mounded, echoing the form of many other border perennials and creating a strong contrast to upright or spiky companions, such as blue oat grass (*Helictotrichon sempervirens*), columbines (*Aquilegia*), and irises. Cushion spurge is particularly good for covering the bare lower stems of alliums and lilies (*Lilium*).

Griffith's spurge is more upright but spreads to form broad clumps. Use it behind lower mounding or trailing plants, such as coreopsis (*Coreopsis*), hardy geraniums (*Geranium*), and mountain bluet (*Centaurea montana*), then consider adding some contrast with spiky, vertical partners,

Euphorbia 'Nothowlee' (Blackbird) and *Imperata cylindrica* 'Rubra'

such as anise hyssops (*Agastache*), crocosmias (*Crocosmia*), Culver's root (*Veronicastrum virginicum*), or 'Karl Foerster' feather reed grass (*Calamagrostis × acutiflora*).

Robb's spurge is also a spreader but it's lower growing, making a handsome ground-cover under shrubs. It can be a bit too aggressive to pair well with small, delicate companions but it looks wonderful as a filler around larger, more sturdy partners, such as bugbanes (*Cimicifuga*), goatsbeard (*Aruncus dioicus*), or medium-size to large ferns and hostas. It can hold its own with other spreaders, such as ajugas (*Ajuga*), 'Ice Dance' sedge (*Carex*), lily-of-the-valley (*Convallaria majalis*), and sweet woodruff (*Galium odoratum*).

Though euphorbia plants are relatively bold in form, their relatively small, narrow leaves tend to give the plants a fine texture, so they benefit from contrast with large, broad or strappy leaves, like those of daylilies (*Hemerocallis*) or yuccas (*Yucca*) in sun or hostas or Siberian bugloss (*Brunnera macrophylla*) in shade.

Seasonal Features

In mild climates, euphorbias may start flowering in late winter and continue through spring. In northern gardens, they begin blooming later: most in mid- to late spring, but in late spring or early summer for Griffith's spurge. Once they color up, most keep flowering for at least a month. The bloom times of the earlier ones match those of many spring bulbs, including grape hyacinths (*Muscari*), Dutch hyacinths (*Hyacinthus*), and tulips. Most euphorbias also coincide or overlap with bleeding hearts (*Dicentra*), irises, and many other late-spring to early-

Euphorbia 'Froeup' (Excalibur) and *Sedum* 'Purple Emperor'

summer perennials, providing lots of opportunities for colorful combinations.

After their peak flowering period, cut cushion spurge and Griffith's spurge back by about half their height if you'd like to get fresh, bushy regrowth (and to prevent self-sowing of the cushion spurge). The evergreen euphorbias flower on their second-year stems. Once they're done, those stems won't bloom again, so you can cut them off close to the base of the plant as long as there are other, leafy stems left. (If not, then only remove the upper part of the flowering stem by cutting just above the uppermost leaves.)

Through the rest of summer, enjoy your euphorbias as foliage accents. The leaves of herbaceous types often take on showy red to orange colors in cool fall conditions, making them pretty partners for asters, chrysanthemums, and other late bloomers. The evergreen euphorbias remain attractive through fall and winter, as well.

Gaillardia
big, bold, and abundant blooms

Gaillardia × grandiflora 'Oranges and Lemons' and *Perovskia*

Gaillardia × grandiflora 'Sun Devil' with *Echinacea* 'Tiki Torch' and *Agastache* 'Summer Glow'

A Perfect Match

I can see the appeal of the very compact blanket flower cultivars, but in my own garden, I prefer the looser look of the somewhat taller selections. My favorite is 'Oranges and Lemons', which reaches 18 to 24 inches tall. Its large, warm-hued blooms look fantastic against the feathery foliage of Mellow Yellow spirea (*Spiraea thunbergii* 'Ogon').

The big, bold, and abundant blooms of perennial blanket flowers (*Gaillardia aristata* and *G.* × *grandiflora*) are guaranteed to catch the eye in any combination. Their daisy-form flowers are composed of tightly packed "disc florets" in the domed center surrounded by the showy "ray florets," or petals. The plants commonly reach 2 to 3 feet tall, but there are also more-compact selections. Perennial blanket flowers are typically hardy in Zones 3 to 9.

Color Considerations

Classic blanket flowers have a distinctive color pattern in their blooms: red in the center and yellow at the petal tips, as on 'Arizona Sun' and 'Goblin' (also sold as 'Kobold'). They are bright enough to hold their own with brilliant oranges, reds, and yellows, like those of many coreopsis (*Coreopsis*) and daylilies

(*Hemerocallis*). Red-and-yellow blanket flowers also look terrific with blue- to purple-flowered partners, such as perennial salvias (*Salvia*) and sea hollies (*Eryngium*).

You can find blanket flowers in solid colors, as well, including bright yellow 'Mesa Yellow', rusty orange 'Tokajer', and deep red 'Arizona Red Shades', and they are orange-and-yellow selections, too, such as 'Oranges and Lemons'. These fit comfortably into hot-color borders, as well as with blues and purples. You can also make some outstanding partnerships by matching their blooms with colorful foliage partners, such as red or orangey heucheras (*Heuchera*).

Shapes and Textures

Blanket flower plants have a mounded form: somewhat open on the taller types but quite dense on the compact cultivars. Use lower mounded or trailing companions, such as hardy geraniums (*Geranium*), in front of the taller blanket flowers. The dwarf blanket flowers are well proportioned for the front of a border, around the bases of larger partners. Both types benefit from contrast with upright companions. They look particularly good with spiky-leaved co-stars, such as agaves (*Agave*) and yuccas (*Yucca*), and with ornamental grasses.

The daisy-form blooms of blanket flowers echo the shape of many other summer perennials, including echinaceas (*Echinacea*) and rudbeckias (*Rudbeckia*). For variety, consider partners with a plumy form, such as goldenrods (*Solidago*) or Russian sages (*Perovskia*), or spikes, like those of agastaches (*Agastache*) and lavenders (*Lavandula*).

Bloom Buddies
Marvelous Matches for Flowering Combos

Blanket flowers (*Gaillardia*) thrive in full sun and can tolerate poor, dry soil, though they adapt well to typical border conditions (with better soil and more moisture or regular watering) as long as they have good drainage. These compatible perennials also bloom during the blanket flowers' long season.

Agastaches (*Agastache*)

Balloon flower (*Platycodon grandiflorus*)

Catmints (*Nepeta*)

Coreopsis (*Coreopsis*)

Daylilies (*Hemerocallis*)

Echinaceas (*Echinacea*)

Globe thistles (*Echinops*)

Lavenders (*Lavandula*)

Perennial salvias (*Salvia*)

Rough blazing star (*Liatris aspera*)

Rudbeckias (*Rudbeckia*)

Russian sages (*Perovskia*)

Sea hollies (*Eryngium*)

Speedwells (*Veronica*)

Torch lilies (*Kniphofia*)

Verbenas (*Verbena*)

Yarrows (*Achillea*)

Seasonal Features

Blanket flowers typically begin blooming in late spring in southern gardens and early summer in cooler areas. Once they start, they keep sending up new flowers for months—well into fall in most areas, and even into winter in mild climates—especially if you frequently clip off the finished flower heads.

Gaura
a beauty for beds and borders

Gaura
Full sun to light shade; average, well-drained to dry soil

Gaura lindheimeri 'Walsnofou' (Snow Fountain) with *Rudbeckia hirta* 'Cherry Brandy', *Cuphea ignea* 'Starfire Pink', and *Rosa* 'Meipoque' (Pink Meidiland)

Gaura lindheimeri with *Pennisetum setaceum* 'Rubrum', *Miscanthus sinensis*, and *Pennisetum alopecuroides*

A Perfect Match

While gaura's dainty blossoms look marvelous mingling with larger, bolder blooms, the most breathtaking partnership I've seen to date is a bed of 'Siskiyou Pink' underplanted with equally wispy Mexican feather grass (*Stipa tenuissima*). This dreamy duo is perfectly suited for a hot, dry spot and looks lovely for much of the growing season.

Most often known simply as gaura (*Gaura lindheimeri*), this Deep South native also goes by a variety of more whimsical monikers, including appleblossom grass, beeblossom, butterfly flower, and wand flower. By any name, it's a beauty in beds and borders, with long, slender stems that are lined with dainty-looking blooms for most of the growing season. The species typically grows 4 to 5 feet tall and wide, but there are many scaled-down selections better suited to smaller gardens, from 'Whirling Butterflies' (to about 3 feet) down to the 12- to 18-inch-tall Ballerina Series. Gauras are generally hardy in Zones 5 or 6 to 9.

Color Considerations

Gauras commonly have reddish buds and white-aging-to-pink or solid pink flowers. There are often additional touches of color on the leaves, which may be spotted or heavily blushed with red. The open flowers combine beautifully with many other perennials that have white and/or pink blooms, such as 'Magnus' and 'White Swan' purple coneflowers (*Echinacea purpurea*), for instance, or 'Berry Chiffon' or 'Cosmic Evolution' coreopsis (*Coreopsis*).

If you'd like to expand the color palette, consider combining your gauras with blues to purples, like those of balloon flower (*Platycodon grandiflorus*); with yellows, like those of coreopsis; or with blue or silver leaves, like those of blue fescues (*Festuca*) or lamb's ears (*Stachys byzantina*).

In combinations you see up close, you could play up the touches of red in the buds and leaves with red co-stars, such as 'Cherry Brandy' black-eyed Susan (*Rudbeckia hirta*) or 'Cheyenne Sky' switch grass (*Panicum virgatum*).

Shapes and Textures

The very compact gauras create fairly broad mounds with dense bloom spikes. Site them at or near the front of a bed or border, in front of more-upright partners, such as 2- to 3-foot-tall yarrows (*Achillea*). Taller gauras, such as 'Summer Breeze' and 'Whirling Butterflies', tend to have arching flower stems and a more open habit that contrasts with partners that have a distinctly upright form and/or spiky flowers: dense blazing star (*Liatris spicata*), for example, or summer phlox (*Phlox paniculata*).

All gauras look terrific paired with broad, spiky leaves, like those of agaves (*Agave*), bearded irises, or yuccas (*Yucca*), and their small blossoms mingle charmingly with bold blooms, like those of daylilies (*Hemerocallis*) and true lilies (*Lilium*).

Bloom Buddies
Marvelous Matches for Flowering Combos

Gaura (*Gaura lindheimeri*) usually grows best in full sun but may appreciate some afternoon shade in warmer areas. It is well suited to hot, dry sites, though it adapts to moist, fertile borders as long as it has good drainage, especially in winter. Below are just a few compatible companions to consider for beautiful bloom combinations.

Asters (*Aster*)

Blanket flowers (*Gaillardia*)

Caryopteris (*Caryopteris*)

Coreopsis (*Coreopsis*)

Echinaceas (*Echinacea*)

Globe thistles (*Echinops*)

Hardy geraniums (*Geranium*)

Lesser calamint (*Calamintha nepetoides*)

Marguerites (*Anthemis*)

Red valerian (*Centranthus ruber*)

Russian sages (*Perovskia*)

Sea hollies (*Eryngium*)

Summer phlox (*Phlox paniculata*)

Verbenas (*Verbena*)

Yarrows (*Achillea*)

Seasonal Features

In the warmer parts of their growing range, gauras begin blooming in mid- to late spring; in cooler areas, late spring or early summer is more common. Once they begin, they typically continue for months, and even into winter in very mild areas.

Geranium
invaluable as supporting players

Geranium 'Gerwat' (Rozanne) and *Iris pallida* 'Variegata'

Geranium maculatum 'Espresso' and *Helleborus × hybridus*

A Perfect Match

Tired of 'Brookside' hardy geranium sprawling just as it reached peak bloom each June, I finally moved it near the middle of a border to fill an empty spot in between a Golden Spirit smokebush (*Cotinus coggygria* 'Ancot') and a clump of 'Screamin' Yellow' yellow false indigo (*Baptisia sphaerocarpa*). The following year, 'Brookside' wove itself up through its taller companions to make a brilliant blue-purple and yellow combo.

Hardy geraniums (*Geranium*), also known as cranesbills, usually don't play the starring role in perennial combinations, but they're invaluable as supporting players. Two of the most readily available species for full sun (or light shade, in hot-summer gardens) include bloody cranesbill (*G. sanguineum*), with purplish pink, pink, or white flowers on 8- to 12-inch-tall plants, for Zones 3 to 9, and meadow geranium (*G. pratense*), flowering in tints and shades of purple-blue as well as white atop 1- to 2-foot-tall stems, for Zones 4 to 8.

There are many outstanding hybrids, as well. Some of the best known in the purple-blue range include Rozanne ('Gerwat'), to about 18 inches tall, and 'Brookside' and 'Johnson's Blue', which usually reach 18 to 24 inches tall in bloom; all three are generally hardy in Zones 3 to 8. Two among the pinks include pale 'Biokovo' and richer 'Biokovo Karmina', both selections of *G. × cantabrigiense*, for Zones 4 to 9: They generally reach 8 to 12 inches tall in flower. These two are quite adaptable, growing in either sun or shade and tolerating drier conditions than many other geraniums.

A couple of other hardy geraniums that can grow in either sun or shade in Zones 3 to 8 include wild geranium (*G. maculatum*), with pink or white flowers on 1- to 2-foot-tall stems, and bigroot geranium (*G. macrorrhizum*), in shades of pink or white on stems to about 1 foot tall.

Color Considerations

If you're drawn to combinations based on soft colors, use the delicately hued hardy geranium cultivars to complement pastel yellow, pink, peach, light purple, and lavender blue flowers, as well as gray or blue leaves. The purple-blue hardy geraniums are also valuable additions to a blue-themed bed or border with blue false indigo (*Baptisia australis*), catmints (*Nepeta*), columbines (*Aquilegia*), irises, and perennial salvias (*Salvia*), to name just a few possible partners.

The magenta, vivid pink, and richer purple-blue geraniums can hold their own with other perennials in those hues, as well as with yellow flowers and foliage, in bright-colored combinations. They're also excellent for adding a bit of "wow" to primarily pastel borders.

Along with their overall petal hue, quite a few hardy geraniums have at least one other color in their flowers—a white or dark center, for instance, or dark veining. These markings are subtle because the flowers are rather small, but they're worth considering when choosing companions for plantings you'll see at close range. Hybrid 'Patricia', for instance, produces magenta pink flowers that have near-black centers, which look great near

Bloom Buddies
Marvelous Matches for flowering Combos

Flowering mainly in late spring and early summer, hardy geraniums (*Geranium*) coincide or overlap with the bloom periods of many popular perennials. Here are some possible companions that also thrive in sun to light shade and average to moist but well-drained soil.

Ajugas (*Ajuga*)

Baptisias (*Baptisia*)

Bearded iris (*Iris* Bearded Hybrids)

Bellflowers (*Campanula*)

Bluestars (*Amsonia*)

Carolina phlox (*Phlox carolina*)

Columbines (*Aquilegia*)

Coreopsis (*Coreopsis*)

Dianthus (*Dianthus*)

Foxgloves (*Digitalis*)

Lady's mantle (*Alchemilla mollis*)

Lemon lily (*Hemerocallis lilioasphodelus*)

Meadow phlox (*Phlox maculata*)

Meadow rues (*Thalictrum*)

Perennial salvias (*Salvia*)

Pincushion flowers (*Scabiosa*)

Red valerian (*Centranthus ruber*)

Rose campion (*Lychnis coronaria*)

Siberian iris (*Iris sibirica*)

Veronicas (*Veronica*)

Yarrows (*Achillea*)

a dark-leaved partner, such as 'Obsidian' heuchera (*Heuchera*).

Some hardy geraniums contribute color to perennial combos even when not in bloom, thanks to showy foliage. 'Samobor' mourning widow (*G. phaeum*), for instance, has deep purple markings on its green leaves (matching deep purple flowers, too). 'Elizabeth Ann' and 'Espresso' wild geranium (*G. maculatum*) have deep purple new leaves that age to chocolate brown; plants sold as 'Dark Reiter' and 'Midnight Reiter' meadow geranium (*G. pratense*) have superdark young foliage that turns purplish green in summer. There are several selections with yellow foliage, as well, such as the magenta-flowered hybrid 'Ann Folkard', which can look spectacular weaving up through dark-leaved shrubs. Leaf markings and colors tend to be brightest in spring to early summer, making them great matches for early bulbs and a wide range of flowering and foliage partners.

Shapes and Textures

The short hardy geraniums, such as bloody cranesbill and 'Biokovo', have a low-spreading form and work well around upright companions. Hardy geraniums that have a more upright, mounded shape or a loosely clumping form look best a foot or two back from the edge of a bed or border, where they can mingle with their companions and be less likely to sprawl. Rozanne, in particular, looks great weaving up through other perennials, roses, and other

Geranium phaeum 'Samobor' and *Heuchera* 'Plum Pudding'

shrubs. Hardy geraniums are also excellent partners for alliums (*Allium*) and lilies (*Lilium*), complementing the flowers of those bulbs while covering up the uninteresting lower stems.

Shallowly to deeply lobed leaves and relatively small, saucer- to bowl-shaped blooms give hardy geraniums an overall medium to fine texture. They benefit from companions with more distinctive habits and leaf shapes, such as strongly upright plants or companions that have broad leaves (like those of hostas) or spiky foliage (irises, for example). They make charming partners for larger blooms, such as those of peonies; daisy-form perennials, such as marguerites (*Anthemis*); spiky blossoms, like

A Trim in Time

If your hardy geraniums stop flowering, start crowding their companions, or simply look tired or untidy at some point during summer, a quick clip can work wonders.

On the low, spreading types, such as bloody cranesbill (*Geranium sanguineum*) and bigroot geranium (*G. macrorrhizum*), trim lightly to remove the seed heads or finished flowering stems. Upright and trailing types can benefit from a harder cut. If new leaves are already coming up in the middle of the plant, trim the leggy old stems back to that fresh growth; otherwise, cut all the top growth back to about 1 inch above the ground. Within a few weeks, you'll be enjoying the fresh foliage and maybe even more flowers for late summer and fall.

those of perennial salvias (*Salvia*); and clustered flowers, like those of yarrows (*Achillea*).

Seasonal Features

Peak bloom time for most hardy geraniums is late spring and early summer (starting a couple of weeks earlier in warmer zones and later in cooler regions), though they may continue to produce scattered new blooms through the rest of summer. As autumn approaches, the leaves of some geraniums, such as 'Biokovo', bloody cranesbill, and 'Brookside', can turn showy shades of red and orange. In sheltered spots—particularly in mild areas— bigroot geranium and its hybrids may stay evergreen for part or all of winter.

Special Effects

Hardy geraniums fit into beds and borders of all sizes and into some specialized areas, as well.

Groundcover combos. With their low-spreading habit and tolerance of dry shade, bigroot geranium and *G.* × *cantabrigiense* make easy-care groundcovers around shrubs. Pair them with other tough perennials that can tolerate similar conditions, such as bergenias (*Bergenia*) and epimediums (*Epimedium*).

Woodland gardens. Wild geranium looks right at home in a woodland garden with other shade-tolerant natives such as creeping Jacob's ladder (*Polemonium reptans*), foamflowers (*Tiarella*), and fringed bleeding heart (*Dicentra eximia*).

Geranium × *cantabrigiense* 'Biokovo' with *Nepeta* 'Walker's Low' and *Weigela florida (top); Geranium macrorrhizum* 'Bevan's Variety' and *Sedum rupestre* 'Angelina' *(bottom)*

Hakonechloa
gracefully arching foliage

Hakonechloa macra 'Aureola' and *Adiantum pedatum*

Hakonechloa macra 'Beni-kaze' with *Chrysogonum virginianum* and *Heuchera* 'Citronelle'

A Perfect Match

Green-leaved Hakone grasses are more readily available these days, but I'm still a sucker for the bright foliage of striped 'Aureola' and solid-yellow 'All Gold'—particularly in high-contrast combinations. In my own garden, I adore them with rich red or near-black leaves, like those of 'Lava Lamp' heuchera (*Heuchera*) or 'Ravenswing' cow parsley (*Anthriscus sylvestris*). I've also seen them look fantastic behind black mondo grass (*Ophiopogon planiscapus* 'Nigrescens').

Hakone grass (*Hakonechloa macra*), also known as Japanese forest grass, is a true beauty for shady combinations. It generally grows 1 to 2 feet tall, with gracefully arching foliage. The species and cultivars perform best in Zones 5 to 8.

Color Considerations

The green-leaved cultivars of Hakone grass are elegant partners for knockout foliage perennials, such as glowing yellow 'Fire Island' hosta or sparkling silver 'Looking Glass' Siberian bugloss (*Brunnera macrophylla*).

Golden Hakone grass ('Aureola') has brilliant yellow striping that gradually softens to light yellow, while 'All Gold' is a solid, slightly greenish yellow to clear yellow all season. Both are useful for bringing the color of taller, bright-leaved companions, such as 'Sun King' Japanese spikenard (*Aralia racemosa*) or 'Little Honey' oakleaf hydrangea (*Hydrangea quercifolia*), closer to ground level, or for picking up the markings of yellow-variegated companions, such as 'First Frost' or 'Frances Williams' hostas. For a bit more variety, pair golden Hakone grass or 'All Gold' with oranges, like those of 'Brilliance' autumn fern (*Dryopteris erythrosora*) or 'Buttered Rum' foamy bells (× *Heucherella*).

Yellow-variegated and solid yellow Hakone grasses also provide some outstanding opportunities for high-contrast pairings. For foliage partners, consider those with superdark leaves, such as 'Britt-Marie Crawford' bigleaf ligularia (*Ligularia dentata*) or 'Hillside Black Beauty' bugbane (*Cimicifuga simplex*). Rich greens, like those of hellebores (*Helleborus*) and wild gingers (*Asarum*) make gorgeous partners, too, as do blue- or gray-leaved hostas, such as 'Blue Cadet'. Bloomwise, consider co-stars in bright pinks to brilliant reds, such as 'Montgomery' or 'Red Sentinel' astilbes (*Astilbe*), or in blues and purples, like those of grape hyacinths (*Muscari*) or 'Louisiana Blue' woodland phlox (*Phlox divaricata*).

Bloom Buddies
Marvelous Matches for Flowering Combos

Hakone grass (*Hakonechloa macra*) is generally happiest in partial shade and average to moist but well-drained soil, though it can often adapt to brighter or darker conditions. Below are a few of the flowering companions that can complement this fabulous foliage perennial.

Anemones (*Anemone*)

Astilbes (*Astilbe*)

Bugbanes (*Cimicifuga*)

Columbines (*Aquilegia*)

Creeping phlox (*Phlox stolonifera*)

Hardy begonia (*Begonia grandis*)

Hardy geraniums (*Geranium*)

Lady's mantle (*Alchemilla mollis*)

Masterworts (*Astrantia*)

Toad lilies (*Tricyrtis*)

Turtleheads (*Chelone*)

Woodland phlox (*Phlox divaricata*)

Shapes and Textures

Hakone grass plants spread gently by short rhizomes to eventually form broad patches. Their arching leaves give them an elegant, flowing appearance that's lovely around the bases of larger mounds, like those of bugbanes (*Cimicifuga*) or goatsbeard (*Aruncus dioicus*), or upright companions, such as columbines (*Aquilegia*) or perennial lobelias (*Lobelia*).

The slender foliage of Hakone grass works beautifully with a variety of other leaf shapes, but it's particularly pretty with little leaves, like those of ajugas (*Ajuga*) or sweet woodruff (*Galium*

odoratum); with ferny or lacy foliage, like that of astilbes (*Astilbe*); and with broad leaves, like those of hostas or Lenten roses (*Helleborus* × *hybridus*).

Seasonal Features

Hakone grasses contribute foliage interest to combinations throughout the growing season. In later summer, they produce wispy flower heads, too, but those aren't especially showy. As the weather cools, the variegated kinds usually develop pinkish to reddish purple colors, while many green-leaved cultivars turn orangey or red.

Helenium
wonderful for warm colors

Helenium 'Coppelia' and *Sanguisorba tenuifolia* 'Purpurea'

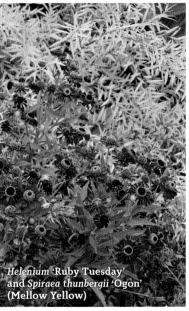

Helenium 'Ruby Tuesday' and *Spiraea thunbergii* 'Ogon' (Mellow Yellow)

A Perfect Match

My go-to companions for heleniums have long been deep purple or chocolate brown flowers or foliage, to contrast with the bright petals and repeat the dark color of the center dome. One of my favorite partnerships so far is the dark purple "catkins" of Japanese burnet (*Sanguisorba tenuifolia* 'Purpurea') mingling with the warm orange blooms of 'Coppelia' helenium.

Heleniums (*Helenium*), also called sneezeweeds or Helen's flowers, are a delight in bright late-summer combinations. Among the best-known species are *H. autumnale*, which typically reaches 3 to 5 feet tall, has yellow-centered yellow flowers, and is hardy in Zones 3 to 8, and *H. flexuosum*, which has dark-centered yellow flowers atop 1- to 3-foot-tall plants and is best suited for Zones 5 to 9. Hybrids between these and other species have produced selections in a range of heights and colors; they're usually hardy in Zones 4 to 8.

Color Considerations

If you enjoy working with warm colors—sunny yellows, clear to reddish oranges, and bright to deep reds—heleniums belong in your plant paint box. They're right at home with other vibrant perennials, such as brilliant red cardinal flower (*Lobelia cardinalis*) and glowing yellow goldenrods (*Solidago*). They're also stunning with intense blues and purples, like those of 'Blue Mirror' Chinese delphinium (*Delphinium grandiflorum*) or 'Vedrariensis' perennial lobelia (*Lobelia × speciosa*).

If you're not comfortable putting two intensely colored flowers right next to each other, use some solid green or purple foliage in between. Dark-leaved companions, such as 'Australia' canna and 'Bishop of Llandaff' dahlia, do a nice job echoing the dark centers of many helenium flowers. The rich colors of heleniums show up beautifully among the tans and browns of ornamental grass flower and seed heads, like those of 'Karl Foerster' feather reed grass (*Calamagrostis × acutiflora*).

Shapes and Textures

Heleniums mostly have an upright habit, though the taller ones may need staking in spring or cutting back by half in early summer to stay that way. It's not unusual for heleniums to drop their lower leaves, especially during dry spells, so it's a good idea to site them behind lower, mounded companions.

The blooms of heleniums echo the shape of rudbeckias (*Rudbeckia*) and other daisy-form flowers, but in a scaled-down size. For contrast, consider spikes, like those of 'Black Adder' anise hyssop (*Agastache*) and torch lilies (*Kniphofia*), or airier partners, such as Russian sages (*Perovskia*) or tufted hair grass (*Deschampsia cespitosa*),

Seasonal Features

While heleniums are traditionally thought of as late-summer perennials, some, such as

Bloom Buddies
Marvelous Matches for flowering Combos

Heleniums (*Helenium*) thrive with lots of sun and rich, evenly moist soil, though they can adapt to average, well-drained soil as long as there aren't extended dry spells. Below are some compatible and complementary perennials that overlap with their main bloom period.

Anise hyssops (*Agastache*)

Bee balms (*Monarda*)

Coreopsis (*Coreopsis*)

Crocosmias (*Crocosmia*)

Daylilies (*Hemerocallis*)

Echinaceas (*Echinacea*)

Goldenrods (*Solidago*)

Japanese burnet (*Sanguisorba tenuifolia*)

Joe-Pye weeds (*Eupatorium*)

Oxeye (*Heliopsis helianthoides*)

Perennial lobelias (*Lobelia*)

Perennial salvias (*Salvia*)

Perennial sunflowers (*Helianthus*)

Rudbeckias (*Rudbeckia*)

Russian sages (*Perovskia*)

Torch lilies (*Kniphofia*)

'Sahin's Early Flowerer', may begin blooming in early summer, and quite a few of the newer hybrids start in midsummer. Once they get going, they typically continue through late summer and even into fall, especially if you regularly clip off the older blooms as they drop their petals. Or let the heads mature in place and enjoy their dark seed heads in your fall combinations.

Helianthus
showy for summer and fall

Helianthus 'Lemon Queen' with *Panicum virgatum* 'Northwind' and *Rudbeckia fulgida*

Helianthus angustifolius and *Aster novae-angliae*

A Perfect Match

It's possible to keep the tall perennial sunflowers more in scale with a small garden if you're willing to cut them back by about half in early summer and again by a third in mid-summer. But really, they're at their best where you have a lot of space to fill, set among shrubs or paired with other sizable late-season perennials. Ironweeds (*Vernonia*) are one of my top picks for flowering partners, because their fuzzy, bright purple blooms look fantastic with the yellow sunflower blossoms.

Perennial sunflowers (*Helianthus*) are valuable for their vibrant yellow, later-season blooms. Two that typically reach 4 to 6 feet tall are many-flowered sunflower (*H. × multiflorus*), for Zones 4 to 8, and willowleaf sunflower (*H. salicifolius*), for Zones 4 to 9. Narrowleaf sunflower (*H. angustifolius*) gets even taller—typically in the range of 6 to 10 feet—and is suited for Zones 5 or 6 to 9. 'Lemon Queen', for Zones 4 to 9, is a popular hybrid that generally grows 6 to 8 feet tall.

Color Considerations

While the color range of perennial sunflowers is limited to shades of yellow, there's no limit to their value as a part of hot-color borders. They're all bright enough to hold their own with rousing red cardinal flower (*Lobelia cardinalis*) or 'Lord Baltimore' hardy hibiscus (*Hibiscus*), for example, or with warm orange

'Coppelia' helenium (*Helenium*) or 'Flame Thrower' echinacea (*Echinacea*). You can also use them to echo the many other yellow-flowered perennials of the summer-into-fall season.

If you're not comfortable mixing strong colors, consider pairing your perennial sunflowers with crisp to creamy whites, such as 'David' summer phlox (*Phlox paniculata*) or white mugwort (*Artemisia lactiflora*). Blues and purples, like those of anise hyssops (*Agastache*) and Russian sages (*Perovskia*), are also beautiful buddies for perennial sunflowers. Lemon yellow 'Lemon Queen' can work well with pink perennials, too, such as 'Gateway' Joe-Pye weed (*Eupatorium maculatum*).

Shapes and Textures

Perennial sunflowers grow in upright clumps. Compact selections, such as 12- to 18-inch-tall 'Table Mountain' willowleaf sunflower, can play nicely near the front of a border, behind lower mounded or trailing companions. Most, though, are better suited to the middle or back of a border with other tall perennials and grasses.

The typical single or semidouble, daisy-form flowers of perennial sunflowers repeat the shape of many other perennials that bloom around the same time, including echinaceas (*Echinacea*) and rudbeckias (*Rudbeckia*). All of the perennial sunflower bloom forms contrast handsomely with spiky partners, such as Culver's roots (*Veronicastrum*) and perennial lobelias (*Lobelia*), and they look wonderful with the plumy heads of 'Dewey Blue' bitter panic grass (*Panicum amarum*), Indian grass (*Sorghastrum nutans*), and many other warm-season ornamental grasses.

Bloom Buddies
Marvelous Matches for flowering Combos

Perennial sunflowers (*Helianthus*) love lots of sun and grow well in average to moist soil, though they can tolerate some drought once established. Below are some perennials that can thrive in the same conditions and overlap with their peak late-summer to early-fall bloom period.

Agastaches (*Agastache*)

Asters (*Aster*)

Caryopteris (*Caryopteris*)

Coreopsis (*Coreopsis*)

Culver's roots (*Veronicastrum*)

Echinaceas (*Echinacea*)

False aster (*Boltonia asteroides*)

Goldenrods (*Solidago*)

Hardy hibiscus (*Hibiscus*)

Heleniums (*Helenium*)

Ironweeds (*Vernonia*)

Joe-Pye weeds (*Eupatorium*)

Perennial lobelias (*Lobelia*)

Rudbeckias (*Rudbeckia*)

Russian sages (*Perovskia*)

Summer phlox (*Phlox paniculata*)

White mugwort (*Artemisia lactiflora*)

Seasonal Features

Some perennial sunflowers, including 'Flore Pleno' and 'Sunshine Daydream' many-flowered sunflowers, may begin blooming in early summer, but most don't start until mid- or late summer, and swamp sunflower and willowleaf sunflower typically hold off until early fall. Once any of these begin, they usually continue flowering for 2 to 3 months, if frost holds off that long.

Heliopsis
sunny summer yellows

Heliopsis helianthoides 'Loraine Sunshine' and *Campanula* 'Sarastro'

Heliopsis helianthoides 'Summer Sun' and *Lobelia cardinalis*

A Perfect Match

I ignored oxeyes for a long time because there are lots of other yellow daisies that don't suffer from the aphids that seem drawn to oxeyes in late summer. The cultivars with interesting foliage have caught my eye, though, because that feature offers additional possibilities for combinations. One of my recent favorites is 'Prairie Sunset' oxeye in front of Diabolo ninebark (*Physocarpus opulifolius* 'Monlo'), to echo this cultivar's deep purple stems and contrast with its gold-and-orange flowers.

Also known as false sunflower or sunflower heliopsis, oxeye (*Heliopsis helianthoides*) grows anywhere from 3 to 6 feet tall, with single, semidouble, or double golden yellow daisies. Oxeye and its cultivars are generally hardy in Zones 3 or 4 to 9.

Color Considerations

If yellow flowers make you smile, a golden garden could be just the project for you. Any of the oxeyes are excellent choices, along with some of the many other summer yellows, such as 'Fireworks' rough goldenrod (*Solidago rugosa*) and threadleaf coreopsis (*Coreopsis verticillata*). Expand the palette a bit with some oranges and ambers, like those of butterfly weed (*Asclepias tuberosa*). If you're feeling particularly brave, turn up the heat with reds and corals, like those of 'Desert Coral' coreopsis, 'Hot Lava' helenium (*Helenium*), and 'Paprika' yarrow (*Achillea*).

Oxeyes are also outstanding with blue or purple flowers, such as balloon flower (*Platycodon grandiflorus*) and sea hollies (*Eryngium*).

For a little extra sophistication, consider pairing oxeyes with companions that have yellow and another color in their flowers: gold-rimmed red 'Dazzler' blanket flower (*Gaillardia × grandiflora*), for instance, or yellow-throated, deep purple 'Bela Lugosi' daylily (*Hemerocallis*).

Variegated oxeyes, such as 'Loraine Sunshine' and 'Sunburst', have bright to creamy white foliage with a network of green veining. Echo the white in the leaves with large and/or taller white flowers, such as 'Becky' Shasta daisy (*Leucanthemum × superbum*) or 'Gentle Shepherd' daylily.

Shapes and Textures

Oxeyes' upright, bushy habit and daisy-form flower shape are similar to those of many summer perennials, so take advantage of other distinctive shapes when choosing companions. Spiky flowers, such as blazing stars (*Liatris*) and torch lilies (*Kniphofia*), are excellent for creating contrast. The slender foliage and airy or fluffy flower heads of ornamental grasses also look terrific with the bold blooms of oxeyes.

Seasonal Features

Oxeyes typically begin blooming in early to midsummer and continue through late summer or early fall, especially if you frequently clip off the dead flowers. Watch out for red aphids: tiny sap-sucking pests that cluster along the upper stems. If you catch them early,

Bloom Buddies
Marvelous Matches for Flowering Combos

Oxeye (*Heliopsis helianthoides*) grows in full sun to light shade and average, well-drained soil. It thrives in rich borders with ample moisture but takes drier conditions. That adaptability, combined with the long bloom season, gives you a large pool of potential companions to consider, including the perennials below.

Agastaches (*Agastache*)

Balloon flower (*Platycodon grandiflorus*)

Blazing stars (*Liatris*)

Blue mist shrubs (*Caryopteris*)

Catmints (*Nepeta*)

Coreopsis (*Coreopsis*)

Daylilies (*Hemerocallis*)

Delphiniums (*Delphinium*)

Echinaceas (*Echinacea*)

Globe thistles (*Echinops*)

Hardy geraniums (*Geranium*)

Heleniums (*Helenium*)

Lavenders (*Lavandula*)

Perennial salvias (*Salvia*)

Rudbeckias (*Rudbeckia*)

Russian sages (*Perovskia*)

Sea hollies (*Eryngium*)

Summer phlox (*Phlox paniculata*)

Torch lilies (*Kniphofia*)

Yarrows (*Achillea*)

squashing them with your fingers or spraying them with insecticidal soap may keep them from getting out of hand; if there are a lot of them, cut the plants back by about one-third to remove the infested stems, and the plants should be in flower again in a few weeks.

Helleborus
four-season favorites

Hellebores

*Partial shade; average,
well-drained soil*

Helleborus × hybridus and
Leucojum aestivum 'Gravetye Giant'

Helleborus × hybridus 'Double
Integrity' with *Iris × robusta* 'Gerald
Darby'

A Perfect Match

Bearsfoot hellebore is particularly distinctive during the colder months, with light green buds and bells over the lacy, deep green leaves. I've seen it look absolutely stunning planted around the bases of shrubs that have colorful winter stems, such as brilliant red 'Cardinal' or bright yellow 'Silver and Gold' dogwoods (*Cornus sericea*). Hybrid hellebores would work well, too, for creating a carpeting effect around the upright shrub stems.

With charming flowers in winter and spring and handsome foliage for the rest of the year, hellebores (*Helleborus*) are invaluable for adding multiseason interest to shady perennial partnerships. They come in two basic types: acaulescent ("stemless"), which send up their mostly leafless flowering stalks right from the ground, and caulescent ("stemmed"), which bloom atop leafy, 2-year-old stems.

The most readily available sort is the acaulescent hybrid hellebores, also commonly known as Lenten roses (*H. × hybridus*, though you'll also see them sold as *H. orientalis*). They generally reach 12 to 18 inches tall, bloom in a range of colors, and are hardy in Zones 4 or 5 to 9. Christmas rose (*H. niger*), another stemless hellebore, typically starts flowering a month or so earlier, has white to pink-blushed blooms to about 1 foot tall, and is hardy in Zones 3 or 4 to 8.

Among the caulescent kinds are bearsfoot hellebore

(*H. foetidus*), also known as stinking hellebore, with deeply cut leaves, and Corsican hellebore (*H. argutifolius*), with toothed, three-part leaves. Both reach 18 to 30 inches tall in bloom, have green flowers, and generally perform best in Zones 6 to 9.

Color Considerations

Along with the pure white and pink-tinged whites of Christmas rose, hybrid hellebores can produce shades of burgundy, deep reds and purples, yellow, and peach, often with intricate shadings or with contrasting spotting or edging. The whites and lighter colors, as well as the greens of bearsfoot and Corsican hellebores, are particularly lovely with blue-flowered partners, such as pulmonarias (*Pulmonaria*) and Siberian squill (*Scilla siberica*), and with white blooms, like those of Allegheny pachysandra (*Pachysandra procumbens*) and snowdrops (*Galanthus*). Try the deep reds and purples with whites or with bright yellows, like those of 'February Gold' daffodils or winter aconites (*Eranthis hyemalis*).

Silver- or gray-leaved partners, such as 'Silver Falls' Japanese painted fern (*Athyrium niponicum* var. *pictum*) and 'Silver Shimmers' pulmonaria (*Pulmonaria*), look terrific with any hellebore in bloom or in leaf, as do perennials with bright yellow foliage, such as 'All Gold' Hakone grass (*Hakonechloa macra*) or 'Gold Heart' common bleeding heart (*Dicentra spectabilis*). The rich greens of hellebore leaves also complement brightly variegated companions, such as 'Banana Boat' broadleaf sedge (*Carex siderosticha*) and 'Stairway to Heaven' creeping Jacob's ladder (*Polemonium reptans*).

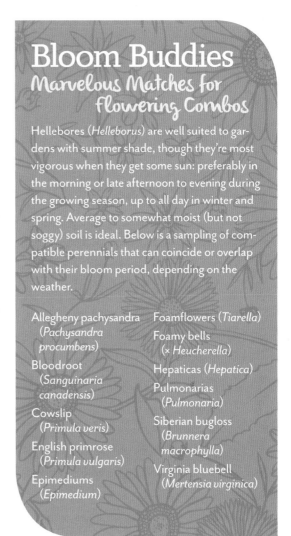

Bloom Buddies
Marvelous Matches for Flowering Combos

Hellebores (*Helleborus*) are well suited to gardens with summer shade, though they're most vigorous when they get some sun: preferably in the morning or late afternoon to evening during the growing season, up to all day in winter and spring. Average to somewhat moist (but not soggy) soil is ideal. Below is a sampling of compatible perennials that can coincide or overlap with their bloom period, depending on the weather.

Allegheny pachysandra (*Pachysandra procumbens*)

Bloodroot (*Sanguinaria canadensis*)

Cowslip (*Primula veris*)

English primrose (*Primula vulgaris*)

Epimediums (*Epimedium*)

Foamflowers (*Tiarella*)

Foamy bells (× *Heucherella*)

Hepaticas (*Hepatica*)

Pulmonarias (*Pulmonaria*)

Siberian bugloss (*Brunnera macrophylla*)

Virginia bluebell (*Mertensia virginica*)

Shapes and Textures

Christmas rose and hybrid hellebore plants have a mounded form, especially in leaf. Use them behind trailing or creeping co-stars, such as spotted deadnettle (*Lamium maculatum*) or woodland sedum (*Sedum ternatum*), and next to or in front of arching or upright partners, such as 'Gilt Edge' toad lily (*Tricyrtis*)

Helleborus × hybridus with *Muscari auscheri* 'Ocean Magic' (left); *Helleborus foetidus* with *Pachysandra procumbens* (above)

or variegated Solomon's seal (*Polygonatum odoratum* 'Variegatum'). The bushier, more upright habit of bearsfoot and Corsican hellebores looks great with lower mounded or carpeting companions, such as pulmonarias and wild gingers (*Asarum*).

The flowers of most hellebores are relatively large and roughly bowl shaped; those of bearsfoot hellebore are a bit smaller and bell-like. They all work well with a variety of other bloom shapes but are particularly pretty with dainty flowers, like the airy sprays of epimediums (*Epimedium*) and forget-me-nots (*Myosotis*).

In leaf, hellebores pair well with lacy or ferny foliage, like that of athyriums (*Athyrium*) or fringed bleeding heart (*Dicentra eximia*), and

with grassy or strappy leaf shapes, like those of 'Oehme' palm sedge (*Carex muskingumensis*) or variegated blue lilyturf (*Liriope muscari* 'Variegata'). The deeply cut leaves of bearsfoot hellebore contrast with broader foliage, like that of bergenias (*Bergenia*), Canada wild ginger (*Asarum canadense*), and hostas.

Seasonal Features

In the warmer parts of their growing range, bearsfoot hellebore and Christmas rose typically start blooming in midwinter, with Corsican hellebore and hybrid hellebores joining them by late winter. In colder areas, the bloom season of all four commonly begins in early to mid-spring. Once the flowers open, they remain attractive for a month or more. After blooming, all of these remain leafy and lovely all the way through fall and for much or all of winter, as well.

Hemerocallis
dependable and adaptable

Hemerocallis '**Milk Chocolate**' and *Physocarpus opulifolius* 'Monlo' (Diabolo)

Hemerocallis '**Autumn Minaret**' and *Rudbeckia fulgida*

A Perfect Match

For too long, I bought into the "oh, daylilies—they're so *common*" attitude. That changed when a fellow gardener shared a piece of his prized 'Milk Chocolate': a hybrid with petals in an odd sort of pinkish brown color. I took it as a challenge to show off the gift in interesting combinations: against 'Grace' smoke-bush (*Cotinus*), for example, to echo the dark buds and dark brush marks on the petals. After that, it didn't take long to be seduced by other hybrids and species.

Daylilies (*Hemerocallis*) are so dependable and adaptable that it's tempting to think of them simply as space fillers in your beds and borders. But these easy-to-please perennials deserve to be appreciated for their beauty, as well, and it's worth taking a little time to choose companions that will enhance them. There are several species and many thousands of hybrids to choose from, most of them hardy in Zones 3 to 9. Heights range from 1 to 6 feet tall, and there's an amazing range of flower forms and colors, too: enough to provide lots of opportunities for delightfully refined to strikingly showstopping combinations.

Color Considerations

While the various yellows and oranges tend to be pretty consistent color-wise, some of the paler tints and deeper shades

Bloom Buddies
Marvelous Matches for Flowering Combos

Daylilies (*Hemerocallis*) have a wonderful ability to adapt to a wide range of growing conditions: from full sun to partial shade and from relatively dry to moist (though not waterlogged) soil. That flexibility, as well as the range of possible bloom times, makes for a wide pool of potential flowering companions. Here's just a sampling of those that can coincide with or overlap the main show.

Agastaches (*Agastache*)

Balloon flower (*Platycodon grandiflorus*)

Bee balms (*Monarda*)

Blazing stars (*Liatris*)

Catmints (*Nepeta*)

Coreopsis (*Coreopsis*)

Echinaceas (*Echinacea*)

Filipendulas (*Filipendula*)

Globe thistles (*Echinops*)

Heleniums (*Helenium*)

Japanese iris (*Iris ensata*)

Meadow rues (*Thalictrum*)

Perennial salvias (*Salvia*)

Pincushion flowers (*Scabiosa*)

Rudbeckias (*Rudbeckia*)

Russian sages (*Perovskia*)

Sedums (*Sedum*)

Shasta daisy (*Leucanthemum × superbum*)

Spike speedwell (*Veronica spicata*)

Stoke's aster (*Stokesia laevis*)

Summer phlox (*Phlox paniculata*)

among the reds, pinks, and purples can fade or bleach out in strong sun, so they often look best in a site with morning sun and afternoon shade, or else in a garden with light all-day shade, especially in southern gardens.

Red, orange, and yellow daylilies contribute vivid splashes of color to hot-color gardens, and there are lots of other vibrant perennials in the same hues that flower around the same time, making it a simple matter to find complementary companions. Though it may seem like a contradiction, adding some dark colors can make the bright ones really pop, so consider including some of the practically black daylilies, such as 'Bela Lugosi' and 'Jungle Beauty', as well. Keep foliage companions in mind, too: dark-leaved perennial partners, such as 'Chocolate' white snakeroot (*Eupatorium rugosum*), for the bright daylilies, and yellow foliage, like that of 'Golden Arrow' mountain fleeceflower (*Persicaria amplexicaulis*), for the darker hybrids.

Where softer colors prevail, you'll be spoiled for choice among the many ivory, cream, buttery yellow, peach, soft pink, and lavender daylilies. Choose perennial partners that flower in tints of the same colors or in slightly darker shades, for a bit of variety: creamy yellow 'Wedding Band' daylily with clear yellow 'Crème Brulee' coreopsis (*Coreopsis*), for instance. Pastel daylilies are beautiful with soft blues and purples, too, such as balloon flower (*Platycodon grandiflorus*), catmints (*Nepeta*), and Russian sages (*Perovskia*). Gray-, blue-, and silver-leaved companions look lovely with pastel daylilies, as do partners with gray- or silvery purple foliage, such as purple sage (*Salvia officinalis* 'Purpurascens') or 'Vera Jameson' sedum (*Sedum*).

Shapes and Textures

Daylilies start the season as vase-shaped clumps, with spiky foliage that eventually arches out from the center of the plant. Young daylilies, with just one or a few "fans" of leaves, may keep a spiky look through the season, but once the plants have been in the ground for a few years, they develop an overall mounded form by summer. Fill in around them at the front to middle of the border with low, broad mounds or spreaders, such as catmints, hardy geraniums (*Geranium*), sedums (*Sedum*), and verbenas (*Verbena*). Next to or behind the daylilies, use upright companions, such as summer phlox (*Phlox paniculata*) and Culver's roots (*Veronicastrum*), for more variety in height and form.

The leaves of daylilies are long and relatively slender. Most have a strappy look, but some of the narrowest ones are almost grass-like; either way, they make a pleasing contrast to the many perennials with fine- to medium-textured foliage, as well as to broad-leaved partners, such as hostas, lady's mantle (*Alchemilla mollis*), and ligularias (*Ligularia*). Daylily foliage repeats the strong shapes of other spiky-leaved plants, such as irises and ornamental grasses.

Hemerocallis 'Barbara Mitchell' with *Echinacea purpurea* 'Razzmatazz', *Hydrangea paniculata* 'Dvppinky' (Pinky Winky), *Delphinium elatum*, and *Persicaria polymorpha*

Though they vary somewhat in size and shape—from funnel or trumpet shaped to starry to almost round—the attention-grabbing flowers of daylilies are all on the bold side. Established plants produce so many buds that the clumps can have a big impact even from quite a distance, holding their own with other substantial summer blooms, like those of blazing stars (*Liatris*), echinaceas (*Echinacea*), mulleins (*Verbascum*), and rudbeckias (*Rudbeckia*). At

Exploring More Options: Partners beyond Perennials

Daylilies (*Hemerocallis*) make ideal partners for spring-flowering bulbs. There's plenty of room around them early in the season for crocuses, daffodils, giant onion (*Allium giganteum*), grape hyacinths (*Muscari*), summer snowflake (*Leucojum aestivum*), and tulips; later in the season, the expanding daylily leaves will cover the declining bulb foliage.

Excellent for Echoes

Besides the main bloom color—which can be pretty much anything except true blue—daylily (*Hemerocallis*) flowers usually have a yellow, orangey, or green "throat" where the petals join. Many hybrids also have one or more other kinds of markings or patterns, with tints and shades of one hue or two or more different colors creating blends, bands, edgings, halos, or other interesting features.

These extra colors can be a superb source of inspiration for choosing beautiful companions. A yellow-leaved or -flowered perennial, such as golden oregano (*Origanum vulgare* 'Aureum') or 'Zagreb' threadleaf coreopsis (*Coreopsis verticillata*), for instance, would work well with a yellow-centered daylily, such as bright red 'Red Razzmatazz' (*right*) or rosy pink 'Rosy Returns'. Or if you're working with a daylily that has white midribs or edges in its blooms, such as purplish pink 'Prairie Blue Eyes', consider a co-star with white flowers, like those of gaura (*Gaura lindheimeri*), or bright silver leaves, like those of 'Powis Castle' artemisia (*Artemisia*).

closer range, enjoy the contrast they provide to smaller-flowered, slender-spiked, or plumed partners, such as astilbes (*Astilbe*), knautias (*Knautia*), mountain fleeceflower (*Persicaria amplexicaulis*), pincushion flowers (*Scabiosa*), and speedwells (*Veronica*).

Seasonal Features

In northern gardens, midsummer is the peak season for daylilies; in the South, it's usually late spring to early summer. There are also species and hybrids that bloom weeks earlier or later than the main show, though, so you need to know just when to expect flowers from your chosen plants before you can choose companions that will be sure to bloom at the same time. Or pair your daylilies with partners that have colorful foliage, which will be there

whenever your daylilies open. Another option is to choose perennial co-stars that bloom over a long period, such as catmints (*Nepeta*) and coreopsis (*Coreopsis*), so there's a good chance that they will overlap.

Most daylilies bloom over a period of 3 to 4 weeks, but it's possible to enjoy their showy blossoms for much longer if you choose "reblooming" (also known as recurrent or remontant) cultivars, which may produce a second show in late summer to early autumn or even repeated flushes of bloom through summer and fall. Besides possibly adding some fresh flowers to the late-season garden, daylilies may contribute some foliage interest when the leaves of "deciduous" types turn yellow in fall. Semi-evergreen and evergreen types can stay green for part or all of winter in the South but often get discolored by winter cold north of Zone 8.

138 HEMEROCALLIS

Hemerocallis fulva and *H.* 'Stella d'Oro' with *Sedum acre* and *Nepeta* 'Walker's Low'

Heuchera
for foliage or flowers—or both!

Heuchera 'Silver Scrolls' with *Brunnera macrophylla* 'Jack Frost' and *Hosta* 'Fire and Ice'

Heuchera 'Berry Timeless' and *Nepeta* 'Walker's Low'

A Perfect Match

I had mixed luck with hybrid heucheras at first, but many newer ones—especially those that include hairy alumroot (*H. villosa*) in their breeding—have proven vigorous and reliable in my garden. I particularly like making matches with the orangey ones, such as 'Caramel' and 'Southern Comfort': to harmonize with orangey or yellow flowers, such as coreopsis (*Coreopsis*), for instance, or for contrast with purple-blue catmints (*Nepeta*) or hardy geraniums (*Geranium*).

Not so long ago, options for heuchera (*Heuchera*) combinations were pretty limited. If you fancied colorful flowers, you chose coral bells (*H. sanguinea*); if you were more interested in foliage, you considered selections of the species often called alumroots (*H. americana*, *H. micrantha*, and *H. villosa*). Since then, busy plant breeders have dramatically expanded the range of heuchera hybrids and cultivars that have fantastic foliage and/ or eye-catching flowers. Most reach about 1 foot tall in leaf and 18 to 24 inches tall in bloom.

Heucheras typically perform best in Zones 3 or 4 to 8. In northern gardens and in coastal areas with moderate summers, many heucheras (particularly those with dark-colored leaves) can perform well with all-day sun, especially if the soil doesn't get too dry. Generally speaking, though, heucheras are happiest in partial shade: with light shade all day, or with sun in the morning or late afternoon and midday shade.

Color Considerations

Flower-wise, color options among the heucheras include reds, pinks, and white. Match them with partners that have similar colors—pink-flowered 'Peppermint' at the feet of pink 'Monsieur Jules Elie' peony (*Paeonia lactiflora*), for example, or white-flowered 'Autumn Bride' heuchera with white-variegated 'Francee' hosta. Or enjoy some variety by letting them mingle with yellows, like those of lady's mantle (*Alchemilla mollis*), or blues to purple-blues, like those of perennial salvias (*Salvia*).

If you're focusing on combinations with foliage heucheras, start with cultivars that have solid-colored leaves, or choose cultivars with secondary colors in their foliage. (Many selections, for instance, have silvery, deep purple, or dark red veining, or an overall silvery cast.) Keep in mind that base colors, shadings, and markings can change subtly or dramatically through the growing season, so don't depend just on pictures when picking heucheras for your combinations: See the plants in person, if you can, or grow them in a holding bed for the first year before settling on color companions.

High-impact contrasts. If dramatic differences give you a thrill, start with a heuchera that has bright yellow foliage, such as 'Citronelle' or 'Lime Marmalade', then match it with a dark-leaved partner, such as black mondo grass (*Ophiopogon planiscapus* 'Nigrescens') or 'Espresso' wild geranium (*Geranium maculatum*). Or choose a companion with intense red, hot pink, or purple-blue flowers, such as 'Fireball' bee balm (*Monarda*), 'Mrs. Bradshaw' geum (*Geum chiloense*), 'Glow' astilbe (*Astilbe*), or 'Sarastro' bellflower (*Campanula*).

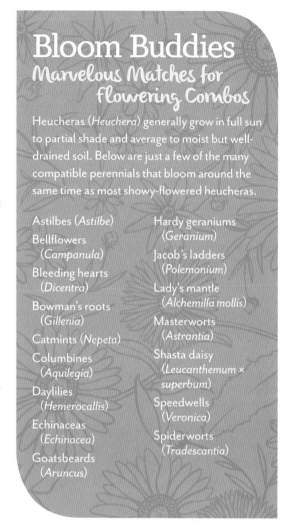

Bloom Buddies
Marvelous Matches for Flowering Combos

Heucheras (*Heuchera*) generally grow in full sun to partial shade and average to moist but well-drained soil. Below are just a few of the many compatible perennials that bloom around the same time as most showy-flowered heucheras.

Astilbes (*Astilbe*)

Bellflowers (*Campanula*)

Bleeding hearts (*Dicentra*)

Bowman's roots (*Gillenia*)

Catmints (*Nepeta*)

Columbines (*Aquilegia*)

Daylilies (*Hemerocallis*)

Echinaceas (*Echinacea*)

Goatsbeards (*Aruncus*)

Hardy geraniums (*Geranium*)

Jacob's ladders (*Polemonium*)

Lady's mantle (*Alchemilla mollis*)

Masterworts (*Astrantia*)

Shasta daisy (*Leucanthemum × superbum*)

Speedwells (*Veronica*)

Spiderworts (*Tradescantia*)

The reverse approach works, too: Start with a deep purple or intensely red heuchera selection, such as 'Blackout', 'Obsidian', or 'Fire Alarm', and combine it with bright yellow leaves, like those of golden meadowsweet (*Filipendula ulmaria* 'Aurea'); with boldly variegated foliage, like that of 'Snow Cap' broadleaf sedge (*Carex siderosticha*); or with bright silver leaves, like those of 'Powis Castle' artemisia (*Artemisia*).

Heuchera 'Tiramisu' and *Pachysandra procumbens (left);*
Heuchera 'Plum Pudding' and *Hosta* 'Guacamole' *(above)*

Or contrast their dark leaves with vivid white or golden yellow blooms, like those of 'Kim's Mop Head' purple coneflower (*Echinacea purpurea*) or 'Zagreb' threadleaf coreopsis (*Coreopsis verticillata*).

Elegant echoes. In small gardens, or in beds you see up close, use dark- or bright-leaved heucheras to echo similar hues in the flowers of perennial partners. Cultivars with bronzy, brown, dark red, deep purple, or practically black leaves are ideal for picking up those colors in the flowers and/or foliage of companions: the spotting or banding in the blooms of many daylilies (*Hemerocallis*) and true lilies (*Lilium*), for example, or the dark centers of rudbeckias (*Rudbeckia*) and many heleniums (*Helenium*). Orangey heucheras, such as 'Southern Comfort', make a marvelous echo for the newer fronds of autumn fern (*Dryopteris erythrosora*) or the

flowers of 'Terracotta' yarrow (*Achillea*), while yellowish heucheras, such as 'Lime Rickey', repeat the yellow flowers of lady's mantle, for instance, or the chartreuse centers of 'Striptease' hosta.

Choose a mood. If you have a particular color palette in mind, pick foliage heucheras to emphasize the theme. For a sultry sun border, for instance, pair deep red- and purple-leaved heucheras with flowering partners in rich reds, scarlet, coral, and deep orange, such as 'Alabama Jubilee' daylily, 'Hot Papaya' echinacea (*Echinacea*), and 'Redhot Popsicle' torch lily (*Kniphofia*). Deep purple to near-black heucheras, such as silver-veined 'Blackberry Ice' and pink-spotted 'Midnight Rose', are also an excellent complement to flowering companions in magenta to pink, such as 'Bressingham Flair' Armenian cranesbill (*Geranium psilostemon*) or 'Red Fox' spike speedwell (*Veronica spicata*). If a softer look is more to your liking, try 'Caramel' and other peachy heucheras with pastel pinks, apricots, yellows, lavenders, and blues, like those of 'Heidi' yarrow (*Achillea*), Rozanne hardy geranium (*Geranium* 'Gerwat'), 'Ruffled Apricot' daylily, and 'Sunrise' echinacea.

Shapes and Textures

Heuchera plants have a broad, mounded form. In larger borders, they work well along the front edge; in smaller areas, use them behind lower trailing or carpeting plants, such as creeping sedums (*Sedum*) or spotted deadnettle (*Lamium maculatum*). Taller companions with somewhat arching habits, such as Hakone grass (*Hakonechloa macra*), Solomon's seals (*Polygonatum*), and toad lilies (*Tricyrtis*), make a particularly nice complement to heucheras.

In bloom, the individual flower stems of heucheras are quite upright, but they tend to be so abundant that the overall effect is more like a cloud of tiny blossoms: charming set against taller, large-leaved companions, such as hostas, or mingling with bolder blooms, like those of dwarf daylilies or compact Shasta daisies (*Leucanthemum* × *superbum*).

Heuchera leaves are typically broad, with somewhat scalloped or ruffled edges. They're excellent for adding some textural contrast to the many ferny- or lacy-leaved shade perennials, such as astilbes (*Astilbe*), bleeding hearts (*Dicentra*), bugbanes (*Cimicifuga*), and goatsbeards (*Aruncus*). The foliage and form of heucheras also add variety when paired with plants that have slender, spiky, and/or strappy leaves, such as daylilies, irises, and New Zealand hair sedge (*Carex comans*).

Seasonal Features

Heuchera foliage is around early enough to harmonize or contrast with spring bulbs and spring-blooming perennials, and it continues to add interest through the rest of the growing season. In most areas, the leaves look good through winter, as well.

Heucheras with showy flowers typically peak in late spring and early summer in warmer areas and early to midsummer in northern zones. The foliage selections, too, bloom at some point during summer; clip off the bloom stalks if you think they detract from the foliage. *H. villosa* cultivars and hybrids tend to flower in late summer to early fall.

Heuchera 'Caramel' and *Geranium* 'Gerwat' (Rozanne)

Hibiscus
flamboyant flowers

Hibiscus 'Fantasia' with *Amsonia hubrichtii* and *Vernonia noveboracensis*

Hibiscus 'Kopper King' and *Phlox paniculata* 'Nora Leigh'

A Perfect Match

It took a while for me to warm up to hardy hibiscus because the huge blooms seemed ridiculously out of scale with other perennial flowers, and the whites and reds were just too bright for my liking. It took 'Plum Crazy', with rich purplish pink blooms and purplish lobed leaves, to make me a hardy hibiscus fan. I've added others since then, but I still adore 'Plum Crazy' with the pink-tinged plumes of 'Dallas Blues' switch grass (*Panicum virgatum*) or with purple coneflowers (*Echinacea purpurea*).

The flamboyant flowers of hardy hibiscus (*Hibiscus*) are guaranteed to steal the show in any garden. Those grown as perennials are most often hybrids of rose mallow (*H. moscheutos*) and other North American species. These heat lovers can reach anywhere from 2 to 8 feet tall, depending on the cultivar, with broad or deeply cut leaves and 4- to 12-inch-wide, saucer-shaped blooms, usually in white or shades of pink or red. Hardy hibiscus generally perform best in Zones 5 to 10.

Color Considerations

Hardy hibiscus flowers offer some excellent reds, ranging from bright, as on 'Lord Baltimore', to deep, as on 'Cranberry Crush'. Go for bold red-and-yellow pairings with partners such as giant coneflower (*Rudbeckia maxima*) or golden lace (*Patrinia scabiosifolia*). Or repeat the reds with other red blooms, like those of cardinal flower (*Lobelia cardinalis*) or 'Ruby Tuesday' helenium (*Helenium*), or with red-tipped switch grasses (*Panicum virgatum*), such as 'Prairie Fire'.

Hardy hibiscus selections with white petals and deep red centers, such as 'Luna White', also make wonderful partners for red flowers and red-and-green leaves. Pure white 'Blue River II' and other white hibiscus are stunning with other later-summer whites, too, such as Culver's root (*Veronicastrum virginicum*), false aster (*Boltonia asteroides*), or 'Morning Light' miscanthus (*Miscanthus sinensis*).

Pinks range from pale 'Cherub' to clear pink 'Peppermint Schnapps' to intense 'Jazzberry Jam'. Match them with some of the many other summer and fall pinks: cultivars of purple coneflower (*Echinacea purpurea*) and summer phlox (*Phlox paniculata*), for example. Whites and clear yellows look lovely with the pinks, as do icy blue grasses, such as 'Dewey Blue' bitter panic grass (*Panicum amarum*).

Shapes and Textures

In form, foliage, and flowers, hardy hibiscus are big and bold. They can hold their own in big borders with other substantial perennials, such as Joe-Pye weeds (*Eupatorium*) and ironweeds (*Vernonia*). Tall ornamental grasses, such as miscanthus and switch grasses, match the hibiscus in size but make a pleasing textural contrast in leaf and bloom. Spiky and plumy flower heads, like those of feather reed grasses (*Calamagrostis*) and white mugwort (*Artemisia lactiflora*), also make a pleasing contrast to the broad blooms of hibiscus, as do daisy-form flowers, like those of asters and heleniums.

Bloom Buddies
Marvelous Matches for Flowering Combos

Hardy hibiscus (*Hibiscus*) grow in full sun to light shade. They thrive in rich, moist soil but can adapt to average, well-drained soil as long as there aren't extended dry spells. Their long bloom period gives you a wide pool of potential matches to choose from, including the compatible perennials below.

Culver's roots (*Veronicastrum*)

Eupatoriums (*Eupatorium*)

False aster (*Boltonia asteroides*)

Golden lace (*Patrinia scabiosifolia*)

Goldenrods (*Solidago*)

Heleniums (*Helenium*)

Ironweeds (*Vernonia*)

New England aster (*Aster novae-angliae*)

Obedient plant (*Physostegia virginiana*)

Perennial lobelias (*Lobelia*)

Perennial sunflowers (*Helianthus*)

Rudbeckias (*Rudbeckia*)

Summer phlox (*Phlox paniculata*)

Swamp milkweed (*Asclepias incarnata*)

Turtleheads (*Chelone*)

White mugwort (*Artemisia lactiflora*)

Seasonal Features

Hardy hibiscus plants are late risers, often not sprouting until late May or even June, so there's plenty of space around them for spring-blooming bulbs. The hibiscus begin flowering in mid- to late summer, continuing into early fall, at least, or even until frost.

Hosta
endless options for creative combos

Hosta 'Summer Lovin'' and Hakonechloa macra 'All Gold'

Hosta sieboldiana 'Elegans' and Aruncus 'Misty Lace'

A Perfect Match

If I had to pick just one hosta for perennial matchmaking, it would have to be a selection with solid yellow leaves—most likely 'Sun Power'. Its spring color is a slightly dull greenish yellow, but by early summer, the leaves turn bright yellow and stay that way for months: fantastic for contrasting with richly colored flowering and foliage partners, or for echoing yellow markings in companion blooms or leaves.

Hostas (*Hosta*) have a wonderful way of making any gardener look good. These dependable perennials pair beautifully with so many different partners that even beginners can create designer-quality combinations with them. And there are so many sizes and color choices that hostas can never get boring!

Long-lived and generally trouble-free (except for slugs and deer), hostas thrive in Zones 3 to 8 or 9, in sites with light all-day shade or morning sun and afternoon shade. You can find a place for them even if your yard is sunny, though: Site them on the north or east side of a taller perennial or shrub that will shield them from the most intense sun. Ample moisture helps hostas tolerate more sun; in full shade, they can adapt to rather dry soil. August lily (*H. plantaginea*) actually does best with sun because it needs more energy to produce the large, sweetly fragrant flowers that it is known for. Hostas with solid yellow or yellow-variegated leaves also tend to look best with a few hours of direct sun each day, while those with deep green, blue, or white-variegated leaves are good choices for shadier sites.

Keep in mind that some hostas produce their trumpet- or funnel-shaped flowers on stems barely taller than their leaves, while others hold them up high. When you're checking the tag or catalog description for a hosta you're considering, make sure it's clear whether the given height refers to the leaves or the flowers.

Color Considerations

For the most part, you'll be focusing on foliage, rather than flowers, when it comes to planning hosta combinations. The basic color range includes green, yellow, and blue, but there's lots of variety within those colors, plus combinations of edging, centering, and striping with those colors, as well as with white and cream.

Besides varying from cultivar to cultivar, the appearance of hosta base colors and markings varies depending on the age of the leaves and the amount of light they get. Yellows may darken to green or pale to cream or white, for instance, and greens may lighten to chartreuse, yellow, or almost white. As you gain experience with the way particular hostas perform in your garden, you can tweak your combinations to take advantage of these variations. But for the most part, you'll get pleasing pairings by choosing companions based on how the hostas look in spring to early summer.

Lush and lovely greens. Solid green hostas are particularly useful as calming complements to perennials with showy white, cream,

Bloom Buddies
Marvelous Matches for flowering Combos

Here's a sampling of flowering perennials that make interesting partners for leafy hostas and that thrive in the partial shade and average to moist but well-drained soil that hostas enjoy.

Astilbes (*Astilbe*)

Bergenias (*Bergenia*)

Corydalis (*Corydalis*)

Daylilies (*Hemerocallis*)

Epimediums (*Epimedium*)

Foamflowers (*Tiarella*)

Foamy bells (× *Heucherella*)

Hardy geraniums (*Geranium*)

Hellebores (*Helleborus*)

Irises (*Iris*)

Lilies (*Lilium*)

Meadow rues (*Thalictrum*)

Meadowsweet (*Filipendula ulmaria*)

Pulmonarias (*Pulmonaria*)

Rodgersias (*Rodgersia*)

Solomon's plume (*Smilacina racemosa*)

Solomon's seals (*Polygonatum*)

Spiderworts (*Tradescantia*)

Spotted deadnettle (*Lamium maculatum*)

or yellow leaf markings, such as 'Evergold' Japanese sedge (*Carex oshimensis*), 'Stairway to Heaven' creeping Jacob's ladder (*Polemonium reptans*), or variegated Solomon's seal (*Polygonatum odoratum* 'Variegatum'). Or use green hostas as contrasting companions for silver-leaved perennials, such as 'Looking Glass' Siberian bugloss (*Brunnera macrophylla*) and 'Silver Shimmers' pulmonaria (*Pulmonaria*), or bright yellow foliage, like that of 'Citronelle' heuchera (*Heuchera*) and Bowles' golden sedge (*C. elata* 'Aurea').

Cool blues. 'Blue Cadet', 'Halcyon', and other "blue" hostas have green leaves with a waxy coating that gives them a power blue to gray appearance. Their color is best in late spring to early or midsummer, turning more greenish toward the end of the growing season. They make lovely partners for pastels, such as peachy-leaved 'Caramel' heuchera, purple-blue or pink-flowered hardy geraniums (*Geranium*), and the butter-colored bells of yellow or straw foxgloves (*Digitalis grandiflora* and *D. lutea*). Blue hostas are exquisite with white-flowered perennials, such as 'Deutschland' astilbe (*Astilbe*); silver and gray leaves, like those of 'White Nancy' spotted deadnettle (*Lamium maculatum*); and bright yellow foliage, like that of golden meadowsweet (*Filipendula ulmaria* 'Aurea').

Sunny yellows. 'August Moon', 'Sun Power', 'Zounds', and other hostas with solid yellow leaves are so eye-catching that they tend to be the stars of any combination. Create a high-impact effect by partnering them with bright blooms and leaves, such as red-and-yellow wild columbine (*Aquilegia canadensis*) or magenta pink 'Bevan's Variety' bigroot geranium (*Geranium macrorrhizum*). Or try them with dark green or deep purple foliage companions, such as black mondo grass (*Ophiopogon planiscapus* 'Nigrescens') or 'Black Scallop' common ajuga

Hosta 'Blue Cadet' with *Iris pallida* 'Variegata', *Geranium maculatum* 'Espresso', and *Cornus sericea* 'Sunshine' *(above)*; *Hosta* 'Frances Williams' and *Viola labradorica* *(right)*

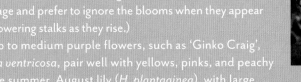

Don't Forget the Flowers

Though best known for their foliage, hostas can also contribute floral interest to your combinations. Most bloom at some point during summer:
Whether that's early, mid-, or late summer varies by species and cultivar, so if
you want to include the blooms in your plans you'll need to do some
research as to the height, color, and timing of the flowers of the selections
you're considering for combinations. (Some gardeners feel that the flowers
detract from the foliage and prefer to ignore the blooms when they appear
or even cut off the flowering stalks as they rise.)

Hostas with deep to medium purple flowers, such as 'Ginko Craig',
'Kabitan', and *Hosta ventricosa*, pair well with yellows, pinks, and peachy
colors in mid- to late summer. August lily (*H. plantaginea*), with large,
fragrant flowers, is one to consider if you'd enjoy some white in your late-summer to early-fall
combinations with other later bloomers, such as Japanese anemones (*Anemone*)—as shown at
right—and turtleheads (*Chelone*). August lily and its hybrids show off well against a background
of deep green or deep purple foliage.

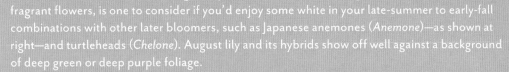

(*Ajuga reptans*). Yellow-leaved hostas are lovely
with blue to purple flowers, too—think of bellflowers (*Campanula*) or hardy geraniums, for
instance—as well as whites. They also do a great
job echoing the yellow centers of daisy-form
flowers, like those of blue and white wood
asters (*Aster cordifolius* and *A. divaricatus*).

Magical multicolors. Many hosta cultivars
have two or more colors in each leaf: edgings,
centers, and streaks or other subtle to striking
markings in shades of green, yellow, cream,
or white on the main green, blue, or yellow
leaf color.

Those with relatively restrained white
markings, such as 'Francee', pair particularly
well with white-flowered co-stars, while those
with lots of white, such as 'Fire and Ice' and
'Undulata Univittata', tend to look best close to
solid green or blue leaves, so there's a bit of

space between their attention-grabbing foliage
and any flowering companions.

Cream- and yellow-variegated hostas are
quite showy, and they, too, do a wonderful job
of echoing flowering and foliage companions in
white, cream, or yellow: Consider cream-and-
blue 'Blue Ivory' hosta with 'Camelot Cream'
common foxglove (*Digitalis purpurea*), for
instance, or yellow–and–blue-green 'Frances
Williams' hosta with the chartreuse flowers
of lady's mantle (*Alchemilla mollis*). Cream- and
yellow-variegated hostas can also combine
comfortably with blues, purples, pinks, and
peach-colored blooms and leaves.

Shapes and Textures

Besides their lovely leaf colors and flowers, hostas contribute distinctive forms and textures to

your combinations—so distinctive, in fact, that you'll mostly want to find contrasts for them.

The plants themselves usually have a broadly mounded habit, but some, such as 'Krossa Regal' and 'Regal Splendor', are distinctly vase shaped: narrow at the base, arching out to a wide top. The mounded forms contrast with both carpeting and strongly upright plants; the vase-shaped forms work well with those, too, and with other mounded forms.

The individual leaves of hostas offer interesting shapes. While some smaller cultivars, such as 'Dragon Tails' and 'The Razor's Edge', have long, narrow leaves that make them look more like sedges (*Carex*) than hostas, most cultivars have lance- to heart-shaped, oval, or rounded foliage. These broad shapes contrast nicely with slender leaves, like those of daylilies (*Hemerocallis*) and sedges, as well as small, lobed, or lacy foliage.

Hosta 'Blue Hawaii' and 'Warwick Comet' with *Adiantum*

Hostas generally have an overall bold texture, making them a great choice for contrast with the many fine- and medium-textured flowering and foliage perennials: Think of spiky-leaved irises and spiky-flowered foamflowers (*Tiarella*); the multileaflet leaves of bugbanes (*Cimicifuga*); the finely cut foliage of fringed and Western bleeding hearts (*Dicentra eximia* and *D. formosa*) and ferns; the small flowers of hardy geraniums, masterworts (*Astrantia*), and toad lilies (*Tricyrtis*); and the plumy blooms of astilbes (*Astilbe*) and goatsbeards (*Aruncus*).

As far as the flowers go, you can repeat their shapes with other funnel- or trumpet-shaped blooms, such as those of daylilies or true lilies (*Lilium*), or you can contrast them with saucer-shaped, cupped, clustered, daisy-form, spiky, or plumy flowers.

Seasonal Features

Hostas start sprouting when the weather is still cool, but their leaves are very sensitive to below-freezing temperatures in both spring and fall. In between, they're beautiful foliage features in beds and borders throughout the frost-free season, and their flowers may add interest in summer and early fall.

Toward the end of the growing season, cooling temperatures can cause the leaves to turn a pale yellow to rich golden color if they don't get nipped by frost first. The change is hard to predict, but when it happens, the color is a lovely addition to the reds, oranges, golds, and purples of epimediums (*Epimedium*), foamflowers, and hardy geraniums, as well as other fall-colored perennials and shrubs.

Hosta 'Emerald Tiara' and *Primula sieboldii*

Exploring More Options: Partners beyond Perennials

There's a fair bit of empty space around hostas in spring, but there's no need to look at bare soil: Use the space closest to the base of each clump for early bulbs, such as daffodils, grape hyacinths (*Muscari*), and snowdrops (*Galanthus*). Eight to 12 inches out from the hosta crown, plant bulbs that bloom in mid- to late spring, such as tulips and summer snowflake (*Leucojum aestivum*). And 12 to 18 inches out, use late-spring and summer bloomers: camassias (*Camassia*), true lilies (*Lilium*), surprise lilies (*Lycoris*), and tall alliums (*Allium*). The hostas do a great job hiding the declining foliage of early bulbs, then they cover and support the lower stems of later bloomers.

Special Effects

Single clumps or small groups of hostas work well as accents or fillers in beds and borders, presenting endless opportunities for eye-catching perennial combinations. These versatile plants are also very useful in some specialized settings.

Asian-style gardens. Native to China, Japan, and Korea, hostas look right at home in Japanese or Zen gardens. Stick with the solid greens and blues or very subtly variegated species and hybrids, and concentrate on combinations based on shapes and textures, rather than contrasting colors. Epimediums, ferns, hellebores (*Helleborus*), irises, and mosses look perfectly at home with hostas in this sort of soothing setting.

Covering the ground. Larger groupings of hostas can serve as excellent growing-season groundcovers around shrubs and under trees. Use mostly green- and blue-leaved hostas with a few solid yellows or variegates for variety. Or mix the hostas with multiplant drifts of other sturdy, space-filling perennials, such as ajugas (*Ajuga*), bigroot geranium (*Geranium macrorrhizum*), golden creeping Jenny (*Lysimachia nummularia* 'Aurea'), Lenten roses (*Helleborus* ×

hybridus), ostrich fern (*Matteuccia struthiopteris*), and sweet woodruff (*Galium odoratum*).

Hosta 'Brother Stefan' and *Athyrium niponicum* var. *pictum*

Iris
endless possibilities

*Iris 'Raspberry Blush' and
Gypsophila repens 'Rosea'*

Iris sibirica 'Caesar's Brother'
and *Spiraea thunbergii* 'Ogon'
(Mellow Yellow)

A Perfect Match

One of my all-time favorite irises is 'Gerald Darby'. It's a selection of *Iris × robusta*, which is a hybrid of two North American species: *I. versicolor* and *I. virginica*. Its graceful, purple-blue flowers are charming, and the dark stems are interesting, too, but its best feature is the rich purple blush on the young leaves. The color is usually gone by early summer, but through spring, the showy foliage makes a fantastic partner for early bloomers, such as white 'Thalia' daffodils.

Among the most well-known irises are the Bearded Hybrids, derived from German iris or common flag (*Iris germanica*). They're available in a rainbow of flower colors and a wide range of heights—from Miniature Dwarf Bearded, to 8 inches in bloom, up to Tall Bearded types, which can reach 3 to 4 feet in bloom— with big, bold blooms that include a fuzzy center strip (the beard) on each lower petal. Bearded irises are usually hardy in Zones 3 to 10. Sweet or Dalmatian iris (*I. pallida*), for Zones 4 to 8 or 9, has a similar flower form but only in a purple-blue color; it blooms on stems 2 to 3 feet tall.

Siberian iris (*I. sibirica*) and its hybrids, for Zones 4 to 9, usually reach 2 to 3 feet in foliage and flower. Shades of blue to purple, yellow, and white are the most common flower colors. Their green leaves are long and slender: more grasslike than those of the bearded and sweet irises. Their flowers tend to look a bit more refined, too.

Bloom Buddies
Marvelous Matches for Flowering Combos

Here's a sampling of suggested companions for each of the most common kinds of irises, based on their bloom times and growing conditions.

Partners for Bearded Hybrids or sweet iris (*Iris pallida*) in full sun and average to dry soil:

Baptisias (*Baptisia*)

Catmints (*Nepeta*)

Dianthus (*Dianthus*)

Euphorbias (*Euphorbia*)

Mulleins (*Verbascum*)

Oriental poppy (*Papaver orientale*)

Partners for Bearded Hybrids, sweet iris, or Siberian irises (*I. sibirica*) in full sun to light shade and average to somewhat moist, well-drained soil:

Bellflowers (*Campanula*)

Bluestars (*Amsonia*)

Columbines (*Aquilegia*)

Delphiniums (*Delphinium*)

Foxgloves (*Digitalis*)

Hardy geraniums (*Geranium*)

Lady's mantle (*Alchemilla mollis*)

Lupines (*Lupinus*)

Peonies (*Paeonia*)

Perennial salvias (*Salvia*)

Speedwells (*Veronica*)

Partners for Japanese iris (*I. ensata*) in full sun to light shade and moist but well-drained soil:

Astilbes (*Astilbe*)

Bee balms (*Monarda*)

Daylilies (*Hemerocallis*)

Globeflowers (*Trollius*)

Shasta daisy (*Leucanthemum × superbum*)

Swamp milkweed (*Asclepias incarnata*)

Japanese iris (*I. ensata*, also sold as *I. kaempferi*) blooms a bit later than the Siberians, with large, broad flowers in shades of blue, purple, pink, and white on 2- to 4-foot stems. Japanese iris is recommended for Zones 4 to 9.

Color Considerations

Oh, the endless possibilities for making glorious color combinations with irises! While some flower in a single, solid hue, most include at least one other color: darker or lighter veining or edging, for instance, or white and/or yellow toward the center, or different-colored petals in the same bloom. Choosing companions that repeat these secondary colors is an easy way to make eye-catching pairings. Below are some other ideas to keep in mind when working with irises in color combinations.

Based on blues. As with lots of other "blue" flowers, irises tend to be more on the purple-blue side, with an infinite range of lighter tints and darker shades. Many are blue enough to satisfy folks who appreciate that hue, though,

Iris ensata and *Stachys officinalis (above)*; *Iris* 'Flavescens'
and *Lysimachia punctata* 'Alexander' *(right)*

and their bloom times overlap with many
other beautiful flowers in the same color
range, so late spring to early summer is an ideal
time to indulge in blue-based combinations or
an entire blue border.

Blues can be hard to see from a distance,
especially if they're against a dark fence or
deep green shrubs, so it's a good idea to keep
them near your house or along a walkway,
where you can admire them up close. Consider
adding a touch of white, too, in the form of
white flowers or white-variegated or bright
silver leaves, for a bit of variety. Tucking in just
a few yellow flowers and chartreuse or yellow-
variegated foliage partners among the blues
can serve the same purpose.

Working with white. Irises offer some of
the most pristine whites you can find in the
world of flowers, making them invaluable for
visual impact in white-based groupings and gardens. Besides white flowers, consider partners

with white-variegated, silvery, gray, or blue
foliage. A planting like this would look particularly striking in a lightly shaded spot or against
a dark-colored background.

Pretty in pastels. There are so many options
here—from near-whites with just the slightest
touch of color to pale pinks, peachy oranges, buttery yellows, baby blues, and soft lavenders—
and they all look lovely together. Pastel color
schemes work particularly well with the mid- to
late-spring-flowering irises, because their delicate tints tend to hold up best when the weather
is still cool and the sun isn't too strong. When
you're putting together a perennial border based
on pale pastel colors, think about including some
irises or companions with slightly richer shades
(such as a few medium pinks, yellows, or lavenders), and perhaps some purple foliage, to add a
little intensity to the scene.

Iris ensata 'Variegata' with *Physostegia virginiana* 'Vivid' and *Lobelia* × *speciosa* 'Vedrariensis' *(left)*; *Iris pallida* 'Variegata' and *Alchemilla mollis (above)*

Think pink. A whole bed or border based on pink? Definitely! It's almost *too* easy with the many tints and shades available among bearded irises and the other pale pink to magenta perennials that bloom around the same time, such as hardy geraniums (*Geranium*) and peonies. Keep the look light with silver- and gray-leaved companions or add intensity with some dark-foliage partners, such as Fine Wine weigela (*Weigela florida* 'Bramwell').

Other companionable colors. Yellows are most often associated with late-summer gardens, but you can enjoy the same sunny cheerfulness earlier in the growing season with the pale to intense yellows available in the bearded and Siberian irises. Combine them with other yellows and white; with warm reds and oranges; or with pastel blues and pinks. If you prefer things more on the moody side, check out some of the practically black bearded irises,

such as 'Before the Storm' and 'Superstition'. Match them with equally dark partners, such as black mondo grass (*Ophiopogon planiscapus* 'Nigrescens') and 'Obsidian' heuchera (*Heuchera*), or contrast them with silver foliage and white flowers.

Look to the leaves. Some irises offer intriguing foliage colors that you can use to repeat or harmonize with the primary or secondary colors of blooming companions. Many bearded irises have a blue or gray cast to their leaves, particularly in spring to midsummer, and sweet iris foliage is especially good as a blue-green accent among green and silver leaves or pastel flowers. Sweet iris also offers two outstanding foliage selections: variegated sweet iris (*I. pallida* 'Variegata'), with creamy yellow and blue-green striping, and 'Argentea Variegata' sweet iris, with ivory white and blue-green striping. Variegated Japanese iris

(*I. ensata* 'Variegata') also has vividly white-striped leaves.

Shapes and Textures

The blooms of most irises tend to be on the big and bold side, holding their own with other in-your-face flowers, such as those of giant onion (*Allium giganteum*) and peonies. For contrast, combine them with partners that have small, airy, or spiky blooms, such as catmints (*Nepeta*).

The leaves of irises may be slender and grasslike or wider and swordlike—ideal for repeating the shapes and textures of ornamental grasses and other spiky plants, such as daylilies (*Hemerocallis*), phormiums (*Phormium*), and yuccas (*Yucca*). For contrast, consider bedmates with foliage that is broad, like that of hostas; rounded to oblong, like that of upright sedums (*Sedum*); fine, like that of perennial candytuft (*Iberis sempervirens*); or ferny, like that of astilbes (*Astilbe*). Perennials with rounded to mounded forms, like hostas and peonies, are also very useful for adding contrast to irises.

Seasonal Features

Get a jump on the iris season by pairing some of the Miniature Dwarf Bearded and Standard Dwarf Bearded hybrids with other spring bulbs and perennials and with low-growing groundcovers, such as creeping sedums, which will help to keep spring rains from splashing mud onto the beautiful iris blooms. Late spring to early summer is prime iris time for most areas (make that early into late spring for those of you in the South), followed by Japanese iris into midsummer.

"Reblooming" bearded irises, such as white 'Immortality', blue-and-white 'Clarence', pink 'Pink Attraction', and bright yellow 'Pure as Gold', may surprise you with fresh flowers in late summer and fall, especially if the soil is relatively fertile and rainfall has been regular.

Variegated irises remain showy well into autumn, and Siberian iris leaves turn shades of yellow as temperatures cool, looking lovely with rich pink and purple asters and other fall-colored perennials and shrubs.

Spread the Wealth

Most irises bloom for only a few weeks, and the start and duration of the flowering period for any given iris can vary by a week or more from year to year, depending on the weather conditions. That means that it's possible for an iris and its companion to perfectly complement each other one year and miss each other completely the next.

To increase your chances of enjoying a splendid show, include more than one iris cultivar in a bed or border, if you have the space. Instead of three 'White Swirl' Siberian iris (*Iris sibirica*), for instance, consider one 'White Swirl', one 'Fourfold White', and one 'Gull's Wing'. Take full advantage of partners with colored foliage in your iris bloom combinations, too, so you'll be guaranteed some pretty pairings even if the various flower-based groupings don't exactly coincide.

Iris pallida 'Argentea Variegata' with *Salvia nemorosa* 'Caradonna', *Salvia argentea*, and *Geranium* 'Brookside' *(top)*; *Iris sibirica* 'Super Ego' and *Rosa* 'Radrazz' (Knock Out) *(bottom)*

Special Effects

While irises can fit into pretty much any site or garden style, there are a few places where they're particularly worth considering.

Cottage gardens. It's hard to imagine the blowsy beauty of a classic cottage-style planting without at least a few irises—especially the Bearded Hybrids and Siberians. Complete the theme with other traditional cottage-garden perennials, including dianthus (*Dianthus*), lady's mantle (*Alchemilla mollis*), lupines (*Lupinus*), peonies, and perennial salvias (*Salvia*).

Rain gardens. Slightly sunken and planted with tough perennials, rain gardens are designed to capture water from gutter downspouts, giving it a chance to soak in and rejoin the natural groundwater instead of running off into the sewer system. Rain-garden plants need to be able to tolerate dry periods as well as occasionally saturated soil. Japanese irises are well suited to the lowest parts of these gardens, where the soil tends to stay moist the longest, while Siberians can work well closer to the edge. Hardy hibiscus (*Hibiscus*), Joe-Pye weeds (*Eupatorium*), perennial lobelias (*Lobelia*), and cinnamon and royal ferns (*Osmunda cinnamomea* and *O. regalis*) are just a few compatible companions for irises in rain gardens.

Exploring More Options: Partners beyond Perennials

Shrubs and vines can be very useful as background plants for medium-height to tall irises. Some that usually flower during peak iris season include hybrid clematis (*Clematis*), lilacs (*Syringa*), roses, rhododendrons (*Rhododendron*), and viburnums (*Viburnum*). Take advantage of those with colorful foliage, too, to harmonize or contrast with your irises. A few that look particularly pleasing with irises include yellow-leaved spireas (*Spiraea*) and dark-leaved elderberries (*Sambucus nigra*) and weigelas (*Weigela*).

Kniphofia
magnificent accents

Kniphofia uvaria 'Flamenco' and *Allium* 'Lucy Ball'

Kniphofia 'Shining Sceptre' and *Salvia forsskaolii*

A Perfect Match

Torch lilies are so dramatic in both form and color that it can be easy for them to steal all of the attention when they're in bloom. That's not necessarily a bad thing: They make great seasonal accents. But I think they look fantastic paired with equally striking spikes—particularly in shades of purple-blue, like those of 'Blue Boa' or 'Purple Haze' agastache (*Agastache*).

Looking to add some drama to your perennial pairings? You can't miss with the bold spikes of torch lilies (*Kniphofia*)! Also known as poker plants, red-hot pokers, and tritomas, these distinctive beauties produce rosettes of slender, spiky leaves and stout stems topped in clusters of small, tubular blooms. There are several species of these African natives and many more hybrids, varying in height and hardiness, though most can grow in Zones 5 or 6 to 9.

Color Considerations

Torch lilies typically have two or three colors in each spike: deepest on the buds and palest on the oldest blossoms. The classic progression is from red to orange to yellow, but you can find other variations, as well as selections that are mostly one color, such as coral 'Red Rocket' or bright yellow 'Lemon Popsicle'.

Bloom Buddies
Marvelous Matches for Flowering Combos

Torch lilies (*Kniphofia*) grow in full sun to light shade. They appreciate average to moist but well-drained soil in summer but prefer to be on the dry side in winter. Below are some compatible perennials that usually overlap or coincide with their peak bloom period.

Agastaches (*Agastache*)

Blanket flowers (*Gaillardia*)

Blazing stars (*Liatris*)

Catmints (*Nepeta*)

Coreopsis (*Coreopsis*)

Daylilies (*Hemerocallis*)

Echinaceas (*Echinacea*)

Globe thistles (*Echinops*)

Goldenrods (*Solidago*)

Heleniums (*Helenium*)

Perennial lobelias (*Lobelia*)

Perennial salvias (*Salvia*)

Rudbeckias (*Rudbeckia*)

Russian sages (*Perovskia*)

Sea hollies (*Eryngium*)

Yarrows (*Achillea*)

All but the palest torch lilies are stunning with other reds, oranges, and yellows in "hot" combinations. Stick with shades of any one color—bright orange 'Mango Popsicle' torch lily with orange 'Julia' echinacea (*Echinacea*), for example, or orange-red 'Fire Glow' torch lily with 'Desert Coral' coreopsis (*Coreopsis*). Or build a whole border around torch lilies paired with other perennials in warm reds, oranges, and yellows, along with dark flowers and leaves, like those of 'Jungle Beauty' daylily (*Hemerocallis*) and 'Mocha' heuchera (*Heuchera*).

Torch lilies look terrific with blue- to purple-flowered partners: Try bright yellow 'Lemon Popsicle' torch lily with rich purple-blue 'Caradonna' perennial salvia (*Salvia nemorosa*), for instance, or pale yellow 'Percy's Pride' torch lily with lighter purple-blue 'Walker's Low' catmint (*Nepeta*). Ivory, pale yellow, peachy, and soft coral torch lilies also look lovely with other perennials with flowers or foliage in similar pastel hues, as well as with soft pinks and whites.

Shapes and Textures

Torch lilies form broad, dense mounds of slender, upright to arching leaves. For contrast, consider carpeting or trailing companions or those that form looser, airier clumps, such as blanket flowers (*Gaillardia*) or coreopsis (*Coreopsis*).

Once torch lilies begin to bloom, the leafless, upright stems and elongated flower clusters have a very vertical effect. Repeat their form with other spiky-flowered perennials, such as agastaches (*Agastache*) or blazing stars (*Liatris*), or add contrast with other flower forms, such as the broad clusters of yarrows (*Achillea*); daisy-form flowers, like those of echinaceas and rudbeckias (*Rudbeckia*); and airy sprays or plumes, like those of goldenrods (*Solidago*) or Russian sages (*Perovskia*).

Seasonal Features

In mild areas, the earliest torch lilies may begin in late spring; elsewhere, they may not start until early to midsummer. Many keep going for 2 or 3 months, especially if you clip off the finished bloom stems close to the base.

Lamium
for flowers and foliage

Lamium maculatum 'White Nancy' and Hakonechloa macra 'Aureola'

Lamium maculatum 'Anne Greenaway' and Heuchera 'Lime Marmalade'

A Perfect Match

Of all the various flower and foliage color options, my favorite of the spotted deadnettles is the classic 'White Nancy'. Its crisp white blooms and strongly silver leaves are invaluable for sprucing up shady spaces around plain green partners, such as ferns, hostas, Siberian bugloss (*Brunnera macrophylla*), and wild gingers (*Asarum*).

Spotted deadnettle (*Lamium maculatum*) does double duty in shady gardens with small but abundant pink or white blooms in spring to early summer and silver-marked green, yellow, or green-and-yellow leaves for the rest of the year. It grows in spreading, 6- to 8-inch-tall carpets and is generally hardy in Zones 3 or 4 to 8.

Color Considerations

Match the blooms of your chosen cultivar with companions in similar colors: white-flowered 'White Nancy' spotted deadnettle with foamflowers (*Tiarella*) and Solomon's seals (*Polygonatum*), for instance, or soft pink 'Cosmopolitan' or 'Pink Chablis' with fringed bleeding heart (*Dicentra eximia*). Or expand your white or pink palette to include springy yellows, like those of daffodils and lady's mantle (*Alchemilla mollis*), and blues, like those of forget-me-nots

(*Myosotis*), grape hyacinths (*Muscari*), and Jacob's ladders (*Polemonium*).

All of the spotted deadnettles have at least a bit of bright silver to silvery white in their leaves, so you can use them to echo silvery-leaved partners, such as pulmonarias (*Pulmonaria*). Similarly, 'Anne Greenaway', 'Beedham's White', Golden Anniversary ('Dellam'), and other spotted deadnettles with yellow or yellow-and-green leaves are ideal for repeating the effect of other bright yellow–leaved perennials, such as 'Sun Power' hosta. Be cautious about using silver-and-green or yellow-and-green spotted deadnettles right next to variegated companions, though, because the effect can be somewhat chaotic.

For a dramatic contrast, pair any of the spotted deadnettles with rich green leaves, like those of bergenias (*Bergenia*); with deep purples to near-blacks, like those of black mondo grass (*Ophiopogon planiscapus* 'Nigrescens'); or with reds, like those of 'Fire Alarm' heuchera (*Heuchera*).

Shapes and Textures

The low, spreading habit of spotted deadnettles makes them superb for filling around larger mounded or upright partners, such as astilbes (*Astilbe*), ferns, and toad lilies (*Tricyrtis*). Or combine them with other spreading perennials, such as ajugas (*Ajuga*) and 'Ice Dance' sedge (*Carex*), for a beautiful mixed groundcover under hydrangeas (*Hydrangea*) and other shrubs.

Spotted deadnettle leaves are quite small, so they benefit from contrast with larger, broader leaves, like those of heucheras, hostas, hybrid hellebores (*Helleborus* × *hybridus*), and Siberian bugloss (*Brunnera macrophylla*).

Seasonal Features

The main bloom period for spotted deadnettle is mid- or late spring to early summer, but the plants may continue to produce some flowers through the rest of the growing season, particularly in cooler weather. The foliage is lovely as soon as it sprouts, and it remains showy through fall; in milder parts of the growing range, the plants may remain attractive through much or even all of winter.

Lavandula

not just for herb gardens

Lavandula × intermedia 'Provence'
and *Echinacea purpurea* 'White Swan'

Lavandula angustifolia 'Blue Cushion'
and *Alchemilla mollis*

A Perfect Match

I love the look of lavenders with roses, lady's mantle (*Alchemilla mollis*), and other traditional cottage-garden companions. But in my own garden, I have the best luck growing it with other plants that do well in drier-soil spots, such as artemisias (*Artemisia*) and thymes (*Thymus*). My current favorite partner for purple-flowered lavenders is the wispy, golden blond flower and seed heads of Mexican feather grass (*Stipa tenuissima*).

Lavenders (*Lavandula*) are delightfully fragrant, of course, but when it comes to combinations, you'll focus on their spiky flowers and slender foliage. Height can range from 1 to 3 feet in flower, depending on the selection. Two of the hardiest kinds are English or common lavender (*L. angustifolia*) and hybrid *L. × intermedia*, sometimes referred to as lavandin. Both are generally recommended for Zones 5 to 8 or 9, though lavandin tends to be more tolerant of hot and humid conditions.

Color Considerations

The gray to silvery cast of their leaves makes lavenders excellent for repeating the effect of other gray-greens, grays, and silvers, like those of artemisias (*Artemisia*). But it's the flowers—particularly the tints and shades of blue to purple—that folks love most about lavenders. They're a natural choice for sunny borders based on

with a variety of pinks, from soft 'Bath's Pink' dianthus (*Dianthus*) to magenta rose campion (*Lychnis coronaria*). White-flowered companions, such as gaura (*Gaura lindheimeri*) and Shasta daisy (*Leucanthemum × superbum*), are also terrific with any color of lavender.

Shapes and Textures

Lavenders are mostly mounded in form, developing a looser look once they begin to bloom. Set them behind carpeting, trailing, or low-mounded partners, such as creeping sedums (*Sedum*) and thymes (*Thymus*). The short, narrow leaves give the plants a fine texture that benefits from some contrast with broader foliage, like that of bearded irises or 'Big Ears' lamb's ears (*Stachys byzantina*).

Spiky in bloom, lavenders add welcome variety among the many daisy-form flowers of summer. They also add contrast to combinations that feature broad bloom clusters, like those of upright sedums and yarrows (*Achillea*), or small, rounded flowers, like those of dianthus (*Dianthus*) and hardy geraniums (*Geranium*). Lavenders look right at home with ornamental grasses, too.

Seasonal Features

English lavenders bloom first—usually in mid- to late spring in warmer climates and late spring to early summer in cooler areas—with lavandin selections joining in several weeks later. Flowering continues through much or all of summer, depending on the cultivar. The foliage typically sticks around through winter; however, it may drop or be damaged in exposed sites, especially in colder regions.

those colors, with partners such as globe thistles (*Eryngium*) and sea hollies (*Echinops*). They also work well with a wide range of yellows, and even with bright to peachy oranges, like those of butterfly weed (*Asclepias tuberosa*) or 'Terracotta' yarrow (*Achillea*).

The blue-purple lavenders—and the white- and pink-flowered ones, as well—are charming

Leucanthemum
classic summer daisies

Leucanthemum × *superbum* 'Goldfinch' and *Coreopsis verticillata* 'Moonbeam'

Leucanthemum × *superbum* 'Becky' and *Lilium* 'Lavon'

A Perfect Match

The brilliant white petals of 'Becky' Shasta daisy are so bold that I tend to stick with "safe" partners, such as blue-purple flowers or white-variegated leaves. But now that I've seen it paired with the fiery red flowers of 'Jacob Cline' bee balm (*Monarda*), I'm looking forward to finding a place for that traffic-stopping combo in my own garden!

The large, single, semidouble, or double blooms of Shasta daisy (*Leucanthemum* × *superbum*) are a can't-miss addition to cheery summer combinations. Though your color choices are limited to white and yellow with glossy, deep green leaves, there's a variety of heights: from 'Tinkerbelle', at about 1 foot, to 'Amelia' and Becky', which are usually in the 3- to 4-foot range. Hardiness can vary, too, but most Shasta daisy selections are recommended for Zones 4 to 8.

Color Considerations

Most Shastas have brilliant white blooms with bright yellow centers. They're stunning in a white border or moon garden with other white-flowered perennials. White Shasta daisies are also lovely with white-variegated partners, such as 'Morning Light' miscanthus (*Miscanthus sinensis*) and variegated

Bloom Buddies
Marvelous Matches for Flowering Combos

Shasta daisy (*Leucanthemum × superbum*) selections generally perform best with full sun and average to moist but well-drained soil, though they can adapt to light shade, especially in hot-summer areas. Below is a sampling of perennial partners that will complement them during the usual early- to midsummer peak bloom time.

Bee balms (*Monarda*)

Bellflowers (*Campanula*)

Blazing stars (*Liatris*)

Catmints (*Nepeta*)

Coreopsis (*Coreopsis*)

Daylilies (*Hemerocallis*)

Delphiniums (*Delphinium*)

Echinaceas (*Echinacea*)

Perennial salvias (*Salvia*)

Rudbeckias (*Rudbeckia*)

Russian sages (*Perovskia*)

Speedwells (*Veronica*)

Spiderworts (*Tradescantia*)

Summer phlox (*Phlox paniculata*)

Yarrows (*Achillea*)

Japanese iris (*Iris ensata* 'Variegata'); silvers and grays, like those of 'Big Ears' lamb's ears (*Stachys byzantina*) and 'Powis Castle' artemisia (*Artemisia*); and cool blue leaves, like those of 'Dewey Blue' bitter panic grass (*Panicum amarum*) and 'Elijah Blue' blue fescue (*Festuca glauca*).

For a simple but memorable color echo, combine your chosen Shastas with perennials that have yellow flowers or solid yellow or yellow-variegated foliage to pick up their yellow bloom centers.

Along with the many white Shasta daisies, there are some with yellow petals that age to paler yellow or creamy white, such as 'Banana Cream' and 'Goldfinch'. Both the whites and the yellows are gorgeous with blues and purples, like those of 'Blue Fortune' anise hyssop (*Agastache*) or 'Blue Paradise' summer phlox (*Phlox paniculata*), and with soft to rosy pinks, like those of purple coneflowers (*Echinacea purpurea*).

Shapes and Textures

Shasta daisies have an upright to broad-mounded habit in bloom. For contrast, use them behind lower mounded, carpeting, or trailing plants, such as coreopsis (*Coreopsis*) and hardy geraniums (*Geranium*), and next to or behind more vertical companions, such as delphiniums (*Delphinium*) and speedwells (*Veronica*).

The large flowers of Shasta daisies are excellent for repeating the form of other summer daisies. For variety, consider spiky companions, too, such as perennial salvias (*Salvia*), and partners with loose bloom clusters, such as catmints (*Nepeta*). Ornamental grasses are excellent companions for both the single-flowered Shastas and those with fluffy or frilly forms, like 'Aglaia' and 'Real Glory'.

Seasonal Features

Shasta daisies vary a bit in their bloom times; most, though, start in late spring in southern gardens and early summer elsewhere. Once they begin, they're typically in flower for about 8 weeks, though they may keep going into late summer or even early fall, especially if you keep the finished flowers clipped off.

Liatris
showstopping spikes

Liatris spicata with Rudbeckia fulgida, Perovskia, Echinacea purpurea, and Leucanthemum × superbum

Liatris spicata 'Alba' with Perovskia atriplicifolia

A Perfect Match

Dense blazing star is undeniably eye-catching in any summer combination, but to my mind, it's tough to beat the perfect pairing of its fuzzy pinkish purple spikes with the broad, purplish pink blooms of purple coneflowers (*Echinacea purpurea*): a lovely harmony of color with a dramatic contrast in flower forms.

Also known as gayfeathers, blazing stars (*Liatris*) have straight, upright stems clad in slender, green leaves and are lined at the top with fluffy-looking flower heads. There are several species of these native North American beauties to choose from, ranging in height from about 2 feet to the more usual 4 to 5 feet. All are recommended for Zones 3 to 9.

Color Considerations

Blazing stars bloom mostly in shades of pinkish purple. They're a bit uncomfortable right next to reds and true blue but can look terrific with bright to pastel shades of other colors: from bright orange butterfly weed (*Asclepias tuberosa*) to peachy 'Sienna Sunset' coreopsis (*Coreopsis*), for instance, and golden yellow oxeye (*Heliopsis helianthoides*) to buttery 'Sunshine' Shasta daisy (*Leucanthemum × superbum*). They also make intriguing combinations with other pinkish purple to rosy pink perennials, such as 'Franz Schubert' summer phlox (*Phlox paniculata*) and purple coneflowers (*Echinacea purpurea*).

Both the pinkish purple and the white-flowered blazing stars work well with white-flowered partners, such as baby's breath (*Gypsophila paniculata*) and rattlesnake master (*Eryngium yuccifolium*). White blazing stars make a beautiful match for silvery, white-variegated, or blue foliage, like that of 'Powis Castle' artemisia (*Artemisia*), 'Snow Fairy' bluebeard (*Caryopteris divaricata*), or 'Heavy Metal' switch grass (*Panicum virgatum*).

Shapes and Textures

Very vertical in form, blazing stars make a dramatic contrast for most other plant shapes. Their spikes are a perfect partner for rudbeckias (*Rudbeckia*) and other daisy-form flowers, as well as for large-petaled blooms such as daylilies (*Hemerocallis*) and true lilies (*Lilium*). Or go for companions with broad clusters of tiny blooms, such as Joe-Pye weeds (*Eupatorium*) or upright sedums (*Sedum*). Blazing stars also look right at home among ornamental grasses.

Seasonal Features

Bloom time varies by season and climate. Dense blazing star (*L. spicata*) and prairie blazing star (*L. pycnostachya*) usually bloom in early to midsummer in southern gardens and mid- to late summer elsewhere. For late-summer to early-fall combinations, consider later-blooming species, such as meadow blazing star (*L. ligulistylis*) or rough blazing star (*L. aspera*).

Ligularia
marvelous for moist sites

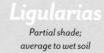

Ligularia dentata 'Othello' and *Athyrium niponicum* var. *pictum*

Ligularia dentata 'Britt-Marie Crawford' and *Hydrangea arborescens*

A Perfect Match

I never had much luck with ligularias until I planted 'Britt-Marie Crawford' bigleaf ligularia. Its leaves stay darker for longer than others I've tried, and it seems more forgiving of dry spells than the spiky-flowered types. This selection is a great match for Japanese painted fern (*Athyrium niponicum* var. *pictum*), echoing the purple stems while contrasting with the silvery gray parts of the fern fronds.

Most perennials aren't big fans of wet soil, but ligularias (*Ligularia*) are happy to call those sites home. They can usually adapt to average moisture levels, too, as long as they get some shade. Two of the best-known options are bigleaf ligularia (*L. dentata*), with rounded foliage and clusters of orangey yellow flowers, and 'The Rocket', sometimes listed under narrow-spiked ligularia (*L. stenocephala*) or Shavalski's ligularia (*L. przewalskii*), with triangular leaves and spikes of yellow flowers. These and related selections are generally recommended for Zones 4 to 8.

Color Considerations

There are lots of options for outstanding foliage combinations with ligularias and shade-loving companions. Echo the deep red to purple leaf stalks and leaf undersides of bigleaf ligularias with

In flower, ligularias pair well with other rich hues, such as vibrant red cardinal flower (*Lobelia cardinalis*) or 'Jacob Cline' bee balm (*Monarda*), orange Mardi Gras helenium (*Helenium* 'Helbro'), or intense purple-blue delphiniums (*Delphinium*).

Shapes and Textures

Ligularias are bold in color and equally bold in size and shape. Standard selections form leafy mounds that easily reach 3 to 4 feet tall and wide (even wider in ideal conditions), with bigleaf ligularia typically about 4 feet in bloom and 'The Rocket' topping out at 5 to 6 feet. They're dramatic as accents among low-growing perennials or at the back of large borders. If you'd like to enjoy their foliage and/or flowers in smaller areas, look for compact cultivars, such as 'Bottle Rocket' or 'Osiris Café Noir'.

The broad leaves of ligularias contrast handsomely with grassy or strappy leaves, like those of irises and sedges (*Carex*), and with lacy leaves, like those of astilbes (*Astilbe*) or ferns. The flowers look great with equally large blooms, like those of daylilies (*Hemerocallis*) or true lilies (*Lilium*).

dark-leaved companions, such as 'Plum Pudding' heuchera (*Heuchera*). To complement the selections that have purple leaf tops, such as delightfully dark 'Britt-Marie Crawford', use partners that have purple-and-green foliage, such as 'Iron Butterfly' foamflower (*Tiarella*) or 'Samobor' mourning widow geranium (*Geranium phaeum*).

Both green- and dark-leaved ligularias can look great with gray to silvery leaves, like those of 'Ghost' fern (*Athyrium*); with bright yellow foliage, like that of 'All Gold' Hakone grass (*Hakone macra*); or with vibrantly variegated leaves, like those of variegated Japanese iris (*Iris ensata* 'Variegata').

Seasonal Features

The leaves of ligularias are attractive through the growing season. The purple-leaved cultivars are at their darkest from spring to midsummer; after that, most turn bronzy green, especially in shade. Peak flowering is usually mid- to late summer, though it may begin earlier in mild climates.

Lilium
fabulous flowers in glorious colors

Lilium 'Lavon' and 'Conca d'Or' with *Phlox paniculata* 'Blue Paradise'

Lilium 'Olina' with *Heliopsis helianthoides* 'Loraine Sunshine', *Veronicastrum virginicum*, and *Miscanthus sinensis* 'Variegatus'

A Perfect Match

Though I was disappointed to find out that 'Landini' Asiatic lily is not the true black that many catalog pictures show, I still enjoy its deliciously dark red that shades to deep burgundy toward the center. It's outstanding in contrast with bright blooms and even better as an echo for dark-leaved partners, such as 'Marooned' coleus (*Solenostemon scutellarioides*) or 'Molten Lava' heuchera (*Heuchera*).

Bulbs have a wonderful way of giving you a lot of flower power without taking up much border space. Early bloomers, such as crocus and daffodils, make great perennial partners for spring; for stunning summer combinations, look to the lovely lilies (*Lilium*). There are many species and even more hybrids to choose from; make your decision based on the height, color, and bloom time you need. Most of the widely available kinds are hardy in Zones 3 or 4 to 8.

Color Considerations

Lilies come in an amazing range of bright to pastel hues—pretty much anything except blues and violets. Some are one solid color; others have two, three, or even more colors in each bloom, giving you additional options for complementary companions. The Asiatic Hybrids, in particular, frequently have deep

Bloom Buddies
Marvelous Matches for Flowering Combos

Lilies (*Lilium*) generally grow well in full sun to partial shade with average to moist but well-drained, compost-enriched soil (ideally on the acidic side). Bloom times also vary, depending on the species or hybrid; below are just some of the many potential flowering partners.

Partners for early to midsummer (with Asiatic, Orienpet, and Trumpet Hybrids, for example):

Agastaches (*Agastache*)

Astilbes (*Astilbe*)

Bee balms (*Monarda*)

Blazing stars (*Liatris*)

Catmints (*Nepeta*)

Coreopsis (*Coreopsis*)

Daylilies (*Hemerocallis*)

Delphiniums (*Delphinium*)

Echinaceas (*Echinacea*)

Meadow rues (*Thalictrum*)

Perennial salvias (*Salvia*)

Rudbeckias (*Rudbeckia*)

Shasta daisy (*Leucanthemum* × *superbum*)

Speedwells (*Veronica*)

Torch lilies (*Kniphofia*)

Partners for late summer to early fall (with Oriental lilies, for example):

Asters (*Aster*)

Bugbanes (*Cimicifuga*)

Chinese astilbe (*Astilbe taquetii* 'Superba')

Echinaceas (*Echinacea*)

Ironweeds (*Vernonia*)

Japanese anemones (*Anemone*)

Japanese burnet (*Sanguisorba tenuifolia*)

Joe-Pye weeds (*Eupatorium*)

Russian sages (*Perovskia*)

Summer phlox (*Phlox paniculata*)

---

purple smudges, speckles, or other markings that you can emphasize with dark-leaved partners. Some other secondary color features to look for include a dark blush on the backs of the petals (especially on the Trumpet and Aurelian Hybrids, such as 'African Queen' and 'Golden Splendor'); bright yellow centers, as on 'Corso' and 'Satisfaction'; and golden yellow markings, as on gold band lily (*L. auratum* var. *platyphyllum*) and 'Legend'.

Concentrated combos. Asiatic lilies, in particular, offer you lots of options for bold colors, including rich red, as on 'Montenegro'; brilliant orange, as on 'Orange County'; and glowing yellow, as on 'Yellow Power'. Concentrate your combinations on one or two of those colors, or combine all of those warm hues in one traffic-stopping border with other hot-colored summer perennials, such as bee balms (*Monarda*), crocosmias (*Crocosmia*), rudbeckias (*Rudbeckia*), and torch lilies (*Kniphofia*). Complement them with intense blues to purples, like those of 'Blue Mirror' Chinese delphinium (*Delphinium grandiflorum*) or 'Caradonna' perennial salvia (*Salvia nemorosa*), or add depth with superdark flowers and leaves, like those of 'Midnight Oil' daylily (*Hemerocallis*) or 'Obsidian' heuchera (*Heuchera*).

Delicate pastels. If you prefer your perennials on the softer side, there are plenty of more delicate tints. Pinks are particularly abundant, from pale 'Elodie' to rosy 'Toronto', as well as creamy to lemony yellows, like those of 'Big Brother' and 'Lesotho', and peachy oranges, including 'Peach Butterflies' and 'Orange Cocotte'. All are lovely with other perennials that have pink, soft yellow, or peach flowers or foliage, and with cool blues and purples, like those of catmints (*Nepeta*) and Russian sages (*Perovskia*). Complete the effect with silver-gray to blue leaves, like those of 'The Blues' little bluestem (*Schizachyrium scoparium*) and many baptisias (*Baptisia*), and with the buff to tan heads of ornamental grasses, such as 'Karley Rose' Oriental fountain grass (*Pennisetum orientale*) and 'Karl Foerster' feather reed grass (*Calamagrostis × acutiflora*).

Elegant whites. Quite a few lilies have some white in their blooms, but those with all-white flowers, such as 'Casa Blanca' and 'Navona', are especially elegant in evening gardens and white borders with Shasta daisy (*Leucanthemum × superbum*) and other snowy-petaled perennials. Enhance the effect with white-lined leaves, like

those of 'Rigoletto' miscanthus (*Miscanthus sinensis*) and variegated Japanese iris (*Iris ensata* 'Variegata'), and with bright silver foliage, like that of 'Powis Castle' artemisia (*Artemisia*). White lilies are also beautiful with pastel-flowered partners.

Shapes and Textures

The straight, upright stems of lilies look great rising through or behind lower mounded or loosely clumping companions, such as Bowman's roots (*Gillenia*), ferns, hardy geraniums (*Geranium*), and hostas. Planting taller lilies among or behind shrub roses, spireas (*Spiraea*), and other small to medium-size shrubs can help to support the stems and minimize the need for staking.

Lilium 'Tom Pouce' with *Astrantia major, Hydrangea quercifolia* 'Little Honey', and *Anthriscus sylvestris* 'Ravenswing' *(left); Lilium* 'Freya' with *Veronica grandis, Symphytum × uplandicum* 'Axminster Gold', and *Juniperus communis* 'Gold Cone' *(above)*

Individual lily blooms can be anywhere from a few inches wide to a foot or more across, depending on the species or hybrid. Balance their bold forms with other large flowers or flower heads in the same border: Some good candidates include daylilies (*Hemerocallis*), echinaceas (*Echinacea*), and garden phlox (*Phlox paniculata*). Spiky flower heads are wonderful for providing visual variety to broad lily blooms, whether you choose plump spikes, like those of blazing stars (*Liatris*) and torch lilies, or slender ones, like those of Culver's roots (*Veronicastrum*) and speedwells (*Veronica*). Or pair them with companions that have a loose, airy, or plumy form, such as gaura (*Gaura lindheimeri*), Russian sages, or tufted hair grass (*Deschampsia cespitosa*).

Seasonal Features

Unlike many hardy bulbs, lily bulbs are available for either spring or fall planting, and you may even find some started in pots in spring, making it easy to incorporate them into combinations without much advance planning. Bloom times vary among the species and hybrids. The Asiatic Hybrids start in early to midsummer, for example, while Aurelian, Orienpet (Oriental-Trumpet), and Trumpet Hybrids generally start in midsummer, and Oriental Hybrids and rubrum lily (*L. speciosum* var. *rubrum*) bloom in late summer to early fall. Regardless of the type, the bloom period usually lasts around 2 to 3 weeks (somewhat longer on well-established clumps).

Lilium 'Orange County' with *Rosa glauca*, *Clematis*, and *Hosta* 'Sun Power' (*above*); *Lilium* 'Black Beauty' with *Eupatorium maculatum* and *Calamagrostis* × *acutiflora* 'Karl Foerster' (*right*)

Lobelia
vertical spikes to catch the eye

Lobelia siphilitica **and** *Rudbeckia fulgida*

Lobelia cardinalis
and *Imperata cylindrica* '**Rubra**'

A Perfect Match

One of my favorite partners for cardinal flower so far is Japanese blood grass (*Imperata cylindrica* 'Rubra') because it provides an intriguing echo of spiky form and red-and-green coloring. Eventually, though, I plan to replace the blood grass with a red-tipped selection of our native switch grass (*Panicum virgatum*), such as short 'Cheyenne Sky' or tall 'Huron Solstice'.

Perennial lobelias (*Lobelia*) are excellent for drawing attention—and butterflies and hummingbirds, as well—to your later-summer combinations. Two of the hardiest species include cardinal flower (*L. cardinalis*), which reaches 3 to 5 feet in bloom, and great blue lobelia (*L. siphilitica*), at 2 to 3 feet tall. These two native North American species can cross with each other and with other species to produce hybrids that are normally sold under the names *L. × gerardii* and *L. × speciosa*. Cardinal flower, great blue lobelia, and their hybrids are generally hardy in Zones 3 to 8.

Color Considerations

Brilliant red cardinal flowers—and many hybrids, too, such as rich purple 'Vedrariensis' perennial lobelia—are top-notch companions for other intense colors. Pair them with flowering

Bloom Buddies
Marvelous Matches for Flowering Combos

Perennial lobelias (*Lobelia*) bloom best in full sun to partial shade (morning sun and afternoon shade, or light all-day shade) with compost-enriched soil that's on the moist side. Here are some compatible companions with bloom times that usually overlap with cardinal flower (*L. cardinalis*), great blue lobelia (*L. siphilitica*), and their hybrids.

Astilbes (*Astilbe*)

Bee balms (*Monarda*)

Culver's roots (*Veronicastrum*)

Daylilies (*Hemerocallis*)

Echinaceas (*Echinacea*)

Eupatoriums (*Eupatorium*)

Fleeceflowers (*Persicaria*)

Ligularias (*Ligularia*)

Lilies (*Lilium*)

Oxeye (*Heliopsis helianthoides*)

Rattlesnake master (*Eryngium yuccifolium*)

Rudbeckias (*Rudbeckia*)

Spiderworts (*Tradescantia*)

Summer phlox (*Phlox paniculata*)

Swamp milkweed (*Asclepias incarnata*)

Torch lilies (*Kniphofia*)

White' dense blazing star (*Liatris spicata*).

Great blue lobelia is a beautiful addition to softer color schemes. It pairs well with pink to peachy-flowered perennials, such as pink turtlehead (*Chelone lyonii*) and 'Peach Magnolia' daylily (*Hemerocallis*), and with a wide range of yellows, too, from soft yellow 'Pineapple Popsicle' torch lily to golden yellow oxeye (*Heliopsis helianthoides*). Blue-and-white is also a marvelous match.

Shapes and Textures

With their very vertical plant habit, the perennial lobelias look great rising between or behind mounded or loosely clumping partners, such as hostas and spiderworts (*Tradescantia*). Their strongly spiky flower form offers an interesting contrast to plumy perennials, such as astilbes (*Astilbe*); to daisy-form flowers, like those of echinaceas (*Echinacea*); and to large, broad blooms, like those of daylilies (*Hemerocallis*) and true lilies (*Lilium*). Their bold effect adds variety to combinations with fine-textured companions, such as ferns or ornamental grasses.

Seasonal Features

Perennial lobelia selections with deep purple leaves, such as 'Black Truffle', are eye-catching as soon as they start growing. For most, though, the show starts a bit later: early to midsummer for cardinal flower and mid- to late summer for great blue lobelia, with the hybrids usually somewhere around midsummer. Once they begin, perennial lobelias continue blooming for about 6 weeks: through much of summer, at least, and possibly into early fall.

partners in clear to golden yellows, like those of ligularias (*Ligularia*) and rudbeckias (*Rudbeckia*), or with clear to rusty orange blooms, like those of 'Mango Popsicle' torch lily (*Kniphofia*) or 'Mardi Gras' helenium (*Helenium*). For a strong contrast, try cardinal flower with white-blooming perennials, such as 'Becky' Shasta daisy (*Leucanthemum* × *superbum*) or 'Floristan

Lychnis
delightfully daring colors

Lychnis
*Full sun to partial shade;
average, well-drained soil*

*Lychnis × arkwrightii 'Vesuvius'
with Carex elata 'Aurea'
and Cryptotaenia japonica f. atropurpurea*

Lychnis coronaria with Stipa tenuissima and Geranium 'Brookside'

A Perfect Match

A large drift of rose campion is traffic stopping in bloom but not much to look at when it finishes flowering. I prefer to scatter the plants through a bed or border, where they can rise out of hardy geraniums (*Geranium*), Mexican feather grass (*Stipa tenuissima*), or other lower companions to provide spots of color when in bloom and then "disappear" when they're past their prime.

Lychnis (*Lychnis*), also commonly called campion, offers some distinctly different options for both flowers and foliage. Two- to 4-foot-tall Maltese or Jerusalem cross (*L. chalcedonica*), for instance, has green leaves and bright red flowers, while 12- to 18-inch-tall Arkwright's campion (*L. × arkwrightii*) commonly has bronzy to purple leaves and vivid orange to orange-red blooms. And then there's rose campion or mullein pink (*L. coronaria*, also known as *Silene coronaria*), with magenta flowers atop 2- to 3-foot-tall stems over fuzzy, silver foliage. All of these are generally hardy in Zones 3 to 9.

Color Considerations

The reds and oranges of Maltese cross and Arkwright's campion are stunning with other saturated colors. Try them with flowering partners in brilliant yellow, like that of 'Hyperion' daylily

speedwell (*Veronica prostrata*); orangey- to red-leaved heucheras (*Heuchera*); and deep purples, like those of 'Bishop of Llandaff' dahlia or 'Black Truffle' cardinal flower (*Lobelia cardinalis*).

Rose campion's usual magenta color, as well as the variant with pink-and-white blossoms (sold as 'Angel's Blush' or var. *oculata*), can be pleasing additions to combinations featuring other pink perennials, such as 'Red Fox' spike speedwell (*Veronica spicata*). Magenta rose campion makes a striking echo for pink-and-white flowers, too, like those of 'Lollypop' lily (*Lilium*). Magenta, pink-and-white, and pure white ('Alba') rose campion all show up well among purples and blues, like those of lavenders (*Lavandula*) and sea hollies (*Eryngium*). The white form, in particular, is exquisite with other white-flowered perennials.

Shapes and Textures

The upright stems of the various types of lychnis work well between, behind, or in front of mounded companions, such as artemisias (*Artemisia*) and heucheras. For a contrast in flower form, pair them with spikes, like those of speedwells (*Veronica*); with tiny or airy blossoms, like those of catmints (*Nepeta*); and with large, broad blooms, like those of daylilies (*Hemerocallis*) and true lilies (*Lilium*).

Seasonal Features

Maltese cross and Arkwright's campion are at their peak bloom for about 6 weeks, starting in late spring to early summer. Rose campion tends to begin slightly later (in early to mid-summer) and flowers for about 8 weeks.

(*Hemerocallis*); warm orange, like that of 'Orange Passion' echinacea (*Echinacea*); or rich purples and blues, like those of perennial salvias (*Salvia*). Colorful foliage options include bright yellow–leaved perennials, such as 'Aztec Gold' creeping

Miscanthus
dramatic border accents

Miscanthus sinensis 'Morning Light' and *Aster cordifolius*

Miscanthus sinensis 'Strictus' and *Helianthus* 'Lemon Queen'

A Perfect Match

One of my favorite easy-care pairings is 'Morning Light' miscanthus with giant coneflower (*Rudbeckia maxima*). The slender leaves of the grass offer a striking textural contrast to the broad coneflower foliage in summer, then make an elegant backdrop for the coneflower's bold blooms in summer and for its large, dark seed heads in fall.

Miscanthus (*Miscanthus sinensis*), also called Japanese silver grass or maiden grass, can be an interesting addition to later-season combos for foliage color and texture. Generally hardy in Zones 4 or 5 to 9, this warm-season grass also has reddish to pinkish to tan, whisk-like flower heads that mature to fluffy, white seed heads. Be aware, though, that miscanthus can seed into natural areas, particularly in the eastern half of the United States, so you may want to do an online search to check its invasive status in your state before planting. Or choose a native grass instead: Switch grasses (*Panicum*), for instance, offer some of the same features.

Color Considerations

Green-leaved miscanthus selections, such as 'Adagio' and 'Arabesque', are useful behind or between brightly colored or

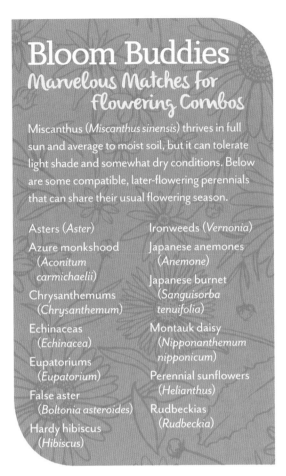

Bloom Buddies
Marvelous Matches for flowering Combos

Miscanthus (*Miscanthus sinensis*) thrives in full sun and average to moist soil, but it can tolerate light shade and somewhat dry conditions. Below are some compatible, later-flowering perennials that can share their usual flowering season.

Asters (*Aster*)

Azure monkshood (*Aconitum carmichaelii*)

Chrysanthemums (*Chrysanthemum*)

Echinaceas (*Echinacea*)

Eupatoriums (*Eupatorium*)

False aster (*Boltonia asteroides*)

Hardy hibiscus (*Hibiscus*)

Ironweeds (*Vernonia*)

Japanese anemones (*Anemone*)

Japanese burnet (*Sanguisorba tenuifolia*)

Montauk daisy (*Nipponanthemum nipponicum*)

Perennial sunflowers (*Helianthus*)

Rudbeckias (*Rudbeckia*)

variegated miscanthus can look great with pink blooms, too.

Shapes and Textures

Many miscanthus selections have a fountainlike form: narrow at the base and wider at the top, with arching foliage that reaches out to all sides. They look striking cascading over lower, upright or mounded companions or contrasted with distinctly vertical partners, such as Culver's roots (*Veronicastrum*) or summer phlox (*Phlox paniculata*). Or start with one of the very upright miscanthus, such as 'Gold Bar', for the vertical effect, and use a mounded partner, such as Arkansas bluestar (*Amsonia hubrichtii*), for contrast.

The flower heads of miscanthus have a fine texture that complements many perennial partners, but they are especially striking with big, bold blooms, like those of hardy hibiscus (*Hibiscus*) and Joe-Pye weeds (*Eupatorium*).

Seasonal Features

Miscanthus clumps are slow to sprout in spring but grow quickly once the soil warms up, so they're usually large enough to contribute to combinations by early summer (in warmer areas) to midsummer (in northern gardens). Some cultivars begin blooming in late summer; most, however, wait until early or mid-fall. Cooler weather usually brings out yellow, bronzy, or reddish leaf colors as the season winds down. Flame grass (*Miscanthus* 'Purpurascens') is particularly prized for its showy autumn colors. Miscanthus leaves and stems eventually turn shades of buff, copper, or tan as they dry in place, and they'll stand through much of winter.

intricately patterned blooms, like those of many daylilies (*Hemerocallis*) and true lilies (*Lilium*).

Miscanthus cultivars with white-centered or white-edged leaves, such as 'Dixieland' and 'Morning Light', are lovely partners for snowy-bloomed perennials, such as 'David' summer phlox (*Phlox paniculata*), or with colored flowers that have white markings. Selections with yellow-banded foliage, such as 'Super Stripe', work equally well with whites, brights, and pastels, but they're particularly charming partners for bright yellow blooms, like those of 'Fireworks' rough goldenrod (*Solidago rugosa*). Any of the

Molinia
graceful perennial grasses

Moor grasses
Full sun to partial shade;
average to moist soil

Molinia caerulea subsp. *arundinacea* 'Skyracer' and *Aster oblongifolius*

Molinia caerulea 'Variegata' with *Amsonia hubrichtii* and *Caryopteris* × *clandonensis* 'Longwood Blue'

A Perfect Match

I like to plant purple moor grasses where they'll be back-lit by the rising or setting sun, because the glow behind the hazy flower heads is stunning. When that's not an option, I look for a dark background, such as a maroon-leaved Japanese maple (*Acer palmatum*) or other tree or shrub with deep green, purple, or red foliage. The backdrop's contrast makes these elegant grasses stand out any time of day.

Lush leaves and airy flower heads make purple moor grass (*Molinia caerulea*) wonderful for adding texture and movement to perennial partnerships. Those classified as *M. caerulea* subsp. *caerulea* reach 12 to 18 inches in leaf and about 3 feet in bloom, while those in *M. caerulea* subsp. *arundinacea*, such as 'Skyracer', are about 3 feet tall in leaf and 6 to 8 feet tall in flower. Moor grasses are suited to Zones 4 or 5 to 8.

Color Considerations

For much of the growing season, moor grasses mostly contribute shades of green to combinations: ideal for separating multicolor flowers that might clash if you plant them right next to each other. The tiny greenish flowers of moor grasses may be tinged with bronze to deep purple; eventually, the heads turn golden to tan as they mature.

Bloom Buddies
Marvelous Matches for Flowering Combos

Selections of purple moor grasses (*Molinia caerulea*) generally grow best in full sun and moist soil, but they can adapt to average, well-drained soil if they get some shade. Here's just a sampling of the many perennials that are lovely complements to their midsummer into fall flower and seed heads.

Anise hyssops (*Agastache*)

Bee balms (*Monarda*)

Crocosmias (*Crocosmia*)

Culver's roots (*Veronicastrum*)

Daylilies (*Hemerocallis*)

Echinaceas (*Echinacea*)

Fleeceflowers (*Persicaria*)

Heleniums (*Helenium*)

Japanese anemones (*Anemone*)

Lilies (*Lilium*)

New England aster (*Aster novae-angliae*)

Perennial lobelias (*Lobelia*)

Rattlesnake master (*Eryngium yuccifolium*)

Rudbeckias (*Rudbeckia*)

Summer phlox (*Phlox paniculata*)

White mugwort (*Artemisia lactiflora*)

One notable selection for foliage color is variegated purple moor grass (*M. caerulea* subsp. *caerulea* 'Variegata'), with cream-and-green-striped leaves. It's a lovely match for Shasta daisy (*Leucanthemum × superbum*), straw foxglove (*Digitalis lutea*), and other white, cream-colored, or light yellow flowers. Try it with blue- to lavender-flowered companions, too, such as catmints

(*Nepeta*) or Rozanne hardy geranium (*Geranium* 'Gerwat'), or with pinks, like those of 'Pink Manners' obedient plant (*Physostegia virginiana*).

Shapes and Textures

Purple moor grasses form upright or vase-shaped clumps of lush leaves, with taller flowering stems topped with loose flower plumes. Because the stems rise well above the leaves and the plumes are so airy, purple moor grasses have a wonderful see-through effect: You can plant the 3-foot ones close to the front of a border or taller ones near the middle of a border and still see the flowers behind them.

In both leaf and in flower, purple moor grasses have a fine texture. The overall wispy quality softens even the boldest blooms or bloom clusters, like those of true lilies (*Lilium*), hardy hibiscus (*Hibiscus*), summer phlox (*Phlox paniculata*), and torch lilies (*Kniphofia*). Set the shorter kinds among echinaceas (*Echinacea*), rudbeckias (*Rudbeckia*), and other daisy-form perennials. Let the taller types mingle with Joe-Pye weeds (*Eupatorium*), 'Lemon Queen' perennial sunflower (*Helianthus*), and other back-of-the border perennials to create a meadow or prairie effect.

Seasonal Features

These cool-season grasses sprout early in the season and begin blooming in mid- to late summer. The flower heads turn into seed heads and last through the rest of the growing season. In fall, the leaves and stems take on rich yellow to golden orange hues. They dry to a tan color but break down fairly quickly, so they usually have little winter interest.

Monarda
showy summer color

Monarda 'Jacob Cline' with *Leucanthemum × superbum* and *Salvia greggii* 'Navaho Bright Red'

Monarda 'Peter's Purple' with *Echinacea purpurea* and *Rudbeckia hirta*

A Perfect Match

When I choose bee balms for my garden, I look for cultivars that have interesting bracts (the leaflike structures around the flower heads) as well as colorful flowers. Red-flowered 'Jacob Cline', for instance, has dark, purplish red bracts that make an excellent echo for purple-leaved shrubs, such as 'Royal Purple' smokebush (*Cotinus coggygria*).

Native to much of North America, bee balms (*Monarda*) are popular with color-loving gardeners and with bees, butterflies, and hummingbirds, too. Common bee balm or Oswego tea (*M. didyma*) typically has red flowers, while wild bergamot (*M. fistulosa*) is lavender pink. Many named selections are hybrids between these and others species, offering a range of colors and heights. Bee balms are usually recommended for Zones 3 or 4 to 8.

Keep in mind that bee balms can be vigorous spreaders: great if you need to fill space but potentially a problem in smaller borders, where they can readily crowd out slower-growing companions. Dividing the clumps every other year and replanting just one piece from each can help to keep bee balms from taking over. Or combine them with other spreading perennials, such as gooseneck loosestrife (*Lysimachia clethroides*) and obedient plant (*Physostegia virginiana*), in a "wild" garden in a side yard or

Bloom Buddies
Marvelous Matches for Flowering Combos

Give bee balms (*Monarda*) full sun to partial shade and average to moist soil, and they'll produce an abundance of eye-catching summer blooms just in time to pair with the flowering perennials mentioned below, among others.

Agastaches
(*Agastache*)

Bowman's roots
(*Gillenia*)

Culver's roots
(*Veronicastrum*)

Daylilies (*Hemerocallis*)

Echinaceas (*Echinacea*)

Hardy geraniums
(*Geranium*)

Heleniums (*Helenium*)

Obedient plant
(*Physostegia
virginiana*)

Perennial lobelias
(*Lobelia*)

Perennial salvias
(*Salvia*)

Rattlesnake master
(*Eryngium
yuccifolium*)

Rudbeckias
(*Rudbeckia*)

Shasta daisy
(*Leucanthemum ×
superbum*)

Summer phlox
(*Phlox paniculata*)

White mugwort
(*Artemisia lactiflora*)

Yarrows (*Achillea*)

backyard border, where they can romp without becoming a problem.

Color Considerations

Many bee balms offer intensely hued blooms, particularly rich reds, like those of 'Gardenview Scarlet' and 'Jacob Cline', as well as fuchsia reds, like those of 'Raspberry Wine'. If you like your borders on the bright side, the reds and fuchsias

can be dramatic partners with brilliant yellows, like those of 'Little Rocket' ligularia (*Ligularia*) and 'Zagreb' threadleaf coreopsis (*Coreopsis verticillata*). Use the red bee balms to repeat the effect of other reds, like those of cardinal flower (*Lobelia cardinalis*) and 'Lucifer' crocosmia (*Crocosmia*), or echo them with red-tipped switch grasses (*Panicum virgatum*), such as 'Shenandoah'.

Pinks are abundant in bee balms, in a variety of shades and tints. Enjoy them in a primarily pink planting with partners such as purple coneflowers (*Echinacea purpurea*), and summer phlox (*Phlox paniculata*) and with white flowers or white-variegated leaves. They're lovely with purple-blue perennials, too, such as anise hyssops (*Agastache*), balloon flower (*Platycodon grandiflorus*), and spike speedwell (*Veronica spicata*).

Shapes and Textures

Bee balms grow in spreading patches of upright stems that work well with either vertical or mounded companions. In bloom, the shaggy flower heads of bee balms have a rounded form. Match them with bold, broad blooms, like those of echinaceas (*Echinacea*) or yarrows (*Achillea*), or create a striking contrast with spiky-flowered partners, such as Culver's roots (*Veronicastrum*), or plumy blooms, like those of filipendulas (*Filipendula*).

Seasonal Features

Peak bloom time for bee balms is usually mid- to late summer, though they may begin in early summer in southern gardens or continue into early fall in cooler areas. Clipping off the finished blooms may encourage more flowers.

Nepeta
charming and adaptable

Nepeta 'Little Titch' and *Sedum* 'Lajos' (Autumn Charm)

Nepeta 'Dropmore' with *Rosa* 'Radcon' (Pink Knock Out)

A Perfect Match

Is there a combination more classic than catmint and roses? The dainty purple-blue blossoms are exquisite with soft pinks and white, but my current favorite partner is a little different: Flower Carpet Amber rose (*Rosa* 'Noa97400a'), with orangey buds opening to golden blooms that age to peachy pink. It reaches only 2 to 3 feet tall, so it works best with a compact catmint, such as Junior Walker ('Novanepjun') or Little Trudy ('Psfike').

Versatile and dependable, catmints (*Nepeta*) are equally at home in formal borders and casual cottage gardens. You may find the most readily available kinds sold under a variety of names, including *N. mussinii*, *N. × faassenii*, and *N. racemosa*. They, along with *N. sibirica*, tend to prefer average to dryish soil, while *N. subsessilis* appreciates a bit more moisture. Catmints vary in height— they reach from 1 to 4 feet, depending on the cultivar—and most often bloom in the purple-blue range, though there are pinks and whites, as well. Most catmints are hardy in Zones 3 or 4 to 8.

Color Considerations

Even when not in bloom, catmints with gray-green leaves provide a charming complement to white and pastel blooms, as well as to brighter silver partners, such as 'Berggarten' common

the blue-purple to lavender blue range. They're practically must-haves for a "blue border," as they peak around the same time as many other favorites in this color range, including bellflowers (*Campanula*), delphiniums (*Delphinium*), lavenders (*Lavandula*), blue flax (*Linum perenne*), and perennial salvias (*Salvia*), to name just a few. The purple-blue catmints—and white ones, too, such as 'Snowflake'—are wonderful with white- or cream-flowered partners, such as feverfew (*Tanacetum parthenium*), Shasta daisy (*Leucanthemum* × *superbum*), and white nettleleaf mullein (*Verbascum chaixii* 'Album'), and with silver foliage or white- or cream-variegated leaves.

You can't miss when pairing catmints with pretty much any pink-flowering partner, from delicately pastel Blushing Maiden dianthus (*Dianthus* 'Valda Judith') to rosy pink red valerian (*Centranthus ruber*) to magenta rose campion (*Lychnis coronaria*). Peachy and salmon colors, like those of 'Peachy Seduction' yarrow (*Achillea*) and Summer Sky echinacea (*Echinacea* 'Katie Saul'), pair perfectly with the purple-blue catmints, as do pale to bright yellows, like those in the flowers of 'Crème Brulee' coreopsis (*Coreopsis*), lady's mantle (*Alchemilla mollis*), and sundrops (*Oenothera fruticosa*) or the leaves of 'Angelina' sedum (*Sedum rupestre*) and golden oregano (*Origanum vulgare* 'Aureum').

Shapes and Textures

Catmints generally form somewhat loose clumps that work well in front of many other plant shapes: particularly distinct ones, such as spiky irises or densely mounded upright

sage (*Salvia officinalis*) and 'Silver Brocade' beach wormwood (*Artemisia stelleriana*). They're also lovely with foliage that's vividly variegated with white or cream, like that of 'Loraine Sunshine' oxeye (*Heliopsis helianthoides*) or 'Frosted Elegance' summer phlox (*Phlox paniculata*).

Of course, it's the flowers that most of us appreciate about catmints: particularly those in sedums. They're especially useful for covering the bases of taller companions that have bare stems or tend to lose their lower leaves, such as baptisias (*Baptisia*), large-flowered alliums (*Allium*), and lilies (*Lilium*).

Though their flowers are held in spiky clusters, the tiny blooms and small leaves give catmints a fine texture overall. Combine them with other airy or wispy plants, such as gaura (*Gaura lindheimeri*) or Mexican feather grass (*Stipa tenuissima*), for a soft, romantic effect. Or create contrast by matching them with large blooms, like those of daylilies (*Hemerocallis*) and peonies, or bold flower forms, such as plump-spiked lupines (*Lupinus*) or rounded common chives (*Allium schoenoprasum*).

Seasonal Features

Catmints may start flowering as early as mid-spring in southern gardens, but the peak bloom period in most areas is late spring to early summer: prime time for combinations with irises, peonies, and many other classic border perennials. After this first flush, many catmints continue to produce some flowers through the rest of summer, at least. If they get floppy or stop blooming by midsummer, cut them back by about half to encourage bushy regrowth and possibly more flowers in late summer and fall, in time to complement Japanese anemones (*Anemone*), upright sedums (*Sedum*), and other late-season bloomers.

Nepeta 'Joanna Reed' with *Geranium* 'Gerwat' (Rozanne), *Veronica spicata* 'Icicle', and *Leucanthemum* × *superbum* 'Becky' *(left)*; *Nepeta* 'Purple Haze' with *Spiraea thunbergii* 'Ogon' (Mellow Yellow) *(below)*

Paeonia
fleeting but fabulous

Peonies
Full sun to light shade; average, well-drained soil

Paeonia 'Smith Opus 1' (Misaka) and *Physocarpus opulifolius* 'Mindia' (Coppertina)

Paeonia lactiflora 'Festiva Maxima' with *Nepeta* 'Novanepjun' (Junior Walker) and *Salvia* 'Snow Hill'

A Perfect Match

While I enjoy trying to find new and interesting flowering companions for my peonies, I find it hard to beat the classic beauty of billowy catmints (*Nepeta*) and bold hybrid peony blooms. No matter what the weather, 'Walker's Low' catmint is at least beginning to bloom when the peonies are open—and when they are both at their peaks, the effect is pure garden magic.

Peonies (*Paeonia*) have a relatively short bloom period, but they're so lovely that it's hard to resist making room for at least one in your garden. There are several different kinds, including herbaceous or garden peonies (*P. lactiflora*: the typical perennial types, which die back to the ground each winter); tree peonies (shrubby kinds, which produce woody stems); and intersectional or Itoh peonies (hybrids between the first two, with some traits of each). Herbaceous peonies are the ones you're most likely to find at your local garden center. They typically reach 2 to 3 feet tall and 3 to 4 feet wide and are hardy in Zones 3 to 7 or 8.

Color Considerations

White, pinks, and reds are the most common flower colors in the hybrid herbaceous peonies. The pure to creamy whites and

Bloom Buddies
Marvelous Matches for Flowering Combos

Herbaceous peonies (*Paeonia*) are most vigorous in full sun, but their flowers may last a bit longer and hold their color better if they get a bit of afternoon shade, especially in the warmest part of their range. There are plenty of other perennials that thrive in similar growing conditions, including those listed below, though it may take a bit of experimenting to find out which ones are most likely to flower at the same time as your chosen peonies. Since peonies can take several years to settle in and flower well after planting or transplanting, it's best to leave them in place and move the other perennials if you want to try them with different partners.

Baptisias (*Baptisia*)

Bearded iris (*Iris* Bearded Hybrids)

Bellflowers (*Campanula*)

Blue flax (*Linum perenne*)

Bluestars (*Amsonia*)

Catmints (*Nepeta*)

Columbines (*Aquilegia*)

Delphiniums (*Delphinium*)

Dianthus (*Dianthus*)

Foxgloves (*Digitalis*)

Hardy geraniums (*Geranium*)

Italian alkanet (*Anchusa azurea*)

Lady's mantle (*Alchemilla mollis*)

Lupines (*Lupinus*)

Masterworts (*Astrantia*)

Perennial salvia (*Salvia* × *superba*)

Pincushion flowers (*Scabiosa*)

Red campion (*Silene dioica*)

Rose campion (*Lychnis coronaria*)

Siberian iris (*Iris sibirica*)

Snow-in-summer (*Cerastium tomentosum*)

Speedwells (*Veronica*)

Tuberous-rooted Jerusalem sage (*Phlomis tuberosa*)

Yarrows (*Achillea*)

light to bright pinks pair particularly well with other white- and pastel-flowered perennials, as well as those with purple-blue blooms, such as 'Caesar's Brother' and 'Super Ego' Siberian irises (*Iris sibirica*). They also look great with blue, gray, or silver foliage, like that of 'Big Ears' lamb's ears (*Stachys byzantina*), or with white- or cream-variegated partners, such as 'Nora Leigh' summer phlox (*Phlox paniculata*).

Match the rich reds and pinks with flowers in equally intense colors, such as sunny yellows and vivid purples, or with vibrant yellow, deep purple, or bright silver foliage. Perennial partners with yellow or chartreuse leaves or flowers—think of golden feverfew (*Tanacetum parthenium* 'Aureum') or lady's mantle (*Alchemilla mollis*), for example—do a nice job drawing attention to the prominent yellow stamens (pollen-bearing structures) in the centers of single-flowered (and some semidouble) peonies.

Shapes and Textures

Peonies form dense, broad mounds that benefit from vase-shaped to narrowly upright companions, such as irises and ornamental grasses,

Paeonia 'Bartzella' and *Allium* 'Globemaster'

for contrast. Leaf shapes vary among the herbaceous hybrids from broad to deeply cut, so the overall foliage texture can range from bold to fine. Contrast the broad-leaved cultivars with partners that have small, spiky, or ferny leaves and set the deeply cut kinds against wide leaves. Peony leaves tend to be smooth and are often glossy, so another way to create eye-catching contrast is with hairy or fuzzy leaves, like those of silver sage (*Salvia argentea*) and rose campion (*Lychnis coronaria*).

The flowers of single-flowered peonies are cupped or bowl shaped, while the semidouble to double types can be so packed with petals that they're practically rounded. Balance their bold appearance with smaller-flowered partners, such as dianthus (*Dianthus*) and hardy geraniums (*Geranium*), or match them with equally dramatic spikes, like those of baptisias (*Baptisia*) and foxgloves (*Digitalis*).

Seasonal Features

In the South, the peak flowering period is mainly in mid-spring (April); in northern gardens, most peonies flower in late spring or at the start of summer. Individual plants typically flower for about a week—a few days more if the weather stays cool or less if there's an early spell of hot weather—but if you have the space for multiple clumps, you can extend the display by several weeks if you include early-, mid-, and late-season hybrids in your garden.

As with many other perennials that bloom around this time, the start and duration of the bloom period is so dependent on the weather that it can be tricky to plan specific combinations with peonies and other flowers. That's not necessarily a problem: Peonies are so fleeting but so special that they deserve to be the star of any garden when they do appear. But if

Bulbs that flower in spring to early summer make excellent bedmates for peonies. Near the crown (the base of the plant), tuck in early bloomers, such as crocus, daffodils, Dutch hyacinths (*Hyacinthus*), and grape hyacinths (*Muscari*); they'll look amazing next to bronzy-to-red new peony shoots. A foot or so out from the crown, interplant with mid- to late-spring bulbs, such as camassias (*Camassia*), summer snow-flake (*Leucojum aestivum*), and tulips, as well as some of the taller alliums (*Allium*), such as purple 'Gladia-tor' and 'Purple Sensation', white 'Mount Everest', and plum-and-white Sicilian honey garlic (*A. siculum*). As the peony leaves expand fully, they'll cover the yellowing bulb foliage.

you would like to try to enhance their beauty, consider perennial partners with colorful foliage, which will look good whatever the weather, or those that bloom over several weeks, at least—such as hardy geraniums and catmints (*Nepeta*)—to increase the odds of their flowering at the same time.

In fall, herbaceous peonies can produce some handsome leaf colors, from soft yellows, peach, and rosy pinks to golds, oranges, reds, and purples. It's hard to predict which ones will turn, and when, and what colors they'll be from year to year. But if and when they do change, they're a wonderful sight among other fall-colored perennials, such as Arkansas blue-star (*Amsonia hubrichtii*) and balloon flower (*Platycodon grandiflorus*), as well as fall-flowering partners, such as asters and chrysanthemums.

Special Effects

Herbaceous peonies make wonderful cut flow-ers: especially those that are deliciously fragrant, such as white 'Duchesse de Nemours' and 'Festiva Maxima', 'Red Magic', and pink 'Sarah Bernhardt'. A fresh-cut bouquet is a memorable gift for a friend (or for yourself), but snipping

flowers from a high-visibility border can spoil the show in your garden. If you'd like to have plenty of peonies for cutting, see if you can find a spot where you could plant a variety of early-, midseason-, and late-flowering cultivars in a row as a low hedge: in a side yard, perhaps, or along a shed or garage wall. Or, if space allows, set aside an entire bed or border just for cut flowers, including peonies as well as asters, blazing stars (*Liatris*), irises, purple coneflower (*Echinacea purpurea*), rudbeckias (*Rudbeckia*), summer phlox (*Phlox paniculata*), yarrows (*Ach-illea*), and other perennials that are ideal for making bouquets.

Paeonia lactiflora '**Karl Rosenfield**' and *Nepeta* '**Walker's Low**'

Panicum
natives for color and texture

Panicum virgatum 'Cheyenne Sky' and *Solidago rugosa* 'Fireworks'

Panicum amarum 'Dewey Blue' with *Eupatorium dubium* 'Little Joe' and *Echinacea purpurea*

A Perfect Match

It's tough to pick just one switch grass as a favorite! At the moment, I'd choose 'Dewey Blue'—partly for its powder blue foliage but mostly for its lacy, arching flower and seed heads. Its fountainlike habit makes it an elegant native substitute for miscanthus (*Miscanthus*), and its height and color make it an excellent companion for tall, later-season bloomers, particularly spiky Culver's roots (*Veronicastrum virginicum*).

Switch grasses (*Panicum*) are superb for adding height, color, and textural interest to perennial partnerships. Most of the named switch grasses are cultivars of *P. virgatum*, but 'Dewey Blue', with silvery blue leaves, is a selection of bitter panic grass (*P. amarum*), also known as coastal switch grass. Most of these North American natives are in the 4- to 5-foot-tall range in bloom, though some are taller or shorter, and they're generally suited for Zones 3 or 4 to 8.

Color Considerations

Some switch grasses, such as 'Emerald Chief' or 'Northwind', are green for most of the growing season. Wonderful with whites and pastels, these greens are also useful as a "neutral" background for multicolor blooms or vividly variegated foliage, or for separating potentially clashing colors.

Quite a few switch grass cultivars—including 'Prairie Fire', Ruby Ribbons ('Rr1'), and 'Shenandoah', among others—start out with green or bluish green foliage but develop red to burgundy leaf tips as summer progresses. They're handy for adding an extra touch of color to summer and fall combinations that feature blooms in bright reds, oranges, and yellows, like those of goldenrods (*Solidago*) and heleniums (*Helenium*).

Beautiful blue-leaved selections are also abundant among the switch grasses. 'Cloud Nine', 'Heavy Metal', and other blues are outstanding with white-variegated partners and with clear to creamy white flowers. Pastel blooms are also wonderful with the blue switch grasses. 'Dallas Blues', which has pinkish flower plumes, is a particularly pretty match for tall-stemmed pink perennials, such as 'Peppermint Schnapps' hardy hibiscus (*Hibiscus*).

Shapes and Textures

The overall habit of these clump-forming grasses is basically vase-shaped (wider at the top than at ground level), though some, such as 'Northwind', are very vertical, and others, like 'Cloud Nine' and 'Dewey Blue', have more of a spreading, fountainlike form. They're all useful for adding visual variety behind or next to broadly clump-forming or mounded perennial partners, such as baptisias (*Baptisia*), bluestars (*Amsonia*), and peonies.

Slender leaves and airy flower heads give switch grass plants a fine texture: ideal for adding contrast to the large blooms or bloom clusters of daylilies (*Hemerocallis*), summer phlox (*Phlox paniculata*), and true lilies (*Lilium*). They also look right at home with daisy-form flowers,

Bloom Buddies
Marvelous Matches for flowering Combos

Switch grasses (*Panicum*) thrive in full sun and can adapt to either moist or dry soil. Here are some medium-height to tall perennials that can make great matches for their late-summer to early-fall flower and seed heads.

Asters (*Aster*)

Culver's roots (*Veronicastrum*)

Echinaceas (*Echinacea*)

False aster (*Boltonia asteroides*)

Golden lace (*Patrinia scabiosifolia*)

Goldenrods (*Solidago*)

Ironweeds (*Vernonia*)

Japanese anemones (*Anemone*)

Joe-Pye weeds (*Eupatorium*)

Oriental lilies (*Lilium* Oriental Hybrids)

Perennial sunflowers (*Helianthus*)

Rudbeckias (*Rudbeckia*)

Summer phlox (*Phlox paniculata*)

White mugwort (*Artemisia lactiflora*)

such as perennial sunflowers (*Helianthus*) and rudbeckias (*Rudbeckia*).

Seasonal Features

These warm-season grasses can be a bit slow to sprout but grow quickly once the weather warms. In later summer, they're topped with open plumes of tiny blooms that mature into cloudlike seed heads. Switch grasses also develop eye-catching fall foliage colors, ranging from yellows to reds and burgundies.

Papaver
big, bold blooms

Poppies
Full sun; average, well-drained soil

Papaver orientale 'Beauty of Livermere' with *Digitalis purpurea* 'Alba' and *Baptisia sphaerocarpa* 'Screamin' Yellow'

Papaver orientale 'Queen Alexandra' and *Paeonia* 'Raspberry Sundae'

A Perfect Match

Oriental poppies are so spectacular in bloom that I often don't even notice what's growing near them. The brilliant reds, scarlets, and oranges are stunning with equally eye-catching bright blues or yellows, but the most memorable combination I've ever seen was much more subtle: purplish pink 'Patty's Plum' poppy against the grayish green, fine-textured foliage of 'Morning Light' miscanthus (*Miscanthus sinensis*).

Though they bloom at the same time as many other eye-catching perennials, poppies (*Papaver*) have a way of stealing most of the attention during their spectacular flowering period. Most perennial poppies are listed as selections of Oriental poppy (*P. orientale*), though they're actually hybrids, varying in color, height, and other traits. Most are recommended for Zones 3 to 7, though some of the newer hybrids may be more tolerant of heat and humidity.

Color Considerations

Many Oriental poppies come in brilliant shades of orange and red. These bold bloomers deserve to be matched with equally intense colors: rich purples and blues, like those of perennial salvias (*Salvia*), for example, or sunny yellows, like those of lemon lily (*Hemerocallis lilioasphodelus*).

'Perry's White', 'Royal Wedding', and other white Oriental poppies are gorgeous with other white flowers, like those of 'Noble Maiden' lupine (*Lupinus*) or 'Snow Thimble' common foxglove (*Digitalis purpurea*). Soft to saturated purple-blues, like those of bellflowers (*Campanula*), catmints (*Nepeta*), and speedwells (*Veronica*), are also exquisite partners for white poppies. Purple-blues can work well with pink-flowered Oriental poppies, from rich 'Raspberry Queen' to soft salmon pink 'Helen Elizabeth'.

Perennials and shrubs with colorful foliage are excellent partners for poppies because you can count on them being there no matter when the poppies bloom. Silver-leaved plants, such as artemisias (*Artemisia*), are stunning with the reds and oranges especially, while pastel to white poppies are wonderful with white-striped leaves, like those of 'Morning Light' miscanthus (*Miscanthus sinensis*), and cool blue foliage, like that of 'Heavy Metal' switch grass (*Panicum virgatum*). Purple-leaved shrubs, such as Wine and Roses weigela (*Weigela florida* 'Alexandra'), are useful for echoing the dark centers of many Oriental poppy flowers.

Bloom Buddies
Marvelous Matches for flowering Combos

Below is a sampling of classic perennials that usually bloom around the same time as Oriental poppy (*Papaver orientale*) and thrive in the same sunny, well-drained sites.

Baptisias (*Baptisia*)

Bearded iris (*Iris* Bearded Hybrids)

Bellflowers (*Campanula*)

Bluestars (*Amsonia*)

Catmints (*Nepeta*)

Columbines (*Aquilegia*)

Delphiniums (*Delphinium*)

Dianthus (*Dianthus*)

Foxgloves (*Digitalis*)

Giant allium (*Allium giganteum*)

Lady's mantle (*Alchemilla mollis*)

Lupines (*Lupinus*)

Maltese cross (*Lychnis chalcedonica*)

Peonies (*Paeonia*)

Siberian iris (*Iris sibirica*)

Speedwells (*Veronica*)

Yarrows (*Achillea*)

Shapes and Textures

At their peak, Oriental poppy plants can fill a lot of space with their broad clumps of lush, hairy, deeply cut leaves, and their plump buds and broad, bowl-shaped blooms complete the bold effect. Match them with other large-flowered perennials, such as irises and peonies, and add some broad spikes, like those of baptisias (*Baptisia*), for variety. Or go for a more subtle contrast with small-flowered companions, such as lady's mantle (*Alchemilla mollis*), and fine-textured ornamental grasses.

Seasonal Features

Oriental poppies jump into growth early in the season and begins flowering in late spring or early summer. After the short bloom period—usually about 3 weeks—the leaves decline quickly and tend to disappear by midsummer, leaving quite a gap in the border. For that reason, it's a good idea to pair them with later-maturing plants, such as daylilies (*Hemerocallis*), gaura (*Gaura lindheimeri*), or Russian sages (*Perovskia*), which can expand to fill the space.

Pennisetum
fluffy flower heads catch the eye

Fountain grasses
Full sun to light shade; average, well-drained soil

Pennisetum alopecuroides with *Solidago rugosa* 'Fireworks', *Aster oblongifolius*, and *Verbena bonariensis*

Pennisetum orientale 'Karley Rose' and *Agastache* 'Purple Haze'

A Perfect Match

One of my favorite fountain grass combos so far is the pink-tinted tails of 'Karley Rose' Oriental fountain grass with the pretty pink saucers of 'Frau Dagmar Hastrup' rose. The grass doesn't start flowering until early or midsummer, so it misses the rose's first flush of flowers in late spring. But 'Frau Dagmar Hastrup' continues to produce new blooms through summer, so there is plenty of opportunity for them to match from midsummer into fall.

The most widely grown fountain grasses (*Pennisetum*) in perennial gardens are selections of *P. alopecuroides* (sometimes known as Chinese fountain grass), usually best suited to Zones 5 to 8, and Oriental fountain grass (*P. orientale*), for Zones 5 or 6 to 9. Both produce clumps of arching leaves, with brushy, spiky flower and seed heads ranging from 1 to nearly 6 feet tall, depending on the cultivar.

Before settling on a fountain grass for your garden, keep in mind that *P. alopecuroides* plants have the potential to produce unwanted seedlings in lawn and gravelly areas, and even in natural areas, depending on the cultivar and climate. If you want to avoid any seedlings, cut off the flower heads before they develop into seeds (especially on 'Moudry' and 'National Arboretum', which are particularly aggressive seeders). Or choose a different grass instead, such as native prairie dropseed (*Sporobolus heterolepis*).

Color Considerations

Green is the primary color for the leaves and emerging flower heads, which then usually age to blond or tan. In all of those stages, they're compatible with any color but are especially useful partners for flowering perennials in vibrant hues, like red, scarlet, orange, hot pink, and magenta, and with multicolor blooms, like those of many blanket flowers (*Gaillardia*).

The flower heads of Oriental fountain grasses—particularly 'Karley Rose'—tend to be tinted pink, making them excellent complements for pink-flowered partners, such as purple coneflower (*Echinacea purpurea*).

Both kinds of fountain grasses are lovely with other pastel perennials—especially soft blues and lavender purples—and with white flowers, too.

Shapes and Textures

Fountain grasses are clump formers that tend to have a mounded outline—broad on most fountain grasses but more upright on selections of Oriental fountain grass. Use them behind lower mounded companions, such as coreopsis (*Coreopsis*); for contrast, set them next to or in front of more upright perennials, such as blazing stars (*Liatris*) or summer phlox (*Phlox paniculata*). They're very useful for covering the uninteresting lower stems of New England aster (*Aster novae-angliae*) and other tall perennials.

The fine-textured foliage of fountain grasses creates a striking contrast to broader leaves and bold flower shapes. The fluffy flower and seed heads of fountain grasses have a soft appearance that's a charming complement to

Bloom Buddies
Marvelous Matches for flowering Combos

Many terrific flowering companions can thrive in the same full sun to light shade and average, well-drained soil conditions that suit fountain grasses (*Pennisetum*). Here are just a few that complement them in midsummer to fall.

Agastaches (*Agastache*)

Asters (*Aster*)

Bee balms (*Monarda*)

Coreopsis (*Coreopsis*)

Culver's roots (*Veronicastrum*)

Daylilies (*Hemerocallis*)

Echinaceas (*Echinacea*)

Globe thistles (*Echinops*)

Joe-Pye weeds (*Eupatorium*)

Lilies (*Lilium*)

Ornamental oreganos (*Origanum*)

Oxeye (*Heliopsis helianthoides*)

Perennial sunflowers (*Helianthus*)

Rudbeckias (*Rudbeckia*)

Yarrows (*Achillea*)

small and/or loosely clustered blooms, like those of gaura (*Gaura lindheimeri*), as well as other daisy-form flowers.

Seasonal Features

These warm-season grasses start growing in mid- to late spring. Oriental fountain grass begins blooming in early to midsummer, while other fountain grasses generally start in late summer; the seed heads then last through fall. In autumn, the foliage of *P. alopecuroides* selections usually turns yellow to golden.

Penstemon
a rainbow of colors

Penstemon 'Prairie Dusk' and Cotinus coggygria 'Royal Purple'

Penstemon 'Sweet Joanne' and Artemisia 'Powis Castle'

A Perfect Match

Foxglove penstemon grows wild in my meadow, so I knew it would do well in my garden, too—unlike many of the brightly colored western species. I first added 'Husker Red', for its red-tinted foliage, then hybrid 'Dark Towers', which is a much deeper purple color in leaf. Their early summer flowers are beautiful in bloom, of course, but their lovely leaves make them useful earlier in the season as colorful companions for 'Thalia' daffodils and other white-flowered spring bulbs.

Penstemons (*Penstemon*), also known as beardtongues, have a reputation for being finicky, and it's true that some are very particular about their preferred climate and growing conditions. Others, though, are much more adaptable, so you can enjoy their funnel-shaped or tubular flowers in pretty much any sunny, well-drained site. Among the most widely adapted species are beardlip penstemon (*P. barbatus*), usually suited to Zones 4 to 8, and foxglove penstemon (*P. digitalis*), for Zones 3 to 8. Both are normally in the 2- to 4-foot-tall range. There are also many hybrids in a range of heights and colors.

Color Considerations

The orange-red blooms of beardlip penstemon are well suited to equally bright-flowered partners, such as clear to golden yellow coreopsis (*Coreopsis*) and orange to red echinaceas (*Echinacea*).

They're also stunning with blues and purples, and with bright yellow foliage.

Foxglove penstemon and hybrids with white to pinkish blossoms are lovely with other white flowers, like those of 'Aqua' dianthus (*Dianthus*); blues to lavender purples, like those of bellflowers (*Campanula*) and bluestars (*Amsonia*); and delicate to rich pinks, like those of 'Apple Blossom' yarrow (*Achillea*) and red valerian (*Centranthus ruber*). Gray, blue, and silvery leaves make great matches, too.

Some selections of foxglove penstemon and its hybrids have reddish green (as on 'Husker Red') to deeper purple foliage (as on 'Dark Towers' and 'Mystica'), extending their usefulness as a color accent through the growing season. Enjoy them as echoes for blooms that have dark centers, such as rudbeckias (*Rudbeckia*), or dark markings, as on many Asiatic lilies (*Lilium* Asiatic Hybrids).

Shapes and Textures

Both foxglove penstemon and beardlip penstemon are clump formers with upright stems. They're ideal for pairing with mounded partners, such as catmints (*Nepeta*) or marguerites (*Anthemis*). For a soft, romantic look, pair their loosely clustered blooms with other small or loosely held blooms, like those of gaura (*Gaura lindheimeri*), and with wispy grasses, such as Mexican feather grass (*Stipa tenuissima*). Or create contrast with bolder bloom and foliage forms.

Seasonal Features

Penstemon species and hybrids vary widely in when and for how long they bloom. Foxglove

Bloom Buddies
Marvelous Matches for Flowering Combos

Penstemons (*Penstemon*) generally thrive in full sun to light shade and average, not especially fertile soil; good drainage is a must. Below are some partners for two commonly grown kinds.

Companions for foxglove penstemon (*P. digitalis*) in late spring to early summer:

Alliums (*Allium*)

Baptisias (*Baptisia*)

Bellflowers (*Campanula*)

Bluestars (*Amsonia*)

Catmints (*Nepeta*)

Dianthus (*Dianthus*)

Hardy geraniums (*Geranium*)

Speedwells (*Veronica*)

Yarrows (*Achillea*)

Companions for beardlip penstemon (*P. barbatus*) in late spring to mid- or late summer:

Agastaches (*Agastache*)

Baptisias (*Baptisia*)

Blanket flowers (*Gaillardia*)

Coreopsis (*Coreopsis*)

Echinaceas (*Echinacea*)

Gaura (*Gaura lindheimeri*)

Lavenders (*Lavandula*)

Perennial salvias (*Salvia*)

Sea hollies (*Eryngium*)

Verbenas (*Verbena*)

Yarrows (*Achillea*)

penstemon, for instance, usually flowers for about 3 weeks in late spring to early summer. Beardlip penstemon typically starts around the same time but continues into midsummer, at least, or even longer if you clip off the finished flower clusters above the leafy part of the stem.

Perovskia
misty blue beauties

Perovskia atriplicifolia 'Little Spire' and *Agastache rupestris*

Perovskia atriplicifolia and *Eryngium yuccifolium*

A Perfect Match

It's easy to make colorful flowering combinations with Russian sages, but recently, I've been more drawn to the look of them with the blonds, golds, and tans of ornamental grasses: next to or in front of 'Karl Foerster' feather reed grass (*Calamagrostis × acutiflora*), for instance, or behind Mexican feather grass (*Stipa tenuissima*).

Their airy habit and hazy blooms give Russian sages (*Perovskia*) a delicate look, but they're surprisingly tough, adapting to a wide range of climates as long as they get lots of sun and good drainage. You'll often see selections listed under *P. atriplicifolia*, but many are hybrids between that species and *P. abrotanoides*. Full-size Russian sages can reach about 5 feet tall and wide: great if you have a lot of room to fill but too large for most home-garden borders. More-compact cultivars, such as Lacey Blue ('Lisslitt'), are in the 2- to 3-foot-tall range, making them easier to match with other border perennials. Russian sages are generally best suited to Zones 5 to 9.

Color Considerations

With their gray-green to silvery leaves, gray-white stems, and purple-blue flowers, Russian sages have a wonderful way of looking good with pretty much any flowering partner. If your color preferences are on the softer side, enjoy them with other cool blues, like those of globe thistles (*Echinops*) and sea hollies (*Eryngium*); with pinks, like those of Joe-Pye weeds (*Eupatorium*) and 'Pink Mist' pincushion flower (*Scabiosa*); with soft yellows, like those of 'Moonlight' golden marguerite (*Anthemis tinctoria*) and 'Sunny Seduction' yarrow (*Achillea*); and with pastel oranges, like those of 'Sienna Sunset' coreopsis (*Coreopsis*) and sunset hyssop (*Agastache rupestris*).

Russian sages are also gorgeous with whites, from bright white 'Becky' Shasta daisy (*Leucanthemum × superbum*) to creamy 'Lime Frost' daylily (*Hemerocallis*) to greenish white 'Green Jewel' purple coneflower (*Echinacea purpurea*). Take advantage of white-variegated foliage partners, too, as well as blue, gray, or bright silver leaves: Think of 'Powis Castle' artemisia (*Artemisia*), for instance, or 'Big Ears' lamb's ears (*Stachys byzantina*).

Russian sages can look terrific with more intense hues. Bright lemon to rich golden partners—such as 'Fireworks' rough goldenrod (*Solidago rugosa*), 'Little Henry' sweet coneflower (*Rudbeckia subtomentosa*), or orange coneflower (*R. fulgida*), for instance—show off beautifully against the purple-blue haze. Or try Russian sages with perennials that bloom in shades of orange to red: many daylilies, echinaceas (*Echinacea*), and torch lilies (*Kniphofia*), for instance.

Shapes and Textures

Though they're commonly sold with perennials, Russian sages are actually shrubs, with a bushy,

Bloom Buddies
Marvelous Matches for flowering Combos

Sun-loving Russian sages (*Perovskia*) perform beautifully in hot, dry, infertile sites but can adapt to borders with more moisture and fertility, as long as they have good drainage. That flexibility, along with their long bloom season, gives you lots of potential partners to choose from for fantastic flowering combinations.

Asters (*Aster*)

Balloon flower (*Platycodon grandiflorus*)

Blazing stars (*Liatris*)

Coreopsis (*Coreopsis*)

Daylilies (*Hemerocallis*)

Echinaceas (*Echinacea*)

False aster (*Boltonia asteroides*)

Gaura (*Gaura lindheimeri*)

Globe thistles (*Echinops*)

Goldenrods (*Solidago*)

Heleniums (*Helenium*)

Japanese anemones (*Anemone*)

Lilies (*Lilium*)

Oxeye (*Heliopsis helianthoides*)

Perennial salvias (*Salvia*)

Rudbeckias (*Rudbeckia*)

Sea hollies (*Eryngium*)

Shasta daisy (*Leucanthemum × superbum*)

Summer phlox (*Phlox paniculata*)

Winecups (*Callirhoe involucrata*)

Yarrows (*Achillea*)

upright to somewhat sprawling habit. (The more the soil is on the moist and fertile side, the more sprawling they are likely to be.) They complement a variety of other plant habits but are particularly interesting contrasted with dense mounds, like those of aromatic aster (*Aster oblongifolius*) or 'Autumn Fire' and other upright sedums (*Sedum*), and with very vertical companions, such as Culver's roots (*Veronicastrum*), 'Northwind' switch grass (*Panicum virgatum*), or summer phlox (*Phlox paniculata*).

Texture-wise, Russian sage plants have an airy, see-through appearance, with lacy leaves and open-branched clusters of tiny blooms. Their fine texture makes them charming partners for other perennials that have small but abundant flowers, such as beardlip penstemon (*Penstemon barbatus*) or gaura (*Gaura lindheimeri*), and for ornamental grasses, for a soft, billowy look. Or use Russian sages to add visual variety among large blooms, like those of daylilies (*Hemerocallis*), true lilies (*Lilium*), and rudbeckias (*Rudbeckia*).

Seasonal Features

In mild climates, Russian sages may start flowering in mid- to late spring; elsewhere, early to midsummer is more common. Once they begin, they can continue for several months—into early fall, at least—though they may take a break at some point in summer. If that happens, cut the plants back by about half to promote bushier regrowth and a new flush of flowers. The foliage may linger well into winter where winters aren't too cold. Even where the leaves drop, the white stems remain to provide off-season interest among dark seed heads, the bleached stems and leaves of many ornamental grasses, and the rich foliage of evergreen shrubs.

Perovskia atriplicifolia **and** *Rudbeckia hirta*

Persicaria
slender spikes to plumy blooms

Fleeceflowers
Full sun to light shade;
average to moist soil

Persicaria amplexicaulis 'Firetail' and *Agastache* 'Blue Blazes'

Persicaria virginiana var. filiformis
'Painter's Palette' and
Cotinus coggygria
'Royal Purple'

A Perfect Match

Along with the various flowering fleeceflowers, this genus offers some beauties prized for their colorful foliage. 'Painter's Palette' jumpseed (*Persicaria virginiana var. filiformis*), for instance, has green leaves that are splashed with cream and marked with red: fantastic against dark foliage, like that of 'Royal Purple' smokebush (*Cotinus coggryia*). I'm a big fan of 'Red Dragon' fleeceflower (*P. microcephala*), too: Its maroon-and-silver leaves are stunning with silver-leaved companions.

Fleeceflowers (*Persicaria*, formerly *Polygonum*) are a diverse group of perennials varying widely in height and habit as well as in growing preferences. Some are rampant spreaders, but there are clump-forming kinds, too. Two well-behaved species worth seeking out for their flowers include mountain fleeceflower (*P. amplexicaulis*), which reaches 3 to 4 feet tall and wide in bloom and has relatively short, slender bloom spikes, and giant fleeceflower (*P. polymorpha*), which reaches about 6 feet tall and wide, or even larger and has showy plumes on shrub-size plants. Both of these are generally hardy in Zones 3 to 8.

Color Considerations

Mountain fleeceflower blooms mostly in shades of reddish pink, though there are also light pink selections. The reddish pinks, such as 'Firetail' and 'Taurus', usually don't look good with pure

Bloom Buddies
Marvelous Matches for Flowering Combos

Here are perennial partners that can thrive in the same full sun to light shade growing conditions as fleeceflowers, with summer bloom times that generally coincide with both giant fleeceflower (*Persicaria polymorpha*) and mountain fleeceflower (*P. amplexicaulis*).

Bee balms (*Monarda*)

Blazing stars (*Liatris*)

'Blue Fortune' anise hyssop (*Agastache*)

Catmints (*Nepeta*)

Culver's roots (*Veronicastrum*)

Daylilies (*Hemerocallis*)

Echinaceas (*Echinacea*)

Feather reed grass (*Calamagrostis × acutiflora*)

Globe thistles (*Echinops*)

Goldenrods (*Solidago*)

Hardy geraniums (*Geranium*)

Joe-Pye weeds (*Eupatorium*)

Meadowsweets (*Filipendula*)

Perennial salvias (*Salvia*)

Rudbeckias (*Rudbeckia*)

Russian sages (*Perovskia*)

Sedums (*Sedum*, upright types)

Summer phlox (*Phlox paniculata*)

Tuberous-rooted Jerusalem sage (*Phlomis tuberosa*)

and globe thistles (*Echinops*)—as well as gray, blue, or silver foliage.

The key color feature of giant fleeceflower is its tiny, creamy white blooms, which are grouped into large clusters (technically known as panicles). They're elegant paired with other whites, with blue flowers, and with gray, silver, and blue-leaved perennials and shrubs. Giant fleeceflower looks terrific with pastels, like peachy daylilies (*Hemerocallis*) and pink swamp milkweed (*Asclepias incarnata*), even as its blooms age through pink to reddish brown. For a particularly high-impact pairing, set it against a dark ground, such as near-black Diabolo ninebark (*Physocarpus opulifolius* 'Monlo'), or try it with hot pink or bright red blooms.

Shapes and Textures

Both mountain fleeceflower and giant fleeceflower have an overall mounded form. Use them to repeat the mounded shapes of other perennials, or pair them with very vertical companions or low, spreading forms for contrast. Their lance-shaped leaves are relatively large but not especially distinctive from a textural standpoint; they do add some variety among broad-, lacy-, needle-, or spiky-leaved partners, though, such as ligularias (*Ligularia*), Arkansas bluestar (*Amsonia hubrichtii*), and ornamental grasses.

The bloom clusters of mountain fleeceflower are undeniably spiky in shape, but they are so slender that the plant has an overall medium to fine texture in bloom. Repeat their form with more substantial spikes, like those of dense blazing star (*Liatris spicata*) and mulleins (*Verbascum*), or contrast them with plumes, daisy-form flowers, or broad-clustered blooms, like those of

reds, but they're vivid enough to hold their own with other flowering perennials in rich purple, yellow, orange, and magenta, as well as with bright yellow, deep purple, or white- or yellow-variegated leaves. They add intensity among softer colors, such as silvery blue flowers—like those of Russian sages (*Perovskia*)

Persicaria polymorpha and *Lilium* 'Black Beauty' *(left); Persicaria amplexicaulis* 'Inverleith' and 'Golden Arrow' with *Panicum virgatum* 'Shenandoah' and *Salvia verticillata* 'Purple Rain' *(above)*

upright sedums (*Sedum*) and yarrows (*Achillea*). In borders you see at relatively close range, the delicate spikes add variety among other perennials with small flowers—such as Bowman's roots (*Gillenia*), hardy geraniums (*Geranium*), and tufted hair grass (*Deschampsia cespitosa*)—without being overpowering.

Use the large plumes of giant fleeceflower to echo other plumes, like those of 'Karl Foerster' feather reed grass (*Calamagrostis* × *acutiflora*) or meadowsweets (*Filipendula*). For contrast, give them other broad or spiky blooms as bedmates: Think of baptisias (*Baptisia*), hardy hibiscus (*Hibiscus*), lilies (*Lilium*), purple coneflower (*Echinacea purpurea*), delphiniums (*Delphinium*), Culver's roots (*Veronicastrum*), and tuberous-rooted Jerusalem sage (*Phlomis tuberosa*), for example.

Seasonal Features

Mountain fleeceflower usually starts flowering in early summer (even late spring, in the warm-est parts of its range) and continues to produce new blooms well into fall. That gives you a large pool of potential companions from which to choose, including summer- and fall-flowering perennials as well as those with colorful foliage (all season or with a fall color change).

Giant fleeceflower has a long flowering period, too, though it's a bit more variable as to when it starts and finishes: late spring into late summer in some areas and early summer into early fall in others. The plant takes several years to reach its full size, so before you commit to choosing permanent companions, consider pairing it with tall annuals—such as cosmos (*Cosmos bipinnatus*), spider flower (*Cleome hassleriana*), and tall zinnias—for the first few seasons. Then select perennial partners with bloom times that coincide with the giant fleeceflower in your garden. Or concentrate on co-stars that will flower in mid- to late summer, which should work anywhere.

Phlox
months of eye-catching color

Phlox carolina 'Miss Lingard' with *Forsythia viridissima* var. *koreana* 'Kumson' and *Physostegia virginiana* 'Miss Manners'

Phlox subulata 'Emerald Cushion Blue' with *Aubrieta* and *Iberis sempervirens* 'Purity'

A Perfect Match

I've seen many marvelous phlox combinations over the years, but the most memorable sight is one I make a point of driving by every year: an eastern redbud (*Cercis canadensis*) underplanted with a carpet of moss phlox (*Phlox subulata*). I don't know if it was by chance or design, but the phlox is a perfect match for that redbud's particular shade of purplish pink, and the sight is absolutely amazing each spring.

Whether you have sun or shade, moist soil or dry, there are at least a few phlox (*Phlox*) that will suit your site. These diverse perennials come in a range of heights, habits, colors, and bloom times. From a gardener's perspective, it's easiest to divide them into two basic groups: those for shade and those for sun, though there are overlaps. The descriptions below touch on some of the most widely available kinds.

Phlox for shade. Creeping phlox (*P. stolonifera*) thrives in partial to full shade. Though it likes soil that's on the moist side, it can adapt well to dry shade. It grows in low, spreading carpets just a few inches tall, with 6- to 12-inch-tall flowering stems topped with light blue, pink, or white flowers through most of spring. Woodland phlox (*P. divaricata*), also known as wild blue phlox or wild sweet William, grows best in light all-day shade or morning sun and afternoon shade; the more moisture it gets, the more sun it can take. It, too, is a spreader, to

Bloom Buddies
Marvelous Matches for Flowering Combos

Here's a sampling of flowering perennials that make great partners for phlox (*Phlox*), based on their bloom times and growing preferences.

Partners for spring bloomers that prefer full sun, such as moss phlox (*P. subulata*):

Basket-of-gold (*Aurinia saxatilis*)

Cushion spurge (*Euphorbia polychroma*)

Perennial candytuft (*Iberis sempervirens*)

Dianthus (*Dianthus*)

Purple rock cresses (*Aubrieta*)

Snow-in-summer (*Cerastium tomentosum*)

White rock cresses (*Arabis*)

Partners for spring bloomers that prefer some shade, such as creeping phlox (*P. stolonifera*) and woodland phlox (*P. divaricata*):

Allegheny pachysandra (*Pachysandra procumbens*)

Bleeding hearts (*Dicentra*)

Epimediums (*Epimedium*)

Foamflowers (*Tiarella*)

Green-and-gold (*Chrysogonum virginianum*)

Jacob's ladders (*Polemonium*)

Pulmonarias (*Pulmonaria*)

Siberian bugloss (*Brunnera macrophylla*)

Snowdrop anemone (*Anemone sylvestris*)

Spotted deadnettle (*Lamium maculatum*)

Wild geranium (*Geranium maculatum*)

Woodland sedum (*Sedum ternatum*)

Partners for early- to midsummer bloomers in sun, such as Carolina phlox (*P. carolina*), meadow phlox (*P. maculata*), and *P. × arendsii*:

Anise hyssops (*Agastache*)

Catmints (*Nepeta*)

Coreopsis (*Coreopsis*)

Delphiniums (*Delphinium*)

Foxgloves (*Digitalis*)

Italian alkanet (*Anchusa azurea*)

Mountain bluet (*Centaurea montana*)

Pincushion flowers (*Scabiosa*)

Red valerian (*Centranthus ruber*)

Rose campion (*Lychnis coronaria*)

Speedwells (*Veronica*)

Yarrows (*Achillea*)

Partners for mid- to late summer bloomers in sun, such as summer phlox (*P. paniculata*):

Asters (*Aster*)

Balloon flower (*Platycodon grandiflorus*)

Bee balms (*Monarda*)

Blazing stars (*Liatris*)

Daylilies (*Hemerocallis*)

Echinaceas (*Echinacea*)

Globe thistle (*Echinops*)

Great blue lobelia (*Lobelia siphilitica*)

Hardy hibiscus (*Hibiscus*)

Heleniums (*Helenium*)

Meadow rues (*Thalictrum*)

Meadowsweets (*Filipendula*)

Mulleins (*Verbascum*)

Obedient plant (*Physostegia virginiana*)

Rudbeckias (*Rudbeckia*)

Russian sages (*Perovskia*)

Stokes' aster (*Stokesia laevis*)

about 6 inches tall in leaf and to 1 foot when it flowers with light purple-blue or white flowers in mid-spring to early summer. Both species are suited to Zones 3 to 8.

Phlox for sun. Moss phlox (*P. subulata*), also known as moss pink or mountain phlox, is one of the earliest bloomers in this group. It forms ground-hugging, 6-inch-tall mats of short, needlelike leaves that are practically smothered in pink, magenta, light purple-blue, or white flowers from mid- to late spring. It thrives in full sun and average to dry soil in Zones 3 to 9. Prairie or downy phlox (*P. pilosa*), for Zones 4 to 9, flowers in shades of pink in late spring to early summer, on spreading carpets of 1- to 2-foot stems.

For later in the season, there are several species that form distinctly upright clumps with relatively sizable bloom clusters at the tops of the stems. Carolina phlox (*P. carolina*) and meadow phlox (*P. maculata*), for Zones 3 to 8, flower in early to midsummer. Both usually reach 2 to 3 feet tall and bloom in a range of pinks and whites. Summer phlox (*P. paniculata*), for Zones 3 or 4 to 8, can be anywhere from 3 to 5 feet tall. Also known as border or garden phlox, it generally starts in midsummer and continues through late summer or even into fall. Pinks and white are the most common colors, but there are also selections in tints and shades of purple-blue, salmon orange, magenta,

Phlox paniculata 'Bright Eyes' and *Veronica (above)*; *Phlox subulata* 'Candy Stripe' and *Armeria maritima* 'Bloodstone' *(right)*

Managing Mildew

It's easy to fall for the huge bloom clusters of summer phlox—and just as easy to be disappointed if your plants end up disfigured by the grayish leaf patches caused by powdery mildew. The easiest solution is to look for cultivars that are resistant to this fungal disease, such as white 'David', purplish pink 'David's Lavender', and many newer hybrids. Another option is to keep your phlox in borders that you see from a distance, so you won't notice the damage.

and crimson red. The upright phlox grow well in average to moist but well-drained soil. They thrive in full sun but perform well in partial shade, particularly in warm-climate gardens.

Color Considerations

Besides the main hue of the flowers, many phlox blooms include at least one other color: a lighter or darker center "eye," for example, or streaking, shadings, or swirls of other colors, or contrasting buds and blossoms. These secondary colors can provide great inspiration for suitable partners. The white flowers of 'North Hills' moss phlox, for instance, have purple markings toward their centers, which you could echo with a dark-leaved heuchera (*Heuchera*), such as 'Black Taffeta'. And phlox flowers with white center markings, like those of lavender purple to purplish pink 'Laura' summer phlox, would look great with a partner that has bright white flowers, such as 'Becky' Shasta daisy (*Leucanthemum × superbum*).

On the softer side. In sun or shade, the pastel hues of phlox pair beautifully with light purples, lavender blues, medium to pale pinks, peaches, soft yellows, and white flowers, as well as gray, peachy, or cream-variegated leaves. If you'd like to add some intensity to the scene, use companions in somewhat deeper shades of those flower colors, bright yellow blooms, or yellow or purple foliage.

Bold and brilliant. The many bright pink, magenta, reddish, purple, and orangey phlox hold their own with other vivid flower colors. They're particularly striking with other hot pinks, blues, and purples, as well as golds and yellows. True red, red-orange, and orange flowers can work with them in the same border, but consider separating them from the phlox with rich purple or blue flowers or green or dark foliage. (Even red and orange phlox tend to be on the pink to magenta side, which can clash uncomfortably right next to clear red, scarlet, and orange.)

White wonders. Phlox offer some of the loveliest white flowers in the perennial world: brilliant, pure whites—such as 'Miss Lingard' Carolina phlox and 'David' and shorter 'Danielle' summer phlox—as well as those that are lightly touched with green, as on 'Jade' summer phlox; barely blushed with pink, as on hybrid 'Miss Jill' (*P. × arendsii*); or with just a hint of blue or lavender, as on 'May Breeze' woodland phlox. Any of these are excellent

Phlox paniculata 'Becky Towe' and *Liriope muscari* 'Silvery Sunproof'

Shapes and Textures

Flower color and bloom time are the most obvious features to consider when you're making matches for your phlox, but it's also worth looking at their plant forms and leaf and flower textures.

Shaping up. Habit-wise, perennial phlox generally fall into one of two shapes: low (anywhere from 6 to 18 inches tall) and spreading, or upright (anywhere from 2 to 5 or even 6 feet tall, depending on the selection) and clump forming.

The low-growing, spreading phlox—such as creeping and woodland phlox for some shade and moss phlox for full sun—work well at the fronts of beds and borders. They do a great job filling in around mounded and vase-shaped companions and make a strong contrast for distinctly vertical partners.

Shorter cultivars of upright-growing phlox—those that are 24 to 30 inches tall—are vertical at first, especially in single clumps. But if you plant them in groups, or if you give single clumps a few years to fill out a bit, the plants have a mounded shape that pairs comfortably with a wide range of perennial companions in the middle of a bed or border. Distinctly upright phlox, particularly the taller cultivars of summer phlox, make strong vertical accents in the middle of a planting and create contrasting backgrounds for shorter mounded and spreading bedmates.

choices for an all-white border, paired with blue, gray, silver, and white-variegated leaves. Or try them with pink and blue flowers, or with yellow blooms and yellow-variegated foliage.

Phlox for foliage. The leaves of some selections, such as 'Becky Towe' and 'Harlequin' summer phlox, are so strikingly variegated that it's best to use them sparingly, as single accents, rather than in multiples. To let them shine, plant them next to and in front of companions that have solid green or dark foliage; that way, you won't have to worry about color clashes between the phlox leaves and flowers and your other perennials.

Textural effects. In leaf, low-growing phlox species have small and/or slender leaves, giving the plants a fine texture: great for contrasting with broad foliage, like that of hostas and heucheras. The leaves of upright phlox range from very narrow to lance shaped, giving the plants a fine to medium texture that benefits from partners with more distinctive leaf shapes: either broad, as on lady's mantle (*Alchemilla mollis*), for instance, or spiky, like the foliage of irises and ornamental grasses.

Though individual phlox flowers aren't very big, they're held in clusters that are relatively large for the size of the plants. Established carpets of the spreaders create sheets of color in bloom, providing a bold effect even with the softer colors and making a striking contrast for spiky companions, such as foxgloves (*Digitalis*). The flower clusters of the upright types range from elongated (on meadow phlox) to domed (as on summer phlox). Repeat their bold form with other large blooms, like those of daylilies (*Hemerocallis*), irises, and true lilies (*Lilium*). For contrast, consider spiky-flowered perennials, such as agastaches (*Agastache*), Culver's root (*Veronicastrum virginicum*), and perennial salvias (*Salvia*), or plumy blooms, like those of astilbes (*Astilbe*) or Russian sages (*Perovskia*).

Seasonal Features

With a bit of planning, you can enjoy phlox combinations from early spring well into autumn. Here are some ideas for planning seasonal pairings; for more specific companion suggestions, see "Bloom Buddies" on page 207.

Thinking spring. Starting with creeping phlox, and then woodland phlox a few weeks later, combinations based on pastel colors are a wonderful way to welcome spring. If you'd like a bit more zip, add rich pink, bright yellow, or

Variations on a Theme

Phlox offer some very interesting color characteristics. The whites, lighter purple-blues, and pinks are pretty consistent, but some of the more unusual colors of summer phlox can vary widely depending on the weather, the age of the bloom, and even the time of day. Those described as orange, for instance, such as 'Orange Perfection' summer phlox, may appear nearly true orange one day and salmon pink to mostly pink on another.

The purple and blue cultivars of summer phlox, such as 'Blue Paradise' and 'Nicky' (also sold as 'Düsterlohe'), are notorious for being variable, appearing blue or purple in the morning, changing to violet in the afternoon, and changing again in the evening. And red summer phlox selections, such as 'Starfire', may sometimes appear true red but are more often on the magenta red side.

So if you're drawn to some of these more unusual hues, don't depend on photographs or descriptions when you're choosing color-based partners; see the flowers for yourself first, at least. Even better, grow the plants in a holding bed for a full season or two so you can observe their colors and variations over time before you start working them into combinations.

white flowers as accents. Some early bloomers that thrive with the shade-adapted phlox include epimediums (*Epimedium*), Siberian bugloss (*Brunnera macrophylla*), and spotted deadnettle (*Lamium maculatum*). Lush new green, yellow, gray, blue, purple, and variegated leaves can all complement these early risers.

In mid- to late spring, moss phlox's colorful carpets make a spectacle in sunny, well-drained sites. Combine several cultivars to create a patchwork effect, or pick just one and pair it with other low-growing companions that thrive in the same conditions, such as bright yellow basket-of-gold (*Aurinia saxatilis*), pink or white dianthus (*Dianthus*), and purple rock cresses (*Aubrieta*).

Color for summer. Carolina phlox and meadow phlox, which peak in early to mid-summer in a range of pinks and whites, associate elegantly with the many other perennial favorites that bloom around the same time in sunny gardens: bellflowers (*Campanula*), foxgloves (*Digitalis*), hardy geraniums (*Geranium*), irises, and perennial salvias, to name a few. And for midsummer on, there are summer phlox to choose from for both hot and cool color schemes, paired with balloon flower (*Platycodon grandiflorus*), echinaceas (*Echinacea*), and mountain fleeceflower (*Persicaria amplexicaulis*), among other summer bloomers.

On into fall. If you snip off the first flower clusters on your summer-blooming phlox as soon as all the blossoms drop, you'll likely enjoy some rebloom into early fall, at least. These bonus blooms add to the autumn spectacle with other late-flowering perennials, such as asters, azure monkshood (*Aconitum carmichaelii*), and Japanese anemones (*Anemone*), as

Phlox divaricata and *Hosta montana* 'Aureomarginata'

well as warm-season ornamental grasses and fall-colored foliage.

A bit of winter interest. Creeping phlox, moss phlox, and woodland phlox may all be evergreen where winters aren't too severe (roughly Zone 6 and south), especially if they're protected from drying wind. Pair them with other evergreen perennials for a textural contrast: Try bergenias (*Bergenia*), hellebores (*Helleborus*), and Robb's spurge (*Euphorbia amygdaloides* var. *robbiae*) with creeping and woodland phlox in areas that are shady in summer. Combine lavenders (*Lavandula*), thymes (*Thymus*), and yuccas (*Yucca*) with moss phlox in sunny sites.

Special Effects

There's a phlox to fit pretty much any bed or border. These versatile perennials also work well in some more specialized settings.

Woodland gardens. Creeping and woodland phlox are perfectly at home with other native wildflowers in the shade of deciduous trees and shrubs. Some wonderful companions in this sort of setting include Canada wild ginger (*Asarum canadense*), crested iris (*Iris cristata*), foamflowers (*Tiarella*), Virginia bluebells (*Mertensia virginica*), wild columbine (*Aquilegia canadensis*), and wood poppy (*Stylophorum diphyllum*).

Butterfly gardens. Phlox produce ample supplies of nectar, and their clustered blooms attract adult butterflies and moths. The spring-blooming species are particularly welcoming for the earliest arrivers. For a later-blooming border that will draw these and other pollinators like a magnet, combine summer phlox

Phlox pilosa and *Itea virginica* 'Sprich' (Little Henry)

with other perennials that are rich in nectar and/or pollen, such as asters, bee balms (*Monarda*), coreopsis (*Coreopsis*), false aster (*Boltonia asteroides*), Joe-Pye weeds (*Eupatorium*), oxeye (*Heliopsis helianthoides*), perennial sunflowers (*Helianthus*), purple coneflower (*Echinacea purpurea*), and swamp milkweed (*Asclepias incarnata*).

Exploring More Options: Partners beyond Perennials

The low-growing, spring-flowering phlox (*Phlox*) are perfect partners for a wide variety of early-flowering bulbs. Creeping phlox and woodland phlox look wonderful with bluebells (*Hyacinthoides*), daffodils, and summer snowflake (*Leucojum aestivum*), while species and hybrid tulips thrive in the same sunny, well-drained soil that moss phlox likes.

Physostegia
abundant summer spikes

Physostegia virginiana and *Sedum* 'Autumn Joy'

Physostegia virginiana 'Miss Manners' and *Leucanthemum* × *superbum* 'Becky'

A Perfect Match

I've been growing 'Miss Manners' obedient plant for about 10 years now, and it truly is perfectly well behaved in the border. Its slender spikes are simply lovely with bold white blooms and with white-variegated foliage, as well: I have it partnered with both 'Miss Lingard' Carolina phlox (*Phlox carolina*) and 'Kumson' greenstem forsythia (*Forsythia viridissima* var. *koreana*), for instance.

The upright stems of obedient plant (*Physostegia virginiana*) are topped with long, spikelike flower clusters. It commonly reaches 3 to 4 feet tall, but you can find more-compact options as well, such as 18-inch-tall 'Crystal Peak White'. Also known as false dragonshead, this adaptable species is native to many parts of North America and is usually recommended for Zones 3 to 9.

Obedient plant tends to spread quickly by creeping roots, especially in rich, moist soil, so it's a challenge to manage in a typical border situation, but there are a few ways you can deal with that trait. One option is to combine it with other creepers, such as bee balms (*Monarda*), blue mistflower (*Eupatorium coelestinum*), 'Silver King' western mugwort (*Artemisia ludoviciana*), and white snakeroot (*E. rugosum*), in a spot where they can spread as they like without crowding out less vigorous companions. Or choose one of the newer cultivars that tend to stay in distinct clumps, such as white 'Miss Manners' or light lavender pink 'Pink Manners'.

Color Considerations

Most color interest in obedient plants comes from the flowers, which are normally pink tinged with a bit of lavender or purple but are bright white on some selections. They can combine well with many other pink or white perennials that flower around the same time, such as Japanese anemones (*Anemone*) and summer phlox (*Phlox paniculata*). Both the pinks and whites look pretty with blues and purples, too.

Yellow-flowered perennials can pair comfortably with white-flowered obedient plants. If you want to use yellows with pink-flowered obedient plants, try to match their intensity (pale yellows with the lighter pinks and lemony yellows with the richer shades).

Variegated obedient plant ('Variegata') is a spectacle in its own right, with purplish pink flowers over green leaves that are widely edged with creamy white. It shows off best in combination with a quieter foliage partner, such as powder blue 'Heavy Metal' switch grass (*Panicum virgatum*).

Shapes and Textures

Their upright stems and spiky flower form give obedient plants a distinctly vertical effect. They provide visual variety next to the many mounded perennials and to a range of flower forms. Contrast them with large, broad or funnel-shaped blooms, for instance, like those of hardy hibiscus (*Hibiscus*), or with daisy-form

Bloom Buddies
Marvelous Matches for flowering Combos

Obedient plant (*Physostegia virginiana*) thrives in moist, fertile soil and full sun but can adapt to drier conditions, especially if the plants get some shade. Below are some compatible flowering companions that can complement them in late summer to early fall.

Asters (*Aster*)

Balloon flower (*Platycodon grandiflorus*)

False aster (*Boltonia asteroides*)

Goldenrods (*Solidago*)

Ironweeds (*Vernonia*)

Japanese anemones (*Anemone*)

Perennial lobelias (*Lobelia*)

Perennial sunflowers (*Helianthus*)

Purple coneflower (*Echinacea purpurea*)

Spiderworts (*Tradescantia*)

Summer phlox (*Phlox paniculata*)

Turtleheads (*Chelone*)

flowers, like those of purple coneflowers (*Echinacea purpurea*).

Seasonal Features

Flowering times vary a bit, depending on the climate and cultivar. In warmer regions, look for flowers starting in midsummer, especially on the earlier-flowering selections, such as 'Miss Manners' and 'Summer Snow'. Late summer is more usual in northern gardens. Once they begin, most obedient plants keep going for about 2 months, into early fall.

Platycodon
charming in bud and in bloom

Platycodon grandiflorus and Heliopsis helianthoides

Platycodon grandiflorus 'Astra Pink' and *Gillenia stipulata*

A Perfect Match

The rich purple-blue blooms of balloon flowers pair well with many summer perennials, but one of my favorite partners for them is any hybrid daylily (*Hemerocallis*), from rich red, gold, or orange to paler peach, pink, or cream. The form of the open flowers is somewhat similar, but there's a difference in size, for variety. Most important, though: Balloon flowers provide one of the few colors you can't get in daylilies!

Balloon flower (*Platycodon grandiflorus*) plants often take a few years to settle in and fill out, but they'll reward your patience. Their distinctive, puffed-up buds open to single, semi-double, or double flowers, usually in purple-blue but sometimes pink or white, on 1- to 3-foot-tall stems. Balloon flowers usually perform well in Zones 3 or 4 to 8.

Color Considerations

Balloon flowers in the purple to blue range complement pretty much any other color. Use them to echo other perennials in the same color range, or pair them with flowering and foliage partners in pastel tints: buttery yellows, like those of 'Sunshine' Shasta daisy (*Leucanthemum* × *superbum*); peachy oranges, like those of 'Caramel' heuchera (*Heuchera*); or a wide range of pinks, from soft pink 'Barbara Mitchell' daylily

(*Hemerocallis*) to rosy pink hummingbird mint (*Agastache cana*).

Purple-blue balloon flowers are also gorgeous with bright to creamy whites. Think of 'Danielle' or 'David' summer phlox (*Phlox paniculata*) or 'Miss Manners' obedient plant (*Physostegia virginiana*), for instance.

Want to work with more intense colors instead? Pair your purple-blue balloon flowers with richer reds, bright to rusty oranges, or sunny yellows to golds: hues you can find in many daylilies, for instance. Or set off the purple-blue flowers with bright yellow foliage, like that of 'Golden Arrow' mountain fleeceflower (*Persicaria amplexicaulis*).

The white- or pink-flowered balloon flowers can pair well with white-, pink-, or blue-flowered companions. They—and the purple-blues, too—also look great with silvery, gray, or blue foliage.

Shapes and Textures

Balloon flowers grow in distinct clumps but tend to have a somewhat sprawling, open effect by bloom time. Taller selections, especially—like 2- to 3-foot-tall 'Mariesii'—benefit from staking or from being cut back by about half their height in early summer. Or pair them with bushy or upright companions that they can mingle with or lean on a bit, such as daylilies (*Hemerocallis*), true lilies (*Lilium*), or summer phlox (*Phlox paniculata*).

Globelike in bud and with a broadly starry outline when open, balloon flowers complement many other flower forms, from spiky blazing stars (*Liatris*) to daisy-form rudbeckias (*Rudbeckia*) to airy Russian sages (*Perovskia*).

Bloom Buddies
Marvelous Matches for Flowering Combos

Balloon flower (*Platycodon grandiflorus*) plants thrive in full sun to light shade and average to moist but well-drained soil: the same conditions that suit many complementary perennials in mid- to late summer.

Bee balms (*Monarda*)
Catmints (*Nepeta*)
Coreopsis (*Coreopsis*)
Daylilies (*Hemerocallis*)
Echinaceas (*Echinacea*)
Heleniums (*Helenium*)
Lilies (*Lilium*)
Obedient plant (*Physostegia virginiana*)
Oxeye (*Heliopsis helianthoides*)

Perennial lobelias (*Lobelia*)
Perennial salvias (*Salvia*)
Rudbeckias (*Rudbeckia*)
Russian sages (*Perovskia*)
Shasta daisy (*Leucanthemum × superbum*)
Summer phlox (*Phlox paniculata*)
Yarrows (*Achillea*)

Seasonal Features

Balloon flowers are notoriously late risers, sometimes not sprouting until spring turns to summer. After that, they grow quickly, and compact kinds may begin blooming in early summer, especially in mild climates; elsewhere, midsummer is more common. They typically keep going for about 2 months, or even longer if you clip off the browned blooms. The leaves turn shades of golden yellow, orange, and/or purple in fall.

Polemonium
graceful early-season blooms

Polemonium boreale 'Heavenly Habit' and Digitalis grandiflora

Polemonium reptans 'Stairway to Heaven' and Heuchera 'Fire Alarm'

A Perfect Match

I've never had much success with keeping the upright Jacob's ladders in my garden for more than a year or two. Creeping Jacob's ladder, on the other hand, has been a dependable performer—even its vividly variegated selections 'Stairway to Heaven' and 'Touch of Class'. Their brightly colored, fine-textured leaves make a great match for rich green wild gingers (Asarum), hellebores (Helleborus), and other foliage partners.

Delicately beautiful Jacob's ladders (Polemonium) are charming complements to other shade-loving perennials. Among the most readily available kinds are P. boreale 'Heavenly Habit', P. caeruleum, and P. yezoense, with upright stems, and creeping Jacob's ladder (P. reptans), with a looser, somewhat sprawling habit. All have similar leaves, with many small leaflets that give them a somewhat ferny appearance, and cup- to bell-shaped blooms, typically in shades of blue but sometimes white. Jacob's ladders are best suited to cooler climates (Zones 3 to 7).

Color Considerations

Most Jacob's ladders bloom in tints of blue. They're wonderful with white or yellow flowers: Try upright Jacob's ladders with 'Snow Thimble' common foxglove (Digitalis purpurea) or lady's mantle (*Alchemilla mollis*), for instance, or creeping Jacob's ladder with foamflowers (*Tiarella*) or wood poppy (*Stylophorum diphyllum*). Pink-flowered partners, such as bleeding hearts (*Dicentra*), are lovely, as well.

Take advantage of colorful foliage partners, too. White- or cream-variegated leaves, like those of 'Patriot' hosta, work well, as do grays and silvers, like those of 'Looking Glass' Siberian bugloss (*Brunnera macrophylla*). Jacob's ladders also match well with yellow variegates, such as 'Eversheen' Japanese sedge (*Carex oshimensis*), and solid yellow leaves, like those of 'Sweet Kate' spiderwort (*Tradescantia*).

Jacob's ladders that have variegated leaflets complement their own blue flowers, creating a stunning combination all by themselves. They show off best next to dark-leaved partners, such as bergenias (*Bergenia*) and Robb's spurge (*Euphorbia amygdaloides* var. *robbiae*).

Shapes and Textures

Jacob's ladders are mounded in leaf, creating ferny clumps that work well at or close to the front of the border. They look great behind or next to lower spreaders, such as European wild ginger (*Asarum europaeum*), and in front of upright to arching partners, such as Solomon's seals (*Polygonatum*) or toad lilies (*Tricyrtis*). In bloom, upright Jacob's ladders develop a more vertical habit that adds variety among mounded companions, such as bleeding hearts and lady's mantle.

Texture-wise, the small leaflets and flowers of Jacob's ladders give the plants a dainty look that contrasts beautifully with hostas and other broad-leaved partners.

Bloom Buddies
Marvelous Matches for Flowering Combos

While Jacob's ladders (*Polemonium*) can thrive in full sun in the coolest parts of their growing range, they generally perform best with morning sun and afternoon shade or light all-day shade with average to moist but well-drained, compost-enriched soil. Below are some companions that can coincide with or overlap their usual bloom period.

Bellflowers (*Campanula*)

Columbines (*Aquilegia*)

Creeping phlox (*Phlox stolonifera*)

Epimediums (*Epimedium*)

Foamflowers (*Tiarella*)

Foamy bells (× *Heucherella*)

Foxgloves (*Digitalis*)

Goatsbeards (*Aruncus*)

Hardy geraniums (*Geranium*)

Lady's mantle (*Alchemilla mollis*)

Lupines (*Lupinus*)

Pulmonarias (*Pulmonaria*)

Siberian iris (*Iris sibirica*)

Woodland phlox (*Phlox divaricata*)

Seasonal Features

Variegated cultivars of Jacob's ladders are showy from the time they emerge, often heavily tinged with pink. Creeping Jacob's ladder usually blooms from mid- to late spring or—in the cooler parts of its growing range—late spring to early summer. Upright Jacob's ladders tend to be at their best in late spring to early summer, extending into midsummer in cool climates.

Polygonatum
sturdy shade lovers

Polygonatum odoratum 'Variegatum' with *Lamium maculatum* 'White Nancy' and *Carex oshimensis* 'Evergold'

Polygonatum biflorum and *Hosta* 'Sagae'

A Perfect Match

A number of years ago, I planted a small pot of dwarf Solomon's seal (*Polygonatum humile*). It didn't do much for the first few years, but it has since spread into a thick and beautiful, 4- to 6-inch-tall carpet at the front of the border. It's a bit too vigorous for delicate companions, such as columbines (*Aquilegia*), but it holds its own well against spreading sedges (*Carex*) and makes a marvelous filler around medium-size to large hostas.

Solomon's seals (*Polygonatum*) are distinctive additions to shady combinations, with gracefully arching, unbranched stems lined by two rows of oval to broadly lance-shaped leaves. They flower, as well, with creamy to greenish white bells, but the blossoms are mostly hidden by the foliage. Common Solomon's seal (*P. × hybridum*), fragrant Solomon's seal (*P. odoratum*), and smooth Solomon's seal (*P. biflorum*) are typically 18 to 30 inches tall and hardy in Zones 3 to 9.

Color Considerations

If you want to take advantage of their white flowers in combinations, plant your Solomon's seals on a slope or in a raised bed so you can more easily see the blooms, or at least plant them in a site where you can see them up close. They're particularly pretty with other white spring bloomers, such as foamflowers

(*Tiarella*); with blues, like those of woodland phlox (*Phlox divaricata*); and with pinks, like those of bleeding hearts (*Dicentra*).

If you're growing Solomon's seals more for their elegant arching habit than for their flowers, enjoy them with any flower color at any point during the growing season. The green-leaved kinds are particularly useful as quiet companions for vividly variegated perennials, such as many hostas, and for bright yellow foliage, like that of 'Citronelle' heuchera (*Heuchera*). Or combine them with other shades of green, gray, silver, and blue for a more subtle interplay of colors, forms, and textures.

Solomon's seals that have variegated foliage are in a class by themselves, adding an element of extra color interest to their elegant form and easy-care nature. The most common cultivar of variegated Solomon's seal, with cream-rimmed foliage, is usually sold as *P. odoratum* 'Variegatum'. Enjoy it as an eye-catching accent among green-leaved partners, or pair it with red-blushed or red-leaved companions, such as 'Fire Alarm' heuchera (*Heuchera*), to contrast with the variegated foliage but echo this Solomon's seal's reddish stems.

Shapes and Textures

The upright-to-arching stems give Solomon's seals a vertical form that adds welcome variety to the many mounded shade perennials, including hostas, Lenten rose (*Helleborus × hybridus*), pulmonarias (*Pulmonaria*), and Siberian bugloss (*Brunnera macrophylla*). They also look terrific rising out of lower, spreading partners, such as creeping phlox and European wild ginger (*Asarum europaeum*). Ferns, fringed

Bloom Buddies
Marvelous Matches for Flowering Combos

Solomon's seals (*Polygonatum*) generally grow best in partial shade (morning sun and afternoon shade or light all-day shade) and average to moist but well-drained soil: the same conditions that suit many other lovely spring bloomers, including those below.

Allegheny pachysandra (*Pachysandra procumbens*)

Bleeding hearts (*Dicentra*)

Columbines (*Aquilegia*)

Creeping phlox (*Phlox stolonifera*)

Crested iris (*Iris cristata*)

Epimediums (*Epimedium*)

Foamflowers (*Tiarella*)

Foamy bells (× *Heucherella*)

Jacob's ladders (*Polemonium*)

Pulmonarias (*Pulmonaria*)

Siberian bugloss (*Brunnera macrophylla*)

Woodland phlox (*Phlox divaricata*)

bleeding heart (*D. eximia*), and other perennials with lacy leaves make a striking textural contrast to the roughly oval Solomon's seal leaves.

Seasonal Features

Solomon's seals sprout early and are in bloom by mid-spring (in warmer areas) to late spring (in cooler regions), typically continuing for 3 to 5 weeks. In fall, the plants turn shades of yellow before going dormant for winter.

Primula
colorful early risers

Primula japonica **and** *Camassia*

Primula veris **and** *Brunnera macrophylla*

A Perfect Match

It's a pity that Siebold primrose (*Primula sieboldii*) is hard to find, because it's certainly not hard to grow. I've seen it in top-notch combinations with ferns, hostas, and other shade-loving perennials, contributing clustered blooms—usually in white or shades of pink—in late spring and then disappearing soon after flowering and returning early the following spring. You don't even miss it during its rest period, as the expanding foliage of its companions quickly fills the space it leaves.

A sure sign of spring, primroses (*Primula*) offer a wide range of cheerful colors for cooler-climate perennial plantings. There are many species and hybrids, but only a few are commonly available at garden centers; most of these are best suited to Zones 3 or 4 to 7 or 8. The earliest kinds, including common or English primrose (*P. vulgaris*) and cowslip (*P. veris*), are typically 6 to 10 inches tall, with single to double flowers in a variety of solid colors and bicolors. Drumstick primrose (*P. denticulata*), for Zones 3 to 8, has flowers in shades of pink, purple, blue, or white in ball-like clusters atop 8- to 12-inch-tall stems. And then there are the "candelabra" primroses, with tiered whorls of flowers on 1- to 2-foot-tall stems, such as red, pink, or white Japanese primrose (*P. japonica*) for Zones 5 to 8. There are also candelabra species and hybrids with orange, peach, pink, purple, or yellow flowers, such as *P. aurantiaca, P. beesianna, P. bulleyana,* and *P. × bulleesiana.*

Color Considerations

Color is so welcome in spring that you really can't make a bad combination with primroses. For a bit of extra sophistication, though, you could stick with tints and shades of one color—pale yellow Belarina Buttercup ('Kerbelbut') common primrose with deeper yellow 'February Gold' daffodil, for instance—or else combine different colors of similar intensity: rosy red 'Miller's Crimson' Japanese primrose with a rich purple Japanese or Siberian iris (*Iris ensata* or *I. sibirica*).

Perennials with yellow, dark, variegated, or blue leaves are particularly useful in primrose combinations, complementing or contrasting with them in flower and then remaining to provide color interest for the rest of the growing season.

Shapes and Textures

Primroses produce rosettes of roughly oblong leaves and mostly have a low, mounded form, though the candelabra types are more vertical when in bloom. For contrast in form, pair them with distinctly upright partners, such as irises, or those with arching stems, such as Solomon's seals (*Polygonatum*). For contrast in texture, look to lacy leaves, like those of astilbes (*Astilbe*) and ferns, or strappy to grassy leaves, like those of irises and sedges (*Carex*).

Seasonal Features

Common primrose, cowslips, and many other low primroses begin blooming at the very start of the growing season: late winter in the mildest parts of their growing range to early

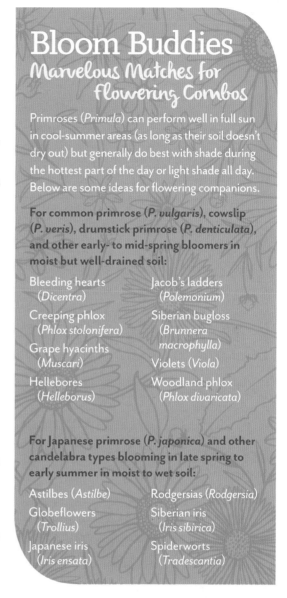

Bloom Buddies
Marvelous Matches for Flowering Combos

Primroses (*Primula*) can perform well in full sun in cool-summer areas (as long as their soil doesn't dry out) but generally do best with shade during the hottest part of the day or light shade all day. Below are some ideas for flowering companions.

For common primrose (*P. vulgaris*), cowslip (*P. veris*), drumstick primrose (*P. denticulata*), and other early- to mid-spring bloomers in moist but well-drained soil:

Bleeding hearts (*Dicentra*)

Creeping phlox (*Phlox stolonifera*)

Grape hyacinths (*Muscari*)

Hellebores (*Helleborus*)

Jacob's ladders (*Polemonium*)

Siberian bugloss (*Brunnera macrophylla*)

Violets (*Viola*)

Woodland phlox (*Phlox divaricata*)

For Japanese primrose (*P. japonica*) and other candelabra types blooming in late spring to early summer in moist to wet soil:

Astilbes (*Astilbe*)

Globeflowers (*Trollius*)

Japanese iris (*Iris ensata*)

Rodgersias (*Rodgersia*)

Siberian iris (*Iris sibirica*)

Spiderworts (*Tradescantia*)

spring elsewhere. Drumstick primrose follows soon after, in early to mid-spring, with Japanese primrose and other candelabra primroses opening in late spring to early summer. The bloom period for most lasts 3 to 4 weeks; candelabra types may continue for 4 to 6 weeks.

Pulmonaria
lovely leaves, beautiful blooms

Pulmonarias
Partial to full shade; average, well-drained soil

Pulmonaria 'Blue Ensign' with Tanacetum vulgare 'Isla Gold'

Pulmonaria saccharata 'Mrs. Moon' and Aruncus aethusifolius

A Perfect Match

I think the silvery pulmonarias look smashing next to dark-leaved heucheras (*Heuchera*), such as 'Blackout' and 'Obsidian'. A Japanese painted fern (*Athyrium nipponicum* var. *pictum*) makes the perfect finishing touch, with deep purple stems to echo the heuchera, silvery fronds to pick up the color of the pulmonaria, and a lacy texture to contrast with both companions.

Whether you use them as stars or supporting players, pulmonarias (*Pulmonaria*)—also known as lungworts—are an excellent choice for shady-garden combinations. Their small but abundant, loosely clustered blooms are their key feature in spring, followed by lush leaves that may be solid green, as on blue lungwort (*P. angustifolia*), or spotted with silver, as on Bethlehem sage (*P. saccharata*) and longleaf lungwort (*P. longifolia*). There are many stunning hybrids, too, with spotted to nearly solid silver leaves. Most pulmonarias reach 8 to 12 inches tall in leaf and 12 to 18 inches in bloom. They're best suited for Zones 3 to 8.

Color Considerations

Pulmonarias commonly produce pink buds that turn purplish and then blue as the flowers open. On some selections, such as

'Raspberry Splash', the hues are very rich; on others, such as 'Roy Davidson', they're distinctly on the pastel side, ranging from pale pink to baby blue. You can also find selections that are one color throughout their bloom period, such as intense 'Blue Ensign', pink 'Bubble Gum', or snowy 'Sissinghurst White'.

These spring beauties pair well with a range of other blues and pinks. If you want to get sophisticated, match the primary color of the pulmonaria with its partners—frosty blue Opal ('Ocupol') with sky blue forget-me-nots (*Myosotis*), for instance. Or echo the buds of those that start off pink with pink-flowering partners, such as bergenias (*Bergenia*), or plants with pinkish leaves, like those of 'Georgia Peach' heuchera (*Heuchera*).

Whites and creams also work well with all pulmonarias in flower. Consider 'Thalia' daffodil to provide white blooms, perhaps, or variegated purple moor grass (*Molinia caerulea* subsp. *caerulea* 'Variegata') for cream-striped leaves. Pulmonarias also look terrific with springy yellows, such as soft yellow bicolor barrenwort (*Epimedium* × *versicolor* 'Sulphureum') or bright yellow 'Tete-a-Tete' daffodils for flowers and cheery Bowles' golden grass (*Milium effusum* 'Aureum') or 'Everillo' Japanese sedge (*Carex oshimensis*) for foliage.

Oranges and reds aren't common colors in spring, but they can make striking partners for some of the more intense blue to purple pulmonarias, such as 'Bertram Anderson', 'Diana Clare', and 'Purple Haze'. For flowers, consider 'Orange Queen' epimedium (*E.* × *warleyense*) or wild columbine (*Aquilegia canadensis*); for foliage, look to selections of foamy bells (× *Heucherella*) or heucheras (*Heuchera*), such as 'Buttered Rum'

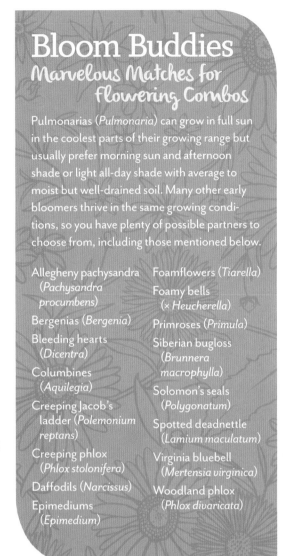

Bloom Buddies
Marvelous Matches for Flowering Combos

Pulmonarias (*Pulmonaria*) can grow in full sun in the coolest parts of their growing range but usually prefer morning sun and afternoon shade or light all-day shade with average to moist but well-drained soil. Many other early bloomers thrive in the same growing conditions, so you have plenty of possible partners to choose from, including those mentioned below.

Allegheny pachysandra (*Pachysandra procumbens*)

Bergenias (*Bergenia*)

Bleeding hearts (*Dicentra*)

Columbines (*Aquilegia*)

Creeping Jacob's ladder (*Polemonium reptans*)

Creeping phlox (*Phlox stolonifera*)

Daffodils (*Narcissus*)

Epimediums (*Epimedium*)

Foamflowers (*Tiarella*)

Foamy bells (× *Heucherella*)

Primroses (*Primula*)

Siberian bugloss (*Brunnera macrophylla*)

Solomon's seals (*Polygonatum*)

Spotted deadnettle (*Lamium maculatum*)

Virginia bluebell (*Mertensia virginica*)

Woodland phlox (*Phlox divaricata*)

or 'Gold Zebra' foamy bells or 'Autumn Leaves', 'Delta Dawn', or 'Southern Comfort' heuchera.

In summer and fall combinations, take advantage of pulmonarias' leaf colors. The solid greens are wonderful with striking silver, cool gray, vivid yellow, or vibrantly variegated foliage. Set off silvery pulmonarias with deep

Pulmonaria saccharata 'Sissinghurst White' and *Scilla siberica*

greens, like those of Robb's spurge (*Euphorbia amygdaloides* var. *robbiae*) or bearsfoot hellebore (*Helleborus foetidus*), or with extra-dark foliage, like that of black mondo grass (*Ophiopogon planiscapus* 'Nigrescens') or 'Chocoholic' bugbane (*Cimicifuga simplex*). Or use the particularly silvery pulmonarias, such as 'Majeste', 'Silver Bouquet', or 'Silver Shimmers', to emphasize the markings of foliage partners with the same color: silver-marked 'Langtrees' Siberian bugloss (*Brunnera macrophylla*), for instance, or silver-marbled 'Plum Pudding' heuchera.

Shapes and Textures

Pulmonarias grow in relatively compact, mounded clumps that are marvelous for filling in around larger mounds, like those of hostas, or around upright partners, such as Solomon's seals (*Polygonatum*) or toad lilies (*Tricyrtis*). If

there's room in front of the pulmonarias, cover the space with low-growing creepers or carpeting companions, such as creeping phlox (*Phlox stolonifera*), European wild ginger (*Asarum europaeum*), or woodland sedum (*Sedum ternatum*).

Broadly oval to lance-shaped leaves give pulmonarias a bold texture that looks terrific next to any of the many fine-textured shade lovers. Pair them with lacy leaves, like those of bugbanes (*Cimicifuga*), Jacob's ladders (*Polemonium*), and ferns, for instance, or with grassy- to strappy-leaved companions, such as crested iris (*Iris cristata*), broadleaf sedge (*C. siderosticha*), or Hakone grass (*Hakonechloa macra*).

Seasonal Features

Pulmonarias jump into bloom early: late winter to early spring in mild climates and early to mid-spring in cooler areas. Once they start, they typically continue for 6 to 8 weeks, overlapping with the bloom times of many other early perennials and spring-flowering bulbs. As the flowers finish, the bloom stems tend to bend down: Cut them off close to the base, if you wish, to tidy the clumps and prevent self-sown seedlings, or simply let the flush of new growth come up and cover them. These leaves generally look good through the rest of the growing season and may even linger well into winter, in mild conditions.

Rudbeckia
go for the gold

Rudbeckia fulgida with Geranium wlassovianum and Pennisetum alopecuroides 'Hameln'

Rudbeckia fulgida with Liatris spicata 'Kobold', Patrinia scabiosifolia, and Echinacea purpurea

A Perfect Match

Dark-leaved shrubs, such as 'Royal Purple' smokebush (*Cotinus coggygria*), and superdark ornamental grasses, such as Vertigo fountain grass (*Pennisetum purpureum* 'Tift 8'), are among my top picks for rudbeckia partners. The bright petals show off beautifully against a deep purple backdrop, and the dark leaves make an excellent echo for the purple-brown to near-black centers of these summer daisies.

The bright blooms of rudbeckias (*Rudbeckia*) are a welcome sight in warm-season beds and borders. There are a number of species to choose from, in a relatively limited range of colors but a variety of heights. Orange coneflower (*R. fulgida*)—which is not actually orange but on the warm side of yellow that's commonly called "gold" in flowers—produces dark-centered, daisy-form flowers atop 2- to 4-foot-tall stems. Sweet coneflower (*R. subtomentosa*) looks similar but grows to about 5 feet. Three-lobed coneflower (*R. triloba*), also known as brown-eyed Susan, has similar-looking but smaller blooms on 2- to 5-foot-tall plants.

Giant coneflower (*R. maxima*), also known as swamp coneflower, is yet another species with dark-centered, golden flowers, but it's distinctive for its blue leaves, which appear mostly near the base of the 5- to 7-foot-tall stems. Two species that can get even taller (to 8 feet) include shining or shiny coneflower

(*R. nitida*), with green-centered, golden flowers, and cutleaf or ragged coneflower (*R. laciniata*), with single or double, green-centered, clear yellow blooms.

All of these species flower from mid- or late summer to early fall and are hardy in Zones 3 to 9, except for giant coneflower, which is recommended for Zones 5 to 9.

Color Considerations

There's nothing subtle about the blooms of rudbeckias. For a traffic-stopping summer show, pair their sunny daisies with other yellow flowers and yellow-variegated grasses. (Use the grasses or other leafy companions to separate warm golden yellows from cooler greenish yellows, which can look a bit awkward right next to each other in borders that you see up close.)

Rudbeckias are also wonderful in exuberant combinations with other vibrant colors, including rich reds, like those of cardinal flower (*Lobelia cardinalis*), and bright to rusty oranges, like those of heleniums (*Helenium*) and torch lilies (*Kniphofia*). They look terrific with blues and purples, from saturated shades, like those of 'Blue Paradise' summer phlox (*Phlox paniculata*) and 'Purple Dome' New England aster (*Aster novae-angliae*), to lighter purple-blues and silvery blues, like those of 'Blue Fortune' anise hyssop (*Agastache*) and globe thistles (*Echinops*).

Shapes and Textures

Most rudbeckias have an upright habit, though 'Goldsturm' and other selections of *R. fulgida* create broad mounds when you plant them in groups of three or more. Giant coneflower's tall, almost leafless flower stems give it a strongly vertical habit, and its broad basal leaves offer bold foliage interest. Other rudbeckias aren't especially distinctive for either

Rudbeckia maxima and *Panicum virgatum* 'Cloud Nine' (above); *Rudbeckia fulgida* with *Pennisetum alopecuroides* 'Piglet' and *Aster laevis* (right)

their habit or their leaves. Their daisy-shaped flowers make them standouts in bloom, though. Repeat their shape with other daisy-form flowers, like those of asters, coreopsis (*Coreopsis*), and echinaceas (*Echinacea*); match them with equally bold blossoms, like those of hardy hibiscus (*Hibiscus*) and lilies (*Lilium*); or go high contrast with strikingly spiky partners, such as blazing stars (*Liatris*) and perennial salvias (*Salvia*).

Seasonal Features

Rudbeckias perk up the summer garden just as many earlier perennials finish their show or take a break, providing welcome color through the warmest part of summer along with other mid- to late summer sun lovers, such as balloon flower (*Platycodon grandiflorus*), daylilies (*Hemerocallis*), and Russian sages (*Perovskia*).

Most rudbeckias continue to open new flowers into early fall, so they pair well with partners that bridge the two seasons, such as Joe-Pye weeds (*Eupatorium*) and goldenrods (*Solidago*). After their colorful petals drop, their center cones stick around into winter, adding interest among the dried skeletons and seed heads of other long-lasting perennials, such as 'Autumn Fire' sedum (*Sedum*), Culver's roots (*Veronicastrum*), and many ornamental grasses.

Special Effects

Native to meadow and prairie habitats, rudbeckias are obvious choices for naturalistic beds and borders. They look right at home with the slender leaves and airy plumes of ornamental grasses: Try little bluestem (*Schizachyrium scoparium*) and prairie dropseed

Rudbeckia subtomentosa 'Henry Eilers' with *Solidago rugosa* 'Fireworks' *(left); Rudbeckia fulgida* with *Aster oblongifolius* and *Panicum virgatum* 'Dallas Blues' *(above)*

(*Sporobolus heterolepis*) with the shorter rudbeckia cultivars, for instance, and Indian grass (*Sorghastrum nutans*) or switch grasses (*Panicum*) with cutleaf, giant, and shining coneflowers.

Add some other perennials with flowers that offer an abundance of nectar and/or seeds, such as bee balms (*Monarda*), heleniums (*Helenium*), and purple coneflower (*E. purpurea*), and your beautiful backyard meadow will do double-duty as a haven for birds, butterflies, and beneficial insects.

Exploring More Options: Partners beyond Perennials

Black-eyed Susan (*Rudbeckia hirta*) can act like a perennial in some areas, but it more often lasts only one or two growing seasons. Its flowers are so pretty, though, that it's worth including it in combinations even if it acts like an annual for you. Also known as Gloriosa daisies, the plants offer a wide range of warm colors, including two-toned yellow 'Prairie Sun' and golden yellow 'Irish Eyes' (both with green centers); light-and-dark red 'Cherry Brandy'; maroon-and-orange 'Chocolate Orange'; and mixes that include yellows, golds, oranges, and rusts, such as 'Cherokee Sunset' and 'Chim Chiminee'. You can find single, semidouble, and double-flowered forms, and cultivars can range from 6 inches to 3 feet in height. They flower for such a long time—from late spring or early summer well into fall—that if they don't make it through winter, they still earn their keep!

Salvia
versatile and dramatic

Perennial salvias
Full sun; average, well-drained soil

Salvia nemorosa 'Caradonna' and *Geranium* 'Brookside'

Salvia nemorosa 'Haeumanarc' (Marcus) and *Allium moly*

A Perfect Match

So many terrific partners for perennial salvias—how to pick just one? My current first choice of companion for any of the blue salvias is pretty much any peachy flower. The first inspiration was a photo of two shades of blue salvias with 'Terracotta' yarrow (*Achillea*). 'Sienna Sunset' coreopsis (*Coreopsis*) is lovely, too, as is sunset hyssop (*Agastache rupestris*).

Ranging from just a few inches tall to sizable, shrubby clumps, and flowering in a rainbow of colors, salvias (*Salvia*) offer a thrilling variety of combination options—so many, in fact, that it can be overwhelming to decide among them, especially if you live south of Zone 6 or 7, where many of the species are fully winter hardy.

Even if you stick with just the "perennial salvias"—*S. nemorosa*, *S. pratensis*, and hybrids of those and other species, usually listed as *S.* × *superba* or *S.* × *sylvestris*—you still have some exceptional plants to enjoy. Blooming primarily in shades of violet to blue, the 1- to 3-foot-tall plants typically peak in late spring to early summer, but they may continue to produce new spikes through summer and/or flower again in fall. The perennial salvias also have aromatic leaves. They are hardy in Zones 3 or 4 to 9.

Another hardy species with fragrant foliage is common or culinary sage (*S. officinalis*). Common sage does flower—it has

Perennial salvias (*Salvia*) typically prefer full sun but can tolerate light shade, and they're wonderfully versatile when it comes to soil conditions, adapting to either dryish or moist (but not soggy) conditions, so there's a wide pool of perennial companions to consider. Here's a sampling of potential co-stars: some that coincide with their main flush of flowers and some that complement their later-season blooms.

- Agastaches (*Agastache*)
- Baptisias (*Baptisia*)
- Bellflowers (*Campanula*)
- Blanket flowers (*Gaillardia*)
- Catmints (*Nepeta*)
- Crimson scabious (*Knautia macedonica*)
- Echinaceas (*Echinacea*)
- Fleeceflowers (*Persicaria*)
- Globe thistles (*Echinops*)
- Hardy geraniums (*Geranium*)
- Heleniums (*Helenium*)
- Jerusalem sages (*Phlomis*)
- Lady's mantle (*Alchemilla mollis*)
- Lavenders (*Lavandula*)
- Maltese cross (*Lychnis chalcedonica*)
- Masterworts (*Astrantia*)
- Meadow rues (*Thalictrum*)
- Meadowsweet (*Filipendula ulmaria*)
- Pincushion flowers (*Scabiosa*)
- Red valerian (*Centranthus ruber*)
- Rose campion (*Lychnis coronaria*)
- Rudbeckias (*Rudbeckia*)
- Russian sages (*Perovskia*)
- Sea hollies (*Eryngium*)
- Sedums (*Sedum*)
- Shasta daisies (*Leucanthemum × superbum*)
- Torch lilies (*Kniphofia*)
- Yarrows (*Achillea*)

light purple-blue blooms in summer—but it's most often grown for its flavorful, gray-green leaves. 'Berggarten' is a selection with more-rounded leaves that are bright silver when new, then aging to gray-green. Purple sage ('Purpurascens'), with dusky purple new foliage and purple-green older leaves, and golden variegated sage ('Icterina'), with showy yellow-and-green leaves, are beautiful, too, but they're often not hardy north of Zone 7, while the species and 'Berggarten' are usually fine in Zones 5 to 9.

Color Considerations

Whether you like your combinations cool and calm or bright and bold, perennial salvias will fit the bill.

On the softer side. Perennial salvias with purple-blue blooms and purple-leaved purple sage are both stunning in pairings with pastel-flowered perennials, such as buttery yellow Anthea yarrow (*Achillea* 'Anblo'); peachy orange 'Ruffled Apricot' daylily (*Hemerocallis*); and pink Lancaster geranium (*Geranium sanguineum* var. *striatum*) and tuberous-rooted Jerusalem sage (*Phlomis tuberosa*). Pink-flowered cultivars of perennial salvias, such as 'Pink Friesland' and 'Rose Queen', tend to be on the richer side of pink, but they, too, pair prettily with light to clear yellows, salmon oranges, and many pinks, as well as a variety of blues and purples.

Blues and whites. Salvia flowers in the blue to purple range are lovely with other blooms in tints and shades of the same hues, such as blue false indigo (*Baptisia australis*), catmints (*Nepeta*), globe thistles (*Echinops*), and sea hollies (*Eryngium*). Enjoy them in an "all

Salvia 'Snow Hill' with *Dianthus* 'Bath's Pink', *Iris* 'Immortality', and *Artemisia* 'Powis Castle'

'Snow Hill' (also sold as 'Schneehugel') and 'Swan Lake', look beautiful with blue- and white-flowered companions.

Bold and brilliant. If "hot" colors are more to your liking, violet-purple to purple-blue perennial salvias work well here. Enjoy them with flowering partners in bright yellows and golds—think of 'Coronation Gold' fernleaf yarrow (*A. filipendulina*), oxeye (*Heliopsis helianthoides*), and 'Zagreb' threadleaf coreopsis (*Coreopsis verticillata*), for example—or with reds and oranges, such as geums (*Geum*), Maltese cross (*Lychnis chalcedonica*), and Oriental poppy (*Papaver orientale*). Magenta blooms, like those of rose campion (*L. coronaria*) and winecups (*Callirhoe involucrata*), are marvelous with the violet to blue perennial salvias.

Shapes and Textures

While common sage forms broad mounds, especially after a few years, most perennial salvias have a more upright appearance due to their abundant, slender flower spikes. Habit-wise,

blue" border, or include crisp whites—such as white rose campion (*Lychnis coronaria* 'Alba') and 'David' summer phlox (*Phlox paniculata*)—as well as silver, gray, and blue foliage, for extra zip. White-flowered perennial sages, such as

Sage Advice

Don't forget to consider colorful foliage companions for your perennial salvias (*Salvia*). For high impact, pair purple-blue perennial salvias with bright yellow to chartreuse leaves, like those of golden oregano (*Origanum vulgare* 'Aureum') or Sunshine Blue blue mist shrub (*Caryopteris incana* 'Jason'); rich red Japanese blood grass (*Imperata cylindrica* 'Rubra'); or coppery New Zealand sedges (*Carex*).

Dark-leaved heucheras (*Heuchera*) make particularly intriguing partners for salvias in plantings that you'll see up close. Pair heucheras with very deep purple leaves, like 'Obsidian', with 'Caradonna' salvia and other salvias that have dark stems. Or use heucheras with silvery purple leaves, such as 'Blackberry Ice' or 'Frosted Violet', to echo the touch of violet in many perennial salvias, such as 'East Friesland' (also sold as 'Ostfriesland') and 'May Night' (also sold as 'Mainacht').

Salvia officinalis 'Berggarten' with *Santolina chamaecyparissus, Thymus vulgaris, Lavandula angustifolia* 'Hidcote', and *Pelargonium* 'Lady Plymouth' *(left); Salvia pratensis* 'Twilight Serenade' and *Scabiosa* 'Butterfly Blue' *(above)*

both work well with low, carpeting partners, such as bloody cranesbill (*G. sanguineum*).

To take advantage of the spiky effect of the flowers, repeat their distinctive shape in the border with companions that have similar bloom forms, such as anise hyssops (*Agastache*) and mulleins (*Verbascum*), or spiky leaves, like those of yuccas (*Yucca*). Or enjoy their contrast with airy bloom clusters, like those of coral bells (*Heuchera sanguinea*) and lady's mantle (*Alchemilla mollis*); big, bold blossoms, like those of alliums (*Allium*) or daylilies (*Hemerocallis*); or broad-clustered or daisy-form flowers, like those of upright sedums (*Sedum*) and marguerites (*Anthemis*).

The strong form of salvia flowers pairs well with wispy-flowered or gracefully arching grasses, such as Mexican feather grass (*Stipa* *tenuissima*), prairie dropseed (*Sporobolus heterolepis*), and tufted hair grass (*Deschampsia cespitosa*).

Seasonal Features

In southern gardens, perennial salvias start flowering in late spring, or even a few weeks earlier; in cooler areas, the show typically starts in early summer. Either way, their timing coincides with that of many classic border perennials, including bellflowers (*Campanula*), catmints, delphiniums (*Delphinium*), dianthus (*Dianthus*), and irises. Common sage is also lovely at this time of year, as new foliage starts emerging as soon as the weather begins to warm up.

It's not unusual for flowering salvias to slow down or even stop producing new blooms during the hottest part of summer, but you can often encourage them to keep going by snipping off the finished spikes. Watering during dry spells can keep them flowering more freely through much of summer. It's pretty likely that they'll have at least some new blooms in late summer and early fall, too, so take advantage of their later show by combining them with other rebloomers, long bloomers, and late bloomers, such as coreopsis (*Coreopsis*), heleniums (*Helenium*), mountain fleeceflower (*Persicaria amplexicaulis*), and rudbeckias (*Rudbeckia*).

Special Effects

In flower, perennial salvias are magnets for butterflies and hummingbirds, and they're also wonderful for attracting bees and other valuable pollinators to your yard. Common sage is an excellent choice for borders based on fragrant plants—think bee balms (*Monarda*), calamints (*Calamint*), lavenders (*Lavandula*), and other scented flowers and foliage—as well as for cottage gardens that include a mix of edible and ornamental herbs, such as artemisias (*Artemisia*), common chives (*Allium schoenoprasum*), feverfew (*Tanacetum parthenium*), lady's mantle, and purple coneflower (*Echinacea purpurea*).

Salvia officinalis 'Icterina' and *Thymus vulgaris*

Exploring More Options: Partners beyond Perennials

If you adore blue flowers, expand your salvia collection with some of the less hardy species as well, and enjoy them as annuals if they don't make it through winter in your area. Mealy-cup sage (*Salvia farinacea*), for instance, flowers abundantly from early or midsummer to frost the very first year, in various shades of blue-purple on 18- to 24-inch-tall plants. For the middle to back of the border, look to hybrid 'Indigo Spires', which usually reaches about 4 feet, or anise-scented sage (*S. guaranitica*), which can get to 6 feet or more; both usually overwinter in Zone 7 and south and peak in late summer and fall.

There are some stunning reds among the annual and tender salvias, expanding your options for hot-color combinations while you're waiting for your hardy perennials to fill in. Consider 'Lady in Red' Texas sage (*S. coccinea*) and 'Furman's Red' autumn sage (*S. greggii*), for example: Both reach about 3 feet tall, with airy bloom spikes that look right at home among hardier perennials from early summer to frost.

Scabiosa
old-fashioned charmers

Scabiosa 'Butterfly Blue' with *Salvia nemorosa* 'Caradonna' and *Iris pallida* 'Argentea Variegata'

Scabiosa 'Pink Mist' and *Salvia* 'Blue Hill'

A Perfect Match

It took me a while to find a color companion that I really enjoyed with the lavender blue of 'Butterfly Blue' pincushion flower, but I finally found a favorite: the deep blue spikes of 'Twilight Blue' meadow sage (*Salvia pratensis*). By chance, I'd moved a clump of the pincushion flower near a drift of the salvia that I'd started from seed the previous year, and I really enjoyed the harmony of color and contrast of form when they flowered together this past spring.

Few perennials can beat pincushion flowers (*Scabiosa*) for the length of their bloom season. For many months—or practically year-round, in mild climates—these cottage-garden classics produce grayish green leaves and 1- to 2-foot-tall stems topped with blue, purple, pink, yellow, or white flowers. Some are selections of *S. caucasica* or *S. columbaria*; others are hybrids. Though sometimes short lived, these perennials are generally hardy in Zones 3 to 9.

Color Considerations

The soft colors of lavender blue 'Butterfly Blue', light pink 'Pink Mist', creamy yellow 'Moon Dance', and other pincushion flowers work best in pastel-based combinations. Pair them with other light to medium tints in the pink to purple to blue range, like those of many hardy geraniums (*Geranium*).

To expand the palette, try your pincushion flowers with soft yellows, like those of 'Happy Returns' daylily (*Hemerocallis*), or pastel oranges, like those of 'Peachy Seduction' yarrow (*Achillea*) and 'Sienna Sunset' coreopsis (*Coreopsis*). Pincushion flowers also make wonderful partners for white or cream-colored flowers, like those of Shasta daisy (*Leucanthemum × superbum*) and 'Snow Hill' perennial salvia (*Salvia*).

Blue-leaved grasses, such as blue fescues (*Festuca*), complement the soft colors of pincushion flowers. Perennials with white-, cream-, or yellow-marked leaves are also lovely partners through the pincushion flowers' extended flowering period.

Shapes and Textures

Pincushion flower plants are mounded at the base, with oval to lance-shaped foliage, but they're relatively loose in bloom, with open-branching flowering stems that carry small, deeply cut leaves. For a contrast in form, use them in front of or next to distinctly upright partners, such as blazing stars (*Liatris*) or summer phlox (*Phlox paniculata*).

The 2- to 3-inch-wide blooms of pincushion flowers are composed of a domed center surrounded by a ruff of short, broad petals. They look lovely next to slender spikes, like those of perennial salvias (*Salvia*) and many speedwells (*Veronica*). For a contrast in size, pair them with larger blooms or bloom clusters, like those of daylilies (*Hemerocallis*), star-of-Persia (*Allium schubertii*), or true lilies (*Lilium*), or let them mingle with tiny blossoms, like those of baby's breath (*Gypsophila paniculata*), catmints (*Nepeta*), or lady's mantle (*Alchemilla mollis*).

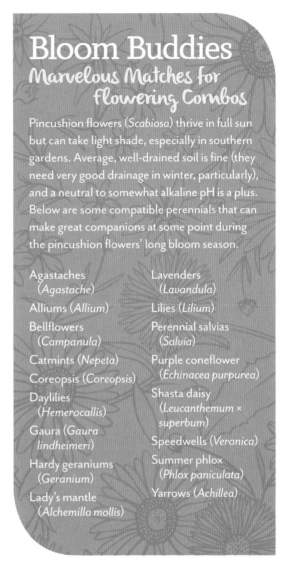

Bloom Buddies
Marvelous Matches for Flowering Combos

Pincushion flowers (*Scabiosa*) thrive in full sun but can take light shade, especially in southern gardens. Average, well-drained soil is fine (they need very good drainage in winter, particularly), and a neutral to somewhat alkaline pH is a plus. Below are some compatible perennials that can make great companions at some point during the pincushion flowers' long bloom season.

Agastaches (*Agastache*)

Alliums (*Allium*)

Bellflowers (*Campanula*)

Catmints (*Nepeta*)

Coreopsis (*Coreopsis*)

Daylilies (*Hemerocallis*)

Gaura (*Gaura lindheimeri*)

Hardy geraniums (*Geranium*)

Lady's mantle (*Alchemilla mollis*)

Lavenders (*Lavandula*)

Lilies (*Lilium*)

Perennial salvias (*Salvia*)

Purple coneflower (*Echinacea purpurea*)

Shasta daisy (*Leucanthemum × superbum*)

Speedwells (*Veronica*)

Summer phlox (*Phlox paniculata*)

Yarrows (*Achillea*)

Seasonal Features

Pincushion flowers typically begin blooming in late spring to early summer and continue well into fall, often until a hard frost. In mild climates, they may continue through winter, as well. Clipping off the spent flower stems helps to keep the plants looking their best.

Sedum
fascinating forms and colors

Sedum spectabile 'Neon' with *Allium thunbergii* and *Amsonia hubrichtii*

Sedum spurium 'Elizabeth' with *Sempervivum* 'Royal Ruby' and *S. arachnoideum*

A Perfect Match

One of my favorite matches for creeping sedums is other low-growing hardy succulents; together, they create a colorful carpet of interesting forms and textures. Ordinary hens-and-chicks (*Sempervivum tectorum*) work well—their distinctive clumps often take on lovely colors in winter, too—and ice plants (*Delosperma*) add extra-showy summer flowers.

With an adaptable, easy-care nature and multiseason features, sedums (*Sedum*)—also known as stonecrops—deserve a place in any garden. There are many hundreds of species and hybrids to choose from, in a range of flower and foliage colors, but for the most part, they fit into just two main categories: spreaders and clump formers. Their winter hardiness varies, but even if you consider only the hardiest species (such as those described below, which are all hardy in Zones 3 to 9), there are still plenty of options for creative combinations.

Spreading sedums, such as *S. rupestre*, Kamschatka sedum (*S. kamtschaticum*), and two-row sedum (*S. spurium*), have slender, trailing stems clad in whorls of needlelike, toothed, or rounded leaves. The stems take root where they touch the soil, producing low, ground-hugging carpets with upward-turned stem tips topped by clusters of small, starry flowers in summer. In flower, most of these are just

Bloom Buddies
Marvelous Matches for Flowering Combos

Pair your sedums (*Sedum*) with flowering partners that are similarly adapted to lots of sun and average, well-drained to dry soil. These compatible companions have bloom times that coincide or overlap with those of the main types of sedums.

Partners for creeping sedums, which mostly bloom in early to midsummer or mid- to late summer:

Ice plants
(*Delosperma*)

Leadwort
(*Ceratostigma plumbaginoides*)

Moss phlox
(*Phlox subulata*)

Mount Atlas daisy
(*Anacyclus pyrethrum*)

Prickly pear
(*Opuntia humifusa*)

Sea thrift
(*Armeria maritima*)

Snow-in-summer
(*Cerastium tomentosum*)

Three-toothed cinquefoil
(*Potentilla tridentata*)

Thymes
(*Thymus*)

Woolly yarrow
(*Achillea tomentosa*)

Partners for upright sedums, which mostly bloom in mid- to late summer or late summer to early fall:

Agastaches (*Agastache*)

Blanket flowers
(*Gaillardia*)

Blazing stars (*Liatris*)

Butterfly weed
(*Asclepias tuberosa*)

Catmints (*Nepeta*)

Coreopsis (*Coreopsis*)

Echinaceas (*Echinacea*)

Gaura
(*Gaura lindheimeri*)

Goldenrods (*Solidago*)

Lavenders (*Lavandula*)

Lesser calamint
(*Calamintha nepetoides*)

Ornamental oreganos
(*Origanum*)

Rudbeckias
(*Rudbeckia*)

Russian sages
(*Perovskia*)

Sea hollies (*Eryngium*)

Yarrows (*Achillea*)

4 to 6 inches tall; when not in bloom, they form patches just 2 to 4 inches tall.

Upright, clump-forming sedums (technically classified in the genus *Hylotelephium* but still commonly sold as *Sedum*) typically reach 18 to 24 inches tall, with thick, oval, bluish or grayish green leaves. Their flowers open in mid- to late summer. The two best-known species here, hardy in Zones 3 to 9, are showy stonecrop (*S. spectabile*), with tiny flowers clustered tightly into broad heads, and orpine (*S. telephium*), with somewhat smaller heads that tend to begin blooming slightly later.

There are many hybrids, too, in a range of flower and foliage colors.

Color Considerations

With sedums, color can come from the flowers, from the foliage, or from both features.

Think pink. Most pink-flowered sedums open on the purplish to reddish pink side, as on 'John Creech' and 'Pink Jewel' two-row sedum and 'Brilliant' and 'Neon' showy stonecrop, though even within one cultivar, the shade of pink can vary depending on the weather and

Sedum 'Autumn Fire' and *Yucca filamentosa* 'Color Guard' *(left)*; *Sedum* 'Xenox' and *Coreopsis* 'Limerock Dream' *(above)*

site conditions. And as they age, the flowers often turn deeper shades of red. This color change can make it tricky if you're trying to put a pink sedum right next to another pink-flowered perennial—they may look good at one time but clash as the flowers mature—so it's smart to separate them a bit with other colors. At any stage, most pink sedums combine well with white, yellow, and rich purple and blue flowers; foliage in shades of green, yellow, blue, deep purple, gray, and silver; and the tans of ornamental grass stems and seed heads.

Working with yellows. The bright yellows—of Kamschatka sedum flowers and 'Angelina' foliage, for instance—make eye-catching accents at the front of a border. Use them to repeat the sunny yellows in the petals or centers, or in the leaf colors or markings, of taller perennial companions. For high-impact pairings, try these bright yellow sedums with vivid pinks, rich blues and purples, vibrant reds and oranges, and crisp silvers and whites. They also make a dramatic contrast with deep purple to near-black leaves, like those of 'Obsidian' heuchera (*Heuchera*) and black mondo grass (*Ophiopogon planiscapus* 'Nigrescens').

On the dark side. If you're a fan of colorful foliage, you need to try at least a few of the purple-leaved sedums in your combinations. They often start the season a purple-tinged blue-gray, darkening as the season progresses to a deep purple to reddish purple on selections such as hybrid 'Purple Emperor and 'Atropurpureum' orpine (*S. telephium* subsp. *maximum*). The leaves make a lovely complement to the plants' own rosy pink blooms, as well as to silver-, gray-, or blue-leaved partners and blue-, purple-, yellow-, or white-flowered companions.

Elegant whites. There are some pleasing whites, too, among the sedums: Consider the flowers of 'Stardust' showy sedum, for example, or perhaps 'Frosty Morn', a selection with white-edged blue leaves and white to pink-tinged blooms. Try them with other white flowers and white-variegated leaves, or with blues, pinks, yellows, peaches, grays, and silvers.

Blue notes. Blue- and gray-leaved sedums are particularly pretty with white or pastel blooms, with other blues and grays, and with silver or deep purple leaves. Don't forget to take their flower colors into account, too, unless you plan to remove the blooms before they open: Depending on the species, they may be white, yellow, or pink, which will influence which companions you choose for them.

Shapes and Textures

The spreading sedums have a low, carpeting form that looks terrific filling in around mounded and upright companions. Clump-forming sedums mostly have upright stems and create broad or rounded mounds; for them, consider low-spreading partners, such as thymes (*Thymus*), or upright companions that have a distinctly vertical or vase-shaped form, such as Mexican feather grass (*Stipa tenuissima*), to provide some contrast.

From a textural perspective, the spreading sedums have tiny leaves that benefit from contrast with larger foliage. The leaves of the upright types are also relatively small, but they're thick and dense, giving them an overall medium to bold texture that adds some solidity to combinations that include lacy or wispy foliage, like that of artemisias (*Artemisia*) and hardy geraniums (*Geranium*). Both types of sedum mix handsomely with partners that have spiky or grassy foliage, such as blue fescues (*Festuca*) and dianthus (*Dianthus*) for the creepers and bearded irises and yuccas (*Yucca*) for the clump formers.

The individual, starry blossoms of sedums are tiny, but they're grouped into showy, flattened to domed clusters. Repeat their shape with taller perennials that have larger flower clusters, such as Joe-Pye weeds (*Eupatorium*) and yarrows (*Achillea*), or with broad, daisy-form blooms, like those of purple coneflower (*Echinacea purpurea*), rudbeckias (*Rudbeckia*), and

Sedum 'Matrona' with *Spiraea japonica* 'Gold Mound', *Ricinus communis*, and *Eupatorium maculatum* 'Gateway'

Shasta daisies (*Leucanthemum*). For contrast, pair them with spiky-flowered perennials, such as blazing stars (*Liatris*), or plumy blooms, like those of Russian sages (*Perovskia*).

Seasonal Features

If you're creating combinations for multiseason or even year-round interest, sedums are a great place to start.

Foliage for spring. Sedums of all shapes and sizes are outstanding for foliage interest in spring, when their fresh growth appears in dense carpets (on the creeping types) or tightly packed rosettes (on the clumping types). The yellows and variegates are so striking at this time that they rival many early bloomers, adding intensity to combinations that feature pastel-flowered perennials; holding their own with vivid reds, oranges, yellows, purples, and blues; and creating a dramatic contrast to deep purple to near-black leaves. The blue-leaved and gray-blue sedums are also quite noticeable in spring, echoing the foliage of baptisias (*Baptisia*), bearded irises, euphorbias (*Euphorbia*), and other blue-leaved perennials and complementing those with silvery leaves and pastel flowers.

A shift in summer. For summer combinations, attention turns from the leaves to the flowers on most sedums. The creeping sedums generally bloom in early to midsummer in warmer regions and mid- to late summer in cooler areas. While most of the upright sedums don't start opening their blooms until mid- or late summer, their clustered buds begin forming (and adding interest) several weeks earlier. (If you'd like to delay their flowering until late

Sedum rupestre 'Angelina' with *Callirhoe involucrata*, *Carex muskingumensis* 'Oehme', and *Origanum vulgare* 'Aureum'

summer or early fall, cut the stems back by about half their height in early summer.)

Fall features. By autumn, the creeping sedums are usually done flowering, but the upright types may still be opening some buds in early fall. October daphne (*S. sieboldii*) doesn't even begin blooming until fall. Cool fall temperatures bring out a wonderful pinkish, purplish, or reddish blush or edging to the leaves of many sedums; others develop shades of yellow, complementing other fall-colored and late-flowering perennials, as well as fall-flowering bulbs, such as colchicums (*Colchicum*).

As the flowers of sedums change into seed heads from late summer through fall, they typically turn reddish to bronzy to brown.

They'll usually disappear on their own on creeping sedums, but you can shear them off if you think they detract from the foliage. On the upright sedums, the seed heads contribute color and form to the fall garden, and some, such as 'Autumn Joy' and 'Autumn Fire', remain standing well into winter, looking wonderful when traced with frost or dusted with snow.

Into winter. While upright sedums die back to the ground or to tight rosettes by the end of fall, most of the creeping types hold on to their leaves through at least the first part of winter. Some are even more striking at this time of year than during the growing season—'Angelina', for instance, turns from bright yellow to brilliant orange at the tips—making them colorful companions for other "evergreen" perennials, such as hens-and-chicks (*Sempervivum*) and yuccas (*Yucca*).

Special Effects

Creeping sedums are particularly valuable for covering the ground in hot, dry sites, where many other perennials fail to thrive: on rocky slopes, for example, or along driveways, or in those narrow, hard-to-maintain strips of

Sedum sieboldii and *Thymus pseudolanuginosus*

ground between the sidewalk and the street. Use a combination of low-growing sedum species and selections to create a tapestry of foliage and flower colors, or combine them with upright sedums and other low-growing, drought-tolerant perennials, such as blanket flowers (*Gaillardia*), ice plants (*Delosperma*), moss phlox (*Phlox subulata*), and sea thrift (*Armeria maritima*) for a bit more variety of heights and shapes as well as colors and bloom times.

Exploring More Options: Partners beyond Perennials

Low-growing bulbs make superb partners for similarly low sedums, providing additional seasonal interest in the same amount of garden space. With creeping sedums, consider early crocus, species tulips, and Turkestan onion (*Allium karataviense*) for spring to early summer, and late-flowering crocuses, such as fall crocus (*Crocus speciosus*), and colchicums (*Colchicum*) for autumn. Interplant upright sedums with hybrid tulips for mid- to late spring and star-of-Persia (*Allium cristophii*) and tumbleweed onion (*A. schubertii*) for late-spring to midsummer interest.

Solidago
bright summer and fall color

Solidago rugosa 'Fireworks' and *Anemone* × *hybrida* 'Honorine Jobert'

Solidago sphacelata 'Golden Fleece' and *Stipa tenuissima*

A Perfect Match

Most goldenrods love sun, but there's also a well-behaved option for shady sites: wreath goldenrod (*Solidago caesia*). Its sprays of blooms add a cheery splash of yellow that's welcome in autumn to complement yellow-variegated hostas and contrast with dark-leaved heucheras (*Heuchera*), such as 'Blackout'. It looks fantastic with perennial foliage that turns color as the weather cools, such as the reds and purples of 'Beni-kaze' Hakone grass (*Hakonechloa macra*).

Goldenrods (*Solidago*) offer welcome variety to the many yellow daisies of late summer. They have a reputation for being aggressive spreaders, but some are just fine for perennial borders. One of the best is 'Fireworks' rough goldenrod (*S. rugosa*), which grows in broad, 3- to 4-foot-tall clumps, with slender sprays of bright yellow blooms. 'Golden Fleece' dwarf goldenrod (*S. sphacelata*) has a similar look but is only 18 to 24 inches tall. A few other well-behaved kinds, with denser, heavily branched bloom clusters, include 2-foot 'Golden Baby' (also sold as 'Goldkind') and 12- to 18-inch-tall 'Little Lemon'. All of these are suited to Zones 4 to 9.

Color Considerations

Goldenrods look great with blue to purple flowers—think of 'Bluebird' smooth aster (*Aster laevis*) or 'Iron Butterfly' narrowleaf ironweed (*Vernonia lettermannii*), for instance—and with blue or purple foliage, like that of 'Prairie Blues' little bluestem (*Schizachyrium scoparium*) or 'Purple Emperor' sedum (*Sedum*).

If you want to keep things light, consider pairing goldenrods with pink-flowered partners, such as Joe-Pye weeds (*Eupatorium*). Use white to make eye-catching companions, too: Consider white flowers, like those of false aster (*Boltonia asteroides*), and white-variegated leaves, like those of 'Morning Light' miscanthus (*Miscanthus sinensis*).

Goldenrods are wonderful with warmer colors, too. For flowers, consider cardinal flower (*Lobelia cardinalis*) or red or orange echinaceas (*Echinacea*) or heleniums (*Helenium*). For reddish foliage, look to 'Burgundy Bunny' fountain grass (*Pennisetum alopecuroides*) or 'Cheyenne Sky' switch grass (*Panicum virgatum*).

Shapes and Textures

The broad, shrubby mounds of 'Fireworks' rough goldenrod work well in the middle of a border, behind lower mounded or carpeting plants and in front of taller perennials, such as Culver's roots (*Veronicastrum*) and feather reed grasses (*Calamagrostis*). Enjoy the lower-growing goldenrods as fillers around larger mounded or upright companions, such as baptisias (*Baptisia*), mountain fleeceflower (*Persicaria amplexicaulis*), and Russian sages (*Perovskia*).

In leaf and in bloom, goldenrods mostly have a fine texture. They contrast well with bold, broad blooms and bloom clusters, like those of echinaceas, hardy hibiscus (*Hibiscus*), and upright sedums (*Sedum*), and with broad,

Bloom Buddies
Marvelous Matches for Flowering Combos

Goldenrods (*Solidago*) generally grow best in full sun and average, well-drained soil, though they can tolerate light shade, too. Below are just some of the many compatible companions to consider for late-summer to early-fall combos.

Asters (*Aster*)

Blanket flowers (*Gaillardia*)

Echinaceas (*Echinacea*)

False aster (*Boltonia asteroides*)

Hardy hibiscus (*Hibiscus*)

Heleniums (*Helenium*)

Ironweeds (*Vernonia*)

Japanese anemones (*Anemone*)

Joe-Pye weeds (*Eupatorium*)

Mountain fleeceflower (*Persicaria amplexicaulis*)

Perennial lobelias (*Lobelia*)

Perennial sunflowers (*Helianthus*)

Rudbeckias (*Rudbeckia*)

Russian sages (*Perovskia*)

Sedums (*Sedum*)

strappy leaves, like those of bearded irises and yuccas (*Yucca*).

Seasonal Features

Some of the compact hybrids begin blooming in midsummer, but most goldenrods start in late summer; 'Fireworks' may not begin until early fall. They typically continue for 4 to 6 weeks, coinciding or overlapping with many other late bloomers and ornamental grasses.

Stachys
touchable textural interest

Lamb's ears
Full sun to partial shade; average,
well-drained to dry soil

Stachys byzantina 'Big Ears' and *Colchicum autumnale*

Stachys byzantina and *Salvia nemorosa* 'Caradonna'

A Perfect Match

I love the look of lamb's ears but get annoyed by their tendency to "melt" in humid summer conditions. Arkansas bluestar (*Amsonia hubrichtii*), one of my favorite matches for it, has its own problem: a tendency to get floppy after flowering. Giving both plants a trim in early summer—by about half for the bluestar and to about 3 inches for the lamb's ears—has been a good solution. Within a few weeks, both leaf out again and look good.

When it comes to lamb's ears (*Stachys byzantina*; also sold as *S. lanata* or *S. olympica*), it's the silvery foliage that steals the show. Also known as woolly betony, it does bloom, with upright, branching, 1- to 2-foot-tall stems that carry tiny pink flowers, but the stalks tend to sprawl as they age. Many gardeners cut them off, or else choose cultivars that produce few or no blooms, such as 'Big Ears' (also sold as 'Helen von Stein') and 'Silver Carpet'. Lamb's ears are usually best suited to Zones 4 to 9.

Color Considerations

Lamb's ears leaves have a dense covering of silky hairs that give them a gray-green to silvery-gray appearance. If you'd like to stick with a restrained color palette, pair them with silvery, gray, or blue-leaved partners, such as artemisias (*Artemisia*), blue fescues (*Festuca*), or yuccas (*Yucca*). To expand that a bit, add bright white to cream-colored flowers, like those of 'Miss Lingard' Carolina phlox (*Phlox carolina*) or Shasta daisy (*Leucanthemum × superbum*), and white or cream-variegated foliage, like that of 'Triple Play' smooth phlox (*P. glaberrima* ssp. *triflora*).

Lamb's ears are outstanding with all tints, tones, and shades of blue to purple flowers, and with any kind of pink you can imagine. They also provide a sparkling setting for red, scarlet, and orange blooms. Lamb's ears look terrific paired with deep green leaves, too, and with dusky purples, like those of purple sage (*Salvia officinalis* 'Purpurascens'). For even more contrast, try a dark-leaved partner, such as deep purple 'Purple Petticoats' heuchera (*Heuchera*).

Shapes and Textures

Typically, lamb's ears grow in spreading carpets 4 to 6 inches tall; 'Big Ears' is 6 to 10 inches tall in leaf. Once the plants are established, they can be moderate to aggressive spreaders, so if you want just an accent patch, divide the plants every few years and replant only a small chunk. Or let them spread and fill in around sturdy, mounded or upright companions, such as daylilies and summer phlox (*P. paniculata*), in a big border. Another way to take advantage of their carpeting habit is to pair them with creeping sedums (*Sedum*), creeping thymes (*Thymus*), and other spreading perennials as a groundcover on a slope or other tough site.

Thick, oval to oblong leaves give lamb's ears a rather bold texture that's excellent for contrasting with tiny leaves, like those of catmints (*Nepeta*) and dianthus (*Dianthus*), and with lacy ones, like those of 'Powis Castle' artemisia (*Artemisia*). They're fantastic with grasses, too.

Bloom Buddies
Marvelous Matches for Flowering Combos

Lamb's ears (*Stachys byzantina*) are quite adaptable but usually prefer full sun to light shade and average, well-drained soil. They can pair well with pretty much any flowering perennial; below is a small sampling of interesting options.

Agastaches (*Agastache*)

Alliums (*Allium*)

Asters (*Aster*)

Bellflowers (*Campanula*)

Blazing stars (*Liatris*)

Bluestars (*Amsonia*)

Catmints (*Nepeta*)

Coreopsis (*Coreopsis*)

Daylilies (*Hemerocallis*)

Dianthus (*Dianthus*)

Echinaceas (*Echinacea*)

Euphorbias (*Euphorbia*)

Hardy geraniums (*Geranium*)

Lavenders (*Lavandula*)

Ornamental oreganos (*Origanum*)

Perennial salvias (*Salvia*)

Phlox (*Phlox*)

Shasta daisy (*Leucanthemum × superbum*)

Speedwells (*Veronica*)

Verbenas (*Verbena*)

Yarrows (*Achillea*)

Seasonal Features

Lamb's ears are lovely foliage features for color and texture in perennial combinations from spring through fall, and even through part or all of winter, in mild areas. Flowers, if they are going to appear, usually peak in early to midsummer, though some may appear earlier or later in the growing season.

Tiarella
beautiful spring bloomers

Tiarella 'Sugar and Spice' and *Hosta* 'Golden Tiara'

Tiarella 'Pacific Crest' with *Heuchera* 'Lava Lamp'

A Perfect Match

"Ordinary" foamflowers are lovely in their own right, but I'm a sucker for the newer selections with interesting leaf shapes and markings. Creeping types with dark stars or splotches, such as 'Appalachian Trail', are fantastic for carpeting the ground around chocolate brown 'Mocha' heuchera (*Heuchera*) and other wide-leaved companions. I've also used 'Pacific Crest' as the trailing plant in container combinations with other shade lovers, such as yellow-leaved 'Maui Buttercups' hosta.

The fuzzy-looking bloom spikes and handsome, heart-shaped to deeply lobed leaves of foamflowers (*Tiarella*) are wonderful for shady borders and woodland gardens. Need a spreader to create a carpet of foliage and flowers? Look for Allegheny foamflower (*T. cordifolia*) or a creeping hybrid, such as 'Pacific Crest' or 'Running Tapestry'. If you'd prefer a kind that will stay in one place, consider Wherry's foamflower (*T. wherryi*; also sold as *T. cordifolia* var. *collina*) or a clump-forming hybrid, such as 'Black Snowflake' or 'Sugar and Spice'. Foamflowers generally reach 4 to 6 inches tall in leaf and about 1 foot in bloom. These North American natives are typically hardy in Zones 3 to 8.

Color Considerations

Foamflowers produce pinkish buds that open to white or pale pink blossoms: perfectly suited for pairing with other pastel pink- or white-flowering partners. Or look for the same colors in foliage companions: white-variegated leaves, like those of 'Touch of Class' creeping Jacob's ladder (*Polemonium reptans*), to complement the white foamflower blossoms, or pinkish to reddish spring leaves, like those of 'Berry Smoothie' heuchera (*Heuchera*), to pick up the pink in the buds. Blue to purple is also exquisite with foamflowers: Consider grape hyacinths (*Muscari*), for example, or woodland phlox (*Phlox divaricata*).

The foamflowers' own foliage continues to add interest long after the blooms are finished. Echo the deep plum to dark chocolate leaf markings with 'Britt-Marie Crawford' bigleaf ligularia (*Ligularia dentata*) or other solidly dark partners. Dark-marked foamflowers look terrific with paler partners, such as bright silver 'Looking Glass' Siberian bugloss (*Brunnera macrophylla*).

Shapes and Textures

Use the vigorous spreaders where you have a lot of space to fill, paired with larger companions such as bugbanes and hostas. Clump-forming or slow-spreading foamflowers are a better choice for small spaces and for pairing with equally restrained companions, such as Jacob's ladders (*Polemonium*) and primroses (*Primula*).

Texture-wise, you can create some striking contrasts with foamflower foliage. Pair broad-leaved cultivars with lacy-leaved partners, such as ferns, or with fine-textured sedges and grasses, such as 'Evergold' Japanese sedge (*Carex oshimensis*). Foamflowers with deeply lobed foliage stand out well against broader leaves, like those of Canada wild ginger (*Asarum canadense*) and hostas.

Bloom Buddies
Marvelous Matches for flowering Combos

Foamflowers (*Tiarella*) can adapt to full shade and average soil but are at their best with partial shade and moist but well-drained, compost-enriched soil that's on the acidic side. Many other beautiful spring bloomers love the same conditions, so you have lots of companions to choose from, including those below.

Ajugas (*Ajuga*)

Allegheny pachysandra (*Pachysandra procumbens*)

Bleeding hearts (*Dicentra*)

Creeping phlox (*Phlox stolonifera*)

Crested iris (*Iris cristata*)

Epimediums (*Epimedium*)

Foamy bells (× *Heucherella*)

Hellebores (*Helleborus*)

Primroses (*Primula*)

Solomon's seals (*Polygonatum*)

Wild columbine (*Aquilegia canadensis*)

Woodland phlox (*Phlox divaricata*)

Seasonal Features

Foamflowers generally begin blooming in mid-spring, or late spring in the coolest parts of their growing range. The peak flowering period usually lasts 4 to 6 weeks, but some hybrids may continue to bloom lightly through summer if the weather's not too hot. Cool autumn weather brings out deep red, burgundy, bronze, or gold hues in the foliage. Foamflower leaves can linger well into the colder months, or even all winter long.

Verbena
months of abundant blooms

Verbena 'Homestead Purple' and *Origanum vulgare* 'Aureum'

Verbena bonariensis with *Pennisetum alopecuroides* and *Solidago rugosa* 'Fireworks'

A Perfect Match

'Imagination' verbena is usually sold as an annual, but I've seen reports of it overwintering in Zone 7 gardens, and it frequently self-sows even in cooler areas. Its easy-care nature and low-growing habit make it one of my go-to plants when I need an inexpensive filler for newly planted perennial beds and borders. 'Imagination' works well with pastel partners, but its brilliant purple blooms are particularly pretty with bright yellow coreopsis (*Coreopsis*), such as 'Early Sunrise'.

Easy, adaptable, and long-flowering, verbenas (*Verbena*)—also known as vervains—are an excellent choice for combinations in hot, sunny sites. Some are perennial only in frost-free areas; others can survive winters in much colder areas. Rose verbena (*V. canadensis* or *Glandularia canadensis*), for instance, as well as 'Snowflurry', may be hardy into Zone 5. 'Homestead Purple' sometimes overwinters as far north as Zone 6, and a number of other hybrids are hardy in Zones 7 and south.

Brazilian vervain (*V. bonariensis*), also known as purpletop vervain or tall verbena, may return from its roots into Zone 6 and frequently self-sows freely, so you may see new plants each year in cooler areas even without replanting. This can be a bonus in some areas but problematic in others, so it's a good idea to do an online search before planting to see if it is considered invasive in your state. Or if you don't want seedlings, consider the compact selection 'Little One', which appears to be sterile.

Even if they're not hardy in your area, verbenas are worth growing as annuals. They're excellent as first-year fillers in new perennial borders or to remedy summer gaps in established plantings.

Color Considerations

Rose verbena can range from rosy pink to purplish pink, so you may want to wait to choose companions until you see the flowers for yourself. They, as well as 'Homestead Purple', can look great with partners in the same pink to purple range, such as blazing stars (*Liatris*), purple coneflower (*Echinacea purpurea*), and summer phlox (*Phlox paniculata*). Clear yellow flowers, like those of 'Moonshine' yarrow (*Achillea*), and partners with bright yellow foliage, such as golden oregano (*Origanum vulgare* 'Aureum'), make for eye-catching companions. For a more elegant effect, try rose verbena with gray to silver leaves, like those of 'Powis Castle' artemisia (*Artemisia*).

If you enjoy very dramatic pairings, combine the rich color of 'Homestead Purple' with equally intense hues: golden yellows, like those of 'Early Sunrise' coreopsis (*Coreopsis*) and rudbeckias (*Rudbeckia*); vivid oranges, like those of Sombrero Adobe Orange echinacea (*Echinacea* 'Balsomador') and butterfly weed (*Asclepias tuberosa*); and even vivid reddish pink to magenta, like that of 'Raspberry Royale' autumn sage (*Salvia greggii*). Vibrant 'Homestead Red' works well with bright oranges, yellows, and purples and with silver- or purple-leaved partners.

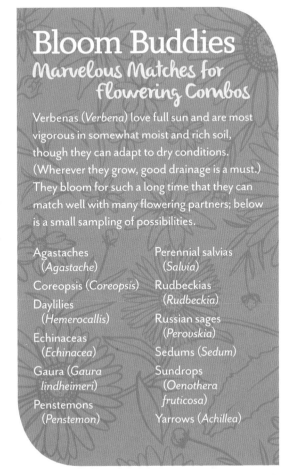

Bloom Buddies
Marvelous Matches for flowering Combos

Verbenas (*Verbena*) love full sun and are most vigorous in somewhat moist and rich soil, though they can adapt to dry conditions. (Wherever they grow, good drainage is a must.) They bloom for such a long time that they can match well with many flowering partners; below is a small sampling of possibilities.

Agastaches (*Agastache*)

Coreopsis (*Coreopsis*)

Daylilies (*Hemerocallis*)

Echinaceas (*Echinacea*)

Gaura (*Gaura lindheimeri*)

Penstemons (*Penstemon*)

Perennial salvias (*Salvia*)

Rudbeckias (*Rudbeckia*)

Russian sages (*Perovskia*)

Sedums (*Sedum*)

Sundrops (*Oenothera fruticosa*)

Yarrows (*Achillea*)

Prefer to work with whites? You'll love 'Snowflurry' as a match for 'White Swan' purple coneflower and other crisp white blooms, as well as with white-variegated, gray, or silver foliage. It's also wonderful with a range of pink, blue, or yellow flowers.

Brazilian vervain, with violet-purple buds and pinkish purple blooms, can work surprisingly well with tints and shades of pretty much any flower color, except perhaps for bright reds. It's lovely mingling with the golden browns and toasty tans of ornamental grass seed heads, like those of 'Karl Foerster' feather reed grass (*Calamagrostis × acutiflora*).

Shapes and Textures

Rose verbena, 'Homestead Purple', 'Snowflurry', and similar verbenas form spreading mounds that are typically 8 to 12 inches tall. On their own, their trailing stems produce flower-filled

Verbena bonariensis with *Heliopsis helianthoides* 'Summer Sun' and *Coreopsis tripteris* (top); *Verbena canadensis* 'Homestead Red' and *Artemisia stelleriana* 'Silver Brocade' *(bottom)*

carpets that look great at the front of a border, on a slope, or cascading over a low wall. Planted around other mounded to upright companions, they often weave among and up through their partners' stems, and their flowers may appear a surprising distance from the main plant.

Brazilian vervain, on the other hand, has a distinctly upright habit, with open-branching stems that give the plant an airy effect. It's usually in the range of 3 to 5 feet tall, though 'Little One' and 'Lollipop' reach only 2 feet tall. Set individual plants between or behind lower companions for some vertical contrast, or use them in groups to create a cloud of bloom in the middle to back of the border.

Individual verbena flowers are tiny but grouped into rounded clusters, creating dense dots of bloom that complement a wide range of other flower forms. Overall, the plants generally have a fine texture. Contrast them with bold forms: dainty 'Snowflurry' with a spiky yucca (*Yucca*) or tightly mounded upright sedum (*Sedum*), for instance. Or go for a soft, romantic look with other airy perennials: Try Brazilian vervain with the open clusters of golden lace (*Patrinia scabiosifolia*), for instance, or with the fluffy tails of 'Karley Rose' Oriental fountain grass (*Pennisetum orientale*).

Seasonal Features

Rose verbena and other trailing types generally flower from spring to frost, or even year-round in mild climates. If the plants do take a summer break, shear them lightly to encourage fresh growth and more flowers. Brazilian vervain usually starts in early to midsummer and continues well into fall.

Veronica
a variety of heights and habits

Veronica 'Eveline' and Achillea 'Pomegranate'

Veronica prostrata 'Trehane' with Geranium sanguineum and Weigela florida 'Alexandra' (Wine and Roses)

A Perfect Match

Though I'm a big fan of yellow-leaved plants, I can understand why those on the greenish yellow side may look a little sickly to some folks. But there are plenty of perennial options with rich yellow leaves that rival the brightest blooms as color accents, such as 'Aztec Gold' prostrate speedwell. It's showy all through the growing season: ideal for echoing the yellow centers or markings of companion flowers, such as 'Snowcap' Shasta daisy (*Leucanthemum × superbum*).

Speedwells (*Veronica*) come in a fairly limited color range, but there are dozens of great garden species, hybrids, and cultivars to choose from for Zones 3 or 4 to 8. Low-spreading speedwells—such as prostrate speedwell (*V. prostrata*) and 'Georgia Blue' (usually listed under *V. umbrosa*)—are mostly 6 to 12 inches tall, forming carpets topped with tiny blooms held in short spikes or loose clusters. Other speedwells, such as spike speedwell (*V. spicata*) and hybrid 'Goodness Grows', have a more upright, clump-forming habit, generally reaching 1 to 2 feet tall with slender, spikelike bloom clusters.

Color Considerations

Speedwells look wonderful in "basically blue" borders with other perennials in the same color range, such as bellflowers (*Campanula*), and they are magnificent with white flowers, such

Bloom Buddies
Marvelous Matches for flowering Combos

Speedwells (*Veronica*) bloom best in full sun but can take light shade with average, well-drained soil.

Partners for carpeting speedwells in mid-spring to early summer:

Bellflowers
(*Campanula*)

Coral bells
(*Heuchera sanguinea*)

Crocuses (*Crocus*)

Daffodils (*Narcissus*)

Dianthus (*Dianthus*)

Euphorbias
(*Euphorbia*)

Irises (*Iris*)

Lady's mantle
(*Alchemilla mollis*)

Moss phlox
(*Phlox subulata*)

Partners for upright speedwells in early to midsummer:

Baby's breaths
(*Gypsophila*)

Carolina phlox
(*Phlox carolina*)

Catmints (*Nepeta*)

Coreopsis (*Coreopsis*)

Daylilies (*Hemerocallis*)

Echinaceas
(*Echinacea*)

Hardy geraniums
(*Geranium*)

Perennial salvias
(*Salvia*)

Pincushion flowers
(*Scabiosa*)

Rudbeckias
(*Rudbeckia*)

Shasta daisy
(*Leucanthemum* ×
superbum)

Yarrows (*Achillea*)

(*Lilium* Asiatic Hybrids), daylilies (*Hemerocallis*), echinaceas (*Echinacea*), and irises are just a few compatible perennial partners that offer many tints and shades of pink, red, orange, and yellow to suit either bright or pastel palettes.

Don't forget about foliage partners, either. Speedwells of any hue can combine well with other perennials with gray to silver foliage. Rich blue and purple-blue speedwells look fantastic with bright yellow-leaved companions, such as 'Sweet Kate' spiderwort (*Tradescantia*).

Shapes and Textures

Carpeting speedwells are a great choice for the front of the border or for planting along a pathway. Pair them with other low growers, such as creeping sedums (*Sedum*); use them as a groundcover; or place them in front of mounded or upright companions, such as heucheras (*Heuchera*) or bearded irises, for contrast.

Upright speedwells add variety to the many other mounded-form perennials. Their spiky flower clusters contrast handsomely with broad-clustered blooms, like those of yarrows (*Achillea*); with daisy-form partners, such as purple coneflower (*E. purpurea*); and with airy partners, such as baby's breaths (*Gypsophila*).

Seasonal Features

Carpet-forming speedwells tend to bloom toward the beginning of the growing season, usually peaking in mid- to late spring or early summer. Upright types tend to flower mostly in early to midsummer, but may have a few blooms through late summer and even into fall, especially if you clip off the finished spikes.

as 'Aqua' dianthus (*Dianthus*). White-flowered speedwells are outstanding with other whites, while the pink speedwells complement many other pink-flowered perennials.

Blue to purple speedwells make great partners for many other colors. Asiatic lilies

Veronicastrum
invaluable vertical accents

Veronicastrum virginicum with *Pennisetum orientale* 'Karley Rose' and *Physocarpus opulifolius* 'Center Glow'

Veronicastrum virginicum 'Temptation', *Liatris spicata* 'Kobold', and *Allium sphaerocephalon*

A Perfect Match

The distinctly upright form of Culver's root clumps makes them an ideal match for tall ornamental grasses. I particularly like the way it looks with the equally vertical 'Northwind' switch grass (*Panicum virgatum*). The grass makes a quiet backdrop for the Culver's root's white flowers in later summer, then creates an appealing contrast when its leaves turn golden yellow and the Culver's root's seed heads age to near-black in fall.

Culver's roots (*Veronicastrum*) can take several years to reach their full size and flowering potential, but they're worth the wait. Hardy in Zones 3 to 8, the plants typically grow 4 to 6 feet tall, with upright stems topped with slender spikes of tiny, densely packed blooms. Those with white to pinkish flowers are usually sold under the botanical name *V. virginicum*; those that are on the bluish to lavender side may be *V. sibiricum*, hybrids, or also listed under *V. virginicum*.

Color Considerations

Culver's roots are particularly pretty in combinations with similar colors. Match the classic white Culver's roots with other white flowers, for instance, such as 'Becky' Shasta daisy (*Leucanthemum* × *superbum*) or 'Casa Blanca' Oriental lily (*Lilium*). For the pastel Culver's roots, consider a partner that's close to the same color or roots combine beautifully with the golden blonds, light browns, and pinkish tans of many ornamental grass flower and seed heads.

Shapes and Textures

Very vertical in both form and flower, Culver's roots are excellent for supplying contrast to perennials with rounded to broad-mounded plant forms, such as baptisias (*Baptisia*), daylilies, and 'Fireworks' rough goldenrod (*Solidago rugosa*). Setting Culver's roots behind mounded partners also helps to hide the lower stems, which may drop their leaves by mid- to late summer.

Culver's roots' slender bloom spikes are valuable for adding variety to broad flowers, like those of hardy hibiscus (*Hibiscus*) and true lilies; to bold bloom clusters, like those of Joe-Pye weeds (*Eupatorium*) and summer phlox; to daisy-form flowers, like those of giant coneflower (*Rudbeckia maxima*) and 'Lemon Queen' perennial sunflower (*Helianthus*); and to rounded flower shapes, like those of bee balms (*Monarda*) and rattlesnake master (*Eryngium yuccifolium*).

Seasonal Features

The selection 'Erica' is exceptional for foliage interest from spring to early summer, with deep purple to burgundy-blushed leaves and stems. Flowering on Culver's roots typically begins sometime in midsummer and continues through late summer or even into early fall, especially if you clip off the finished flower spikes. Or let the spikes dry in place; they and their stems will turn deep brown by late fall and stand for months, providing outstanding winter interest.

Bloom Buddies
Marvelous Matches for flowering Combos

Culver's roots (*Veronicastrum*) thrive in full sun and average to moist soil. They can take partial shade, too, but they're likely to flower less and may need some staking there. These tall treasures bloom in time to make great matches for many other perennials in mid- and late summer.

Bee balms (*Monarda*)
Daylilies (*Hemerocallis*)
Echinaceas (*Echinacea*)
Golden lace (*Patrinia scabiosifolia*)
Hardy hibiscus (*Hibiscus*)
Heleniums (*Helenium*)
Ironweeds (*Vernonia*)

Joe-Pye weeds (*Eupatorium*)
Lilies (*Lilium*)
Perennial lobelias (*Lobelia*)
Perennial sunflowers (*Helianthus*)
Rudbeckias (*Rudbeckia*)
Summer phlox (*Phlox paniculata*)

a darker shade, for added variety. Pale pink 'Erica' and 'Pink Glow' Culver's roots, for example, look great with many selections of purple coneflower (*Echinacea*), while pale purple 'Lavendelturm' (also sold as 'Lavender Towers') is gorgeous with pinkish purple Brazilian vervain (*Verbena bonariensis*) or deeper lavender 'Laura' summer phlox (*Phlox paniculata*).

To expand the palette a bit, consider other pastels, such as light yellows and peachy oranges, like those in many daylilies (*Hemerocallis*), and powder blue foliage, like that of 'Dallas Blues' switch grass (*Panicum virgatum*). Culver's

Yucca
dramatic foliage features

Yucca filamentosa 'Color Guard' and Stipa tenuissima

Yucca rostrata 'Sapphire Skies' and Artemisia 'Powis Castle'

A Perfect Match

Combining strikingly spiky yuccas with "weaving" partners—low-growing companions with slender, trailing stems that can creep through the yuccas' swordlike leaves—is an easy way to make them look at home among more typical border perennials. Magenta-flowered winecups (*Callirhoe involucrata*) are marvelous for this sort of match. Purple 'Imagination' verbena (*Verbena*) also works wonderfully as a weaver.

Yuccas (*Yucca*) produce large, dramatic rosettes of long, swordlike leaves and towering clusters of white, bell-shaped blooms in summer. Some of the hardiest species include Adam's needle (*Y. filamentosa*, also sold as *Y. flaccida*), for Zones 4 to 10; big bend or beaked yucca (*Y. rostrata*), for Zones 5 or 6 to 10; and soapweed (*Y. glauca*), for Zones 3 to 10. In leaf, they're typically 2 to 3 feet tall and wide; in bloom, they can reach 6 to 8 feet tall.

Color Considerations

Leaf colors vary among the yucca species but are usually in the gray-green to blue-green range. For soothing harmony, pair them with perennials that have gray to blue foliage. Just make sure that those partners offer some contrast in texture and/or form—such as rue (*Ruta graveolens*) or blue false indigo (*Baptisia*

Bloom Buddies
Marvelous Matches for Flowering Combos

Yuccas (*Yucca*) thrive in full sun to light shade and average, well-drained soil. Below are just a few compatible perennials that tend to bloom around the same time as sturdy yuccas.

Blazing stars (*Liatris*)

Coreopsis (*Coreopsis*)

Daylilies (*Hemerocallis*)

Echinaceas (*Echinacea*)

Rudbeckias (*Rudbeckia*)

Russian sages (*Perovskia*)

Sea lavender (*Limonium latifolium*)

Summer phlox (*Phlox paniculata*)

australis), which both have fine-textured leaves and dense, mounded plant shapes—so they don't all blend together. Cool blue flowers add to the harmony: Consider catmints (*Nepeta*), lavenders (*Lavandula*), and sea hollies (*Eryngium*). For a bit more zip, look for companions that have silvery leaves, such as 'Powis Castle' artemisia (*Artemisia*), or white flowers, such as 'David' summer phlox (*Phlox paniculata*) or 'White Swan' purple coneflower (*Echinacea purpurea*).

Yuccas' grays and blues look great with pastel pinks, soft yellows, or peachy flowers: 'Bath's Pink' dianthus (*Dianthus*), 'Susanna Mitchell' marguerite (*Anthemis*), and sunset hyssop (*Agastache rupestris*) are just a few examples. For more intensity, select stronger versions of those colors, such as magenta-flowered rose campion (*Lychnis coronaria*) or winecups (*Callirhoe involucrata*), golden yellow 'Zagreb' threadleaf coreopsis (*Coreopsis verticillata*), or brilliant orange butterfly weed (*Asclepias tuberosa*).

Variegated yuccas offer even more possibilities. You could, for example, echo the markings of 'Ivory Tower' Adam's needle with white flowers. Yellow-striped Adam's needles, such as 'Color Guard' and 'Golden Sword', pair beautifully with yellow-petaled or yellow-centered flowers, such as 'Full Moon' coreopsis, 'Moonshine' yarrow (*Achillea*), and 'Becky' Shasta daisy (*Leucanthemum* × *superbum*), as well as a wide range of pink, purple, and orange shades. For a high-contrast effect, pair them with deep purple or maroon leaves, such as dark-leaved sedums (*Sedum*) or purple heart (*Setcreasea pallida*); with bright blues and purples, such as 'Homestead Purple' verbena (*Verbena*); or with rich red or bicolor flowers, such as 'Arizona Sun' blanket flower (*Gaillardia*).

In flower, yuccas' tall bloom clusters show off beautifully against an equally tall or taller green-leaved backdrop, such as an evergreen or deciduous shrub or a sizable ornamental grass, like pampas grass (*Cortaderia selloana*). Color-wise, their white tends to be on the ivory side, so you may want to avoid planting them right next to partners with bright white blossoms; instead, put some space between them with greens or other colors. Consider pairing yuccas with cool purple-blues to silvery blues, such as globe thistles (*Echinops*) and Russian sages (*Perovskia*), or go bolder with bright colors in other large-flowered perennials, such as daylilies (*Hemerocallis*) and summer phlox (*P. paniculata*).

Shapes and Textures

Shape-wise, yucca plants tend to have an overall mounded to rounded outline, but their long, strappy leaves provide a spiky effect, as well. They're so striking that a single yucca in a border may look out of place, yet repeating clumps of yucca along the length of the border can take up a lot of space and may appear too formal. Instead, consider repeating the effect with other perennials that have a similar spiky-mounded effect, such as blue oat grass (*Helictotrichon sempervirens*) or bearded

Yucca filamentosa 'Color Guard' and *Liatris spicata* 'Kobold'

or sweet irises (*Iris* Bearded Hybrids or *I. pallida*). Or echo it with strappy-leaved perennials that have a more upright outline, such as blackberry lily (*Belamcanda chinensis*), 'Dallas Blue' switch grass (*Panicum virgatum*), and rattlesnake master (*E. yuccifolium*).

Yuccas are outstanding for providing contrast to perennials with tiny, ferny, or rounded to oblong leaves, like those of perennial candytuft (*Iberis sempervirens*) and sedums (*Sedum*), or with dainty flowers, such as gaura (*Gaura lindheimeri*). They also add drama rising out of perennials that form low, dense carpets, such as moss phlox (*P. subulata*) and lamb's ears (*Stachys byzantina*), and they make excellent supports for companions with upright but somewhat sprawling habits, such as Rozanne hardy geranium (*Geranium* 'Gerwat') and some penstemons (*Penstemon*). For an especially dramatic contrast, pair them with the globe-shaped blooms of alliums (*Allium*).

Seasonal Features

In warm climates, yuccas flower from early to midsummer; in cooler areas, mid- into late summer. Young plants often take several years to reach flowering size, so you may want to focus on foliage partners, at least at first. Once a rosette sends up a bloom stalk, it will not flower again, but it will produce new rosettes around its base, eventually forming a large clump that is likely to have several flower spikes each year. (Cut off the entire stalk when the flowers drop to tidy the plants and prevent self-sowing.) The foliage of yuccas is attractive all year long.

Hemerocallis 'Milk Chocolate' and 'Nona's Garnet Spider' with *Spiraea thunbergii* 'Ogon' (Mellow Yellow), *Zinnia* 'Profusion Orange', *Eucomis comosa* 'Oakhurst', *Cuphea* 'Firefly', *Lobelia cardinalis* 'Black Truffle', *Tanacetum vulgare* 'Isla Gold', *Patrinia scabiosifolia*, *Corylus avellana* 'Red Majestic', and *Cotinus coggygria* 'Royal Purple'

PART 2

PERENNIAL MATCHMAKING:

Exploring More Options

Making amazing combinations with any perennials always starts the same way: Choose one feature plant and take a good look at all of the attributes it has to offer. You'll learn more about that in Matchmaking 101, starting on page 263. Then you can move on to the fun part: finding compatible companions (see Picking Perennial Partners, starting on page 271).

Whether you're choosing partners for perennials you already grow or considering new ones to try, Finding Design Inspiration, starting on page 277, tells you where to look for great combination ideas and how to tell if they might work for you. Since color is the feature that many of us look to first in our gardens, Exploring Color Effects, starting on page 283, covers the obvious and not-so-obvious ways to create eye-catching color-based plant matches.

Whether you're hoping for a single-season spectacle or a garden that's interesting all year round, check out Creating Combinations for Seasonal Effects, starting on page 295, to find out how seasonal conditions can influence your perennial partnerships. Looking to move beyond perennial-with-perennial pairings? Partners beyond Perennials, starting on page 301, includes tips on choosing and using annuals, shrubs, and more.

When you're ready to turn your dream garden into the real thing, flip to Planting and Caring for Combinations, starting on page 305. The real artistry starts once you get your perennials in the ground and observe the results; then you can use maintenance techniques such as grooming and pruning to fine-tune your favorite combos from year to year.

Gaillardia × grandiflora 'Gallo Red' with *Stachys byzantina, Verbena canadensis* 'Homestead Red', and *Artemisia* 'Powis Castle'

Lavandula angustifolia 'Ellagance Ice' and *Veronica spicata* 'Glory' (Royal Candles)

Coreopsis 'Jethro Tull' and *Nepeta* 'Walker's Low'

Physostegia virginiana 'Pink Manners' and *Echinacea purpurea*

Matchmaking 101:
It's All in the Details

Being a successful perennial matchmaker involves more than simply selecting flowers that might look pretty together. It's about choosing plants that will grow well in the same conditions; that bloom at the same time (or at different times, if you're trying to extend the good looks of your garden by weeks or months); and that offer variety as well as similarities when it comes to sizes, shapes, and colors. That's a whole lot of information to process all at one time, though, especially when you're trying to plan an entire border.

Fortunately, you don't need to juggle all of those details at once. A garden is made of plant groupings, groupings start with pairings, and pairings start with a single plant. When you focus first on just one perennial (one you already have in your yard, perhaps, or one that has caught your eye at your local garden center), the whole design process suddenly seems much more manageable.

Once you've set your sights on a perennial that needs a partner, it's time to go into fact-finding mode: gathering key details about that plant, deciding what effect you want to create with the combination, and then coming up with a list of potential co-stars. I'm still a fan of the old-fashioned pencil-and-paper gardening notebook for keeping track of details when I'm working out combinations. You may prefer to keep your notes on your computer, though, or in an online account where you can gather ideas and plant details, such as Pinterest.

Take a Good Look

Let's start with the plant features that you can see for yourself—in pictures or actually out in the garden.

Color. Flowers tend to be the first features that catch our eye, but they're not the only sources of color. A number of perennials offer colors (other than the usual range of greens) in their leaves: yellows, reds, oranges, and purples in a wide range of tints and shades, as well as striping, edging, spotting, and all sorts of other markings. You may also find unexpected colors in buds, stems, and seed heads. Exploring Color

STRIKING FLOWER FORMS. Pairing spikes with broad, branching flower clusters is an easy way to add visual variety to your combinations. This pairing includes 'Karl Foerster' feather reed grass (*Calamagrostis × acutiflora*) and Joe-Pye weed (*Eupatorium maculatum*).

Effects, starting on page 283, covers in great detail the exciting aspects of working with color when choosing companions. For now, just make a note of the color features your focus plant has to offer.

Leaf and flower forms. Individual leaves and flowers may have distinctive shapes that are worth considering when planning perennial partnerships. Long, narrow leaves, like those of yuccas (*Yucca*), and long, slender flower clusters, like those on foxgloves (*Digitalis*), have a decidedly spiky look, for instance. Leaves that are divided into many smaller lobes or leaflets, as on yarrows (*Achillea*), have a lacy or ferny form, while leaves that are circular to oblong, as on wild gingers (*Asarum*), have a rounded form. Besides spiky, some distinctive shapes among flowers and flower clusters include

cupped to bowl shaped, bell shaped, funnel to trumpet shaped, daisy form, starry, globe or ball shaped, plumes, and umbels (flat-topped to domed clusters). Contrasting forms are valuable for adding variety when you are working with a limited range of flower or foliage colors.

Season. Timing is another key consideration in combinations. While you can't know to the day (or even the week) when a particular perennial is going to begin blooming each year, it's useful to have some idea of when it's likely to start, how long its main flowering period is going to last, and whether the plant is likely to bloom again later in the season.

Select a calendar for recording bloomtime observations from year to year, and make a note of the date when the leaves look good, too: Do they appear early in the growing season, or are they slow to come up, not emerging until late spring or even early summer? Do they remain attractive after the plant blooms, or do they look tattered or even disappear after the flowers finish? You may also notice special seasonal changes, such as a pink, purple, or reddish leaf blush in spring; a shift from green to shades of red, purple, orange, or gold in fall; or leaves that persist through winter. Other noteworthy seasonal features beyond bloom include interesting or particularly long-lasting stems, seed heads, seeds, and berries.

Height. Obviously, if you're hoping to pair two perennials for a spectacular flower show, they need to bloom at around the same height so the flowers are near each other. You can't have *all* of your combinations be the same height, of course, or you'd have a pretty boring border, but you do want the plants to be reasonably in proportion to one another.

When you take into account the height of the flowers, also look at the whole plant. Some perennials produce most of their leaves close to the ground, with their flowers on separate, taller stems. Others bloom atop the same stems that hold the leaves, and still others produce leaves and flowering stems of varying heights. That's why some perennials can be very different heights when they're in bloom compared to when they're not.

Many tall perennials are available in more-compact cultivars, so if you want to use a particular perennial in a combination with a shorter companion, you may be able to find a selection to suit the purpose. It's also possible to reduce the height of some perennials by well-timed pruning, but you have to remember to do that at the right time to get the appropriate effect later in the season. Research and note-taking are key to your success with this method.

Habit. Habit—the overall shape of a plant when you look at it from the side—should be considered when choosing compatible companions. Some perennials, such as summer phlox (*Phlox paniculata*), have a distinctly upright, vertical habit; others may be vase-shaped, mounded, or low spreading or carpeting. Pairing perennials with different habits adds interesting variety even when the plants are not in flower. It also lets you fit more plants into a given area,

because you can tuck mounded plants close to the bases of upright ones or let low-spreading companions fill in around mounded partners.

Textural traits. Texture, in reference to the surface appearance of a plant, may be fine, medium, or bold. (You'll sometimes see the term "coarse" instead of bold, though that's a rather negative word for a positive trait.) Many perennials have a medium texture, but some have particularly small or slender leaves and/or flowers, giving them a "fine" texture: Think of ferns, for instance, or ornamental grasses. Bold perennials, such as ligularias (*Ligularia*), have large, broad leaves or especially large flowers. Texture can also refer to the surface of individual leaves: whether they're smooth (matte or glossy), rough (due to short, bristly hairs), or

MIX IT UP. This late-spring spectacular features Siberian iris (*Iris sibirica*) and two different alliums (*Allium*): 'Purple Sensation' and 'Gladiator'. Though the colors would be the same without the taller 'Gladiator' bloom clusters, it's the variations in height that turn this pretty scene into a memorable match.

CONSIDER CONTRASTING SHAPES. Whether you're making matches of flowers or working mostly with foliage, it's important to include different plant habits and textures, especially as you expand from two-plant pairings to filling a whole border. This scene includes the bold foliage of broad-mounded 'Sun Power' hosta; the strappy, arching leaves of vase-shaped 'Gerald Darby' iris (*Iris × robusta*); the fine-textured, strongly upright leaves of Japanese blood grass (*Imperata cylindrica* 'Rubra'); the small-leaved, carpeting form of 'Dimity' dwarf fleeceflower (*Persicaria affinis*); a broad-bladed mound of plantainleaf sedge (*Carex plantaginea*); and a sprinkling of dainty-flowered forget-me-nots (*Myosotis sylvatica*).

even fuzzy (with silky, closely packed hairs). Thinking about these aspects of texture when you choose a co-star for your focus perennial is another way to mix things up for interest beyond flowers.

Do Your Homework

Even the most potentially stunning combinations aren't worth much if they're not based on perennials that will actually grow in your garden. Once you've been gardening for a number of years in the same place, you can often know at a glance if a given combination is likely to work in your yard, but until then, you'll need to do a bit of research.

Along with this book, it's useful to have at least one or two general perennial encyclopedias from within the last 10 or so years, so they're likely to include currently available plants and up-to-date information. If you're new to gardening in general, it's also handy to have one or more gardening guides written specifically for your state or region, because their writers are likely to have more insight into the particular growing conditions in your area. Online sources can be invaluable, as well, but here, too, try to find sites that are geared toward your local conditions as much as possible. A catalog or Web site that's based in Australia or England may be misleading if you're gardening in Maine or New Mexico—or anywhere in between, for that matter!

Consider the site. Healthy, vigorous perennials that are filled with flowers and lush leaves are beautiful in their own right, so when you pair them with others that thrive in the same light and soil conditions, you're practically guaranteed a gorgeous garden. Granted, plants can be surprisingly adaptable, sometimes performing respectably in much more sun or shade or wetter or drier soil than they normally prefer, depending on the specific conditions available in a particular site. As you gain experience, you can take advantage of your observations and create combinations that look great in your yard but probably wouldn't work well elsewhere. When you're just getting into gardening, though, or when you're designing for a new garden or for a site that you're not fully familiar with, you'll get the best results by choosing partners with very similar light and soil preferences.

Take climate into account. Climate considerations are important. One way to judge whether particular perennials are likely to thrive in your area is by looking at their USDA Plant Hardiness Zone ratings (usually just referred to as their zones). The USDA Plant Hardiness Zone Map is based on average annual minimum temperatures. So if you live in Zone 4, for example, you can guess that a perennial

CHECK THE GROWING CONDITIONS. On paper, you wouldn't expect this combination of 'Snowflake' catmint (*Nepeta*) and variegated sweet flag (*Acorus calamus* 'Variegatus') to work, because catmints typically prefer well-drained soil and sweet flag usually grows in constantly moist to wet soil. It's obviously thriving, though, proving that you can create unexpected pairings if you're open to experimenting. For a similar-looking but more widely adapted match, choose a companion that has more compatible growth needs, such as variegated sweet iris (*Iris pallida* 'Variegata').

rated for Zone 4 is likely to survive an average winter in your area. (Not sure which zone you live in? Turn to the USDA Plant Hardiness Zone Map on page 268 to find out.)

Of course, average minimum temperature is just one factor in determining where a plant will grow. English lavender (*Lavandula angustifolia*), for instance, may survive winter as far north as Zone 3 if the soil doesn't stay wet and if there's a thick blanket of snow to protect it from cold and wind; that same plant,

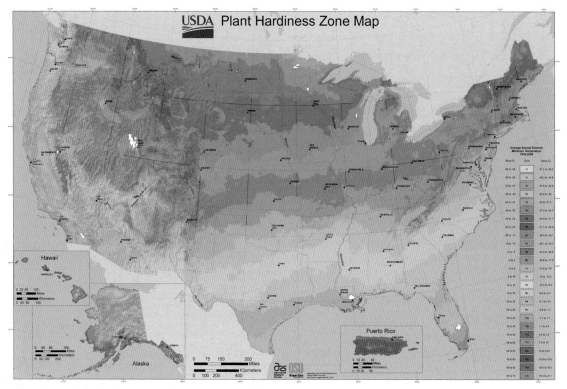

USDA Plant Hardiness Zone Map

Go to http://planthardiness.ars.usda.gov/PHZMWeb/ for an interactive map that will help you focus in on your local climate.

however, may struggle to overwinter in a Zone 6 garden with little or no snow but ample winter rain that keeps the soil moist to wet for months on end. That's why you may find very different zone ratings for the same plant: because different gardeners have varying experiences and take those into account when they write about their favorite plants.

You'll notice that most references don't give a single zone number; instead, they list a range, such as Zones 5 to 9. In this case, it means that the plant is likely to perform well as far north as Zone 5 and all the way south through Zone 9. Again, this rating tends to be

subjective, since the Hardiness Zone Map doesn't take into account other aspects of climate, such as humidity, the amount and seasonal distribution of rainfall, and summer temperatures. There are maps that take one or more of these into account, or that are customized for specific areas of the United States, but they're not consistently used by all writers, so you may or may not be able to find this specialized information for the perennials you're interested in. Don't worry about that, though: Just do your best to find perennials that at least a few books or catalogs agree should be fine in your area.

START SMALL. Plants don't read books or maps, so they don't know where the experts say they will grow or not grow. If you want to create pairings with perennials that may not be dependably winter hardy in your area—as in this pairing of 'Caramel' heuchera (*Heuchera*; Zones 4 to 9) with Mexican feather grass (*Stipa tenuissima*; Zones 6 or 7 to 10)—try them out in small spaces and see how they perform in your particular conditions before depending on them to fill out a drift in a big border.

Tanacetum coccineum 'Robinson's Red'
and *Iris sibirica* 'Caesar's Brother'

Lavandula angustifolia
'Hidcote' with *Stachys byzantina*
and *Artemisia stelleriana*
'Silver Brocade'

Lysimachia nummularia 'Aurea' and
Ajuga reptans 'Valfredda' (Chocolate Chip)

Lilium 'Lollypop' with *Stipa tenuissima*
and *Nigella damascena* 'Cramers' Plum'

Picking
Perennial Partners

Once you've chosen one perennial to start with, and you've made a mental or on-paper list of its key features, it's time to dive into the heart of the matchmaking process: finding it some compatible companions.

From One to Two

Composing a memorable union between any two perennials comes down to one simple factor: variety. A strong contrast—such as golden orange with purple-blue flowers. or spiky leaves with rounded ones—adds obvious drama, while small variations, such as tints and shades of yellow or short-spiked with long-spiked blooms, are much more subtle.

Colors and shapes are the two most obvious features to work with when creating contrast, but traits such as height, habit, and texture also provide interesting opportunities for working variety into a pairing. The greater the differences between two plants, and the larger the number of differences, the more vivid the contrast. That's valuable for grabbing attention,

particularly in a border that you see from a distance or where you really want a "wow" factor. Pairings with less striking differences and with variety in just a few elements—such as a light blue hardy geranium (*Geranium*) with a deep blue perennial salvia (*Salvia*)—are lovely in their own right, but they need to be where you can see them up close to appreciate the small variations.

The process of finding the perfect partner starts with picking the key feature you want to work with on your focus plant, then sorting through possibilities for contrast until you come up with one or more complementary companions. For example: Let's say that a friend gave you a piece of her favorite purple coneflower (*Echinacea purpurea*) when you moved into your house a few years ago. It grows beautifully in your yard, too, and you like it so much that you want to use it as the star of a new border; now you need to find it some equally good-looking friends. So you make a list of what you know about it.

My Purple Coneflower

Rosy pink flowers; orangey center turns bronzy brown

Large daisy-form bloom

Flowers late June through August

3 to 4 feet tall in bloom

Leaves are medium to dark green; broad; rough

Upright habit

Dark brown seed heads in fall and winter

Growing in all-day sun

Average soil

Grows well here in Zone 5

Clearly, the flowers are what make it special, so we'll start with those. What would look nice with its pink color? If you want to play it safe, you could go with a darker shade of pink, or a lighter tint, to get a little variety. Prefer a bit more "wow"? How about a buddy with bright white blooms, or sunny yellow flowers or leaves? Hmm, let's stick with a different pink and set those other ideas aside for now.

Pink with pink is pretty similar, obviously, so it's time to work in some contrast of texture or form: maybe something with tiny flowers to differ from the coneflower's large ones, or something with a spiky or umbel-form bloom to contrast with the coneflower's daisy shape? That still leaves us with lots of possibilities, though, so let's see what other details we can use to narrow down the candidates.

Possible Partners for My Purple Coneflower

Flowers in some shade of pink

Tiny, spiky, plumed, or umbel-form flowers for contrast

2 to 6 feet in flower

Mounded habit and/or narrow or ferny leaves for contrast when the coneflower isn't blooming?

Full sun; average soil

Hardy in Zone 5

Now it's back to the books (or computer), looking for lists or photo galleries of perennials with pink flowers. As you go through them, make a note of those that catch your eye with the bloom sizes and shapes you're considering. When you have six or more possibilities, go back through them to check their heights, flowering times, preferred growing conditions, and hardiness zones against what's on your list. Cross off those that are the wrong size, flower at the wrong time, or need different growing conditions. Here's an example of what your edited list might look like:

Echinacea purpurea and *Phlox paniculata* 'Jeana'

Ideas for Purple Coneflower Partners

'Bath's Pink' dianthus: about 1'; late spring to early summer; full sun; average soil; Zones 3–9

(Too short, too early)

'Dark Towers' penstemon: about 3'; early to midsummer; full sun; average soil; Zones 3–8

(Maybe too early?)

'Gateway' Joe-Pye weed: 5–6'; mid- or late summer to early fall; full sun to partial shade; average soil; Zones 4–9

'Jeana' summer phlox: about 3'; mid- to late summer; full sun to light shade; average soil; Zones 3–8

'Karley Rose' Oriental fountain grass: about 3'; early to late summer; full sun; average soil; Zones 5–8

'Rhineland' astilbe: about 2'; early to midsummer; partial shade; moist soil; Zones 3–8

(Prefers shade)

'Rosy Returns' daylily: about 18"; mid- to late summer; full sun to partial shade; average soil; Zones 4–9

'Saucy Seduction' yarrow: 18–24"; early to late summer; full sun; average soil; Zones 4–8

'Summer Love' agastache: 2–3'; early or midsummer into fall; full sun to light shade; average soil; Zones 6–9

(Not hardy here)

Now you have a list of five possibilities. Remember that you need contrast because the colors are all pretty similar, so take a closer look at the flower sizes and shapes and plant heights to see if you can eliminate any more options. The 'Jeana' summer phlox (*Phlox paniculata*) and 'Saucy Seduction' yarrow (*Achillea*), for example, have small individual flowers, but they're in clusters that are about the same size as purple coneflower blooms, so you might consider crossing them out. 'Rosy Returns' daylily (*Hemerocallis*) is shorter, so there's an element of variety, height-wise, but its flowers are still pretty similar in size to those of purple coneflower; maybe cross that one out, too, or put a question mark next to it.

That leaves you with two solid options that should bloom around the same time as your purple coneflower, also in a shade of pink but in a different shape, and that will grow in the same light and soil conditions: 'Gateway' Joe-Pye weed (*Eupatorium maculatum*), with branching bloom clusters that are larger and taller, and 'Karley Rose' Oriental fountain grass (*Pennisetum orientale*), with brushy pink spikes around the same height as the purple coneflower blooms. Either one could be a great match!

This may seem like a time-consuming process to pair just two plants, and yes, it can be at first. As you gain gardening experience, though, many of the decisions will become automatic. You'll be familiar with the traits and needs of many more plants, so you can eliminate options before you even put them on the list of possibilities.

From Pairing to Planting

Unless you're planning to fill an entire border with just two different perennials, it's time to start including additional companions that will thrive in the same growing conditions. Each time you add a plant to a combination, continue to think about variety, but balance that with some repetition: Repeat the flower form of one plant, for instance, but in a different color, or choose a companion with a similar flower color but a strongly contrasting leaf shape. Then think about how the possible new addition will look with the others you've already chosen, and how it fits into your overall vision for the border.

To carry on with the first example, let's say you've decided to pair your purple coneflower with the 'Karley Rose' Oriental fountain grass, so you have two perennials that are similar in height and color but very different in flower form (one daisy form and one spiky). If you're thinking of a primarily pink border, then add a flower form that varies from the other two, such as the 'Gateway' Joe-Pye weed, with tiny flowers held in large, branching umbels. (It's a different height, as well, which adds additional contrast: much needed since you're working with such similar colors.) Or add variety with a different color but repetition with a similar flower shape. In this case, you might choose a perennial such as Culver's root (*Veronicastrum virginicum*), which has spiky flowers that echo the shape

PRETTY IN PINK. The more limited the color range in a border, the more important it is to add variety with different flower forms and plant heights. The bold, daisy-form blooms of purple coneflower (*Echinacea purpurea*), for instance, contrast charmingly with the brushy spikes of 'Karley Rose' Oriental fountain grass (*Pennisetum orientale*) *(left)* and work well in front of the typically taller 'Gateway' Joe-Pye weed (*Eupatorium purpureum*) *(right)*.

of the grass flower heads but in white instead of pink for variety.

Once you've come up with a grouping of three to five perennials that you think will look good together, it's time to consider the border as a whole. You could repeat that one combination as many times as needed to fill the space or else create variations of it, repeating key plants, colors, and/or shapes to provide an element of unity but adding contrast with plants that have different heights and forms.

If you're relatively new to creating perennial combinations, focus your efforts on two or three main colors and easy-to-find plants that all look good around the same time: late spring to early summer, perhaps, or late summer into fall. As you gain experience and confidence, you can start creating more sophisticated "combinations by swapping out some of the common plants for more unusual selections, expanding the color palette, or extending the season of interest.

Designing on the Fly

Let's be honest: Sometimes you just want to plant, not plan. Filling a whole new border without some sort of advance planning is tricky unless you have a lot of experience, an unlimited budget, and a high tolerance for things not turning out as you expect them to. But if you have some impulse purchases on hand and a small new bed or some space in an existing border to fill, it can be great fun to experiment with some on-the-fly design. Carry those potted perennials out there and move them around until they look good with each other and the perennials around them (as in the photo). You'll still want to keep basic design concepts in mind—balancing contrasts and similarities in height, leaf and flower forms, colors, and the like—but count on your eye rather than your books to tell you what looks good.

The pot labels should tell you how big the plants are eventually going to get, but don't feel like you have to use the recommended spacing. Allow each perennial a bit of room to fill out, of course—particularly if you're planting in spring—but if you set them out fairly close together, they're likely to look good the very first year. In fall or the following spring, move or divide the plants as needed to give them more room, or swap some out to fine-tune the combination.

Pennisetum alopecuroides 'Cassian' with
Schizachyrium scoparium and *Aster ericoides*

Lavandula ×intermedia 'Provence'
with *Stachys byzantina* 'Big Ears' and
Artemisia 'Powis Castle'

Geranium maculatum 'Espresso' with *Viburnum
lantana* 'Aureum' and *Melissa officinalis* 'All Gold'

Hakonechloa macra 'All Gold' with
Mazus reptans, *Myosotis*, and *Viola*

Finding Design Inspiration

If poring over plant lists and researching facts such as heights and hardiness zones sound a bit too much like schoolwork, if you're having trouble narrowing down your plant choices, or if you simply have no idea where you want to start, you'll be happy to know that there are lots of ways to jump-start the combination-creation process. Ideas that you find close to home are often the best because you already know that the plants are likely to grow well in your area. Photos, too, can provide inspiring combination ideas, as long as you keep in mind that they have some drawbacks, as well. (You'll find out more about that in "Pictures *Can* Lie" on page 279.)

Make a Bouquet

If you're already growing some perennials, you probably have the makings of exciting combinations in your own yard. Pick one of your favorite plants, then take a stroll around your beds and borders looking for other perennials with flowers or foliage that might look good with it. Snip pieces from the potential partners, then carry them back to where the favorite is growing and see how they look together. If you're not sure about a particular combination, cut a bit of the favorite plant, too, bring all of the pieces indoors, and live with the bouquet for a few days. If you like the grouping, make a note to move the plants in fall or spring so they're all in one spot.

Take a Tour

Local gardeners are another excellent source of inspiration. Take a walk through your neighborhood to look for beautiful perennial plantings, and take advantage of local garden tours. Bring a notebook and camera with you to record combinations that catch your eye. The gardeners will probably be happy to identify the specific plants for you and tell you where they bought them; if you're lucky, they may even share seeds, cuttings, or divisions.

Just remember to be a courteous visitor: Ask permission before you take pictures, and don't monopolize the garden owners' time on a busy tour day. Instead, ask if he or she would be willing to talk by phone or e-mail, or even possibly allow a private visit on another day.

Can't find a way to directly connect with local gardeners? Do an online search for the name of your town, state, or region and "garden blog" to find the sites of bloggers in your area who write about and post pictures of their gardens.

Botanical gardens and arboreta with perennial borders are worth a visit, as well. Most will have the plants clearly identified with individual labels: a huge help if you'd like to copy a specific combination in your own garden. Or they may have printed planting maps that you can take home with you for future reference.

Visit a Nursery

A great local nursery or garden center—not a big home-improvement store that also happens to sell plants, but an independently owned place staffed with folks who really know their stuff—is a wonderful resource when you're gathering combination ideas. Visit their displays of container-grown plants that are in bloom so you can see the colors for yourself, and carry pots around to test how the flowers and leaves might look together.

ON THE MOVE. Looking at two flowering partners next to each other is a great way to compare their colors and forms. If they're still in pots, you can easily try instant combinations. If they're in the ground, snip some flowers from one and hold them against potential partners until you find a pairing you'd like to try, such as this duo of Mardi Gras helenium (*Helenium* 'Helbro') and 'Little Henry' sweet coneflower (*Rudbeckia subtomentosa*). Perennials don't like to be moved when they're in bloom, so wait until the appropriate season to do the transplanting.

THINK BIG BUT PLANT SMALL. Touring local private and public gardens, so you can see the plants and plantings in person, is an excellent way to learn about what you like and what might work in your own yard. Focus on combinations of two to five perennials that catch your eye, and plan to try out a few each year as time and space allow.

You'll still need to check the pot tags, talk to the nursery staff, or research the mature sizes of the plants because potted perennials tend to be smaller than they'll be once they've settled in your garden for a year or two. You'll also want to confirm the true bloom times, especially if you're shopping in spring, because early-season plants may have been grown in a greenhouse to bring them to bloom more quickly, making them flower several weeks earlier than they might in your garden. If the nursery or garden center has display gardens, so much the better: You'll see the plants actually growing in the ground, reaching their true sizes and flowering at the right times.

Don't limit yourself to a single spring shopping spree, or you'll end up filling your garden

Pictures *Can* Lie

When it comes to successful perennial combinations, seeing isn't always believing if you're depending on photographs.

There are numerous reasons why what you're looking at might not work in your garden—or anywhere, for that matter. A photo shows one moment of time in one place, so you don't know what the combination looked like a week earlier, or a week later, or even when or where it was captured. It might be a pairing of mature perennials that have been growing happily together for several years, or it might be two container-grown perennials that someone set next to each other for a minute and snapped a shot of because they were pretty, regardless of whether or not they'd actually grow together. Or a stunning combination might be a lucky accident—two plants blooming at the same time due to unusual weather conditions that year, for example, or a tall perennial that has sprawled onto a low companion, as with the beebalm (*Monarda*) and lamb's ears (*Stachys byzantina*) shown here—and not something that you could ever plan for.

It's also very easy for the person who took the picture to be intentionally or unintentionally misleading. They may have shot the combination from an unusual angle or in specific lighting conditions that change the appearance of the leaves and flowers. Two leaves or flowers may look amazing in a particular close-up shot but disappointingly different in real life. And, sadly, it's not unheard of for retail catalogs and Web sites to use pictures that have been enhanced—with the colors intensified, for instance, or with extra flowers added to a plant—to improve sales.

So go ahead, drool over those gorgeous photos, but don't set your heart on copying them exactly without doing your homework. Find out if the plants shown will grow in the conditions you can provide and if they really are compatible as far as heights and bloom times. If you still think they'll work, then give the pairing a try for yourself. If not, then use the pictured pairing to inspire your own creation, copying the colors or forms but using perennials that will thrive in your light, soil, and climate.

BE A SMART SHOPPER. Mail-order nurseries are wonderful sources of the newest and most unusual perennials, but shipping prices can add up quickly. It's worthwhile to make regular visits to local nurseries and garden centers to stock up on dependable, time-tested favorites that are well suited to your area. Once you get your borders basically the way you want them, you can fine-tune the combinations with additions of special mail-order acquisitions.

with early bloomers and have little to look at from midsummer on. Instead, make several visits throughout the growing season to pick up plants and combination ideas that will extend the show from spring into fall—and even beyond.

Go for a Nature Walk

Local natural areas offer invaluable opportunities to observe native plants that thrive in your region without supplemental water, fertilizer, or other special care. Try to visit areas that are similar to the conditions in your yard: woodlands if you have a lot of shade, for instance, or meadows if you have sun, or wetlands if you have soggy spots that need sprucing up.

On your walk, you'll see some wonderful spontaneous combinations: not just perennials with perennials, but perennials with annuals, groundcovers, shrubs, vines, and trees. Plants have a remarkable way of putting themselves with partners you might not have thought of yourself, and you can copy those combinations in your own yard. Besides a camera and notebook, take along a regional wildflower guide to help you figure out what plants you're looking at, or go on guided walks with leaders who can identify the plants for you.

By the way, planning combinations based on perennials that naturally grow together is a good way to go, even with plants that aren't native to your local area. If you have good luck growing orange coneflower (*Rudbeckia fulgida*), for instance, you'll probably have success with plants it often grows with in nature, such as butterfly weed (*Asclepias tuberosa*) and little bluestem (*Schizachyrium scoparium*). It takes a bit of research to find this information, though: Try typing the plant's botanical name and the term "natural communities" into a search engine to find out what sort of habitats it grows in, then use those habitat names to track down other perennials that grow there. Some perennials are very particular about where they like to grow, while others can adapt well to a range of conditions; members of the latter group are particularly easy to make combinations with, because there are so many potential partners.

Check Online Resources

An online search engine is a truly valuable tool for finding additional combination ideas. Here are a few more ways to use your favorite search sites to spark your creativity.

- Do a text or image search for "perennial combinations" or the name of a specific plant plus "companions" or "combinations" to find loads of inspiring ideas and pictures of wow-worthy perennial partnerships.

- If you already have a particular design style in mind—formal, cottage garden, or naturalistic, for instance—search for that term plus "perennials" or "perennial combinations" to find the names of other plants that are well suited to that sort of setting.

- Do you have a particular job you want your perennials to do—screen out an ugly view, perhaps, or attract butterflies, or look good in the evening? Try a search phrase such as "perennials for screening," "perennials for butterflies," or "perennials for evening gardens" to find lists of plants that can work well for specific purposes.

LEARN FROM NATURE. Perennials that grow well together in a natural habitat—such as the New York ironweed (*Vernonia noveboracensis*) and Joe-Pye weed (*Eupatorium maculatum*) in this sunny meadow setting—are likely to pair beautifully if you give them similar conditions in your home garden.

Canna 'Phasion' (Tropicanna) and *Coreopsis* 'Limerock Dream'

Iris × *robusta* 'Gerald Darby' and *Cotinus coggygria* 'Royal Purple'

Polygonatum odoratum 'Variegatum' and *Carex siderosticha* 'Snow Cap'

Stachys byzantina with *Thymus praecox* Coccineus Group and *Sedum hispanicum*

Exploring
Color Effects

Features such as flower forms, leaf shapes, and plant habits all play a part in interesting pairings, but color is what draws many of us to perennial combinations. There's a lot of science behind how we perceive color and a good deal of theory behind the art of combining colors to create specific effects. Ultimately, color is a very subjective thing; if you find two hues pleasing together, it doesn't matter whether art or science agrees, because you're the one who'll be enjoying the plants you combine. But if you're new to creating combinations or are at a loss for ideas, classic color themes may provide a useful starting point. Here are some basic concepts to consider when you're working with color-based combinations.

Color by Design

One simple way to approach the subject is by using a color wheel: a visual representation of the colors of the rainbow arranged in a circle.

An artist's color wheel includes three primary colors—red, yellow, and blue—plus the

secondary colors you get by mixing equal amounts of two primaries: orange between red and yellow, green between yellow and blue, and violet (purple) between blue and red. Tucked among those are tertiary or intermediate colors, which include a primary and a secondary color: blue-green, for example, or yellow-orange, or red-violet. Adding white to these hues produces tints (also called pastels, if there's a good deal of white); adding black to hues gives shades; and adding gray (some black and some white) creates tones.

If you decide to delve deeper into color theory, you'll find that there are a number of other ways to explain the ways colors can be described and combined to make other colors. (Computer monitors, for instance, use red, green, and blue as the three primary colors, while printing processes use cyan, magenta, and yellow.) It's all very interesting, but keep in mind that working with color in the garden is much different than on a computer screen or on paper because we're looking at blooms and leaves against all kinds of backgrounds and in many different kinds of light, depending on the time of day and the weather. And the plants themselves are continually varying slightly or dramatically in color, depending on their growing conditions and the age of their flowers and foliage. However, we can still use the basic terms and ideas to approach plant pairings and groupings.

Go monochrome. If you're particularly drawn to one color, that can be a good starting point for a combination or even a whole garden. Technically, no pairing or planting is ever truly monochrome: Even if all the flowers are tints and shades of blue, for instance, there are greens from the various leaves and stems and probably yellows and whites from markings or parts within the blue flowers. Still, the intention is obvious enough that we can think of it as a "blue garden."

Working with one color sounds like an easy way to go, and it usually is if you're working with just a few perennials. You simply need to remember to add contrast with different flower forms, leaf shades, plant habits, and so on, since their colors are so similar, or the combination won't offer much variety to hold your attention. This variety becomes increasingly important as you expand from a pairing to a grouping to a whole garden. Once you try your first monochrome garden, you'll appreciate how much thought goes into creating something that appears to be so simple!

Stick with similarities. Combinations based on colors that are close to each other on the color wheel (also known as analogous colors) can actually be easier than monochrome combos, because there's already some variety in the hues. One way to think of similar hues is

to divide them into "warm" or "hot" colors (reds, oranges, and yellows) and "cool" colors (greens, blues, and purples). Pastels and whites also tend to look good together, creating a very soft, delicate effect. Deep shades paired with black or near-black work well, too, producing a rich, powerful impression. When you work with these sorts of similarities—hot colors, cool colors, pastels, or saturated shades—you're practically guaranteed to come up with pleasing color combinations.

Add drama with contrast. Don't feel like playing it safe? Have fun pairing colors that are directly or almost directly across from each other on the color wheel, such as yellow with

MATCHING IN MONOCHROME. Colorful foliage is a valuable addition to combinations based on one main hue, maintaining the theme as the flowers come in and go out of bloom. This sunny yellow partnership includes cushion spurge (*Euphorbia polychroma*) and 'Circus' heuchera (*Heuchera*).

violet, blue with orange, and red with chartreuse (yellow-green). (These are called complementary and near-complementary colors.) Or try a triadic scheme, using three colors that are spaced at equal intervals around the color wheel, such as red with yellow and blue or red-orange with blue-violet and chartreuse. Dark and light contrasts, such as black with white or red with silver, are also quite striking.

These sorts of groupings tend to be vibrant and attention grabbing: very useful in a border that's seen from a distance. Up close, the effect of high-contrast combinations depends on the viewer: Some people find them cheery and playful, while others may consider them gaudy and chaotic. Again, you're the one living with the plants, so if you enjoy a flamboyant garden, then go for it! If the idea appeals to you but you're not confident with trying high-contrast combinations in high-visibility spots, save them for a side yard or a backyard border and stick with more restrained color schemes out front.

The Colors in the Details

Once you start looking at perennials with an eye toward creating combinations, you'll notice that their most obvious colors aren't the only hues they have to offer. Considering their more

MAKE AN IMPACT. A rich purple iris with a bright orange globeflower (*Trollius*)—why not? If you're new to making high-contrast combinations, starting with a few duos or trios is a good way to experiment with the effect before committing to an entire border *(top)*.

GETTING CENTERED. Multicolored blooms offer lots of opportunities for interesting matches. This pairing of 'Sunset Snappy' blanket flower (*Gaillardia* x *grandiflora*) and dark-leaved 'Amethyst Myst' heuchera (*Heuchera*), for instance, plays off of the daisy's deep red center *(bottom)*.

subtle touches of color can inspire interesting partnerships that lead to truly sophisticated combinations. Focusing on these sorts of subtleties in your combinations is a wonderful way to make even a very small garden worthy of close attention. Taking fine details into account also works well in plantings that you can admire up close: by a door, along a path, or next to your deck, patio, or favorite garden bench, for instance.

Bloom attributes. Petals usually provide the overall color, but if you look closely, you'll notice color in other flower features, as well. The reproductive parts in the center, for instance, are generally yellow, green, bronze, or brown to near-black. It's also quite common for petals to include several tints or shades of one color, or even multiple colors, creating markings such as stripes or bands or a contrasting center "eye."

Flowers include structures called sepals, which cover the petals while the flower is developing. They're often hidden by the petals when the blooms open, but sometimes they peek through not-quite-overlapping petals or are evident when you look at the flower from the side, adding green or other colors to the blossom.

Foliage features. Leaves can be just as valuable as flowers for providing color: even more so, in fact, because leaves are around for most or all of the growing season (sometimes even all year), while blooms are much more fleeting. In the greens alone, there are striking tints, shades, and tones, from green so dark that it's practically black to cool blue-greens and gray-greens and brilliant yellow-greens. Other pigments can add varying amounts of

LOOK TO THE LEAVES. From subtle shadings to bold spots and splashes, leaf markings bring an element of elegance to carefully planned combinations, such as this grouping of silver-and-purple Japanese painted fern (*Athyrium niponicum* var. *pictum*), silver-and-green pulmonaria (*Pulmonaria*), and purple mitsuba (*Cryptotaenia japonica* f. *atropurpurea*).

red and purple to the green, creating moody maroon and rich burgundy, while hairs or waxy coatings on the leaves or air pockets below the surface can make green leaves appear gray, powder blue, or silver.

Like flowers, individual leaves can include multiple colors as well, from subtle shades of one color to distinctive spots, splashes, speckles, and stripes, or contrasting edges or centers. Many variegated leaves are green with white, cream, or yellow markings, but foliage can also show combinations of two or more other colors, such as yellow with red or gray with burgundy.

Additional interesting elements. Other places to look for colors that you can play off of in plant partnerships include buds, leaf and flower stems, fruits, seeds, and seed heads. It's fair also game to consider colorful accessories, such as painted posts, bits of trellising, decorative pots, and other sorts of garden ornaments, as well as nearby features, such as paving, walls, fences, hedges, and arbors.

Color Considerations

Understanding some of the basic facts and theories about color will help you figure out why certain combinations might or might not be pleasing to your eye. But when you actually put two plants next to each other, you'll find that colors can appear and combine very differently in the garden than art and science may lead you to expect. Here are some tips to keep in mind when you're working with specific colors in your combinations.

Rousing reds. By themselves, red flowers are bright and attention grabbing, but in the garden, they may get lost if they're set against lots of green leaves. Adding white flowers and white-variegated and bright silver foliage adds more contrast, but the overall effect of a red, green, and white garden may be more suited for the Christmas season than a summer border. Reds with yellow flowers and leaves, and some orange, too, are equally festive but far better suited to the growing season.

The most interesting "red gardens" usually include maroon, burgundy, and purple foliage to add variety to red flowers and leaves. These foliage colors help to separate violet-reds, pinkish

TAKE ADVANTAGE OF ACCENTS. A favorite garden ornament can become the inspiration for your next great combination. Choose the plants to match the ornament, or use a bit of paint to echo the color of the plant partners.

DON'T BE SHY. Red and yellow—as in this trio of cardinal flower (*Lobelia cardinalis*), Japanese blood grass (*Imperata cylindrica* 'Rubra'), and 'Isla Gold' tansy (*Tanacetum vulgare*)—is a bold combo that's well suited to summer gardens.

IN THE PINK. Soft pinks are beautiful with blues, as in the combination of 'Bevan's Variety' bigroot geranium (*Geranium macrorrhizum*) with 'Ultramarine' forget-me-not (*Myosotis sylvatica*) (*above*). They also make a great match with dark foliage, as on 'Dark Towers' penstemon (*Penstemon*), shown with the pods of 'Cramers' Plum' love-in-a-mist (*Nigella damascena*) (*right*).

reds, and orange-reds, which may not look good right next to each other. It can be a real challenge to find enough red-flowered perennials to make a good show at any one time, so take advantage of annuals, bulbs, and shrubs with red flowers, leaves, stems, or fruits, too.

Tricky pinks. Adding white to red makes pink, but that simple formula hardly does justice to the wide range of pinks available in perennial flowers. Add a little white to pure red and you get a vibrant reddish pink; a lot of white produces a delicate pale pink. If you start with an orangey red, you get coral to salmon to peachy pink; a purplish or bluish red with white can produce hot pinks, fuchsias, or rosy pinks. Adding gray to red produces many more varieties of pink.

There are so many kinds of pink, and so many terms for the various tints, tones, and shades, that depending on written descriptions when you're planning pink combinations can produce very disappointing results. You'll combine two pinks that sound like they should look good together only to find that they're just not quite right to your eye. To further complicate matters, some flowers hold their particular pink from start to finish, while others fade or deepen as they age or as weather conditions change. Seeing particular pink flowers in person—at a garden center, for instance, or in someone else's garden—is the safest way to judge whether the pairing is pleasing to your eye.

Of course, pink flowers can combine beautifully with many other colors, especially when they're similar in intensity: strong pinks with bright yellows, blues, and purples, for instance, and paler pinks with soft yellows and creams, baby blues, lavenders, and peaches. Pairing pinks with reds and oranges is a challenge, but it's worth attempting if you enjoy adventurous combinations. (Adding deep purple or burgundy foliage to a pink-and-orange or pink-and-red combo may be all that's needed to make the flowers look fine together.)

Joyful yellows. There's certainly no shortage of yellow perennials for any time in the growing season. There are greenish yellows, clear yellows, and orangey yellows, from soft ivory to cream to bold, brassy gold: not just in flowers, but in foliage, as well. On petals, the primary yellow may lighten or darken from the outer tip to the attachment point, or it may appear with white or with other colors, such as red, orange, or green. Leaves may be a solid yellow or yellow with green, red, blue, silver, or white. Yellow leaves (often referred to as golden, or as chartreuse if they're a greenish yellow) may hold the same color all through the growing season, develop a reddish or orange blush in cool weather, or turn green or whitish as they age.

With so many perennials in this category to choose from, yellow is a wonderful place to start for a pairing, grouping, or entire garden. Try bright yellow with rich red and orange flowers and dark foliage for a hot tropical look; cool it down with violets and blues; or team it with white for a cheery effect. Softer yellows are outstanding partners for baby blues, pale

YELLOW BEDFELLOWS. Pinks and purples—like those of Joe-Pye weeds (*Eupatorium*) and ironweeds (*Vernonia*)—pair prettily with yellow-flowered partners, such as 'Lemon Queen' perennial sunflower (*Helianthus*); solid yellow foliage, like that of Briant Rubidor weigela (*Weigela florida* 'Olympiade'); and yellow-variegated leaves, like those of 'Oehme' palm sedge (*Carex muskingumensis*).

LEAFY GREENS. When you're making matches within a palette of greens, take advantage of different leaf shapes and textures to bring in some contrast. In this trio, the lacy leaves of autumn fern (*Dryopteris erythrosora*) and a deeper green astilbe (*Astilbe*) play off of the broad, bold leaves of 'Golden Tiara' hosta.

purples, light pinks, and peachy flowers, and with silvery, gray, or blue leaves. Or go for a "yellow garden," based on a range of tints and shades plus greens from the leaves and perhaps a dash of blue, silver, and/or peach.

Active oranges. Though few gardeners would claim orange as their favorite flower color, it can be part of some really interesting and exciting combinations. Bright orange flowers create exuberant groupings with similarly intense yellows, scarlet, and reds, and they look terrific with purple and/or chartreuse foliage. Or use somewhat deeper shades of orange, amber, and rust with reds, violets, and purples, along with dark foliage, to create a sunset-to-twilight combo or border.

Pairing orange with pink may sound awful at first, but it can work; in fact, it can look great! Try putting some purple foliage between these colors, or use the tan seed heads of ornamental grasses instead. Coppery leaves, like those of New Zealand sedges (*Carex*) and some heucheras (*Heuchera*), include touches of both pink and orange, so they, too, can make good blenders.

If you're not comfortable with vivid oranges, consider trying tints instead. Soothing colors, like salmon, apricot, peach, and buff, are lovely with light yellows, pinks, blues, and lavenders in flowers and with greens, blues, grays, and silver in leaves.

Agreeable greens. It's easy to overlook the value of green in plant pairings. It's so common in leaves and stems that we often forget it is there, but it can play a big part in the overall appearance of a combination or planting, particularly when and where flowers are scarce, such as in winter and spring, or in shady areas in summer and fall.

Like other hues, green comes in all sorts of interesting variations, from bright yellow-greens to cool blue-greens, with shades so deep that they're practically black, as well as lighter tints and tones of pale green and gray-greens. With some attention to choosing contrasting shapes and textures, it's possible to make memorable combinations working only within the greens.

Bright and deep greens make a crisp contrast with white, silver, pastels, red, and scarlet, and they make vibrant companions for yellows and oranges. Rich purples and blues get lost against darker greens but look brilliant with yellow-greens (as do reds and oranges). Light greens, blue-greens, and gray-greens blend gently with white, silvers, and pastels.

USING BLUES. Mixing tints and shades of purple and blue, as with dark 'Caradonna' perennial salvia (*Salvia nemorosa*) and paler 'Walker's Low' catmint (*Nepeta*), tends to create a soft, hazy effect. Working in some strong shapes, such as the very vertical stems of just-in-bud Japanese iris (*Iris ensata*), is one way to add some drama; a contrasting background—in this case, 'Royal Purple' smokebush (*Cotinus coggygria*)—is another option.

Enchanting blues. There's something special about blue flowers, so it's not surprising that so many of us are drawn to creating combinations with them. While there aren't many true blue perennials, there are plenty that are on the purple-blue side, and when you consider all the various tints, shades, and tones, there's no lack of great candidates for blue duos and trios, as well as entire beds and borders.

Because blues are so close to greens, it's very easy for them to get lost against a lot of green leaves. Keeping them where you can see them at close range is one way to handle that; setting them against a light background, such as a pale fence or wall, is another. Light-colored companions—such as white and yellow flowers and silver, yellow, and white-variegated leaves—also help to make blue flowers into true standouts. Many blue flowers already include a bit of white and/or yellow in the middle, so pairing them with a white- or yellow-petaled partner and then adding white-and-green, yellow-and-green, or solid yellow foliage is a simple formula for a stunning combination.

Blues with reds can be interestingly attention grabbing or unpleasantly jarring, depending on your taste; either way, they're a strong pairing, and just a touch of one with a lot of the other can go a long way.

Blues are very pretty with pinks, especially

On the Dark Side

When it comes to foliage, "purple" is a very different color than it is in flowers. Chlorophyll is what gives leaves a green appearance, but it's not the only pigment they contain: Anthocyanins (reds and blues) can mask the green to a greater or lesser extent. Because the green is still there, you generally don't get a clear color, like the purple of an iris or aster. Instead, it's usually a shade anywhere from a wine red (burgundy) to reddish brown (maroon) to a chocolate brown to near-black. Features on top of or within the leaves can create grayed purples—as on the younger leaves of 'Purple Emperor' sedum (*Sedum*)—or silvery purples—as on some heuchera (*Heuchera*) cultivars, such as 'Blackberry Ice'. With all of this variation, it's often easier to think of foliage plants in this group as "dark" rather than "purple."

Dark foliage looks great mixed with "hot" colors, such as oranges, golds, yellows, and reds, adding a touch of sophistication that can save the grouping from appearing garish or gaudy. Paired with white, yellow, or pink flowers or yellow or silver foliage, dark leaves create a strong contrast. Dark foliage is often a terrific companion for flowers that include dark centers, spots, bands, or other markings, such as many daylilies (*Hemerocallis*) and true lilies (*Lilium*). And it creates sultry duos with equally dark blooms, as in this pairing of 'Erica' Culver's root (*Veronicastrum virginicum*) and 'Queen of Night' tulip.

The color variations in dark foliage aren't very obvious in a planting you see from a distance, but up close, leaves that lean toward brown can look very different from those that are more of a reddish purple. For that reason, it's a good idea to see the leaves for yourself before you settle on a specific combination. Also, keep in mind that the intensity of leaf darkness can vary by site and season. Purples, reds, and browns tend to be strongest in full sun and on new growth, particularly in cool weather; if they get too much shade, or if the weather gets hot, they may appear a purplish or brownish green.

if you match their intensity (cobalt blue with fuchsia pink, for instance, or baby blue with pale pink). A border based on blues, blue-purples, and pinks with touches of white, gray, and silver is a classic look and easy to design. Or expand to a wider pastel palette of light blues and lavenders with soft yellows, pinks, and peachy flowers combined with accents of blue leaves and cream-variegated foliage. These paler colors are easy to see, so they'll work well even in a border that you view at some distance.

Vibrant purples and violets. Though different gardeners use different terms for the basic colors in this range, we all know these mixes of blue and red when we see them. In many ways, the clear purples and violets act like blues, blending into green leaves and needing lighter flowers, foliage, or backgrounds to help them get the attention they deserve.

Bright purples and violets create exuberant combinations with equally vivid yellow, red, and orange flowers and look amazing with golden to chartreuse foliage. They're great with pinks, too; in fact, it's not unusual for flowers that we call purple or pink, such as cultivars of hardy geraniums (*Geranium*) and phlox (*Phlox*), to include a good amount of both of those colors. Rich reddish purples and violets are absolutely exquisite with deeper shades of gold, orange, red, and other twilight colors. Or set yourself to the challenge of a border based on shades of blues, purples, violets, and red. Adding white or gray to purple and violet gives us lovely varieties of lilac, lavender, and orchid, and these make charming partners for white and pastel selections.

Radiant whites. Oh, the many possibilities for combinations with white! It's hard to beat the crisp, clean effect of a simple white-and-green or white-and-blue pairing, and a white-and-yellow combo is radiant even in shade or twilight. Bright white also adds zip to a border based primarily on pastels. It's outstanding with silvers and creates a strong contrast with reds and purples in both foliage and flowers.

Besides pure white, there are plenty of perennial flowers that are basically white but have touches of green, blue, purple, pink, yellow, or other colors appearing in features such as bands, streaks, stripes, edges, and centers or mixed into the white itself (often most notably in cool weather). It's easy to play off of these additional colors when choosing a companion: a yellow-leaved partner for a white-and-yellow iris, for example.

HIGHS AND LOWS. White flowers are so eye-catching that they can create a glaring effect if there are too many too close together. Mixing their heights so they're separated by some green gives each one space to shine, as in this combination of perennial candytuft (*Iberis sempervirens*) and Florentine iris (*Iris* 'Florentina').

A white garden or moon garden is always a tempting project, and there's no lack of great candidates to work with besides white and almost-white blooms, such as green leaves that are variegated with white or cream. (Cream in leaves tends to be white in hot weather and strong sun and more yellow in cool weather, but it's wonderful either way.) Silver, gray, and blue leaves are also superb with white.

The one drawback to white flowers is that they can look terrible once they're past their peak, so remove the aging blooms as they turn brown. Or keep your whites away from high-traffic spots; you won't notice the discoloration nearly so much from a distance.

Pennisetum alopecuroides 'Cassian' with Rudbeckia fulgida, Echinacea purpurea, Solidago rugosa 'Fireworks', and Panicum virgatum 'Dallas Blues'

Allium 'Gladiator' with Iris 'Edith Wolford', Baptisia sphaerocarpa 'Screamin' Yellow', and Cornus sericea 'Silver and Gold'

Hemerocallis 'Nona's Garnet Spider' and Coreopsis tripteris

Persicaria affinis 'Dimity' with Imperata cylindrica 'Rubra', Brassica oleracea var. tronchuda, Acer palmatum, and Amsonia hubrichtii

Creating Combinations for Seasonal Effects

S ometimes, the inspiration for your combinations may come from the season, rather than specific plants or colors. Each season has its own special considerations that can help to guide your choices: the hues you use, the perennials (and other plants) that you include, and the sites where you focus your efforts.

Spring Things

Spring is a tricky time for planning effective and beautiful combinations because weather has a significant effect on exactly when and for how long things bloom. Flowers that last for weeks in cool conditions may be at their peak for just a few days if there's an unseasonably warm spell. Hot, sunny days also bleach out blooms that are prettily pastel in mostly overcast conditions. Warmer-than-usual weather may significantly speed up flowering on some perennials but not others, even within the same bed, so from year to year, two plants may bloom at the same time, just overlap, or miss each other altogether. But when early-season combinations do work,

you'll know that they were well worth waiting for.

One way to improve your chances of enjoying a delightful spring show is to group your spring combinations in one part of your yard. With many early bloomers in one spot, there will always be *something* looking great. It's a particularly good time to focus your attention on sites that are sunny in spring and shady later, because many shade perennials send up their flowers early in the season. For inspiration, look to your local woodlands to see what's blooming during the spring season.

Including colorful foliage along with the flowers is yet another way to succeed with spring perennial groupings. Blue, yellow, and purplish leaves, in particular, often produce their most intense hues in their new spring growth. They provide a dependable splash of color as early flowers come and go, then still look nice later in the season. Just keep in mind that dark foliage can blend right into bare soil or mulch unless it has other leafy companions nearby to provide a lighter background.

MAKE THE MOST OF SPRING BULBS. Daffodils, grape hyacinths (*Muscari*), and other hardy bulbs do a great job filling the open space that's often so obvious in early-season gardens, adding spots or drifts of color and then disappearing as the perennials emerge and expand.

Color-wise, white flowers are abundant in spring, as are pinks, yellows, and purple-blues, so white and pastel combinations are well suited to the season. Warm colors, such as reds, oranges, and golds, tend to be the least common at this time of year, but there are some, and a small bed of them can supply a dash of summery warmth to your view even on a chilly spring day.

Most spring-blooming perennials are quite short (knee level or lower, especially in early to mid-spring), so think about combining them with early-flowering shrubs and trees for color closer to eye level, too. Spring bulbs make excellent co-stars for perennials, contributing a wide range of flower forms and colors early in the season and then disappearing back below ground by early summer.

Summer Abundance

There's so much going on at this time of year that it's easiest to think of summer as two seasons: early to midsummer and mid- to late summer. The palette of perennials you'll use in your combinations can be very different for each, but there's some overlap, as well, because some early-summer perennials flower again later in the season and some long-flowering selections are in bloom throughout this period.

It's no coincidence that perennial gardens tend to be heavy on late-spring and early-summer bloomers. Most of us are drawn to shopping for plants in mid- to late spring, so retailers make sure their displays are filled with perennials grown to be in bloom around that time. (Often, that means the plants have been in a greenhouse to hurry them into flower; in subsequent years, they'll bloom a few weeks later.) This abundance gives lots of options for early-summer combinations, but when you fill your yard with only those, you won't have much to look at later. If you're hoping to extend your garden's interest past the first big show, make it a point to include some combinations that feature long bloomers, rebloomers, and later-summer perennials, as well, to get a long season of beauty from your beds and borders. Also, check out "Perennial Pruning Basics" on page 307 for tricks you can use to delay or extend the flowering periods of many summer favorites.

The soft colors of spring tend to extend into early summer; later on, they're likely to bleach out unless they're in some midday to afternoon shade. As the weather heats up, so do the hues in sunny gardens: Bright-and-bold combos, with brilliant reds, oranges, and yellows;

SPREAD THE WEALTH. Don't let your beds and borders fizzle out after midsummer. Instead, take advantage of some of the many perennials that don't even begin flowering until hot weather arrives, such as golden lace (*Patrinia scabiosifolia*), Joe-Pye weeds (*Eupatorium*), summer phlox (*Phlox paniculata*), and orange coneflower (*Rudbeckia fulgida*).

saturated jewel tones, such as ruby red, amethyst purple, sapphire blue, and topaz yellow; sunset shades, including deep reds, golds, and oranges; and twilight colors (blues, violets, and purples with touches of magenta, pink, and yellow-orange) are equally appropriate. Mid- to late summer is an especially good time for plantings based mainly on yellows and golds, and there are lots of deep to medium pinks to choose from, as well. In shady areas, summer is a great time to play with interesting foliage color and texture groupings.

Style-wise, early summer is peak season for the traditional cottage-garden look, with classics such as bellflowers (*Campanula*), catmints (*Nepeta*), irises, lady's mantle (*Alchemilla mollis*), and peonies transitioning to summer favorites such as daylilies (*Hemerocallis*) and summer phlox (*Phlox paniculata*). Mid- to late summer is a great time to take inspiration from sunny meadows and pair ornamental grasses with medium-height to tall flowering perennials, such as Joe-Pye weeds (*Eupatorium*), milkweeds (*Asclepias*), and rudbeckias (*Rudbeckia*).

Fall Factors

There's no reason that the end of summer has to mean the end of the gardening season. Early to mid-fall can be a prime time for amazing combinations, especially in sunny gardens. Besides the summer perennials that rebloom, or continue to bloom, in autumn, there are late bloomers that don't peak or even begin to

OPTIONS FOR AUTUMN. Colorful leaves and showy seed heads are excellent complements to fall-flowering perennials. This late-season combination features the tall lavender-purple blooms of Tatarian aster (*Aster tataricus*) behind the coppery fall color of 'The Blues' little bluestem (*Schizachyrium scoparium*) and the dark dots of orange coneflower (*Rudbeckia fulgida*) seedheads.

flower until then, such as many asters and goldenrods (*Solidago*). Seed heads and berries add intriguing shapes and colors.

One fall feature that many perennial gardeners overlook is autumn color changes in leaves. Just like deciduous shrubs and trees, quite a few perennials can produce showy fall foliage colors, including balloon flower (*Platycodon grandiflorus*), bluestars (*Amsonia*), Bowman's roots (*Gillenia*), Culver's roots (*Veronicastrum*), hardy geraniums (*Geranium*), and peonies, as well as most warm-season ornamental grasses. Combined with late bloomers in rich purples, reds, yellows, oranges, and golds, they bring the colors of autumn woodlands and roadsides right to your garden. If those colors are too bright for your taste, more muted tones—lavender, rosy pink, buttery yellow, and peach, perhaps with touches of coral and maroon as accents—are perfectly appropriate.

Winter Wonders

In mild climates, long-flowering and late-flowering perennials can continue to bloom into the winter months, possibly even overlapping with those that typically bloom in spring or even early summer in cooler regions. Elsewhere, it's more common for perennials to have little or no presence in winter, either because they get cut down to tidy the garden in mid- to late fall or they get covered with snow for months.

That doesn't mean that you can't attempt to create combinations or even whole borders that are attractive through typical cold winters, though. You just need to be willing to expand your definition of beauty to include colors like tan, brown, gray, and black and to appreciate features such as dried foliage, interesting "skeletons" (dried stems), and long-lasting seed heads. Many warm-season ornamental grasses, for instance, dry beautifully as autumn progresses, turning from their bright fall colors to shades of buff, golden tan, or pale copper. And if you stop snipping off faded flowers after midsummer, you'll enjoy the intriguingly shaped, brown to black seed heads of durable perennials such as agastaches (*Agastache*), bee balms (*Monarda*), echinaceas (*Echinacea*), and rudbeckias (*Rudbeckia*). These sorts of features look fantastic when dusted with snow or encased in ice, and they also provide welcome shelter and food for birds and beneficial insects through the winter months.

Site a winter combo or border like this where you can admire it through a window

Marking the Seasons

Exactly when each season starts and ends depends on where you live and which definition you use. Though calendars mark the seasons by the equinoxes and solstices (around March 20 for the spring solstice, for instance, and around June 21 for the summer solstice), meteorologists in the Northern Hemisphere define winter as the 3 coldest months, summer as the 3 warmest months, and spring and fall as the periods in between. In many parts of North America, you can think of spring as March through May, summer as June through August, fall as September through November, and winter as December through February. If you live in a particularly mild area, though, your spring perennials may start in February or even earlier; in cold climates, those same flowers may not appear until mid- or late May.

All this variation means that it's impossible to give a definitive bloom time and duration that will apply to a particular perennial wherever it grows in the country. In this book, I use the March-through-May, June-through-August, September-through-November, and December-through-February system for seasons and give general bloom times that apply best to Zones 5 through 7. In warmer areas, figure that they'll be several weeks earlier; in areas to the north, they'll likely be several weeks later.

while you're cozy indoors, and you'll have a great view through the better part of winter. Cut down individual plants as they start to look messy, or wait a bit longer and cut down the whole planting in late winter or early spring to make room for the new growth.

There are some perennials that hold live foliage in a variety of colors through winter, including blue fescues (*Festuca*), Christmas and shield ferns (*Polystichum acrostichoides* and *P. setiferum*), European wild ginger (*Asarum europaeum*), hellebores (*Helleborus*), heucheras (*Heuchera*), lavenders (*Lavandula*), evergreen sedges (*Carex*), and yuccas (*Yucca*), to name a few. Grouped near a doorway, planted along a frequently used path, or combined with evergreen shrubs and groundcovers, they can provide enough interest to help you get through the winter months, then go on to earn their keep with their fresh foliage (and often flowers, too) throughout the growing season.

LINGERING INTO WINTER. Many perennials that look good in late summer through fall hold their dried stems, leaves, and seed heads through much or all of winter. The image above is of the border shown on page 298 as it looks several months later, with the skeleton of aromatic aster (*Aster oblongifolius*), seedheads of purple coneflower (*Echinacea purpurea*), and dried plumes of 'Dallas Blues' switch grass (*Panicum virgatum*) also visible.

Rudbeckia fulgida with *Ipomoea batatas* 'Sweet Caroline Bronze' and *Hibiscus acetosella* 'Maple Sugar'

Allium atropurpureum and *Ajuga reptans* 'Valfredda' (Chocolate Chip)

Coreopsis 'Limerock Ruby' and *Alternanthera dentata* 'Purple Knight'

Caryopteris × clandonensis 'Worcester Gold' and 'Red Sails' lettuce

Partners beyond Perennials

Matching perennials with perennials is a fine way to focus your combinations when you're getting started, but that's just the beginning! Think of all the others plants we gardeners like to grow, including annuals and bulbs in all shapes, sizes, and colors, as well as shrubs and trees with lovely leaves, beautiful blooms, and other showy seasonal features. Pairing them with perennials is basically the same as pairing perennial-with-perennial combos—they need to thrive in the same growing conditions, then offer a balance of harmony and contrast in their colors, forms, and textures—but each of these other plant groups offers additional benefits that you won't get from perennials alone.

Single-Season Companions

Annuals (plants that complete their life cycle within 1 year) and tender perennials (plants that can live from year to year in warm climates but are usually treated like annuals in cooler areas) are versatile partners for hardy perennials. Want to try a color combination but unsure how it will look in your yard? Experiment with a mix of annuals and tender perennials or annuals and hardy perennials in your chosen hues to see how they work together. If the color combination is a dud, try something different next year; if you like it, either repeat it as is or replace the annuals with similar perennials.

Annuals and tender perennials also make terrific placeholders for perennials in newer gardens, allowing you to develop a bed or border over a few years instead of having to buy all of the perennials at one time. Take advantage of them as fillers, too, while you're waiting for newly planted or later-emerging perennials to grow up and out. Tuck cool-season annuals, such as blue lobelia (*Lobelia erinus*), pansies (*Viola × wittrockiana*), and sweet alyssum (*Lobularia maritima*) into empty spaces around just-sprouting perennials and bulbs, for instance. Pull them out in early summer, if the hardy perennials need the space, or replace the spring annuals with coleus (*Solenostemon*

Bulb Buddies

Though we sometimes put bulbs in their own category, all bulbs are perennials: They're specialized structures with modified roots and stems that are meant for storing energy from year to year. Hardy bulbs are those that can survive winter outdoors where you live, including classics such as most crocus, daffodils, tulips, and lilies (*Lilium*). Hardy bulbs make fantastic companions for hardy perennials, greatly expanding your options for exciting spring combinations, supplying extra splashes of color in summer, and providing surprising accents for fall. Best of all, they don't take up much space.

Plant early-blooming bulbs in what would otherwise be empty spaces between your perennials early in the year, either as part of your spring combinations or to provide an extra season of interest to a perennial border you've planned primarily for late summer and fall. Or tuck them into carpeting perennials and groundcovers, as in the pairing of reticulated iris (*Iris reticulata*) and 'Angelina' sedum (*Sedum rupestre*) shown at right.

Hardy summer bulbs, such as alliums (*Allium*) and lilies, look splendid coming up through lower-growing perennial partners: The bulbs contribute height and bold flower forms as well as color, and the perennials do a great job covering up the often-bare lower stems of the bulbs. Fall bulbs, such as late-flowering crocus species and colchicums (*Colchicum*), tend to be quite short but show off perfectly when they're popping up through low-growing perennial partners, such as ajugas (*Ajuga*) and lamb's ears (*Stachys byzantina*).

There are lots of stunning tender bulbs, too. Like annuals and tender perennials, they need to be planted each spring, but at the end of the growing season you can dig them up and store them in a cool but frost-free place if you want to keep them from year to year. Cannas and dahlias are invaluable for adding height and bold textures, as well as interesting foliage, to sunny perennial plantings in summer and fall, while caladiums and tuberous begonias add welcome color to shady borders.

scutellarioides), sweet potato vines (*Ipomoea batatas*), zinnias, and other warm-season annuals and tender perennials if the permanent perennials aren't yet mature enough to fill their allotted spaces.

In shady spaces, add a touch of the unexpected by pairing tropical foliage plants with your hardy perennials. Tropicals come in amazing colors and dramatic variegation patterns: just the thing, where a basically green grouping needs a jolt of excitement. Consider red-, pink-, or silver-leaved rex begonias (*Begonia rex*); bright yellow Rita's Gold Boston fern (*Nephrolepis exaltata* 'Aurea'); purple-and-silver Persian shield (*Strobilanthes dyerianus*); or multicolor croton (*Codiaeum variegatum* var. *pictum*), to name a few of the many dramatic tropicals worth trying.

More Permanent Unions

Chances are, you already have at least a few trees and shrubs in your yard, so why not take advantage of them when you're thinking about creating combinations? Plant low-growing perennials around them as a groundcover, or make them part of a mixed border where you grow them with hardy perennials, annuals, bulbs, and whatever else strikes your fancy.

Woody-stemmed plants can contribute many terrific seasonal features, such as lovely flowers, eye-catching leaves, showy fall color, bright fruits and berries, evergreen foliage, and colorful winter stems. Some of them, including hydrangeas (*Hydrangea*), roses, spireas (*Spiraea*), and weigelas (*Weigela*), are so commonly grown with perennials that they're practically must-haves for mixed borders.

The main challenge of growing shrubs and trees with perennials in the same border is keeping pleasing proportions between the two. If the shrubs are relatively short, the perennials can be, too, but if you're dealing with larger shrubs and small trees, you need some shrub-size perennials as well, such as bugbanes (*Cimicifuga*) and goatsbeard (*Aruncus dioicus*) for shade and perennial sunflowers (*Helianthus*) and tall ornamental grasses for sun.

When you're choosing new woody-plant partners for your perennials in a mixed border, consider those that can withstand hard pruning, such as elderberries (*Sambucus*), ninebark (*Physocarpus opulifolius*), smokebushes (*Cotinus*), smooth hydrangea (*Hydrangea arborescens*), and colorful-stemmed dogwoods (*Cornus*). If they get too big after several years, you can trim them back to 12 to 18 inches before new growth starts in spring. You'll usually lose their flowers that year, but they'll bloom again in the following years, and in the meantime, they'll have lush (and often brightly colored) new growth and be much more in scale with their perennial companions.

SHOWY SHRUBS FOR MIXED BORDERS. Smokebushes (*Cotinus*) and some other deciduous shrubs can tolerate occasional hard pruning to keep them in scale with perennial partners. This bright yellow Golden Spirit (*C. coggygria* 'Ancot'), for example, makes an eye-catching color accent for purple-blue 'Brookside' hardy geranium (*Geranium*) and vibrant 'Screamin' Yellow' yellow false indigo (*Baptisia sphaerocarpa*).

Euphorbia polychroma
and *Heuchera* 'Fire Alarm'

Yucca filamentosa 'Color Guard'
and *Artemisia* 'Powis Castle'

Nepeta 'Novanepjun' (Junior Walker) and
Rosa 'Noa97400a' (Flower Carpet Amber)

Persicaria amplexicaulis 'Golden Arrow'
with *Geranium* 'Ann Folkard', *Oxalis tetraphylla*
'Iron Cross', and *Verbena* 'Homestead Purple'

Planting and Caring
for Combinations

For the most part, you'll plant and maintain your perennial partnerships just as you would if the plants were growing by themselves. But there are a few special considerations that are worth keeping in mind to get the best out of your combinations.

together the first year, so they look good at planting time, and then be prepared to move some of them in the following years.

Once you've been gardening for a while, dividing or transplanting your older perennials in spring or fall gives you opportunities to try out new combinations and to make room for new additions. When you're creating a combination by pairing an established perennial with a new one, consider dividing the established plant at the same time that you add the new partner, so the clumps will be more closely matched in age; this way, they are more likely to stay in proportion as they mature. Or if you don't want to disturb the existing plant, set out three or more of the new ones close together to create a clump that's in good balance, size-wise.

Maturity Matters

Some perennials need 2 or 3 years in one spot before they reach their full size and flowering potential; others, such as baptisias (*Baptisias*) and bugbanes (*Cimicifuga*), may take 4 years or more. The speed at which they fill in depends a great deal on the growing conditions as well as the sizes of the plants you are starting with. If you're beginning a bed or border from scratch, setting out the perennials based on the spacings suggested on their pot tags can leave you with a very bare-looking garden for a few years. (It will leave lots of room for weeds, as well, unless you use annuals or lots of mulch to keep the soil covered.) It's often more satisfying to set the plants closer

Good Grooming

Sometimes the difference between a good combination and a photo-worthy one comes down to a few minutes of attention with your garden shears. To keep perennial pairings in

Holding Beds

One simple garden project—creating a holding bed—can be an invaluable help in creating outstanding combinations. A holding bed, also known as a nursery bed, is a small plot where you can plant young perennials and let them grow for a while before giving them a permanent place. It's a great place for raising seedlings and for pampering small mail-order purchases until they're large enough to go into your garden, as well as for holding excess divisions and impulse plant purchases until you can figure out where you want to use them. It's also an excellent source of instant replacement plants, if you discover that you've lost some perennials after a tough winter or an extended rainy spell.

Though it can be pretty, a holding bed isn't meant to be ornamental: it's a practical space for bulking up small plants and observing new acquisitions to see when they flower and exactly what colors they offer. Instead of depending on photos and secondhand information, you'll see for yourself just how a particular perennial will grow and look in your yard before giving it valuable garden space. And when you're ready to use it in a combination, you can simply dig it out of the holding bed, plant it next to its new companion, and poof—instant combination!

A holding area can be as simple as a few square feet in one corner of your vegetable garden or a separate space with one or more ground-level or raised beds meant specifically to be a short-term home for perennials. If possible, site it close to an outdoor faucet so you can easily provide supplemental water to the young plants during dry spells. Prepare the soil just as you would for any perennial planting, or enrich it with extra compost to get speedier growth on the young plants. When you dig out clumps for use in the garden, fill the holes with a soil-compost mix, then add new plants as you acquire them.

prime condition for as long as possible, regularly trim off dead or discolored leaves (a process sometimes called "deadleafing"). If flowers are the focus of a combination, snip off older blooms as they start to fade or discolor, or cut off entire flowering stems close to the base of the plant when all the flowers are done, unless you also want the seed heads for later-season interest. This "deadheading" not only tidies the plants, but it may also extend their main bloom period or encourage them to flower again later in the growing season, and it may encourage them to produce fresh leafy growth. Perennials that we prize for their foliage, such as heucheras (*Heuchera*) and hostas, also produce flowers that may spoil the effect of a foliage-based grouping; in that case, you may want to clip off the flowering stems as soon as they appear.

Medium-size to tall perennials may need some help to hold their upright form and produce their flowers at the height you expect. If you find that certain plants are sprawling and spoiling your carefully planned combinations, gently propping them up with half-hoop supports, linking stakes, or Y-stakes may salvage their pairings for the current season. Next year, consider staking them soon after new growth begins; using pruning techniques, as explained below; or giving them shrubs or sturdy perennials as companions for natural support. Or accept that the flowers are going to sprawl, then plan accordingly or just enjoy the often surprising and delightful combinations they can create on their own that way (as long as they're not smothering their bedmates, of course).

Perennial Pruning Basics

Some well-timed snips with your pruning shears can work wonders with many perennials, changing their height and shape, influencing their bloom time, and affecting the size and distribution of their flowers. Here are just a few ways you can use pruning as part of your combination-care routine; for more specific tips, see the individual plant entries, starting on page 2. (*Note:* Don't try these techniques with daylilies [*Hemerocallis*], torch lilies [*Kniphofia*], true lilies [*Lilium*], or other perennials with nonbranching flowering stems, or you'll remove the flowers for that year, too!)

To make plants shorter and bushier. When you remove the stem tips of perennials

that have growth points along their stems, you encourage those points to produce side shoots, making for lower, bushier plants. That's not something you need to do with spring-blooming perennials, which naturally tend to be short, but it's a big help with summer and fall perennials that might otherwise tend to sprawl once they start flowering, such as chrysanthemums, New England aster (*Aster novae-angliae*), and upright sedums (*Sedum*).

TIME FOR A TRIM. Many spring and early-summer perennials respond well to a bit of pruning when they finish flowering. Even if they don't bloom again later in the year, they'll look much tidier and may be less prone to flopping. Arkansas bluestar (*Amsonia hubrichtii*), for instance, stays bushier through the rest of the growing season, and lamb's ears (*Stachys byzantina*) produces fresh new leaves that are less likely to "melt" in humid summer weather.

Perennial pruning can take the form of light trimming—removing just 1 to 2 inches from the tips—starting in mid-spring. Do this once or twice on perennials that flower in early to midsummer; repeat the process once or twice, a few weeks apart, in early summer on later bloomers. Or simplify matters for the later bloomers with a single hard pruning in early summer, cutting them back to about half their height at that time.

To affect flowering. When you prune perennials to control their size, you're also changing the way they flower, to some extent. One possible result is a delay in flowering time, which can be very useful if you'd prefer your mid- to late-summer perennials to flower a few weeks later for an impressive late-summer to fall display. Some good candidates for this sort of pruning include chrysanthemums, heleniums (*Helenium*), ironweeds (*Vernonia*), Joe-Pye weeds (*Eupatorium*), and perennial sunflowers (*Helianthus*). Shear the whole clump by about

PERENNIAL PRUNING EFFECTS. It's worth experimenting with pruning techniques on your later-flowering perennials to vary their heights, shapes, and bloom times. In the border above, for instance, the clump of Culver's root (*Veronicastrum virginicum*) on the right was left untrimmed and began flowering in early July. The clump on the left, cut back by half its height in early June, was shorter and bushier and began flowering a few weeks after its neighbor.

half once in early summer to delay the bloom time by a week or two, or in midsummer to delay it by a month or so. Or trim off just the shoot tips every few weeks from mid- to late spring into midsummer; most perennials will start flowering 3 to 4 weeks after the last trim.

Perennials that tend to have a few, mostly straight stems in each clump—cardinal flower (*Lobelia cardinalis*), Joe-Pye weeds, and summer phlox (*Phlox paniculata*), for example—produce fewer but larger flowers or flower clusters than bushier plants with many-branched stems, and those flowers appear at the tops of the plants. That's fine when you're working only with tall plants in a combination or when you're looking for a real spectacle: In that case, stake the plants instead of pruning them, or give them sturdy companions to lean on. If you're looking to pair them with shorter plants, though, the same approach you'd use for delaying bloom times can also produce smaller flower clusters that are more evenly distributed over the plant and in better proportion to shorter companions.

EXTENDING THE SHOW. In larger borders, shearing half of the plants in a particular grouping can stretch the bloom display by several weeks, at least. In the photo at left, the purple coneflower (*Echinacea purpurea*) plants in front were cut back by about two-thirds in late June, just before they began to bloom. By mid-September, those plants were contributing fresh flowers to the border while those behind them were filled with seedheads. The photo at right shows a large drift of 'Lemon Queen' perennial sunflower (*Helianthus*). The front half was cut back by about half in late June, producing bushier growth that supported the taller, unpruned stems at back. The pruned stems began blooming in late August, about a month after those at the back.

Chelone lyonii 'Hot Lips' with *Lobelia siphilitica* and *Persicaria virginiana* 'Painter's Palette'

Hosta 'Mostly Ghostly' and *Myosotis sylvatica*

Aruncus 'Misty Lace' and *Heuchera* 'Blackout'

Sedum sieboldii and *Thymus pseudolanuginosus*

Troubleshooting Perennial Combinations

If a particular perennial combination turns out exactly as you'd envisioned, it's a magical thing. Don't be too disappointed, though, when things don't work out quite as you'd hoped. Careful planning and good plant care go a long way, but you're still working with many factors that are beyond your control, such as weather, light, time, and the natural variability of living things. And don't forget insect and disease problems, marauding deer, lawn-mower mishaps, or carelessly thrown basketballs, which can put any carefully planned combination out of commission for the season. Still, those factors aren't unique to making perennial partnerships: They're all part of the fun and challenge of any sort of outdoor gardening.

When that perfect combination does happen, take the time to admire your own brilliance, and take lots of pictures, too. If it doesn't work out as well next year, at least you have the memory (and the photographic evidence) that it was a worthy idea. If it *does* turn out beautifully several years in a row, you may end up getting bored with it and want to see if you can possibly improve on it, or perhaps try something totally different in that spot. Creating customized combinations is one place where home gardeners have a distinct advantage over professional garden designers. The pros need to rely on dependable plants and time-tested combinations that are likely to look respectable every year, for at least the first few years, with only basic care. When you live with a combination and see it every day, in a wide variety of light and weather conditions, and can watch how it changes from year to year, you have the opportunity to add, move, or remove plants to fine-tune the composition and come up with exciting new partnerships that are perfectly suited to your site, your skills, and your aesthetic preferences.

If a combination doesn't satisfy you, you need to figure out *why* before you can decide on *how* to improve it. It's usually not a matter of starting over from scratch; often, it's just a matter of moving a few plants around to get the results you're looking for.

WORK IN STAGES. It's easy to get carried away with creating a garden, but trying to fill a big space on a small budget often ends up producing less than spectacular results. Instead of attempting a big area all at once, consider planting it in stages: Work from one end to the other, or dig and plant just the back half first. Once you get that part looking good, then expand the border over the next few years, using divisions of some of the fast growers, moving some clumps that are getting crowded, and adding some new combinations as you go.

Size Issues

In new and young gardens, especially, disappointments can be due to too-ample plant spacing. Generous spacing gives each plant room to reach its full size and beauty and reduces the need for frequent division, which is a reasonable way to go if your goal is a low-maintenance and relatively low-cost garden and you're willing to wait for the beautiful combinations you hoped for. However, it can mean several years of a sparse-looking garden, where the plants aren't even close enough to touch, let alone mingle their leaves and flowers to create pleasing partnerships.

There are a few ways you can use "proper" spacing and still get good combinations fairly quickly. If you start with large plants—in 2-gallon pots, for instance, instead of quarts or half-gallon sizes—you'll spend more money, but they'll make an impact much sooner. Or, you could put extra effort into preparing the site, loosening the soil deeply and digging in plenty of compost, and then water regularly after planting to encourage speedy growth.

What if you've already planted and are unhappy with sparse-looking results? If you can afford to buy more perennials, tuck in a few more clumps of the slower growers to help them fill their space fast and keep them in balance with more vigorous companions. Or, consider adding relatively inexpensive, seed-grown annual transplants or buy packets of fast-growing kinds that you can sow right around the existing perennials. For the front of a sunny border, for instance, think of low growers like bush-type nasturtiums (*Tropaeolum majus*) or compact zinnias. For the middle, consider Texas sage (*Salvia coccinea*) or tall zinnias; for the back, spider flower (*Cleome hassleriana*) or annual sunflowers (*Helianthus annuus*) can work well. Choose plants in heights and colors that complement the combinations you were originally going for, and you may find that you like the effect so much that you repeat it in following years. Or, leave out the annuals once the perennials have filled out in a few years.

Getting the heights right is another important consideration for combinations, especially if you want the flowers of two perennials to bloom next to each other or if you want one plant to act as a background for another. Heights will change as the plants mature and can vary from year to year depending on the weather, but the information on the pot tag or catalog description will give you a good idea of what to expect. If certain plants are still too short after the first couple of years, replacing them with taller cultivars is the simplest solution. If they're consistently too tall, a bit of summer pruning (as explained in "Perennial Pruning Basics," starting on page 307), is an easy way to reduce their size a little—or a lot—without having to replace them.

Color Concerns

Color issues can make what should be an eye-catching combination into a cringe-worthy one. If you've used several different flower colors in one area and are concerned that the effect is too "busy," it may help to replace a few so you end up with similar intensities—all rich shades, for instance, or all pastels—to keep the muddle to a minimum. Though it may seem counterintuitive, adding one more color, in the form of foliage, can help to unify a mix of bloom colors. Deep purple foliage is an excellent complement to an assortment of bright hues, while silver, grays, and blues can help to link softer colors.

Sometimes, flower and foliage colors don't turn out the way you expected from what you saw in a photograph. Weather conditions can have a lot to do with that: Petals that have rich colors when the weather is cool or cloudy may bleach to paler tints in strong sunshine. The age of the flowers and foliage matters, too. It's not unusual for petals to lighten or darken as the blooms mature, and colored or variegated leaves, in particular, often change their hues or markings as the growing season progresses. These subtle or dramatic differences can be frustrating if you're trying to create a combination for a specific color effect. Once you get used to the changing colors, you can take advantage of them when you make new perennial pairings, but that doesn't help when you're disappointed in an existing combination. In that case, you may need to replace the problem plant. Or, if all of the colors are fading or scorching in strong sun, you could try moving the whole combination to a site that will get some midday to afternoon shade.

Every once in a while, you may find that one of your carefully chosen perennials blooms in a completely different color than

you were expecting. Most perennial cultivars are vegetatively, or asexually, propagated (that is, reproduced by division, cuttings, or tissue culture), so they should be genetically identical. However, mutations that occur during production or in the garden can change flower colors and other traits as well; that's how new cultivars can come about, in fact. Other "named" perennials are seed strains, meaning that the seed-grown plants are normally similar in appearance. As they're not genetically identical, though, they can each be slightly (or occasionally very) different.

These sorts of variations are interesting to observe and can produce some delightful surprises. And they're a distinct bonus if you're going for a loose cottage-style or naturalistic look in your garden. But when it's really important to you to get a particular color for a combination, using vegetatively propagated cultivars is the best way to go. To be extra-sure, buy new or replacement plants when they are in bloom, so you can see exactly what you're getting.

BALANCE HARMONY WITH CONTRAST. When you're working with a limited range of colors, it's important to include a range of flower heights, forms, and sizes so the blooms don't all blend together. This pairing of 'Prairie Dusk' penstemon (*Penstemon*) and 'Walker's Low' catmint (*Nepeta*), for instance, is charming but very subtle: Adding more of the slender, deep blue spikes of 'Caradonna' perennial salvia (*Salvia nemorosa*) or the purple globes of 'Ambassador' allium (*Allium*) would make it more dramatic grouping (*top*).

QUICK FIXES. Need to spruce up a bland combination? Add a garden ornament for an instant result while you're pondering a more permanent solution. Ornaments or decorative pots (with or without plants in them) are also handy for supplying spots of color while you're waiting for flowers to start blooming, or where you need to fill holes in later-season border (*bottom*).

Timing Problems

When you're new to working with plant combinations, it's natural to be drawn in by pictures of flowery partnerships and to want to recreate them in your own garden. It seems a bit unfair, then, that many of the most enticing images focus on spring and early-summer perennials, such as irises, peonies, and poppies (*Papaver*). Many of these gorgeous perennials also have relatively short flowering periods, lasting just a few days to a week or two, and their timing and duration depend a good deal on the weather conditions. There's nothing wrong with attempting combinations with these spectacular but short-lived beauties, as long as you accept that there's a fair chance they may not bloom at the same time every year.

Basing many of your combinations on longer-flowering perennials greatly increases the odds that you will be happy with the results. While one or two partners may start earlier or flower longer than their companions, they're likely to overlap for a good amount of time and make a lovely show during that period. If you find that they're missing each other completely, try

VARIATIONS ON A THEME. Differences in color, height, and other characteristics are fairly common among seedlings of species perennials. If you buy three pots of 'October Skies' aromatic aster (*Aster oblongifolius*), for example, you can reasonably expect all three to have lavender-blue flowers on mounded plants around 18 inches tall. But if you buy three pots of seed-raised aromatic aster, each one may be slightly more bluish or purplish, with a looser or bushier form, and anywhere from 1 to 3 feet tall—as you can see in the grouping above.

TIMELY TRIMMING. Want to bring a touch of freshness to your late-season combinations without adding any new plants? Try giving earlier-blooming perennials a good trim, down to just a few inches above the ground, as soon as they finish flowering. This can encourage columbines (*Aquilegia*), hardy geraniums (*Geranium*), catmints (*Nepeta*), perennial salvias (*Salvia*) and some other late-spring to midsummer bloomers to produce a lush new leaves and possibly even another round of flowers for fall. Rozanne ('Gerwat') geranium, for instance, can end up flowering with asters and other late perennials well into mid-fall, in addition to contributing showy autumn foliage colors.

different species or cultivars to find one that flowers earlier, later, or for a longer period so it coincides with the others. Or, see if deadheading will help: On some perennials, regularly pinching or clipping off the flowers as they finish blooming will encourage new ones to form, extending their flowering period for a few more weeks or even months. It's worth doing a little research to see if this simple solution might be the answer to making your combination work without changing any of the plants.

When you're creating a combination for midsummer, late summer, or fall, it can be worth experimenting with different times and amounts of pruning to delay the bloom times of one or more perennials in the partnership. If you were hoping to pair the showy blooms of purple coneflower (*Echinacea purpurea*) with some late-summer grasses, for instance, but your coneflowers have mostly gone to seed by August, consider cutting them back by about half their height in early summer next year to delay their bloom period by several weeks. You can find out more about timing techniques in "Perennial Pruning Basics," starting on page 307.

The more experience you get in working with perennial combinations, the more you'll come to appreciate the value of good-looking foliage as a key player in successful plant partnerships. While leaves can change through the season, varying in color and freshness, they tend to be much more consistent than flowers from week to week and year to year. If you're getting frustrated with flowering perennials that don't dependably bloom when you expect them to, consider adding a plant with colored or variegated foliage to the combination. That way, you're sure to have a colorful combo even if only one plant is in bloom. And if the flowers do all appear at the right time, then the foliage is there, too, to enhance the show.

Texture Troubles

Maybe you have a combination—or a whole border—with the right mix of plant sizes and colors at the time you hoped for, but it still lacks that "wow" factor. In that case, you may need to consider the less-obvious features of texture and form.

First, consider the various flower sizes and shapes you've included. Daisy-form and bowl-to cup-shaped blooms are so prevalent among perennials that it's easy to end up with too many of them, and even using different colors may not provide enough of the necessary contrast. Replacing some of those ordinary shapes with spiky flowers, like those of blazing stars (*Liatris*), spike speedwell (*Veronica spicata*), or torch lilies (*Kniphofia*), may be all you need to add that professional-designer touch to your combinations. Mix up the flowers sizes, as well. Too many small flowers can create an indistinct, hazy effect—pretty if that's what you're going for but possibly a bit boring if you were hoping for more visual impact.

Also, take a good look at the leaves and see if their shapes are too similar. It's common to overuse lacy or ferny foliage in shady areas or grassy and strap-like leaves in sunny spots, because those shapes are so common in those sorts of settings. It's also easy to end up with too many "medium-textured" leaves—those

Give Seeds a Chance

My own favorite way to acquire out-of-the-ordinary perennials is by growing them from seed. I don't know why so many people—even well-experienced gardeners—are intimidated by the prospect of raising their own plants. It's true that some can require a good bit of patience, but while you're waiting for those, you can enjoy the experience of watching faster ones sprout and grow, and then add them to your combinations within just a year or two.

Growing perennials from seed doesn't require a greenhouse, or even indoor plant lights. Many perennial seeds spout quickly in warm conditions, so you can sow them in pots outdoors in May or June, transplant them to individual pots in June or July, and then move them to a holding bed—or even directly into your garden, if they're big enough—in fall or spring. Other perennials need, or at least tolerate, a period of cold temperatures before they sprout, so late summer to mid-fall is another good window of opportunity for seed-sowing. Leave the pots outdoors for the winter, in a spot protected from mice, water them occasionally if they don't get rain or snow, and then watch for sprouts once the weather begins to warm up again.

SHAPING UP. This late-summer trio of 'Eva Cullum' garden phlox (*Phlox paniculata*), 'Prairie Jewel' tall boneset (*Eupatorium altissimum*), and New York ironweed (*Vernonia noveboracensis*) offers lots of color, but it could be more even interesting if it included a strongly contrasting flower form. Replacing the boneset with the slender spikes of white Culver's root (*Veronicastrum virginicum* 'Album'), for instance, would keep the white color but provide a more dramatic accent.

not distinctive in either size or shape—in any combination. Sometimes, swapping out just one plant for another that has strongly contrasting foliage is all it takes to turn a lackluster combo into a show-stopper.

The Ho-Hum Effect

As you gain confidence in creating combinations, it's easy to get snooty about using "common" perennials, like 'Goldsturm' orange coneflower (*Rudbeckia fulgida*), 'Palace Purple' heuchera (*Heuchera micrantha*), or 'Walker's

Low' catmint (*Nepeta*). But to be fair, common plants are common for good reasons. They're easy to produce, so they're relatively inexpensive and widely available, and they can tolerate a range of growing conditions without much pampering, so they're likely to be pretty for a reasonably long period without much attention. Unless you have a tiny garden or lots of time and money to lavish on your yard, basing the largest part of your beds and borders on easy-to-find, reasonably priced, dependable perennials is a sensible way to go.

Once your plantings are pretty well established, though, and your combinations are mostly working out as you'd planned, you may find yourself wanting something a bit different: more interest later in the year, for instance, or some out-of-the-ordinary perennials to give your garden a bit more sophistication. The solution could be as simple as changing the time you go plant shopping. If you normally haunt your favorite garden center only in May and June, you may be missing out on some neat species and cultivars that are available only in summer or fall, so try to visit at least once in later summer and fall to see if they have new plants in stock.

Also, keep in mind that most garden centers are limited to offering only what their usual wholesale sources make available from week to week and year to year. If you visit a nursery that grows its own plants, you may find a wider variety of perennials at any given time. Or, make a day trip once (or a few times) a year to garden centers outside of your usual shopping range. Traveling just 25 to 50 miles away may get you to places that buy from different wholesalers, introducing you to a

SOMETHING SPECIAL. Investing a few unusual perennials now and then is a good way to spruce up your garden if you're getting a little bored with the plants you have. Pair your new treasures with more common perennials to add an element of the unexpected to your combinations—as in this partnership of striking shredded umbrella plant (*Syneilesis aconitifolia*) with relatively ordinary 'Black Scallop' common ajuga (*Ajuga reptans*).

BEYOND THE OBVIOUS. Once you're pleased with the combinations you have, challenge yourself to see if you can improve on them with features that add interest before and after their peak period. This duo of cushion spurge (*Euphorbia polychroma*) and 'Golden Sword' Adam's needle (*Yucca filamentosa*), for example, provides a sunny yellow combo when the spurge is flowering in spring, then continues to add textural interest, and an interesting color echo, too, well into fall.

whole new range of species and cultivars your local sources don't carry.

Then there's the Web, of course, where you can track down pretty much any perennial you could ever hope to grow. Mail-order nurseries are a boon to those who love to grow the very newest cultivars and unusual species. The challenge of growing uncommon plants well and using them in beautiful combinations is a surefire remedy for gardening ennui. It can come at a high price, though. The plants themselves may not be hugely expensive, but shipping prices can be astronomical, often totaling more than the cost of the perennials themselves. Still, it's a good thing to support small specialty nurseries, especially, who are willing to invest time and care into nurturing unusual plants for discerning

collectors. And, it may be the only way you can get your hands on the amazing new perennial selection that you saw in the latest issue of your favorite gardening magazine.

If you're looking for new perennial sources to try or want to read other gardeners' reviews before you order, check out the Garden Watchdog at http://davesgarden.com/products/gwd/. To find a source for a specific plant, try searching for it through PlantScout at http://daves garden.com/products/ps/.

PHOTO CREDITS

All photos are by Nancy J. Ondra except for the following:

Don Avery, Vermont
46 left, 194 left and right, 259

Daniela Baloi, Ohio
30 right, 55 right, 122

Kylee Baumle, Ohio
39, 79

Frank Bittman, Pennsylvania
155 right, 202

Lisa Bowman, Indiana
244 left

Megan Cain, Wisconsin
creativevegetablegardener.com
ix

Freda Cameron, North Carolina
18, 98 right, 183 left

Rob Cardillo, Pennsylvania
10 (Morris Arboretum), 12 left (Heronswood Nursery), 27 (Scott Arboretum), 35 left (Landscape Arboretum of Temple University), 40 left (New York Botanical Gardens), 40 right (Ondra garden), 45 (Ondra garden), 54 (Chanticleer), 57 right (Chanticleer), 64 right and left (Chanticleer), 69 left (Fordhook Farm), 80 right (New York Botanical Gardens), 100 (New York Botanical Gardens), 102 left (Fordhook Farm), 107 right (David Culp garden), 113 (Southlands Nursery), 115 (Ondra garden), 116 left (Chanticleer), 124 left (Inta Krombolz garden), 128 right (Temple), 148 right (Locus Flevum), 150 (Plant Delights Nursery), 151 (Chanticleer), 152 (Plant Delights Nursery), 159 right (Chanticleer), 185 right (Morris Arboretum), 200 left (Chanticleer), 222 right (Chanticleer), 224 left (Longwood), 238 left (Temple), 265 (Chanticleer), 267 (Morris Arboretum), 271 (Fordhook Farm), 276 bottom right (Linden Hill Gardens), 279 (Ondra garden), 296 (Chanticleer)

Christopher Carrie, North Carolina
167 left, 179 left

Alison Conliffe, Washington
80 left

Larry Conrad, Wisconsin
82

Darcy Daniels, Oregon
darcydaniels.com
92 right, 188 left, 190

Diana Davis, Massachusetts
83 left

Janet Davis, Ontario, Canada
vii bottom, 101, 159 left, 212, 214 left

Mark Denee, Ontario, Canada
49 right, 123 top, 177 left, 206 right, 231 right

Gail Eichelberger, Tennessee
213

Barbara W. Ellis, Maryland
91 right, 220 right

Alex Feleppa, New York
96 left

Gatsby Gardens, Illinois
92 left, 165 right, 171 left

Frances Garrison, Tennessee
42, 114

Cathy Gaviller, Alberta, Canada
153 left

Sue Gaviller, Alberta, Canada
Not Another Gardening Blog
142 right

Mark Golbach, Wisconsin
55 left

Peter Herpst, Washington
203 right

Judy Hertz, Illinois
28 right

Pam Hubbard, Pennsylvania
74 left

Christine Hunter, Pennsylvania
118 right

Wendy Kremer, Virginia
153 right

John Markowski, New Jersey
46 right

Nick McCullough, Ohio
69 right

Jean McWeeney, Louisiana
244 right

Carol Michel, Indiana
28 left

Janice Miller-Young, Alberta, Canada
26, 167 right, 270 top left

Gregory Nelson, Kansas
2 right

Pam Penick, Texas
Digging
24 right, 257 right, 304 top right

Kristine Peterson, California
118 left

Kathy Purdy, New York
coldclimategardening.com
57 left, 208 left

Amy Rich, Indiana
248 left

Lorraine Roberts, Ontario, Canada
Plant Paradise Country Gardens
87 left, 137, 171 right

Tammy Schmitt, Virginia
110

Ellen Sousa, Massachusetts
THBFarm.com
175 left

Jenny Stocker, Texas
183 right

Kathy Stoner, California
116 right

Three Dogs in a Garden Photography, Ontario, Canada
140 left, 161 right, 200 right, 216 left, 253 left

Melanie Vassallo, New York
224 right, 230 left

Carolyn Walker, Pennsylvania
94 right, 146 left, 222 left

Skyler Walker, Washington
31 left

Sue Webel, Connecticut
94 left, 144 right, 185 left

Scott Weber, Oregon
6, 72 left, 98 left, 196 right, 203 left, 205 right, 257 left, 304 bottom right

Julie Witmer, Pennsylvania
31 right, 49 left, 139

VaLynn Woolley, Washington
120 left

INDEX

Boldface page numbers indicate photographs or illustrations. <u>Underscored</u> references indicate boxed text, charts, and graphs.

GENERAL INDEX

Boldface page numbers indicate photographs or illustrations. <u>Underscored</u> references indicate boxed text, charts, and graphs.

31901060005115